Interrogating Sources

Questions: Any time you encounter a source, you will want to ask the same questions historians ask. Depending on the nature of the source you are working with, the answers may range from the obvious to the unobtainable.

- *When was this source produced and under what circumstances?*
- *Who produced this source?*
- *What purpose was this source created to serve?*
- *Who was the audience for this source?*
- *What is the point of view in this source?*

Checklists in each chapter help you dig deeper and ask the right questions of specific source types:

1. CONGRESSIONAL HEARINGS AND REPORTS, page 8
2. PHOTOGRAPHS, page 36
3. NEWSPAPER ARTICLES, page 61
4. AUTOBIOGRAPHIES, page 85
5. ADVERTISEMENTS, page 107
6. DIARIES, page 131
7. SONG LYRICS, page 155
8. PUBLIC ART, page 182
9. COURT DOCUMENTS, page 204
10. PRESIDENTIAL TAPES, page 227
11. CONGRESSIONAL SPEECHES, page 250
12. INTRODUCTIONS TO BOOKS ON HISTORY, page 275
13. POLITICAL CARTOONS, page 296

Limitations: When working with any source, follow the same principles that historians do and be aware of the limitations of historical evidence:

- *Sources are incomplete.* You will never have all the sources for any single historical moment, and no single source can tell the whole story.
- *Sources have limits to what they can tell you.* You must consider what you can and cannot logically conclude from a source.
- *Sources have biases, which must be accounted for.* Do not dismiss the source's bias or adopt it in your interpretation. Instead, identify the bias and use it as evidence of one viewpoint.
- *Sources can conflict.* Never hide or dismiss sources that complicate or contradict your interpretation. Either revise your interpretation or explain why conflicting evidence does not alter your interpretation.

Additional Resources

Refer to Appendix I for help **avoiding plagiarism** when writing about sources. See Appendix II for help **documenting your sources**.

Going to the Source

The Bedford Reader in American History

FOURTH EDITION

Going to the Source

The Bedford Reader in American History

VOLUME 2: SINCE 1865

Victoria Bissell Brown

Grinnell College

Timothy J. Shannon

Gettysburg College

Bedford/St. Martin's

A Macmillan Education Imprint

Boston • New York

For Bedford/St. Martin's

Vice President, Editorial, Macmillan Higher Education Humanities: Edwin Hill
Publisher for History: Michael Rosenberg
Senior Executive Editor for History: William J. Lombardo
Director of Development for History: Jane Knetzger
Developmental Editor: Tess Fletcher
Production Editor: Louis C. Bruno Jr.
Production Supervisor: Robert Cherry
Executive Marketing Manager: Sandra McGuire
Copy Editor: Lisa Wehrle
Director of Rights and Permissions: Hilary Newman
Photo Editor: Felice Pilchik
Senior Art Director: Anna Palchik
Text Design: Claire Seng-Niemoeller
Cover Design: William Boardman
Cover Art: The Civil Rights Act of 1964, Courtesy of U.S. National Archives and Records Administration
Composition: Achorn International, Inc.
Printing and Binding: RR Donnelley and Sons

Manufactured in the United States of America.

0   9   8   7   6   5

f   e   d   c   b   a

For information, write: Bedford/St. Martin's, 75 Arlington Street, Boston, MA 02116 (617-399-4000)

ISBN 978-1-319-02750-6

Acknowledgments

Acknowledgments and copyrights appear on the same page as the text and art selections they cover; these acknowledgments and copyrights constitute an extension of the copyright page. Text acknowledgments continue on pages 370–71. It is a violation of the law to reproduce these selections by any means whatsoever without the written permission of the copyright holder. At the time of publication all Internet URLs published in this text were found to accurately link to their intended Web site. If you do find a broken link, please forward the information to history@macmillan.com so that it can be corrected for the next printing.

Preface

We live in an age of raw data. Every day we are bombarded with unexpurgated leaks, unfiltered images, and unedited texts. That access has fueled even our students' skepticism about how others—experts, officials, scholars, the press—use sources, and how they interpret and present them to us. Increasingly, we doubt the reliability of others' interpretation; we want to see the sources ourselves, whether we are studying the present or the past. *Going to the Source* recognizes that students need tools for interpreting historical sources, and that acquiring those tools can give students an appreciation for the ethical methods we all can use to produce trustworthy interpretations of documents.

Collections of historical documents can no longer claim to provide a pedagogical service simply by making primary sources from the past available to faculty and students. The problem students face today is not getting their hands on documents; the problem is learning how to sift through them, assess them, and understand them. *Going to the Source* is designed to assist teachers with that problem in at least three ways:

First, each chapter centers on a very specific event or definable era so that students can immediately see the importance of context when analyzing any document.

Second, each chapter offers only one type of source, such as newspaper articles, diaries, or song lyrics, so that students can focus on the qualities unique to each type of source. Each chapter is designed to expose students to historians' processes and to encourage active interrogation of the sources at hand. Toward that end, we include a chapter on how to use and interpret secondary sources. We also give students the opportunity to work with a variety of source types on one topic by providing a "capstone" chapter in each volume where students can engage in historical analysis on an issue that spans several decades and draws from the different sorts of documents discussed in earlier chapters.

Finally, the architecture of every chapter guides students toward a disciplined analysis of sources by offering a contextual introduction; a discussion of "Using the Source," which focuses on both the value and the limitations of the type of source in the given chapter; and a "Source Analysis Table," which offers an analytical grid intended to push students beyond the cherry-picking approach to data analysis that they instinctively distrust (but often replicate). "The Source" section then presents that chapter's selection of documents or images, followed by a set of analytical questions that can stimulate both written assignments and class discussion. The Source Analysis Tables for each chapter are available for download on the Instructor Resources tab on our catalog page: macmillanhighered.com/brownshannon/catalog.

Underscoring our message that document analysis demands understanding of the broader context, we conclude each chapter with two sections: "The Rest of the Story," which reveals later developments in the chapter's story and connects it to larger themes in U.S. history; and "To Find Out More," which points students to additional primary, secondary, and online sources for further study of that chapter's topic.

Two appendices give students an edge when writing papers, whether brief homework assignments or full-length research papers. Appendix I, "Avoiding Plagiarism," shows students how and why they need to keep track of sources, take careful notes, and acknowledge sources where appropriate. Appendix II, "Documenting the Source," provides guidelines and examples for following *Chicago Manual of Style* citation methods.

NEW TO THIS EDITION

This new edition of *Going to the Source* reflects several changes in the book's content and structure inspired by feedback we received from more than two dozen U.S. survey instructors. Each volume of this new edition offers one entirely new chapter topic and one chapter revised to include fresh sources. In Volume 1, a new Chapter 4 introduces students to the use of secondary sources by examining the material culture of the Great Lakes borderlands through a journal article from the *William and Mary Quarterly*. Chapter 5, now titled "The Sound of Rebellion," has been updated with five new songs from Revolutionary America. In Volume 2, a new Chapter 12 explores secondary sources by examining economic decline in the 1970s while demonstrating the value of historians' introductions in professional works of history. Chapter 4 has been streamlined to provide a broader view of ethnic females' experiences with settlement houses through three immigrant memoirs from the progressive era. We hope these revisions enhance the value of this reader for both faculty and students.

ACKNOWLEDGMENTS

We would like to thank the following reviewers who guided us in our revisions with their suggestions and comments: Elliott Bowen, Binghamton University; Margaret Brown, Brevard College; Mary Ann Caton, University of Pittsburgh at Titusville; Amy Curry, Lone Star College at Montgomery; Benjamin Dettmar, Adrian College; Neal Dugre, University of Houston-Clear Lake; Amy Foster, University of Central Florida; Aram Goudsouzian, University of Memphis; Martin Halpern, Henderson State University; Jay Hester, Sierra College; Dave Hochfelder, University at Albany; George Jarrett, Cerritos College; Greg Kaster, Gustavus Adolphus College; Kelly Kennington, Auburn University; April Merleaux, Florida International University; Matthew Osborn, University of Missouri-Kansas City; Kathryn Ostrofsky, Angelo State University; Emily Rader, El Camino College; Thaddeus Romansky, Sam Houston State University; Paul Rubinson, Bridgewater State University; Scott Stephan, Ball State University; Jeremy Vetter, University of Arizona; and Andrew Wehrman, Marietta College.

We extend our thanks to the editorial staff at Bedford/St. Martin's: Michael Rosenberg, publisher for history; Jane Knetzger, director of development for history; Bill Lombardo, executive editor; Emily DiPietro, our encouraging developmental editor for this edition; Tess Fletcher, the editor who patiently brought this edition into home port; Mary Posman, our deft editorial assistant; our copyeditor, Lisa Wehrle; the book's designer, Claire Seng-Niemoeller: and Lou Bruno, our efficient production editor. In thanking our current colleagues at Bedford we do not forget our previous editors, including Laura Arcari, Heidi Hood, and Sara Wise, and Michelle McSweeny whose work was so valuable in earlier editions. A very special thanks also to Katherine Kurzman, our original sponsoring editor. This book never would have happened without her impetus and the sponsorship of Charles H. Christensen, former president of Bedford/St. Martin's.

We have been greatly aided in our endeavors by the librarians at Gettysburg College, including Chris Amadure, Karen Drickamer, Linda Isenberger, and Susan Roach, as well as the Government Documents librarians at the University of Iowa, Marianne Mason and John Elson, and the staff in the archives section of the Minnesota Historical Society. Staff assistance from Rebecca Barth and Marna Montgomery is gratefully acknowledged, as is the advice we received from colleagues who answered questions and read drafts of chapters. We are particularly grateful to Brendan Cushing-Daniels, Tom Dublin, William Farr, Matt Gallman, Jim Jacobs, Mary Lou Locke, Gerald Markowitz, Barbara Sommer, Char Weise, Mark Weitz, and Robert Wright. The assistance of students and former students was invaluable in this project, and we owe much to Maggie Campbell, David Fictum, Katie Mears, April Mohler, Amy Scott, Lauren Rocco, and Meg Sutter.

Finally, of course, we owe thanks to our families, who encouraged us throughout this process and regularly offered much-needed relaxation from our labors. Thanks to Jim, Colleen, Caroline, Daniel, and both of our Elizabeths.

Victoria Bissell Brown
Timothy J. Shannon

About the Authors

Victoria Bissell Brown (Ph.D., University of California, San Diego) is Professor Emeritus, Grinnell College. In addition to editing Jane Addams's autobiography, *Twenty Years at Hull-House* for Bedford/St. Martin's, she is the author of *The Education of Jane Addams* and articles on Addams, on Woodrow Wilson and gender, and on female adolescents in the Progressive Era. She is currently working on a social history of the American grandmother in the twentieth century.

Timothy J. Shannon (Ph.D., Northwestern University) is professor of history at Gettysburg College, where he teaches Early American, Native American, and British history. His books include *Iroquois Diplomacy on the Early American Frontier, Atlantic Lives: A Comparative Approach to Early America,* and *Indians and Colonists at the Crossroads of Empire: The Albany Congress of 1754,* which received the Dixon Ryan Fox Prize from the New York State Historical Association and the Distinguished Book Award from the Society of Colonial Wars. He is also the editor of *The Seven Years' War in North America: A Brief History with Documents* for Bedford/St. Martin's. His articles have appeared in the *William and Mary Quarterly,* the *New England Quarterly,* and *Ethnohistory.*

Brief Contents

Contents

Library of Congress, Prints and Photographs Division.

3	**Reading the 1894 Pullman Strike: Chicago's Daily Papers Report the News** *54*

Historic Pullman Foundation.

Private Collection/J. T. Vintage/
Bridgeman Images.

Library of Congress, Prints and Photographs Division.

Courtesy of the Arhoolie Foundation.

Courtesy National Archives.

8 | Painting a New Deal: U.S. Post Office Murals from the Great Depression   *175*

9

Challenging Wartime Internment: Supreme Court Records from *Korematsu v. United States*   *197*

National Portrait Gallery, Smithsonian
Institution/Art Resource, NY.

Cecil Stoughton. White House Photographs. John F. Kennedy Presidential Library and Museum, Boston.

Library of Congress, Prints and Photographs Division.

---

12 Introducing the Seventies: Historians Explore Economic Decline   *267*

© Bettmann/CORBIS.

| 13 | **Drawn to Summits: Political Cartoons on President Reagan and the Arms Race**   *289* |

Richard Wallmeyer.

Nina Leen/The LIFE Picture Collection/Getty Images.

CAPSTONE	**Organizing Their Lives: Women, Work, and Family, 1950–2000** 316

Going to the Source
The Bedford Reader in American History

CHAPTER 1

Political Terrorism during Reconstruction

Congressional Hearings and Reports on the Ku Klux Klan

E lias Thomson was an old man in 1871. Born a slave in Spartanburg County, South Carolina, he had lived his entire life on the plantation of Dr. and Mrs. Vernon. When he gained his freedom in 1865, he continued to live there, farming land he rented from his former masters. Thomson's daily life after the war must have gone on much the same as it did before, but freedom did bring some opportunities he was anxious to seize, even at his advanced age. In particular, the ratification of the Fifteenth Amendment in March 1870 guaranteed him the right to vote. Thomson exercised that right in the fall of 1870, casting his ballot in the state and congressional elections for the Republican ticket.

Late one night the following May, a group of men disguised in hoods appeared on his doorstep. They dragged him from his home and told him to start praying, for "your time is short." When Thomson refused, they pointed pistols at his head and asked him, "Who did you vote for?" Thomson responded that he had voted for Claudius Turner, a neighbor whom he held in high esteem. The disguised men told him he had made the wrong choice and whipped him. They told Thomson to remain silent about what had happened and left him with a final warning: "We will have this country right before we get through."

Thomson was one of many Southern men and women to suffer at the hands of the Ku Klux Klan between 1867 and 1871. In fact, his hometown of Spartanburg, South Carolina, was at the center of one of the most violent and prolonged outbreaks of Klan activity during Reconstruction. The Klan had first appeared there in 1868, using intimidation, arson, whippings, sexual assault, and murder to keep potential Republican voters away from the polls in that year's election. Despite such efforts, the state government remained in the hands of the Republicans, and the Klan temporarily receded as a public threat in 1869.

Klan violence rose again, however, with the next election in 1870, and it became more intense as white and black Republicans tried to mobilize the vote. In addition to intimidation and physical assaults on potential black voters, Klansmen burned black churches, schools, and homes and murdered black men who had enrolled in the state militia. In several counties of the Carolina up-country, the inland piedmont region where white and black populations were roughly equal or whites held a slight majority, the Klan conducted these crimes without fear of prosecution. Local sheriffs failed to make arrests, and if they did, white juries refused to deliver guilty verdicts. In some up-country counties, such as Spartanburg, state Republican officials estimated that practically the entire white adult male population belonged to the Klan or sympathized with it.

The Ku Klux Klan was of very recent origins in 1871 but had spread quickly throughout the former Confederate states. It was founded in 1867 by a group of Confederate veterans in Pulaski, Tennessee, who initially intended for it to be nothing more than a social club, similar to the Freemasons and other secret fraternal orders popular with American men in the nineteenth century. Like the Freemasons, early Klan members created their own ritual, costume, and hierarchy from a mishmash of precedents in ancient mythology: the name "Ku Klux" was derived from the Greek word *kuklos*, meaning circle, and one of the titles in the organization was "Grand Cyclops," named after a figure in Greek mythology. As the Klan spread, however, it acquired a different purpose. In Tennessee and the Carolinas in 1868, local "dens" of the Klan began to act as vigilantes, calling themselves "regulators" or "night riders" who enforced law and order according to local custom rather than the dictates of the postwar state governments created by Congress and the Republican Party. Local Klansmen operated autonomously and rarely cooperated with one another beyond the county level. Regardless of that fragmentation, the primary targets of the Klan's terrorism remained the same: any blacks who challenged white supremacy by daring to vote, teach, or acquire land; and "carpetbaggers," white Northerners who came to the South seeking their fortunes or taking positions in the Reconstruction state governments.

The violence and intimidation the Klan visited upon freedmen, freedwomen, and white Republicans seriously challenged the federal government's plans for the postwar South. After passing the Civil Rights Act of 1866, congressional Republicans had pegged their hopes for Reconstruction on enfranchising the former slaves as full and equal U.S. citizens. In this manner, the freedmen would become a core constituency for the Republican Party in the South and prevent the defeated Confederates from reassuming control there. The ratification of the Fourteenth Amendment in 1868 made this plan part of the Constitution by granting former slaves U.S. citizenship and guaranteeing them equal protection under the law. When some Southern states failed to extend their franchise to the freedmen, Republicans in Congress responded with the Fifteenth Amendment, which prohibited states from denying the right to vote to any citizen because of "race, color, or previous condition of servitude."

Republicans had great success in passing their legislative agenda for Reconstruction in Washington, D.C., but the enforcement of those laws in the South remained very much in question. The twenty thousand federal troops stationed

Figure 1.1 Racial Violence in the Reconstruction South *Political cartoonist Thomas Nast condemns the Ku Klux Klan and other perpetrators of racial violence in this illustration from the magazine* Harper's Weekly. *At the center, a black couple kneeling under the words "Worse Than Slavery" cradle their dead child, while a schoolhouse burns and a lynched figure hangs in the background. A hooded Klansman and "White League" supporter clasp hands over their work. The federal government intervened by passing the Ku Klux Klan Act and launching a congressional investigation of racial violence in the South.* Source: Library of Congress, Prints and Photographs Division.

in the South in 1867 were not nearly enough to pacify regions such as the Carolina up-country, where the Klan was at its greatest strength. Furthermore, military officers were reluctant to assume control over matters of law enforcement without specific requests from civilian authorities to do so lest they alienate the defeated Southern white population even further. As news of the Klan's expansion and pervasive influence in the South made its way to the nation's capital, Republican leaders agreed that federal action against it was necessary.

In a special message to Congress in December 1870, President Ulysses S. Grant noted that the Klan and similar organizations were using violence to prevent citizens from voting in the Southern states. Acting on a request he had received from the governor of North Carolina, he asked Congress to investigate the matter. Congress formed a committee to review affairs in North Carolina and then, in April 1871, created another, much larger committee to expand the investigation into other states. This latter group, titled the Joint Select Committee to Inquire into the Condition of Affairs in the Late Insurrectionary States, had twenty-one members—seven senators and fourteen representatives—thirteen of whom were Republicans and eight of whom were Democrats.

At approximately the same time it formed the Joint Select Committee to investigate the Klan, Congress also passed the Ku Klux Klan Act. This law gave the president the power to use federal troops and courts to protect the lives, property, and rights of U.S. citizens in the South. For the first time, crimes committed by private persons against other citizens became eligible for prosecution under federal rather than state law. Provisions included in the Ku Klux Klan Act effectively gave the president the ability to declare martial law in any state or region he deemed under Klan influence. The most controversial of these provisions concerned suspension of the writ of habeas corpus, a cornerstone of civil liberties in the United States. The writ of habeas corpus protects citizens from unlawful imprisonment by requiring that any person placed under arrest be charged with a specific crime and placed on trial. By allowing the president to suspend this writ, Congress made it possible for suspected Klansmen to be jailed indefinitely. Many congressmen, even some Republicans, questioned the constitutionality of this provision and of the Ku Klux Klan Act in general, but the majority who supported the law believed that the Klan could not be defeated without such powerful measures.

Members of Congress formulated and debated this legislation in Washington while African Americans in the South confronted the Klan face to face. Casting a ballot or even expressing an interest in voting could put a former slave's life in jeopardy. Those who joined militias, held office, or tried to improve their economic circumstances faced similar reprisals, and the promise of assistance from Washington must have seemed far off indeed. In 1871, a showdown was brewing between the Ku Klux Klan and the federal government that placed people like Elias Thomson squarely in the middle of the battle to determine Reconstruction's fate.

Using the Source: Congressional Hearings and Reports

The Joint Select Committee undertook one of the most far-reaching congressional investigations ever conducted up to that time. During the summer and fall of 1871, it heard testimony from witnesses in Washington, D.C., and sent subcommittees to interview witnesses throughout the South. Most of its work was concentrated on North Carolina and South Carolina, where the activities and effect of the Klan were reported to be most severe, but committee members also visited Alabama, Florida, Georgia, Mississippi, and Tennessee, compiling thousands of pages of testimony. In February 1872, the Joint Select Committee submitted this testimony and its reports to Congress. The majority report, signed by every Republican on the committee, endorsed the Ku Klux Klan Act of 1871 and recommended continuing the president's powers to combat the Klan through the use of federal troops, courts, and suspension of the writ of habeas corpus. The minority report, signed by every Democrat on the committee, did not deny the existence of Klan-related violence but blamed it on misguided federal Reconstruction policy, which had left the Southern states in the hands of carpetbaggers and former slaves.

What Can Congressional Hearings and Reports Tell Us?

Since its publication in 1872, historians have found the thirteen volumes of the Joint Select Committee's report a remarkably detailed and comprehensive source for studying Reconstruction in the South. One of its chief advantages as a source is its sheer size. The committee conducted its work thoroughly, and the hundreds of witnesses who testified before it represented a broad spectrum of Southern society: white and black, rich and poor, male and female, Republican and Democrat. One historian has called their testimony "the richest single source" for understanding Southern society during the Reconstruction era. In the case of African Americans, testimony before the committee provides invaluable first-person narratives of what the transition from bondage to freedom was like.

Another advantage of working with this source has to do with the methods by which the Joint Select Committee collected its evidence. Its procedures resembled legal hearings: oaths were administered to witnesses, and witnesses were subjected to cross-examination, all in meetings open to the public. No witnesses appeared anonymously or gave secret testimony. Although those procedures may have prevented many from testifying for fear of reprisals, they nevertheless lent an air of authenticity to the witnesses' descriptions of the Klan that was not accorded to rumors or sensationalistic stories reported in the press. The Klan conducted its terrorism under cover of night and in disguise. By its very nature, it did not submit willingly to public scrutiny. For the most part, however, the witnesses who appeared before the committee in Southern towns and counties were eyewitnesses to the Klan's activities, making their testimony the most complete and reliable account of this secret organization's operations during Reconstruction.

The disadvantages associated with using the Joint Select Committee's report stem mostly from its inherent political biases. The Republicans who dominated the Joint Select Committee by a two-to-one margin were most interested in finding evidence that the Klan was a conspiratorial organization bent on depriving black and white Republicans of their civil and political liberties. Such evidence could be used to justify imposing martial law in those regions affected by the Klan. Democrats accused the Republicans of using the committee to drum up stories of Klan brutality and lawlessness that could be publicized to Republican advantage in the upcoming election of 1872. Although the Democrats on the committee could not deny the violence of the Klan, they used their questioning of witnesses to cast doubt on its political motives, depicting Klansmen instead as isolated, ill-advised characters pushed to extremes by desperation and offended honor. It is important to remember that Congress had already passed the Ku Klux Klan Act when the Joint Select Committee conducted its work. Given that the committee's majority was made up of the same Republicans who had passed that piece of legislation, how likely was it that the committee's findings would challenge its enforcement? By passing the Ku Klux Klan Act *before* its investigation of the Klan, Congress clearly anticipated the outcome of the Joint Select Committee's work.

As you read the testimony, you will quickly realize that neither the Republicans nor the Democrats on the Joint Select Committee resembled neutral fact finders; each side brought an agenda to the proceedings. Consider, for example, these excerpts from the testimony of D. H. Chamberlain, the Republican attorney general of South Carolina, given before the committee in Washington, D.C., on June 10, 1871. A good historian quickly learns to read between the lines of such evidence, looking carefully at the questions as well as the answers to determine what biases and ulterior motives are contained in this source.

D. H. Chamberlain, sworn and examined.

By the Chairman:

> *Question:* How long have you been a resident of the State?
>
> *Answer:* I have been a resident there since December, 1865.
>
> *Question:* Please go on and state to the committee the knowledge you have acquired, from your official position, as to the efficiency with which the laws are executed throughout the State of South Carolina, and the protection afforded to life and property in the State. Make your statement in general terms.
>
> *Answer:* The enforcement of the law has, from time to time, been very much interrupted and disturbed from special causes; lately by what are popularly known as Ku-Klux operations. . . .

An oath to tell the truth similar to that given in a court of law

Republican senator John Scott of Pennsylvania chaired the committee and typically initiated the questioning

Invites Chamberlain to speak freely about law enforcement

By Mr. Van Trump:

Question: You say you went to South Carolina in 1865?

Answer: Yes, sir.

Question: How long after the termination of the war; what part of the year?

Answer: I went in December, 1865.

Question: From where did you go?

Answer: From Massachusetts. I had been in the Union army during the war. I settled at Charleston in December, 1865, and remained there, and my residence is there now, although I have to be at the capital of the State most of the time.

Returns to the subject of Chamberlain's background, seeking to discredit him as a carpetbagger

Philadelph Van Trump, a Democratic representative from Ohio, typically led the cross-examination

Source: United States Congress, *Report of the Joint Select Committee to Inquire into the Condition of Affairs in the Late Insurrectionary States*, vol. 2, *South Carolina, Part 1* (Washington, DC: Government Printing Office, 1872), 48–51.

One other disadvantage to bear in mind about the Joint Select Committee's report is that even though the committee's hearings had the appearance of legal proceedings, the committee did not work with the same standards of evidence as a court of law. In particular, the Republican majority of the committee was willing to accept hearsay, what someone had heard but not personally witnessed, as evidence. Democrats on the committee objected, likening it to accepting rumors and gossip as facts. They accused local Republican officials of coaching witnesses, and they equated the $2-a-day allowance the committee paid to witnesses with bribery. In the thousands of pages of testimony in the Joint Select Committee's report, some witnesses do appear more reliable than others.

Congressional hearings have remained a part of our national politics, and today they are often televised. They serve an important role in the legislative process by acting as fact-finding investigations for members of Congress. They also provide an opportunity for congressional leaders to push their own political agendas before large audiences, regardless of the testimony they are hearing from witnesses. The Checklist questions on page 8 will help you read congressional hearings and reports with a critical eye that takes into account the politics as well as the issues involved in such sources.

CHECKLIST: Interrogating Congressional Hearings and Reports

☐ What issue or legislation is the hearing investigating?

☐ Who is the witness providing the testimony? Where is the witness from, and why is he or she testifying?

☐ What does the witness say in his or her testimony?

☐ Who are the members of Congress conducting the hearings? What do you know about their backgrounds and political affiliations?

☐ How reliable does the testimony appear to be? Is it based on first-hand experience, personal opinion, or hearsay?

☐ What bias is evident in the questions being asked of the witness?

☐ What measures do the congressional investigators recommend in their report on the testimony they have heard? If there is a minority report, how does it differ in its interpretation of the testimony and its recommendations for action from the majority report?

Source Analysis Table

Source	Personal Information	Description of the Klan's Activities and Motives	Reliability of Evidence Provided
WITNESS TESTIMONY			
1. Samuel T. Poinier			
2. D. H. Chamberlain			
3. Elias Thomson			
4. Lucy McMillan			
5. Mervin Givens			

(continued)

Source	Description of the Klan	Assessment of Federal Response to the Klan
COMMITTEE REPORTS		
6. Majority Report		
7. Minority Report		

The Source: Testimony and Reports from the Joint Select Committee to Inquire into the Condition of Affairs in the Late Insurrectionary States

The testimony that follows is taken from the Joint Select Committee's investigation of the Ku Klux Klan in South Carolina. Sources 1 and 2 come from testimony heard in Washington, D.C., whereas Sources 3, 4, and 5 are from testimony heard in Spartanburg, South Carolina. Sources 6 and 7 are excerpts from the committee's majority and minority reports, respectively, which were completed after the investigation was over.

WITNESS TESTIMONY

1   *Testimony of Samuel T. Poinier,* Washington, D.C., June 7, 1871

Poinier was a Republican newspaper editor and a federal tax collector in South Carolina at the time of his testimony.

Samuel T. Poinier sworn and examined.

By the Chairman:[1]

> *Question:* Please state in what part of South Carolina you reside.
> *Answer:* In Spartanburg County, the most northern county in the State.
> *Question:* How long have you resided there?
> *Answer:* Since February, 1866; a little over five years.
> *Question:* From what part of the United States did you go to South Carolina?
> *Answer:* I went there from Louisville, Kentucky. . . . I went there in 1866 with

no intention whatever of remaining. I went entirely for social reasons, to marry, and I was persuaded to stay there. My wife was a native of Charleston, and I found her up in Spartanburg after the war, where a large number of Charleston people went during the bombardment of the city. . . .

> *Question:* Were you in the Union Army?
> *Answer:* Yes, sir: I went out from Kentucky.

---

[1] Republican senator John Scott from Pennsylvania.

Source: United States Congress, *Report of the Joint Select Committee to Inquire into the Condition of Affairs in the Late Insurrectionary States*, vol. 2, *South Carolina, Part I* (Washington, DC: Government Printing Office, 1872), 25–28, 33–34.

Question: Proceed with your statement.

Answer: Just before our last campaign,[2] it was May a year ago, I . . . identified myself publicly with the republican party. I made my paper a republican paper. I did everything I could in the last State election for the reelection of Governor Scott[3] and our other State officers. From that time I have been in very deep water. . . . I was ordered away last fall, immediately after our last election, in November. It was soon after the first appearance of this Ku-Klux organization, or whatever it is. Soon after these outrages occurred in our county I received a note ordering me away from there, stating that I must leave the county; that all the soldiers of the United States Army could not enable me to live in Spartanburg. . . . Two days prior to our election, a party of disguised men went, at night, and took out two white men and three negroes, one of them a colored woman, and whipped them most brutally. Two of them were managers of the box[4] at that election; and the men told them that if they dared to hold an election at that box they would return and kill them. That was the first appearance of any trouble in the State. . . .

Question: Were those people of whom you spoke in disguise?

Answer: They were all in disguise. One of the colored men who were whipped swore positively as to the identity of some of them, and the parties were arrested, but nothing could ever be done with them; they proved an *alibi*, and some of them have since gone to Texas. . . .

Question: Go on and state any similar occurrences in that county since that time. . . .

Answer: Since that time outrages of that nature have occurred every week. Parties of disguised men have ridden through the county almost nightly. They go to a colored man's house, take him out and whip him. They tell him that he must not give any information that he has been whipped. They tell him, moreover, that he must make a public renunciation of his republican principles or they will return and kill him. . . .

Question: Do the facts that have transpired and the manner in which they have occurred satisfy you of the existence of the organization in that portion of South Carolina?

Answer: Yes, sir; I have no doubt of it in the world. I have received anonymous communications signed by the order of "K.K.K.," directing me to leave the county, stating that I could not live there; that I was a carpet-bagger. But personally I have never met with any trouble.

By Mr. Van Trump:[5]

Question: You have a connection with the partisan press there?

Answer: Yes, sir. I am editing a republican paper.

[2] The election of 1870.

[3] Robert K. Scott was the Republican governor of South Carolina.

[4] Ballot box.

[5] Democratic representative Philadelph Van Trump from Ohio.

Question: Do you advocate the cause of the negro in your paper?

Answer: Not the negro especially. I advocate the general principles of republicanism.

Question: You support the whole republican doctrine in your paper?

Answer: So far as general principles go, I do. I do not approve or uphold the State government in many of its acts; but, so far as the general principles of republicanism are concerned, I uphold it very strongly. I advocate the right of the colored people to vote and to exercise their civil and political privileges. . . .

Question: These men who assert that their object is to put down the negro and get possession of the Government are prominent men, are they not?

Answer: Yes, sir.

Question: Can you name a single man?

Answer: Well, I cannot name anybody specially who has made such a remark, but I hear it in the hotels.

Question: Have you yourself heard them make the remark?

Answer: I have heard the remark made; it is a common thing.

Question: Is it not rather an uncommon remark?

Answer: It is not, there.

Question: You cannot recollect the name of a single person who has made that declaration?

Answer: No sir, I cannot recall any now.

2   *Testimony of D. H. Chamberlain,*
Washington, D.C., June 10, 1871

Chamberlain was a Republican and the attorney general of South Carolina.

D. H. Chamberlain, sworn and examined.

By the Chairman:

Question: How long have you been a resident of the State?

Answer: I have been a resident there since December, 1865.

Question: Please go on and state to the committee the knowledge you have acquired, from your official position, as to the efficiency with which the laws are executed throughout the State of South Carolina, and the protection afforded to life and property in the State. Make your statement in general terms.

Answer: The enforcement of the law has, from time to time, been very much interrupted and disturbed from special causes; lately by what are popularly known as Ku-Klux operations. There have been a great many outrages committed, and

Source: Report of the Joint Select Committee, vol. 2, South Carolina, Part I, 48–51.

a great many homicides, and a great many whippings. I speak now, of course, of what I have heard; I have never seen any outrages committed myself; I am simply stating what I believe to be fact. . . .

Question: In what part of the State are these offenses committed which you attribute to the influence of this organization?

Answer: Notably in Spartanburg, Newberry, Union, and York Counties; those are the principal counties that have been the scenes of these disturbances. But they have extended into Laurens, Chester, and Lancaster Counties.[1] . . .

Question: Have there been any convictions for these offenses in the State, so far as your information goes; offenses committed by these organized bands?

Answer: No sir, no convictions, and no arrests, except in the case of this wounded Ku-Klux.[2] . . .

By Mr. Van Trump:

Question: You say you went to South Carolina in 1865?
Answer: Yes, sir.
Question: How long after the termination of the war; what part of the year?
Answer: I went in December, 1865.
Question: From where did you go?
Answer: From Massachusetts. I had been in the Union army during the war. I settled at Charleston in December, 1865, and remained there, and my residence is there now, although I have to be at the capital of the State most of the time.

By Mr. Stevenson:[3]

Question: When did it first come to your knowledge that this organization existed in the State of South Carolina?

Answer: It would be difficult to say. My conviction that there is such an organization has grown up very gradually. . . . I cannot fix the date exactly.

Question: Had you any knowledge of the fact that there were acts of violence and disorders in that State about the time of the election in 1868?

Answer: Yes, sir.

Question: Had you any information of the sending of arms at that time into that State?

Answer: O, I remember that a great many arms were purchased by private individuals, if you refer to that. I know that at the time, during the canvass,[4] there was considerable excitement when it was understood that the democrats,

---

[1] All seven of these counties were in the piedmont, or up-country, region of South Carolina, where the black and white populations were roughly equal.

[2] Chamberlain is referring to a Klansman wounded during a raid on the Newberry County Courthouse. He was jailed and then released on bail and subsequently either died while in the care of a friend or was spirited away by friends to avoid prosecution.

[3] Republican representative Job Stevenson from Ohio.

[4] Campaigning for votes.

as we call them, were arming themselves with Winchester and Henry rifles, or something of the kind.

    Question: Repeating rifles?

    Answer: Yes, sir. . . .

By Mr. Blair:[5]

    Question: Did you have any actual knowledge of the fact that the democrats were then arming?

    Answer: No, sir.

    Question: Then you make this statement as a rumor merely?

    Answer: Well, yes, sir; I should use, perhaps, a little stronger term than rumor. I had heard it so often that it came to be a belief with me, but it was hearsay. . . .

    Question: Was it a common report that those arms all went into the hands of democrats?

    Answer: As I heard it, it was understood that those arms were imported into the State upon order of individuals. I do not know but a republican might have had his order filled, but the belief was that they were generally ordered by democrats.

By Mr. Stevenson:

    Question: You have no knowledge of any general arming among the republicans at that time?

    Answer: No, sir.

    Question: You were a republican, then, were you not?

    Answer: Yes, sir.

By Mr. Blair:

    Question: Did not the republicans have arms?

    Answer: O, yes.

By Mr. Van Trump:

    Question: Did not the negroes have arms?

    Answer: Yes, sir; it is very common for people to have their shot-guns, to have some kind of arms. I suppose that in this instance people thought that there was an unusually large number brought in at a particular time, and that they were not for sporting purposes. They were repeating rifles.

    Question: Have you been a politician for any part of your life?

    Answer: No, sir; I do not think I have ever been a politician.

    Question: Have you never heard a thousand rumors during an election that had no foundation in fact?

    Answer: Yes, sir; many of them.

    Question: Got up for excitement merely?

    Answer: Yes, sir.

[5] Democratic senator Frank Blair from Missouri.

3 **Testimony of Elias Thomson,**
Spartanburg, South Carolina, July 7, 1871

Elias Thomson (colored) sworn and examined.

By the Chairman:

> *Question:* Where do you live?
> *Answer:* Up on Tiger River, on Mrs. Vernon's plantation.[1]
> *Question:* What do you follow?
> *Answer:* Farming.
> *Question:* Do you live on rented land?
> *Answer:* Yes, sir.
> *Question:* How much have you rented?
> *Answer:* I think about fifty acres.
> *Question:* How long have you been living there?
> *Answer:* Ever since the surrender; I never left home.
> *Question:* Have you ever been disturbed any up there?
> *Answer:* Yes, sir.
> *Question:* How?

Answer: There came a parcel of gentlemen to my house one night—or men. They went up to the door and ran against it. My wife was sick. I was lying on a pallet, with my feet to the door. They ran against it and hallooed to me, "Open the door, quick, quick, quick." I threw the door open immediately, right wide open. Two little children were lying with me. I said, "Come in gentlemen." One of them says, "Do we look like gentlemen?" I says, "You look like men of some description; walk in." One says, "Come out here; are you ready to die?" I told him I was not prepared to die. "Well," said he, "Your time is short; commence praying." I told him I was not a praying man much, and hardly ever prayed; only a very few times; never did pray much. He says, "You ought to pray; your time is short, and now commence to pray." I told him I was not a praying man. One of them held a pistol to my head and said, "Get down and pray." I was on the steps, with one foot on the ground. They led me off to a pine tree. There was three or four of them behind me, it appeared, and one on each side, and one in front. The gentleman who questioned me was the only one I could see. All the time I could not see the others. Every time I could get a look around, they would touch me on the side of the head with a pistol, so I had to keep my head square in front. The next question was, "Who did you vote for?" I told him I voted for Mr. Turner—Claudius Turner, a gentleman in the neighborhood. They said, "What did you vote for him for?" I said, "I thought a good deal of him; he was my neighbor." I told them I disremembered who was on the ticket besides, but they had several, and I voted the ticket. "What did you do that for?" they said. Says I, "because I thought it was right." They said, "You thought it

---

[1] The Vernons were Thomson's former masters.

Source: Report of the Joint Select Committee, vol. 2, South Carolina, Part I, 410–15.

was right? It was right wrong." I said, "I never do anything hardly if I think it is wrong; if it was wrong, I did not know it. That was my opinion at the time and I thought every man ought to vote according to his notions." He said, "If you had taken the advice of your friends you would have been better off." I told him I had. Says I, "You may be a friend to me, but I can't tell who you are." Says he, "Can't you recognize anybody here?" I told him I could not. "In the condition you are in now, I can't tell who you are." One of them had a very large set of teeth; I suppose they were three-quarters of an inch long; they came right straight down. He came up to me and sort of nodded. He had on speckled horns and calico stuff, and had a face on. He said, "Have you got a chisel here I could get?" I told him I hadn't, but I reckoned I could knock one out, and I sort of laughed. He said, "What in hell are you laughing at? It is no laughing time." I told him it sort of tickled me, and I thought I would laugh. I did not say anything then for a good while. "Old man," says one, "have you got a rope here, or a plow-line, or something of the sort?" I told him, "Yes; I had one hanging on the crib." He said, "Let us have it." One of them says, "String him up to this pine tree, and we will get all out of him. Get up, one of you, and let us pull him up, and he will tell the truth." I says, "I can't tell you anything more than I have told. There is nothing that I can tell you but what I have told you and you have asked me." One man questioned me all this time. One would come up and say, "Let's hang him a while, and he will tell us the truth"; and another then came up and said, "Old man, we are just from hell; some of us have been dead ever since the revolutionary war." . . . I was not scared, and said, "You have been through a right smart experience." "Yes," he says, "we have been through a considerable experience." One of them says, "we have just come from hell." I said, "If I had been there, I would not want to go back." . . . Then they hit me thirteen of the hardest cuts I ever got. I never had such cuts. They hit me right around my waist and by my hip, and cut a piece about as wide as my two fingers in one place. I did not say a word while they were whipping, only sort of grunted a little. As quick as they got through they said, "Go to your bed. We will have this country right before we get through; go to your bed," and they started away. . . .

Question: Who is Claudius Turner?

Answer: He is a gentleman that run for the legislature here. He was on the ticket with Mr. Scott.

Question: The republican ticket?

Answer: Yes, sir; the radical[2] ticket. . . .

By Mr. Van Trump:

Question: Explain to me, if you can, if the object of this Ku-Klux organization is to intimidate the colored people, why they were so particular as to make you promise, under penalty of death, that you would never disclose the fact that you had been visited; do you understand why that is?

---

[2] Radical Republicans were known for their support of black suffrage and the disenfranchisement of former Confederate military and civilian officers.

Answer: I can explain this fact this far: You know when they said to me to not say anything about this matter, I asked them what I must say, and when I asked, "What must I say? I will have to say something," they said, "What are you going to say?" I said, "What must I say?" He said, "Are you going to tell it?" I told them, "I have to say something, of course, and what must I say; what can I say?" Then they said, looking straight at me—

Question: Why is it that so often in giving your testimony you have to get up and make gesticulations like an orator? Have you been an orator?

Answer: No, sir, but I was showing the way they did me, and what they said to me. They said, "You just let me hear of this thing again, and we will not leave a piece of you when we come back."

Question: To whom have you talked lately about this case, or consulted here in town?

Answer: I have not consulted much about it.

Question: How long have you been waiting to be examined?

Answer: Since Tuesday about 10 o'clock.

Question: Have any white republicans been to see you?

Answer: No, sir; nobody at all.

Question: Did you see them?

Answer: I don't know who the republicans are here. I may have seen some.

Question: Do you pretend to say that since Tuesday you have not talked with any white about your case?

Answer: With none about the Ku-Klux matter.

4 | *Testimony of Lucy McMillan,*
Spartanburg, South Carolina, July 10, 1871

Lucy McMillan (colored) sworn and examined.

By the Chairman:

Question: Where do you live?

Answer: Up in the country. I live on McMillan's place, right at the foot of the road.

Question: How far is it?

Answer: Twelve miles.

Question: Are you married?

Answer: I am not married. I am single now. I was married. My husband was taken away from me and carried off twelve years ago.

Question: He was carried off before the war?

Answer: Yes, sir; the year before the war; twelve years ago this November coming.

Source: Report of the Joint Select Committee, vol. 3, South Carolina, Part II, 604–7.

Question: How old are you now?

Answer: I am called forty-six. I am forty-five or -six.

Question: Did the Ku-Klux come where you live at any time?

Answer: They came there once before they burned my house down. The way it happened was this: John Hunter's wife came to my house on Saturday morning, and told they were going to whip me. I was afraid of them; there was so much talk of Ku-Klux drowning people, and whipping people, and killing them. My house was only a little piece from the river, so I laid out at night in the woods. The Sunday evening after Isham McCrary[1] was whipped I went up, and a white man, John McMillan, came along and says to me, "Lucy, you had better stay at home, for they will whip you anyhow." I said if they have to, they might whip me in the woods, for I am afraid to stay there. Monday night they came in and burned my house down; I dodged out alongside of the road not far off and saw them. I was sitting right not far off, and as they came along the river I knew some of them. I knew John McMillan, and Kennedy McMillan, and Billy Bush, and John Hunter. They were all together. I was not far off, and I saw them. They went right on to my house. When they passed me I run further up on the hill to get out of the way of them. They went there and knocked down and beat my house a right smart while. And then they all got still, and directly I saw the fire rise.

Question: How many of these men were there?

Answer: A good many; I couldn't tell how many, but these I knew. The others I didn't. . . .

Question: What was the reason given for burning your house?

Answer: There was speaking down there last year and I came to it. They all kept at me to go. I went home and they quizzed me to hear what was said, and I told them as far as my senses allowed me.

Question: Where was this speaking?

Answer: Here in this town. I went on and told them, and then they all said I was making laws; or going to have the land, and the Ku-Klux were going to beat me for bragging that I would have land. John Hunter told them on me, I suppose, that I said I was going to have land. . . .

Question: Was that the only reason you know for your house being burned?

Answer: That is all the reason. All the Ku-Klux said all that they had against me was that I was bragging and boasting that I wanted the land. . . .

By Mr. Van Trump:

Question: Do you mean to say that they said they burned the house for that reason?

Answer: No sir; they burned the house because they could not catch me. I don't know any other reason. . . .

Question: Who was John Hunter?

Answer: He is a colored man. I worked for him all last summer. I worked with him hoeing his cotton and corn.

---

[1] Another freedman who testified before the committee in Spartanburg.

Question: What was he doing with these Ku-Klux?
Answer: I don't know. He was with them. . . .
Question: How did you come to be named Lucy McMillan?
Answer: I was a slave of Robert McMillan. I always belonged to him.
Question: You helped raise Kennedy and John?[2]
Answer: Not John, but Kennedy I did. When he was a little boy I was with him.
Question: Did he always like you?
Answer: Yes, sir. They always pretended to like us.
Question: That is while you were a slave?
Answer: Yes, sir, while I was a slave, but never afterward. They didn't care for us then.

[2] Sons of Robert McMillan.

5   *Testimony of Mervin Givens,*
Spartanburg, South Carolina, July 12, 1871

Mervin Givens (colored) sworn and examined.

By Mr. Stevenson:

Question: Your name in old times was Mery Moss?
Answer: Yes, sir; but since freedom I don't go by my master's name. My name now is Givens.
Question: What is your age?
Answer: About forty I expect. . . .
Question: Have you ever been visited by the Ku-Klux?
Answer: Yes, sir.
Question: When?
Answer: About the last of April.
Question: Tell what they said and did.
Answer: I was asleep when they came to my house, and did not know anything about them until they broke in on me.
Question: What time of night was it?
Answer: About twelve o'clock at night. They broke in on me and frightened me right smart, being asleep. They ordered me to get up and make a light. As quick as I could gather my senses I bounced up and made a light, but not quick enough. They jumped at me and struck me with a pistol, and made a knot[1] that you can see there now. By the time I made the light I catched the voice of them, and as soon as I could see by the light, I looked around and saw by the size of the men and voice so that I could judge right off who it was. By that time they

[1] Bump.

Source: Report of the Joint Select Committee, vol. 2, South Carolina, Part II, 698–700.

jerked the case off the pillow and jerked it over my head and ordered me out of doors. That was all I saw in the house. After they carried me out of doors I saw nothing more. They pulled the pillow-slip over my head and told me if I took off they would shoot me. They carried me out and whipped me powerful.

Question: With what?

Answer: With sticks and hickories. They whipped me powerful.

Question: How many lashes?

Answer: I can't tell. I have no knowledge at all about it. May be a hundred or two. Two men whipped me and both at once.

Question: Did they say anything to you?

Answer: They cursed me and told me I had voted the radical ticket, and they intended to beat me so I would not vote it again.

Question: Did you know any of them?

Answer: Yes, sir; I think I know them.

Question: What were their names?

Answer: One was named John Thomson and the other was John Zimmerman. Those are the two men I think it was.

Question: How many were there in all?

Answer: I didn't see but two. After they took me out, I was blindfolded; but I could judge from the horse tracks that there were more than two horses there. Some were horses and some were mules. It was a wet, rainy night; they whipped me stark naked. I had a brown undershirt on and they tore it clean off. . . .

By Mr. Van Trump:

Question: There were, then, two men who came to your house?

Answer: Yes, sir; that was all I could see.

Question: Were they disguised?

Answer: Yes, sir.

Question: How?

Answer: They had on some sort of gray-looking clothes, and much the same sort of thing over their face. One of them had a sort of high hat with tassel and sort of horns.

Question: How far did John Thomson live from there?

Answer: I think it is two or three miles.

Question: Were you acquainted with him?

Answer: Yes, sir.

Question: Where?

Answer: At my house. My wife did a good deal of washing for them both. I was very well-acquainted with their size and their voices. They were boys I was raised with. . . .

Question: Did you tell anybody else it was John Thomson?

Answer: I have never named it.

Question: Why?

Answer: I was afraid to.

Question: Are you afraid now?

Answer: I am not afraid to own the truth as nigh[2] as I can.

Question: Is there any difference in owning to the truth on the 12th of July and on the 1st of April?

Answer: The black people have injured themselves very much by talking, and I was afraid.

Question: Are you not afraid now?

Answer: No, sir; because I hope there will be a stop put to it. . . .

Question: Do you think we three gentlemen can stop it?

Answer: No, sir; but I think you can get some help.

Question: Has anybody been telling you that?

Answer: No, sir; nobody told me that. . . .

Question: Why did you not commence a prosecution against Thomson and Zimmerman?

Answer: I am like the rest, I reckon; I am too cowardly.

Question: Why do you not do it now; you are not cowardly now?

Answer: I shouldn't have done it now.

Question: I am talking about bringing suit for that abuse on that night. Why do you not have them arrested?

Answer: It ought to be done.

Question: Why do you not do it?

Answer: For fear they would shoot me. If I were to bring them up here and could not prove the thing exactly on them, and they were to get out of it, I would not expect to live much longer.

[2] Near.

COMMITTEE REPORTS

 ## Majority Report of the Joint Select Committee to Inquire into the Condition of Affairs in the Late Insurrectionary States, February 19, 1872, Submitted by Luke P. Poland

Poland was a Republican representative from Vermont.

The proceedings and debates in Congress show that, whatever other causes were assigned for disorders in the late insurrectionary States, the execution of the laws and the security of life and property were alleged to be most seriously threatened

Source: Report of the Joint Select Committee, vol. 1, Reports of the Committee, 2–3, 98–99.

by the existence and acts of organized bands of armed and disguised men, known as Ku-Klux. . . .

The evidence is equally decisive that redress cannot be obtained against those who commit crimes in disguise and at night. The reasons assigned are that identification is difficult, almost impossible; that when this is attempted, the combinations and oaths of the order come in and release the culprit by perjury either upon the witness-stand or in the jury-box; and that the terror inspired by their acts, as well as the public sentiment in their favor in many localities, paralyzes the arm of civil power. . . .

The race so recently emancipated, against which banishment or serfdom is thus decreed, but which has been clothed by the Government with the rights and responsibilities of citizenship, ought not to be, and we feel assured will not be left hereafter without protection against the hostilities and sufferings it has endured in the past, as long as the legal and constitutional powers of the Government are adequate to afford it. Communities suffering such evils and influenced by such extreme feelings may be slow to learn that relief can come only from a ready obedience to and support of constituted authority, looking to the modes provided by law for redress of all grievances. That Southern communities do not seem to yield this ready obedience at once should not deter the friends of good government in both sections from hoping and working for that end. . . .

The law of 1871[1] has been effective in suppressing for the present, to a great extent, the operations of masked and disguised men in North and South Carolina. . . . The apparent cessation of operations should not lead to a conclusion that community would be safe if protective measures were withdrawn. These should be continued until there remains no further doubt of the actual suppression and disarming of this wide-spread and dangerous conspiracy.

The results of suspending the writ of *habeas corpus* in South Carolina show that where the membership, mysteries, and power of the organization have been kept concealed this is the most and perhaps only effective remedy for its suppression; and in review of its cessation and resumption of hostilities at different times, of its extent and power, and that in several of the States where it exists the courts have not yet held terms at which the cases can be tried, we recommend that the power conferred on the President by the fourth section of that act[2] be extended until the end of the next session of Congress.

For the Senate:	For the House of Representatives:
John Scott, Chairman	Luke P. Poland, Chairman
Z. Chandler[3]	Horace Maynard[4]

---

[1] The Ku Klux Klan Act.

[2] To suspend the writ of habeas corpus.

[3] Republican senator from Michigan.

[4] Republican representative from Tennessee.

BENJ. F. RICE[5]   GLENNI W. SCOFIELD[6]

JOHN POOL[7]   JOHN F. FARNSWORTH[8]

DANIEL D. PRATT[9]   JOHN COBURN[10]

                                    JOB E. STEVENSON

                                    BENJ. F. BUTLER[11]

                                    WILLIAM E. LANSING[12]

[5] Republican senator from Arkansas.
[6] Republican representative from Pennsylvania.
[7] Republican senator from North Carolina.
[8] Republican representative from Illinois.
[9] Republican senator from Indiana.
[10] Republican representative from Indiana.
[11] Republican representative from Massachusetts.
[12] Republican representative from New York.

7   *Minority Report of the Joint Select Committee to Inquire into the Condition of Affairs in the Late Insurrectionary States,* February 19, 1872, Submitted by James B. Beck

Beck was a Democratic representative from Kentucky.

The atrocious measures by which millions of white people have been put at the mercy of the semi-barbarous negroes of the South, and the vilest of the white people, both from the North and South, who have been constituted the leaders of this black horde, are now sought to be justified and defended by defaming the people upon whom this unspeakable outrage had been committed. . . .

There is no doubt about the fact that great outrages were committed by bands of disguised men during those years of lawlessness and oppression. The natural tendency of all such organizations is to violence and crime. . . . It is so everywhere; like causes produce like results. Sporadic cases of outrages occur in every community. . . . But, as a rule, the worst governments produce the most disorders. South Carolina is confessedly in the worst condition of any of the States. Why? Because her government is the worst, or what makes it still worse, her people see no hope in the future. . . . There never was a Ku-Klux in Virginia, nobody pretends there ever was. Why? Because Virginia escaped carpet-bag rule. . . .

Source: Report of the Joint Select Committee, vol. 1, Reports of the Committee, 289, 463–64, 514–16, 588.

The Constitution was trampled under foot in the passage of what is known as the Ku-Klux law; a power was delegated to the President which could be exercised by the legislative authority alone; whole communities of innocent people were put under the ban of executive vengeance by the suspension of the writ of *habeas corpus* at the mere whim and caprice of the President; and all for what? For the apprehension and conviction of a few poor, deluded, ignorant, and unhappy wretches, goaded to desperation by the insolence of the negroes, and who could, had the radical authorities of South Carolina done their duty, just as easily have been prosecuted in the State courts, and much more promptly and cheaply, than by all this imposing machinery of Federal power, through military and judicial departments. . . .

. . . The antagonism, therefore, which exists between these two classes of the population of South Carolina does not spring from any political cause, in the ordinary party sense of the term; but it grows out of that instinctive and irrepressible repugnance to compulsory affiliation with another race, planted by the God of nature in the breast of the white man, perhaps more strongly manifested in the uneducated portion of the people, and aggravated and intensified by the fact that the Negro has been placed as a *ruler* over him. . . .

We feel it would be a dereliction of duty on our part if, after what we have witnessed in South Carolina, we did not admonish the American people that the present condition of things in the South cannot last. It was an oft-quoted political apothegm, long prior to the war, that no government could exist "half slave and half free." The paraphrase of that proposition is equally true, that no government can long exist "half black and half white." If the republican party, or its all-powerful leaders in the North, cannot see this, if they are so absorbed in the idea of this newly discovered political divinity in the negro, that they cannot comprehend its social repugnance or its political dangers; or, knowing it, have the wanton, wicked, and criminal purpose of disregarding its consequences, whether in the present or in the future, and the great mass of American white citizens should still be so mad as to sustain them in their heedless career of forcing negro supremacy over white men, why then "farewell, a long farewell," to constitutional liberty on this continent, and the glorious form of government bequeathed to us by our fathers. . . .

The foregoing is a hurried, but, as we believe, a truthful statement of the political, moral, and financial condition of the State of South Carolina, under the joint rule of the Negro and the "reconstructive" policy of Congress.

FRANK BLAIR

T. F. BAYARD[1]

S. S. COX[2]

JAMES B. BECK

---

[1] Democratic senator from Delaware.

[2] Democratic representative from New York.

P. Van Trump

A. M. Waddell[3]

J. C. Robinson[4]

J. M. Hanks[5]

[3] Democratic representative from North Carolina.
[4] Democratic representative from Illinois.
[5] Democratic representative from Arkansas.

Analyzing Congressional Hearings and Reports

1. How did the descriptions of the Ku Klux Klan differ between witnesses examined in Washington, D.C. (Sources 1 and 2), and those examined in South Carolina (Sources 3, 4, and 5)? How would you explain those differences?

2. Briefly compare the nature of evidence presented in the testimony. How did it differ between black and white witnesses? In what ways did the Klan's attacks on blacks differ from those on white Republicans? What do you think accounts for such differences?

3. What patterns did you find in the cross-examination of witnesses? How did Van Trump and other Democrats on the committee seek to discredit or shape the testimony they heard, and do you think they succeeded in any instances? Which witnesses do you think were most successful in answering their cross-examinations? Did any of the witnesses contradict themselves?

4. Consider whether the majority and minority reports (Sources 6 and 7) could have been written before the committee heard any witnesses. Using your notes from the second portion of the table on page 10, do you think any of the congressmen sitting on the committee had their minds changed about the Ku Klux Klan or the federal government's response to it by the testimony they heard? What specific examples or passages from the reports support your answer?

5. What does this source tell you about the limits of federal power during Reconstruction? According to the testimony and reports, what accounted for the breakdown of law and order in South Carolina, and how was it most likely to be restored? How did Republicans and Democrats differ in this regard?

6. Using the testimony you have read here, describe the social and economic conditions faced by African American men and women in the South during Reconstruction. What evidence do Thomson, McMillan, and Givens (Sources 3, 4, and 5) provide of the ways in which African American men and women valued and acted on their freedom after 1865 and of the limits whites tried to impose on that freedom?

The Rest of the Story

As noted in the Joint Select Committee's majority report, the Ku Klux Klan Act of 1871 did succeed in suppressing the Klan's activities in those regions where it was enforced. In October 1871, while the Joint Select Committee was still at work, President Grant suspended the writ of habeas corpus in nine South Carolina counties, including Spartanburg, and sent in federal troops to arrest approximately fifteen hundred suspected Klansmen. Even more Klansmen fled the region to avoid prosecution. In a series of trials managed by Amos Akerman, attorney general of the United States, in late 1871 and in 1872, approximately ninety Klansmen were sentenced to prison terms ranging from three months to ten years. Most of those given long sentences were released within a year or two, under amnesty offered by Grant. Overall, very few Klansmen were ever brought to meaningful justice for their crimes, but by the election of 1872, reports of Klan terrorism had declined considerably, and the organization's ability to intimidate black voters appeared to have been broken.

During the 1920s, the Ku Klux Klan was revived by whites who felt threatened by Catholic and Jewish immigrants as well as by African Americans. At its peak, this version of the Klan included three million members and spilled beyond the South into western and northern states. After ebbing in the 1940s, the Klan surged again during the civil rights movement of the 1950s and 1960s. This incarnation was much smaller than its predecessor in the 1920s but more violent in its resistance to racial equality. Today, a number of white supremacist organizations continue to call themselves the Ku Klux Klan, but they are poorly organized and constantly at odds with one another and with similar hate groups on the far right of American politics.

In the larger story of Reconstruction, the Ku Klux Klan Act and the congressional investigation of the Klan appeared to be shining examples of how the federal government and African Americans in the South acted in partnership to advance the cause of racial justice and equality in the United States. Unfortunately, these successes were short-lived. During his second term, Grant reduced the number of federal troops in the South, and the Republicans split between a liberal faction still committed to racial equality and a more conservative faction willing to jettison Reconstruction policies and black voters in return for political compromises with Democrats on other issues.

The third branch of the federal government did not help African Americans in their pursuit of equality either. In two cases from the 1870s, the Supreme Court interpreted the Fourteenth Amendment in such a way that it severely restricted the federal government's ability to intervene on behalf of private citizens when their civil and political rights were violated. In the *Slaughterhouse Cases* (1873), the Court ruled that the Fourteenth Amendment protected only those rights that were derived directly from the federal government, most of which dealt with matters of interstate or foreign travel or business; the civil rights of most concern to blacks in the South still fell under the jurisdiction of state courts and law enforcement. In *United States v. Cruikshank* (1876), the Court ruled that the Fourteenth Amendment empowered the federal government only to prosecute violations of civil rights by the states, not by individual persons (violations in that category still fell under state jurisdiction). The combined effect of these two decisions was to place responsibility for protecting the rights of the South's African American population under the authority of the state governments, while making any federal intervention on their behalf similar to that pursued under the Ku Klux Klan Act unconstitutional.

After the last of the former Confederate states had fallen back into Democratic hands in 1877, Southern whites found new ways to confine blacks to second-class citizenship. Insulated from federal intervention by the Supreme Court's decisions and congressional indifference, Southern states passed laws that disenfranchised blacks by imposing poll taxes and literacy tests. They also erected a system of social segregation known as Jim Crow laws that limited black access to education and economic opportunity. When blacks challenged this system, mobs and night riders responded with the same methods used by the Klan, most notably lynching and arson, to prevent any sustained resistance to white rule. Not until the civil rights movement of the 1950s would the federal government again embrace the cause of racial justice in the South with the same vigor it had shown during its battle against the Klan in 1871.

To Find Out More

Resources on Reconstruction

"America's Reconstruction: People and Politics after the Civil War." *Digital History*. University of Houston. http://www.digitalhistory.uh.edu/exhibits/reconstruction/.

Miller, Stephen F. *The Freedmen and Southern Society Project*. University of Maryland. http://www.history.umd.edu/Freedmen.

Report of the Joint Select Committee to Inquire into the Condition of Affairs in the Late Insurrectionary States. 13 vols. Washington, DC: Government Printing Office, 1872.

Tourgée, Albion W. *The Invisible Empire*. 1880; repr., Baton Rouge: Louisiana State University Press, 1989.

Secondary Sources on Reconstruction and the Struggle for Racial Equality

Foner, Eric. *Reconstruction: America's Unfinished Revolution, 1863–1877*. New York: Harper and Row, 1988.

Hahn, Steven. *A Nation under Our Feet: Black Political Struggles in the Rural South from Slavery to the Great Migration*. Cambridge, MA: Belknap Press, 2003.

Rable, George C. *But There Was No Peace: The Role of Violence in the Politics of Reconstruction*. Athens: University of Georgia Press, 1984.

Trelease, Allen W. *White Terror: The Ku Klux Klan Conspiracy and Southern Reconstruction*. New York: Harper and Row, 1971.

CHAPTER 2

Picturing a Western Myth

Photography and the Blackfeet Indians

I n 1996, Elouise Cobell, a member of the Blackfeet tribe of Native Americans and founder of the Blackfeet National Bank, filed a federal lawsuit to force the U.S. Department of Interior to provide a full accounting of its century-long oversight of native lands. Cobell, a trained accountant and director of the Blackfeet Reservation Development Fund Inc., took this drastic action because she "got fed up" with the federal government's chaotic bookkeeping and evasive answers to questions she asked about the workings of the Indian Trust Fund, which was created in the late nineteenth century to manage Native Americans' land.

This lawsuit, which was finally settled in 2010, points to both failures and successes in Native American history. The U.S. government failed to honor the autonomy of native tribes and failed to negotiate an honest economic settlement with them, but tribes and their members succeeded in surviving U.S. government encroachments onto their lands and into their cultures, and tribes such as the Blackfeet continue to challenge federal control of their communities.

At the end of the nineteenth century, few Americans, white or native, would have predicted any success for the nation's surviving 250,000 tribal people. Native Americans' friends and foes shared the belief that the nation's indigenous population was a "vanishing" people, destined to become extinct or to abandon tribal cultures, adopt modern modes of life, and assimilate as individuals, not as tribal members, into white society. Indeed, the policy of the U.S. government was to teach—or force—Native Americans to give up their tribal identities and follow the government's dictate to "walk the white man's road."

Ironically, it was the U.S. government that created the greatest obstacles to Blackfeet efforts to modernize while maintaining tribal identity and tribal customs. From 1855 to 1895, treaties with the Blackfeet denied the tribe and its members their economic autonomy. In those decades, the Blackfeet signed treaties allowing the U.S. government to build roads, railroads, telegraph lines, military posts, missions, schools, and "government agencies" throughout Blackfeet territory; the tribe also granted white settlers access to minerals, water, and, of course, acreage. In sharp contrast to all other "civilized" business deals of the day, the government did not pay the Blackfeet in actual cash funds that tribal members could bank, invest, and use to design their own approach to modernization. Instead, the U.S. government agreed to provide "useful goods and services" and to create programs promoting the "civilization and Christianization" of the Blackfeet. Moreover, all government payments were made according to the U.S. government's timetable and were sometimes withheld if the government had other priorities. As a result, treaties with the United States did not give the Blackfeet independent access to the economic resources that would have allowed them to create their own style of assimilation.

In the four decades between 1870 and 1910, between the close of the Civil War era and the opening of Glacier National Park, the problems with federal Indian policy became clear to the Blackfeet. In these decades, buffalo disappeared from the northern Montana grasslands, partly because whites overhunted buffalo for sport and partly because the only economic activity left to the Blackfeet lay in supplying buffalo meat to the tribe and selling buffalo hides to whites. So they, too, overhunted. At the same time, more than twenty thousand land-hungry white settlers poured into the Montana Territory, occasionally meeting with violent resistance from the Blackfeet and fighting off that resistance with the help of the U.S. Army. Military reprisals against Blackfeet resistance were so harsh in these years that a *New York Times* editorial denounced the killing of women and children as a tactic for pacifying the Blackfeet.

The combination of food shortages, smallpox, and conflict with whites reduced the Blackfeet population from 8,000 in 1855 to 2,500 in 1880. Another 20 percent died of starvation in the winter of 1884 when the federal government failed to deliver food allotments owed in exchange for land. The starving remainder of the Blackfeet nation negotiated two major land sales to the government in 1887 and 1895. By the turn of the century, the 2,000 surviving residents of the Blackfeet reservation still owned 1.5 million acres of grazing land, but they had relinquished ownership of the western mountains, lakes, and streams that had been a vital source of the tribe's spiritual and dietary nourishment. In each of the two major land sales, the Blackfeet received $1.5 million, half what they asked for. Again, payment never came as a direct infusion of capital that the tribe could control and invest; it was always in the form of goods and services controlled and distributed by the Bureau of Indian Affairs, by then a famously corrupt arm of the federal government.

As white ranchers, farmers, and miners were moving onto Blackfeet lands, an emerging lobby of white conservationists was increasingly alarmed that uncontrolled development would destroy the West's natural beauty and resources. The conservationists realized that they could protect pockets of the region

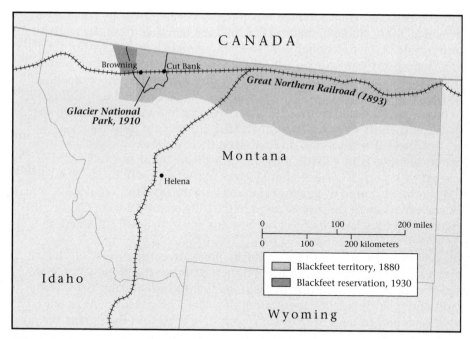

Map 2.1 Glacier National Park and the Blackfeet, 1880–1930 *This map shows the reach of the Great Northern Railway and its connecting lines by 1909, on the eve of congressional approval for Glacier National Park. With the railway lines already built, advocates for the national park could argue that tourists would have easy access to the park's natural beauty and manufactured luxuries. As the map indicates, the Blackfeet had given up millions of acres of land by 1909, and they would give up even more after the park was built.*

by appealing to Americans' nostalgia for the vanishing wilderness. In 1910, conservationists joined with the Great Northern Railway Company, which stood to profit from tourism trade in Montana. Together, they won congressional approval for Glacier National Park, 1,600 square miles of alpine beauty that had once formed the "backbone" of the Blackfeet's world (see Map 2.1). The Great Northern financed the construction of roads and trails, two magnificent hotels, and a series of smaller "chalets" and tourist-friendly camps around the park. In less than a decade, aggressive marketing increased tourism to Glacier National Park from four thousand visitors in the summer of 1911 to almost twenty thousand in the summer of 1920. Advertisements for Glacier National Park promised tourists a "wilderness experience," including glimpses of the "vanishing" Blackfeet Indian. Countless brochures, calendars, postcards, and magazine layouts featured photographs of the Blackfeet, described as "specimens of a Great Race soon to disappear." The publicity campaign was so successful that the image of the Blackfeet, with their feathered headdresses and buffalo-hide tipis, became the standard image of all American Indians, despite great variations in dress and housing among Native Americans.

The Blackfeet tribe survived this modern development by adapting to its demands. Every summer, members of the tribe relocated from the reservation, just outside Glacier National Park, to live in designated areas within the park. The Great Northern Railroad paid these tribal members to occupy traditional tipis and wear costumes that twentieth-century whites thought of as authentic. Although publicity stills occasionally depicted a Blackfeet man spearing a fish or holding his bow and arrows, the rules governing national parks actually denied Blackfeet their treaty rights to hunt and fish in their old territory.

For those Blackfeet who profited from their summertime performances as historical artifacts in a living museum, this pragmatic use of their culture was layered with irony. Glacier National Park's marketing myth of the "vanishing" Indian was reinforced by government policy on the Blackfeet reservation, where federal agents spent the money owed to the tribe on programs to dissolve tribal identity and transform Blackfeet hunters into the individualized American family farmer.

As part of the government's effort to put Native Americans "on the white man's road," the Dawes Severalty Act of 1887 made it U.S. policy to encourage all natives to divide tribally held lands into individually held, 160-acre plots and to farm independently from the tribe. The government promised to hold each plot of land in trust for twenty-five years and then grant the land as well as citizenship to the former tribal member who had individually farmed that land. To oversee this policy, the Dawes Act established the Indian Trust Fund, whose poor accounting procedures were at the heart of the modern Blackfeet suit against the U.S. government. Furthermore, the Dawes Act, which was hailed in 1887 as a reform that would assimilate Native Americans into American culture, failed to acknowledge economic and environmental realities. The family plot ideal that the Dawes Act promoted was wholly unsuited to Montana's hot, dry summers and long, cold winters. Direct payments to purchase grazing herds would have made more sense. Indeed, the most prosperous Blackfeet were those with white fathers who brought their own livestock to graze for free on their Blackfeet mothers' tribal grasslands. In a 1900 report, the U.S. Commissioner of Indian Affairs admitted that only 500 acres on the Blackfeet reservation were under farm cultivation.

In the first three decades of the twentieth century, as the Great Northern Railroad was eulogizing the passing of a "Great Race," the Blackfeet were not in fact vanishing, nor were they strictly adhering to the government's assimilation plan. Instead, they were striving to create an alternative method of survival that retained tribal integrity while using the opportunities presented by the surrounding white society. An excellent example of the Blackfeet's creativity in this regard is their adaptation of the Sun Dance. Christian missionaries and federal agents regarded the Sun Dance as a blatant display of "heathen worship" that had to be exterminated if the Blackfeet were ever to assimilate. Other whites, including the managers of Glacier National Park, were fascinated by the Blackfeet's elaborate ritual of sacred vows to the holy sun. By the beginning of the twentieth century, the Blackfeet had rescheduled the Sun Dance to coincide with the Fourth of July, turning it into a major tourist attraction that the church and the government dared not oppose. In this way, as well as other ways, the Blackfeet preserved their tribal traditions while adapting to the demands of modern life.

Using the Source: Photographs

The Great Northern Railroad used photographs to sell its images of the "vanishing" Blackfeet to the American public. In fact, the belief that Native Americans were on the verge of extinction inspired a great many nineteenth-century photographers to pile their bulky cameras, tripods, glass plates, developing chemicals, and darkroom tents onto the backs of horses and venture out West. Thus, a modern technology was used to document the existence of those thought to be threatened by modernity. The photographs that have survived as tangible documents can help us appreciate the complex blend of old and new that resulted in survival for tribes like the Blackfeet.

Photographs are one of the most modern types of documents available. For centuries, people have consulted written texts, paintings, sculptures, music, and all sorts of manufactured artifacts to reconstruct human life in the past, but not until the 1840s did technological invention make it possible to capture and preserve an image of a physical object. Photographs thus revolutionized human access to the past, giving every viewer a unique window on people and places long gone.

Native Americans became the subjects of photographs as early as the 1850s, when Indian delegations to Washington, D.C., were regularly photographed as part of the official record of treaty negotiations. Joseph Henry, the first secretary of the Smithsonian Institution, tried to raise government funds in 1867 to build a complete photographic record of the "principal tribes of the U.S." by arguing that "the Indians are passing away so rapidly that but few years remain within which this can be done, and the loss will be irretrievable . . . when they are gone."

Henry was not granted his funds, so photography of Indians proceeded in a haphazard way, driven by technology and influenced by commercial, cultural, and personal motives. Native warriors went to portrait studios in the 1860s, where they sat motionless for the eighty seconds required to capture an image on a glass plate. Professional photographers in the West, burdened by early technology's requirement that they develop every photo within ten minutes of taking it, still managed to capture images of people in their native environments.

Thanks to the introduction of George Eastman's handheld "box" camera in 1888, photography became the pastime of amateurs as well as the business of professionals, and the "vanishing" Indian continued to be a favorite photographic subject into the twentieth century. Today, there are more than ninety thousand photographs at the National Museum of the American Indian (NMAI) at the Smithsonian Institution in Washington, D.C., and that museum holds just one of dozens of photographic archives in the United States that serve, according to one historian, as "a collective witness to Indian transitions."

What Can Photographs Tell Us?

Photographs are a valuable historical source for an obvious reason: they give us visual access to a wealth of information on the natural world, material culture, social life, and human emotion. Photographs allow us to gather subtle details about life in the past that cannot be gathered from any other source. The camera, as we all know, doesn't lie, but we also know that every camera has an angle. More precisely, every camera has a photographer operating it, a person who brings some mix of cultural attitudes, personal emotions, economic motives, and artistic assumptions to the picture-taking process. When reading a photograph for evidence of the past, we cannot afford to regard the camera as a neutral technology or the photograph as a purely "objective" witness. We must regard every photograph as the creative product of a photographer's point of view and must put each photograph into the context in which it was taken.

Imagine, for example, how distorted our view of Blackfeet life in the early twentieth century would be if the only surviving photographs were the publicity shots commissioned for Glacier National Park. The highly skilled, world-famous photographers, such as Edward S. Curtis and Roland Reed, who created these photographs for companies like the Great Northern Railway, often manipulated the scene by blocking out signs of modern life and paying tribal people to dress in anachronistic costumes and pose in a wistful or stoic stance. Thanks to the improvements to the easy-to-use box camera in the 1890s, we also have access to somewhat more candid images of the Blackfeet on their own reservation, outside the gates of Glacier National Park. These amateur photographs, probably taken by store merchants or U.S. Indian agents, did not block out modern life or the Blackfeet's accommodation to that life.

Consider this detail from an amateur photograph on the facing page, taken around 1930 at a traditional tribal dance on the reservation, where the audience included tourists from Glacier National Park. On the one hand, it provides a wealth of evidence on the blending of native culture with modern American culture. On the other hand, it raises a host of unanswerable questions about the thoughts and feelings of those who appear in the photo.

Although this photograph offers valuable information on the Blackfeet's incorporation of American products into daily tribal life, it cannot tell us the relationship between the material objects and the tribal women. Does the automobile signify the natives' own prosperity, or is it a sign of white wealth derived from Blackfeet land? Do the American flags denote the Blackfeet's deference to governmental power, their patriotism, or their calculated use of

Consider the meaning of the American flags

Important clue for dating the photo

What is the significance of farm machinery next to a tipi?

Note the use of sunglasses

Source: Minnesota Historical Society.

white icons in tribal rituals? Such questions remind us that photographs alone cannot reveal all we want to know about the objects in front of the camera. The Checklist questions on page 36 will help you evaluate photographs as historical evidence.

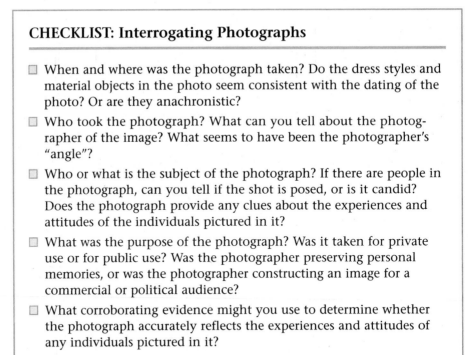

CHECKLIST: Interrogating Photographs

☐ When and where was the photograph taken? Do the dress styles and material objects in the photo seem consistent with the dating of the photo? Or are they anachronistic?

☐ Who took the photograph? What can you tell about the photographer of the image? What seems to have been the photographer's "angle"?

☐ Who or what is the subject of the photograph? If there are people in the photograph, can you tell if the shot is posed, or is it candid? Does the photograph provide any clues about the experiences and attitudes of the individuals pictured in it?

☐ What was the purpose of the photograph? Was it taken for private use or for public use? Was the photographer preserving personal memories, or was the photographer constructing an image for a commercial or political audience?

☐ What corroborating evidence might you use to determine whether the photograph accurately reflects the experiences and attitudes of any individuals pictured in it?

Source Analysis Table

The photographs you will be examining include commercial photographs used for publicity by the Great Northern Railway Company and shots taken by amateur photographers on the Blackfeet reservation outside Glacier National Park. By comparing them, you can consider the ways in which traditional Blackfeet culture became a marketing tool for whites, the ways in which traditional native culture continued to have meaning for the Blackfeet, as well as the ways in which the Blackfeet adapted to modern market society.

	Signs of Traditional Culture	Signs of Modern Society
COMMERCIAL GLACIER NATIONAL PARK PHOTOS		
1. Greetings from Glacier National Park		
2. Great Northern Railway Calendar		
3. Blackfeet and Park Golfers		
4. Spearfishing in Glacier National Park		
5. Two Guns White Calf Reading		

(continued)

	Signs of Traditional Culture	Signs of Modern Society
AMATEUR RESERVATION PHOTOS		
6. Old Ration Place		
7. Blackfeet Performance		
8. Family at Sun Dance Encampment		
9. Students with Their Harvest		
10. Mad Plume Family Harvest		
11. Blackfeet Girl at Glacier National Park Switchboard		
12. Sewing Class at the Cut Bank Boarding School		

The Source: Photographs of the Blackfeet at Glacier National Park and on the Reservation, 1890–1930

COMMERCIAL PHOTOGRAPHS FROM GLACIER NATIONAL PARK

1

Greetings from Glacier National Park, c. 1920

The following photo was used in a variety of Glacier National Park publicity materials throughout the 1920s. This photo appeared at the top of park stationery and on the front of specialized brochures sent to convention participants. It was often accompanied by the words "Ki-tuk-a, Stum-ik-Us-tsi-kai-yi" and "Ok-yi! Ik-so-ka-pi," along with the translation: "Us Indians will be glad to see you at Glacier Park this summer and next summer too" and "We shake hands with you!" Typically, the photo's caption promised that the men in the photo would be at the Glacier National Park train station to greet conventioneers when they arrived.

Source: Minnesota Historical Society.

2   *Great Northern Railway Calendar,* 1923

The Great Northern Railway Company made extensive use of commercial photographs of the Blackfeet in this popular form of advertising.

Source: Minnesota Historical Society.

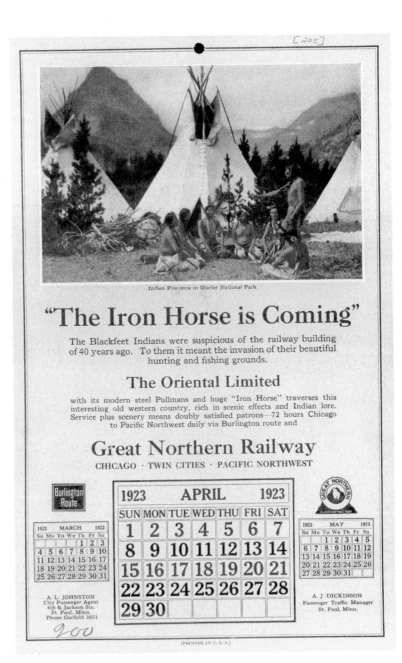

3 *Blackfeet and Park Golfers,* c. 1930

Blackfeet sometimes served as caddies for Glacier National Park golfers, but this undated publicity photo does not depict the natives in that role.

Source: Minnesota Historical Society.

4   *Spearfishing in Glacier National Park,* date unknown

Although it made for an impressive publicity shot, the Blackfeet art of spearfishing could not actually be pursued in Glacier National Park.

Source: Minnesota Historical Society.

5 | *Two Guns White Calf Reading,* date unknown

Two Guns White Calf often appeared in Glacier National Park publicity shots. Here, Tomer Hileman posed him reading a book by Zane Grey, a famous writer of western stories.

Source: Minnesota Historical Society.

AMATEUR PHOTOGRAPHS TAKEN ON BLACKFEET RESERVATION IN MONTANA

6   *Old Ration Place,* date unknown

Blackfeet sale of tribal lands to the U.S. government was paid for in food rations. After the buffalo disappeared, Blackfeet gathered each week for the one and a half pounds of beef, the half pound of flour, and small amounts of beans, bacon, salt, soda, and coffee that were allocated to each man, woman, and child.

Source: Montana Historical Society Research Center Photograph Archives, Helena, MT.

7   *Blackfeet Performance,* c. 1930

This photo from the Great Northern Railway's photo archives does not appear to have been used for Glacier National Park publicity. It suggests that park visitors in the 1930s took day trips to the reservation to view Blackfeet performances. This gathering may have been a combined celebration of the Blackfeet's Sun Dance and the Fourth of July.

Source: Minnesota Historical Society.

8   *Family at Sun Dance Encampment,* 1908

Blackfeet traveled to a central location on the reservation for the annual Sun Dance. This 1908 photo, taken at that year's Sun Dance encampment, shows one family's display of finery and prized possessions.

9 | *Students with Their Harvest,* 1912

This photo and the next reflect the government's effort to encourage Blackfeet vegetable farming in the decades following the 1887 Dawes Act. The students shown here attended the Cut Bank Boarding School, where sailor suits were the regulation uniform.

10   *Mad Plume Family Harvest,* c. 1920

Albert and Susan Mad Plume and members of their family display their harvest for a photographer. They were among the full-blooded Blackfeet who supported the government's plans for agricultural self-sufficiency.

11 *Blackfeet Girl at Glacier National Park Switchboard,* c. 1920

This photo, probably taken in the 1920s, is from the Great Northern Railway's photo archive but was not used for publicity. It suggests that some Blackfeet were hired into jobs at Glacier National Park that gave them training in marketable skills.

Source: Minnesota Historical Society.

12   *Sewing Class at the Cut Bank Boarding School,* 1907

At government-sponsored boarding schools, Blackfeet were taught to use modern technology and encouraged to assimilate into American culture. Native recollections of these schooling experiences vary widely; some former students have very positive memories, whereas others report being made to feel inferior.

Source: Courtesy of the Sherburne Collection, University of Montana Archives.

Analyzing Photographs

1. What are the differences in the ways that tradition and modernity are depicted in the commercial photographs taken in Glacier National Park and in the amateur photographs taken on the reservation? How do you explain those differences?

2. What do the amateur photographs taken on the reservation tell us about the Blackfeet tribe's incorporation of modern material goods into their daily lives?

3. Can the commercial photographs be used as evidence that the Blackfeet supported the development of Glacier National Park on their traditional tribal lands?

4. If the publicity photos taken at Glacier National Park are inauthentic representations of Blackfeet life, how can they contribute to our historical knowledge about Native Americans?

5. Every photograph calls up a variety of stories in our minds. Write two different "stories" to describe what might be going on in the photographs in Sources 3 and 9. What additional evidence would you seek to test the validity of your stories?

6. Imagine finding a box of old and completely unidentified family photographs in the attic of the house you just moved into. What steps would you take to figure out who was in the photos, when the photos were taken, and who took them?

The Rest of the Story

In December 2009, the Obama administration settled the lawsuit brought by Elouise Cobell in 1996 on behalf of her tribe, the Blackfeet, and all other Indian people in the United States. At the time of the settlement, Attorney General Eric Holder stated, "Over the past thirteen years, the parties have tried to settle this case many, many times, each time unsuccessfully. But today we turn the page. This settlement is fair to the plaintiffs, responsible for the United States, and provides a path forward to the future." It took another year, however, for Congress to agree to allocate the $3.4 billion agreed upon as restitution for the $150 billion withheld from Indian people by the U.S. Department of Interior.

The year-long delay in funding the suit's settlement was just one more step in a long history of problems between Native Americans and the U. S. government. At the heart of Cobell's original suit was the 1887 Dawes Act, which theoretically allocated 160 acres of reservation land to individual Native American families, including the Blackfeet in Montana, but then held that land "in trust" for twenty-five years. In addition, the "surplus" reservation land that was not broken up for family plots was leased to white ranchers, farmers, and mining companies. When Indian families were unable to survive on their 160-acre plots (and prevented from selling the land outright), the government stepped in and leased those lands to whites who had the resources to extract the water and minerals and to buy grazing herds. Cobell's lawsuit asked: What has the Department of Interior done with all the money from more than a century of leasing and selling off Indian lands? Can the government produce accounts proving that Native Americans were properly recompensed for their lands?

Long before Cobell raised these questions, the U.S. government had openly admitted that it could not possibly account for all the monies extracted from Indian lands because of a long history of mismanagement, theft, and document destruction within the Bureau of Indian Affairs. Back in 1929, the General Accounting Office had reported that "numerous expenditures [have been] made from these funds" that did not go to Indian landowners and conceded that the trust fund's accounting methods were so poor that it was impossible to certify that "the Indian received the full measure of benefit to which he was entitled." More than sixty years later, a 1992 congressional report titled "Misplaced Trust: The Bureau of Indian Affairs' Mismanagement of the Indian Trust Fund" again confirmed a history of inadequate accounting and payment practices.

In 1999, Judge Royce C. Lamberth, the U.S. district judge then charged with overseeing this case, indicated his skepticism about the federal government's reliability by transferring jurisdiction over the Indian Trust Fund from the Department of Interior to the U.S. district court. Frustrated with the government's obstruction tactics in the case, the judge ruled that the Interior Department's "degenerate tenure as Trustee-Delegate for the Indian Trust . . . is shot through with bureaucratic blunders, flubs, goofs and foul-ups, and peppered with scandals, deception, dirty tricks and outright villainy, the end of which is nowhere in sight."

The $3.4 billion agreed upon in the 2010 settlement was predictably far less than the amount Cobell estimated was owed for the extraction of water and minerals and the use of grazing lands over the decades. Some Native Americans have criticized the settlement because it will pay out millions of dollars to those who have worked on the case for more than a decade, including Cobell herself. Back in 2003, when the suit was still embattled, the Blackfeet awarded Cobell the status of "warrior." After the settlement was announced, some charged her with profiting from the case. Blackfeet Tribal Chairman Willie Sharp Jr., however, asked the critics in the National Congress of American Indians, "Where were all these armchair Cobell authorities over fifteen years ago? Why didn't they do something then? She was the only one," Sharp argued, to take action and see the case through to the end. Now that Congress has agreed to fund the settlement, it will be used to pay lawyers and to award sums of about $1,000 to $1,500 to individual members of various tribes. That may not sound like a great deal of money to some, but it is if you live in the Blackfeet community of Browning, Montana, where unemployment and poverty continue to testify to the legacy of the Dawes Act.

To Find Out More

Photographs of Native Americans

Bush, Alfred L., and Lee Clark Mitchell, eds. *The Photograph and the American Indian*. Princeton, NJ: Princeton University Press, 1994.

Great Northern Railway Company archives. Minnesota State Historical Society, St. Paul, MN. htpp://www.mnhs.org/library/. Contains the commercial photographs of Blackfeet used in advertising Glacier National Park.

Farr, William E. *The Reservation Blackfeet, 1882–1945: A Photographic History of Cultural Survival*. Seattle: University of Washington Press, 1984. Contains amateur photographs taken on the reservation.

Johnson, Tim, ed. *Spirit Capture: Photographs from the National Museum of the American Indian*. Washington, DC: Smithsonian Institution Press, 1998. Excellent collection of photographs of members of various Native American nations.

Secondary Sources on Blackfeet Indian History

Dippie, Brian W. *The Vanishing American: White Attitudes and U.S. Indian Policy*. Middletown, CT: Wesleyan University Press, 1982.

Ewers, John C. *The Blackfeet: Raiders on the Northwestern Plains*. Norman: University of Oklahoma Press, 1967.

Harrod, Howard L. *Mission among the Blackfeet*. Norman: University of Oklahoma Press, 1971.

Rosier, Paul. *Rebirth of the Blackfeet Nation, 1912–1954*. Lincoln: University of Nebraska Press, 2001.

Spence, Mark David. *Dispossessing the Wilderness: Indian Removal and the Making of the National Parks*. New York: Oxford University Press, 1999.

Other Resources on the Blackfeet Nation and Native Americans

Blackfeet Nation. http://www.blackfeetnation.com. Offers information on the Blackfeet today.

Cobell v. Salazar. http://www.cobellsettlement.com. Elouise Cobell's site regarding the suit against the U.S. government.

Hirschfelder, Arlen, and Martha Kreipe de Montano, eds. *The Native American Almanac: A Portrait of Native America Today*. New York: Prentice Hall General Reference and Travel, 1993.

National Museum of the American Indian. http://www.nmai.si.edu. Includes resources on Native American history and contemporary life.

NativeWeb. http://www.nativeweb.org. Articles and links on Indians in the past and present.

U.S. Bureau of Indian Affairs. http://www.bia.gov. Historical and contemporary documents on Native Americans, along with an index to relevant government and other Web sites.

U.S. Census Bureau. http://factfinder.census.gov/home/aian/index.html. Recent population data on Native Americans.

Welch, James. *Fools Crow*. New York: Viking Press, 1986. A highly praised novel that tells the story of the Blackfeet tribe through the eyes of a young male tribe member coming of age in the decades after the Civil War.

CHAPTER 3

Reading the 1894 Pullman Strike

Chicago's Daily Papers Report the News

Victor Harding was working as a reporter for the *Chicago Times* in the summer of 1894 when the Pullman labor strike tied up rail lines from Lake Michigan to the Pacific Ocean. On the night of July 5, when federal troops marched into Chicago to break the strike at its center, Harding mounted a horse and rode up and down the city's miles of railway track to witness the uprising of thousands of unemployed workers. He saw twenty railcars overturned at Forty-third Street, saw gangs of boys with iron pipes destroy a railway switching mechanism, and watched the smoke billow up from railcars set afire. Harding noted that few of the rioters were railroad workers and even fewer police were taking action to stop the rebellion. Chicago seemed headed for a conflagration, and the unions, the railway companies, the police, and the army seemed unable to stop it.

The Pullman strike had begun eight weeks earlier, in May 1894, as a peaceful labor protest against a single Chicago employer. On its face, there was nothing remarkable about this particular local strike against the Pullman Palace Car Company. Although all labor strikes were illegal in the United States in this industrializing era, that fact did not silence the thousands of workers' protests staged in the three decades following the Civil War. The Pullman strike might have erupted and been put down like countless others. Instead, uniquely combustible conditions in the early summer of 1894 ignited it, causing this local strike to explode first into a national labor boycott of more than twenty railroads and then into a violent confrontation between the federal government, the railroad companies, and American workers. A singular mix of employer resistance, government aggression, worker bitterness, and general economic desperation transformed the Pullman strike into a pivotal event, intensifying debates about the rights of employers and workers in an industrialized democracy and about the role of government in labor disputes.

Long before the strike, the Pullman Palace Car Company and its president, George Pullman, were famous. Pullman had perfected the passenger railcar, providing comfortable seats and sleeper cars to the traveling public in the 1870s and 1880s. Pullman's cars were so popular and his business dealings so shrewd that by 1890 three-fourths of the nation's railroads were under contract to carry only Pullman passenger cars, and the brand name "Pullman" had become synonymous with "passenger car." In addition to the fame of his product, George Pullman was well known for creating the "model" industrial town of Pullman, Illinois, just fifteen miles south of Chicago.

Some observers admired the town's array of 1,400 redbrick rental units, which ranged from boardinghouses and two-bedroom tenements to four-bedroom homes. Others praised its modern system of water, gas, and sewage. Still others, however, criticized the town George Pullman built because it lacked any elected government and because the company exercised paternalistic control over the company-owned schoolhouse, shopping arcade, library (where borrowers had to pay a member's fee), and hotel (the fanciest building in town and the only place where alcoholic beverages could be sold). Some critics also complained that George Pullman owned the only church building in town and set the rent too high for working-class congregations, thereby forcing workers to attend churches in neighboring towns. Pullman, however, was firm on the subject of rent in Pullman town: this real estate endeavor was no charity. Investors in the Pullman Land Association were assured of a steady 5 percent return on their shares in the town's rental properties.

Pullman workers experienced both boom and bust in the year before their strike. The World's Columbian Exposition, held in Chicago in 1893 to celebrate industrial progress in the United States, momentarily stimulated full employment and high wages in Pullman town, but the New York stock market crash that same year led to the bankruptcy of sixteen thousand businesses nationwide, including hundreds of railroads. The depression of 1894 was the worst the United States had ever suffered in its tumultuous economic history, and the worst it would suffer until 1929.

In the town of Pullman itself, the 1894 depression caused layoffs, wage cuts, and increased resentment over the company's housing policies. During the exposition's boom time, fewer than 40 percent of the 4,500 Pullman workers had chosen to live in the company town. Most chose to live in neighboring towns, with lower rents, greater personal independence, and the opportunity to buy their own homes. When the depression began, the Pullman Palace Car Company laid off workers, cut wages by as much as 40 percent, and then gave rehiring preference to those workers who agreed to take up residence in Pullman town, where the rents were not reduced at all. Bitterness over these practices grew because management salaries did not decline during the depression and because those who owned stock in the company were still receiving their guaranteed annual dividends of 8 percent. Angry that they were bearing more than their fair share of the economic depression, Pullman workers joined the American

*Figure 3.1 **Pullman Workers Head for Home*** *This photo shows Pullman workers on a regular workday, headed toward their homes just south across Florence Boulevard, which was named for Pullman's daughter. These factory buildings have been demolished, but the brick houses that workers rented have become valued properties in today's housing market.* Source: Historic Pullman Foundation.

Railway Union (ARU) early in 1894 and voted to strike on May 11, after George Pullman and his managers refused to negotiate with the union over wages or rents.

It was no accident that this conflict was centered in the midwestern city of Chicago, which had become a transportation nexus by 1894. On one side of the struggle, the railroad owners belonged to voluntary collectives like the General Managers' Association (GMA), which represented the twenty-four railroads with terminals in Chicago. GMA members secretly set wage scales and work rules for its member railway lines and negotiated with a few highly skilled workers in small craft unions while blacklisting all workers who tried to form industry-wide unions. On the other side of the struggle was the ARU, a brand-new, national, "industrial" union in which skilled, semiskilled, and unskilled railroad workers joined together in one industry-wide association. Railway owners feared the potential power of the ARU, which first appeared in 1893 and claimed 150,000 members by 1894. Just weeks before the Pullman strike began, the ARU reached a favorable settlement in a strike against the Great Northern Railroad, and the members of the GMA understood that this new union was the player to beat.

In late June 1894, the ARU, led by its charismatic president, Eugene V. Debs, transformed the local strike in Pullman into a national struggle within the railway industry. By then, the local strike had been under way for six weeks, and public sympathy lay with the workers, who appeared to be battling a stubborn, paternalistic employer. Debs and the ARU hoped for a great victory by refusing to handle any Pullman cars on the railway lines, thereby forcing George Pullman to the negotiating table. The railway owners in the GMA, however, strengthened Pullman's hand by claiming that their railways were contract-bound to carry Pullman cars. So, if workers refused to attach Pullman cars to their trains, then the railways would be forced to cease all railway service, not just Pullman car service. The GMA was betting that public sympathy would turn against the workers if a boycott of Pullman cars disrupted all vital arteries of trade, travel, and mail service.

The chaos resulting from the boycott lasted from June 26 to July 10, but those two weeks brought a bloody end to the ARU's national effort and the local Pullman strike. During the first week of the showdown, nearly 100,000 railway workers refused to handle Pullman cars, and the GMA's twenty-four railway companies refused to run trains without Pullman cars. As a result, vital trade arteries in twenty-seven states were stalled and snarled, which meant delays and disruptions for travelers, manufactured goods, fuel, livestock, produce, and—most important—the U.S. mail. During the second week of the standoff, control of events shifted from the railway workers to the federal government.

In the summer of 1894, officials in President Grover Cleveland's administration were in no mood to negotiate with workers. In the wake of the stock market crash, the gross national product was down by almost 10 percent, national unemployment was climbing above 15 percent, and the United Mine Workers had just rallied 125,000 miners to a nationwide coal strike. Moreover, the highest officials in the administration had worked as lawyers for railway companies and shared railway owners' philosophical belief that labor unions infringed on employers' property rights. Even if administration officials had been more sympathetic to labor unions, the federal government in 1894 had no formal mechanism for mediating disputes between labor and management. For all these reasons, no one in the White House viewed arbitration of the strike as an option. Instead, on July 2, a federal judge issued sweeping injunctions forbidding the ARU from interfering with rail service, from interrupting U.S. mail service, or from inducing railway workers to withhold their labor. Working in cooperation with the GMA, the U.S. attorney general's office effectively declared all ARU activity to be illegal. It then dispatched more than sixteen thousand federal troops to enforce the court orders.

The injunctions and the appearance of troops in various cities sparked the strike's first violence, including street protests, attacks on railway property, fires in rail yards, and violent confrontations between prolabor demonstrators and authorities. Armed but ill-trained federal marshals clashed with those who had been left unemployed and disaffected by the nationwide economic depression. Across the country, fifty-one people died and more than five hundred were arrested in street skirmishes, although only a handful of those associated with violence were ARU members. On July 10, seventy-one union leaders— including Debs—were arrested and charged with violating the federal injunctions against organizing strike actions. With its leaders in jail and troops on the streets, ARU members could not sustain their boycott and Pullman workers could not sustain their strike. By July 19, the trains were running, and the Pullman Palace Car Company was ready to hire anyone who pledged not to join a union.

Using the Source: Newspaper Articles

The old saying that "newspapers are the day books of history" certainly holds true in the case of public events such as the Pullman strike. Although there exists an array of primary sources on the strike, including court proceedings, judicial rulings, government testimonies, speeches, pamphlets, and even novels, it is the daily newspaper articles on the strike that allow us to watch events as they unfolded and to feel the passions of the moment. When incidents like the Pullman strike occur in today's world, we have an array of information sources we can turn to—television, radio, the Internet, Twitter, and, of course, printed newspapers and magazines—but in 1894, newspapers were the community's prime vehicle for both chronicling and shaping events. It is because of newspapers' importance as a record of past events that historians so often include newspapers among their sources.

By the time of the Pullman strike, urban newspapers had become a vital part of American public life. In the thirty years following the Civil War, the number of U.S. cities with populations of more than 50,000 had increased from sixteen to fifty-eight; by 1890, 19 percent of Americans lived in these sizable urban communities. Chicago's population alone had grown from almost 300,000 in 1870 to more than one million in 1890. In this expanding sea of strangers, newspapers offered not only a basis for common knowledge about civic affairs and influential people but also a means by which city dwellers could identify with (or against) strangers across town.

At the same time, urban newspapers in the United States in the late nineteenth century had become big businesses that competed for readers by charging one or two cents for a ten-page daily. In Chicago in 1890, there were twenty-six daily newspapers, with circulation rates between 10,000 and 230,000 each. Nine of those newspapers provided general news in English, ten offered the news in a foreign language, and the rest provided financial or neighborhood news. Then, as now, information was a commodity that these newspapers sold, although late nineteenth-century newspapers were much less subtle than today's newspapers when inserting editorial opinion into news stories. After all, in a city like Chicago, where the competition was fierce, a newspaper's editorial slant was as important as its information in winning readers' loyalty.

What Can Newspaper Articles Tell Us?

The best way to appreciate the value of newspapers as a historical source is to think about how difficult it would be to reconstruct an event in the past without the benefit of newspapers. Despite their biases and inaccuracies, newspapers give us basic information about the *who*, *what*, *when*, *where*, and *how* of events in the past. By gathering information from various newspaper articles, we can construct a more complete, accurate record of events than any single newspaper can offer.

In addition to providing information, daily newspapers can also be an excellent gauge of the public climate at the time an event actually occurred. A fiery news article can both reflect and create the mood in a community. Although newspapers cannot tell us what their readers were thinking, they can tell us what information and opinions readers were being exposed to, and circulation figures can indicate the popularity of different editorial positions on an event. In Chicago, eight of the city's nine daily English-language newspapers opposed the ARU's use of the railway boycott to aid the Pullman strikers. Only one newspaper, the *Chicago Times*, supported the union. Although the *Times* lost most of its commercial advertising during the strike, its circulation rose from just 40,000 to more than 100,000 in the heat of the boycott, suggesting that its editorial stance won over new readers, if only temporarily.

The advantages of newspapers—providing local details, reflecting the immediate climate, and appealing to a particular readership—are the very reasons we must also be cautious in using the information we find in newspapers. The key disadvantage of newspapers as a source is that reporters are "on deadline" and do not always have time to recheck their facts. Information gathered in the heat of the moment may be wrong or incomplete.

The second disadvantage of using newspapers as a historical source is that they offer editorial bias as well as the news. This problem was particularly acute in the 1890s, during the era of "yellow journalism," when newspaper publishers inflated, exaggerated, and even fabricated "facts" to attract readers. As the rise in circulation at the *Chicago Times* indicates, the buying public often rewarded publishers for slanting the news to suit readers' existing loyalties and opinions.

To appreciate the role of editorial bias in shaping news reporting during the Pullman strike, consider these excerpts from the *Chicago Tribune* and the *Chicago Times* on June 30, 1894, four days after the national railway boycott began and three days before U.S. troops were called up. Notice the ways in which each reporter's language, as well as his choice of content, served to shape each story:

CHICAGO TRIBUNE, JUNE 30, 1894

"Law is Trampled On"

With the coming of darkness last night Dictator Debs' strikers threw off the mask of law and order and began the commission of acts of lawlessness and violence. A Pan Handle train carrying seven sleeper cars was flagged at Riverdale, and the engineer and fireman, under threat of being killed if they moved, were forced to hold the train while a mob of 800 men detached the Pullmans. . . . The mob grew in numbers and resisted efforts of the train men to recouple the Pullmans.

CHICAGO TIMES, JUNE 30, 1894

"Mail Trains Must Move"

At noon today United States Marshall Byington received telegraphic instructions . . . to move all mail trains that were being detained in this city on account of the Pullman boycott. He . . . notified the . . . American Railway Union . . . giving them until 2 p.m. to decide whether or not they would offer any interference. A committee of strikers called on [Byington] an hour later and informed him that the trains would be allowed to proceed. . . . Passenger trains on the Ohio & Mobile roads were allowed to go out this morning without sleepers.

It is easy to tell from these two paragraphs that the *Chicago Tribune* was opposed to the ARU boycott and the *Chicago Times* supported it. The more difficult task is to piece together a single, plausible version of events from such varying and possibly inflated stories. We cannot assume that the version that appeared in the majority of papers is the most accurate, nor can we assume that the story whose editorial bias we agree with is the most accurate. Newspapers can alert us to events, but we often have to consult other sources, such as police reports or sworn testimony, to establish a reliable version of those events.

Although the language used in news reports may be biased, it can also offer useful evidence regarding the political and emotional climate at the moment. For example, the *Tribune*'s passionate prose about "Dictator Debs" acting in the "darkness" of night may not accurately depict the ARU's president during the Pullman strike, but it does suggest the heightened tempers in Chicago. In addition, the fact that Chicago newspapers covered their front pages with strike stories in late June and early July of 1894 constitutes historical evidence. The sheer quantity of coverage, and the size of the headlines, conveyed a sense of crisis, and the more frightening the boycott appeared, the more likely people were to turn against the ARU and support the federal troops. So, although sensational coverage in newspapers has to be corroborated, it also serves as its own kind of historical evidence.

The newspaper stories you will be examining in this chapter are a seven-day sample from the sixty-six-day Pullman strike, representing coverage in the *Chicago Tribune* and the *Chicago Times*. The *Tribune* was a staunchly Republican newspaper with a probusiness leaning, and it strongly opposed the ARU boycott. It was the city's oldest newspaper in 1894, and its daily circulation of 75,000 was the third largest in the city. The *Chicago Times*, a boycott supporter, was the second-oldest newspaper in Chicago. It had been a Republican newspaper with low circulation until it was purchased by a Democratic politician in 1893 and adopted a prolabor stance. The Pullman strike gave the *Times* an opportunity to capture a new, working-class audience. In using these newspapers to trace events and emotions in the Pullman strike, you will want to take this background information into consideration. In addition, keep in mind the following Checklist questions, which provide general guidelines for examining newspaper articles.

CHECKLIST: Interrogating Newspaper Articles

☐ When was the article written? What effect might the timing of the article have on its perspective?

☐ In what newspaper did the article appear? What does the article reveal about the sympathies of that newspaper's publisher?

☐ Does the article have a "byline" giving the reporter's name? Is it clearly marked as an individual's or as the newspaper's editorial opinion?

☐ Who was the audience for this article? What assumptions can you make about the newspaper's readership from the slant of the article?

☐ How factual is the article? How much of the article could be verified by checking other newspapers or other types of sources?

☐ What biases can you detect in the article's choice of language? What do these biases reveal about the time in which the article was written? What do they reveal about the author and publisher of the article?

Source Analysis Table

The fourteen news stories you will be examining from the *Chicago Tribune* and the *Chicago Times* differ in both factual claims and editorial bias. Factual claims are statements of names, dates, and events that you could verify by consulting other sources, such as police records, sworn testimony, or other news stories. Editorial bias becomes apparent in the newspaper's choice of words or omission of some information and its emphasis on other information that is intended to encourage the reader to sympathize with one side in the boycott and to dislike the other side. The accompanying table gives you space to note examples of factual claims from each news article and examples of editorial bias.

Date and Source	Factual Claims	Editorial Bias
May 12, 1894 *1. Chicago Tribune*		
2. Chicago Times		
May 15, 1894 *3. Chicago Tribune*		
4. Chicago Times		
June 26, 1894 *5. Chicago Tribune*		
6. Chicago Times		
June 28, 1894 *7. Chicago Tribune*		
8. Chicago Times		

Date and Source	Factual Claims	Editorial Bias
July 1, 1894 *9. Chicago Tribune*		
10. Chicago Times		
July 7, 1894 *11. Chicago Tribune*		
12. Chicago Times		
July 15, 1894 *13. Chicago Tribune*		
14. Chicago Times		

The Source: Chicago Newspaper Articles on the Pullman Strike, May 12, 1894–July 15, 1894

FIRST FULL DAY OF THE LOCAL PULLMAN STRIKE

1   *Chicago Tribune,* May 12, 1894, page 1

PULLMAN MEN OUT

DISCHARGES THE CAUSE

Committeemen Laid Off and Their Comrades Act

Two thousand employees in the Pullman car works struck yesterday, leaving 800 others at their posts. This was not enough to keep the works going, so a notice was posted on the big gates at 6 o'clock . . . saying: "These shops closed until further notice."

Mr. Pullman said last night he could not tell when work would be resumed. The American Railway Union, which has been proselyting for a week among the workmen, announces that it will support the strikers. Just exactly how, Vice-President Howard would not say. He intimated, however, that the trainmen on the railways on which are organized branches of the union might refuse to handle any of the Pullman rolling stock. It is not believed, however, that such action will be taken and it is equally impossible to see how the union can otherwise aid the strikers.

The walk-out was a complete surprise to the officials. . . . Mr. Pullman had offered to allow the men the privilege of examining the books of the company to verify his statement that the works were running at a loss. When the men quit work at 6 o'clock Thursday evening none of them had any idea of striking. . . . But the Grievance Committee of Forty-six held a session at the Dewdrop Saloon in Kensington which lasted until 4:30 o'clock in the morning. At that time a ballot was taken which resulted: 42 to 4 in favor of a strike. A second ballot was unanimous. So a messenger was sent to the freight car builders to order them to stop, and all seventy-five walked out of the big gate. One department at a time, the men went out so that by 10 o'clock 1500 men were out. Thirteen hundred and fifty men kept at work until noon, but only 800 came back after lunch. . . .

Included among the strikers were 400 girls from the laundry, sewing-rooms, and other departments. In the afternoon, everyone—men, women, and children—put on their best clothes and assembled on the ball grounds. They stood in groups or rolled around in the grass, making no demonstration and acting in a subdued manner.

2   *Chicago Times,* May 12, 1894, page 1

PULLMAN MEN OUT

Nearly 4,000 Throw Down Their Tools and Quit

Refuse to Strike Another Link Till Wrongs Are Righted

Firing Three Men Starts It

Almost the entire force of men employed in the Pullman shops went out on strike yesterday. Out of the 4,800 men and women employed in the various departments there were probably not over 800 at work at 6 o'clock last evening. The immediate cause of the strike was the discharge or laying off of three men in the iron machine shop. The real but remote cause is the question of wages over which the men have long been dissatisfied and on account of which they had practically resolved to strike a month ago.

The strike of yesterday was ordered by a committee of forty-six representing every department at the Pullman works. This committee was in session all night Thursday night, and finally came to the conclusion to order a strike 4:30 o'clock yesterday morning. The vote stood 42 in favor of a strike and 4 against.

The terms upon which the men insist before returning to work are the restoration of the wage scale of 1893, time and one-half for overtime, and no discrimination against any of those who have taken a prominent part in the strike.

The position of the company is that no increase in wages is possible under the present conditions. . . . The position of the men is that they are receiving less than a living wage, to which they are entitled. . . . President George M. Pullman told the committee that the company was doing business at a loss even at the reduced wages paid the men and offered to show his books in support of his assertion.

FOURTH DAY OF THE LOCAL PULLMAN STRIKE

3   *Chicago Tribune,* May 15, 1894, page 8

THEY MAY GO HUNGRY

Grocers Threaten to Cut Off Credit for Pullman Strikers

It will soon be a question of how to get food with the Pullman strikers if the strike continues much longer. A committee of the Kensington grocerymen, who furnish supplies for the men, told the Grievance Committee yesterday they were in a peculiar position. To extend credit to men on an indefinite strike meant ruin, while to refuse credit probably would mean a boycott when the men resumed work and began to earn money. So the grocers wanted to know how long the strike was going to last. . . . The strikers' committeemen said they had no means of knowing, so there the matter rests. The Arcade Mercantile Company,[1] which ran a strictly cash concern in the market and a credit place in the Arcade, closed up the credit branch. . . . Eugene V. Debs, President of the American Railway Union, is certain that the strikers will win. He said so several times yesterday but absolutely refused to give reasons for his supreme confidence. He still hints darkly at what will happen if the union should refuse to handle Pullman cars.

"Why," he said, "the boys all over the country are clamoring to tie up the Pullman cars. They are in an inflammable mood and longing for a chance to take part in this affair. . . . The whole country is in an inflammable condition. . . . When a man gets $2 a day he can live and is therefore a coward—afraid to try to get more—but when he gets cut down to $1.40 or $1 he gets desperate. The difference between that and nothing is so slight he feels he has almost nothing to lose and everything to gain by a strike. . . . "

The strikers are following the advice of their leaders to stay at home and let whiskey alone. Morning, noon, and night the streets in Pullman and Kensington are as quiet and deserted as of a Sunday. There are no groups at the street corners; no loafers in the saloons. Even at the headquarters the crowd rarely exceeds 200 men, and these sometimes become bored and go home, leaving the hall empty. . . . John S. Runnells, general counsel for the Pullman company, said yesterday: "The statement made in some of the newspapers that after a while there would be a great number of evictions at Pullman and consequent scenes of excitement is entirely untrue."

[1] In Pullman.

4   *Chicago Times,* May 15, 1894, page 1

SKIMS OFF THE FAT

Pullman Company Declares a Dividend Today

Quarterly 2 Per Cent Thrives at the Men's Expense

Full Pockets Swallow $600,000 While Honest Labor Is Starving

Today the Pullman company will declare a quarterly dividend of 2 per cent on its capital stock of $30,000,000 and President George M. Pullman is authority for the statement that his company owes no man a cent. This despite the assertion of Mr. Pullman that the works have been run at a loss for eight months. Six hundred thousand dollars to shareholders, while starvation threatens the workman.

H. J. Pingrey, vestibule builder at the Pullman shops, has worked or reported daily for work since Jan. 1, till the strike, and during that time has been able to put in eighty days, for which he received $100. During that time he paid back to the company $40 for house rent and still owes $10 on that account.

The Rev. Mr. Oggel, who preaches in the beautiful green stone church on Watt Avenue, hard by the Pullman shops, marveled greatly in his sermon of Sunday night that Pingrey and his fellow workmen should have been so foolish as to go on a strike. The Rev. Mr. Oggel draws about $40 a week salary paid by Pullman workmen, and house rent free, to expound the gospel of Christ. . . .

Another matter which caused a ripple of excitement among the men was the announcement made by a committee representing the merchants . . . that under the existing circumstances . . . they could not give further credit to the strikers for goods. . . . Mr. Heathcoate[1] told the committee that . . . no individual merchant need hope to avert the certain boycott which would follow his refusal to give his customers credit. . . . "These are the merchants who have made a living out of the working men here for years and now when our time of trouble comes, they abandon us almost before we have a chance to ask for accommodation; we are not asking them for charity."

[1] ARU local president.

FIRST DAY OF THE NATIONAL ARU BOYCOTT OF PULLMAN CARS

5   *Chicago Tribune,* June 26, 1894, page 8

BOYCOTT IS ON TODAY

American Railway Union Begins Its Fight on Pullman

The American Railway Union at noon today will begin a test of its strength with railways using the Pullman Palace Car company's sleeping and dining-room cars. At that hour the boycott of Pullman cars ordered by the union will go into effect. Though its purpose is to force the Pullman company to consent to an arbitration of the Pullman strike, its manifestation will be nothing more or less than a fight with the railways in which the Pullman company will take no part.

The railway lines have already been told through the press that they must haul no Pullman cars in their trains. They have accepted the implied challenge and yesterday their representatives in joint meeting voted to stand together as one and resist the union's demand. Their contracts with the Pullman company . . . impose a penalty for failure to haul the Pullman cars and they will certainly haul them, say the managers. Representative men among them declare the boycott will amount to but little. . . . George M. Pullman yesterday made a statement of his company's position. It contained no offer to arbitrate the strike.

6   *Chicago Times,* June 26, 1894, page 1

UNITED TO FIGHT

Railway Managers Arrayed against the A.R.U.

In the big fight which will open between the Pullman Palace Car company and the American Railway union at noon today, Mr. Pullman will have the concerted aid of all the railroad companies which use his cars. At a meeting of the board of general managers of the railroads running into Chicago, the following resolutions were adopted:

" . . . That it is the sense of this meeting that the said proposed boycott, being confessedly not in the interest of any employees of said railroad companies, or on account of any grievance between said railroad companies and said employees, is unjustifiable and unwarranted. . . . That we hereby declare it to be the lawful right and duty of the said railway companies to protest against said proposed boycott; to resist the same in the interest of their existing contracts and for the benefit of the traveling public, and that we will act unitedly toward that end."

THIRD DAY OF THE NATIONAL RAILWAY BOYCOTT

7   *Chicago Tribune,* June 28, 1894, page 1

DEBS IS A DICTATOR

His Warfare on the Railroads Is Waged Effectively

The American Railway Union became aggressive yesterday in its efforts to force a settlement between Mr. Pullman and his striking employees. By calling out their switchmen, it threw down the gauntlet to the Erie, Grand Trunk, Monon, Eastern Illinois, Northern Pacific, Wisconsin Central, Chicago Great Western, Baltimore and Ohio, Pan-Handle, and Santa Fe railroads. It continued the warfare commenced the night before against the Illinois Central and continued it so successfully that the road had to abandon its suburban service at 9 o'clock. Its freight service was at a standstill all day and the same is practically true of other roads. In no case, however, did the strikers prevent the departure of any regular passenger trains from Chicago. . . .

Debs' master stroke, however, occurred at midnight, when every employee on the Santa Fe belonging to the American Railway Union was ordered out. . . . Whether the men will obey the mandate will be learned today. . . .

So far no marked violence has been attempted. Two hundred policemen put in the day in various railroad yards, but their services were not needed.

Chief Brennan says he has 2,000 men who can be massed at any point inside of an hour.

8   *Chicago Times,* June 28, 1894, page 1

NOT A WHEEL TURNS IN THE WEST

Complete Shutdown of All Roads in the Territory beyond the Missouri River

Chicago Center of Eastern Trouble

It May Be the Biggest Tie-Up in All History

All the western half of the United States has begun to feel the paralysis of the American Railway Union's boycott of Pullman. From the Missouri River to the Pacific Coast, from the Canadian to the Mexican line, there is scarcely a railway that has not been gripped by the boycott. At every important division point in the west, southwest, and northwest, there are trains blockaded because the American Railway Union men will not run them with Pullman cars attached and the railway managers will not allow them to run otherwise. Some roads are absolutely and utterly blockaded, others feel the embargo slightly yet, but it grows in strength with every hour. It is spreading eastward from Chicago, too. No man can tell what the end will be. . . . This is the end of the second day. This, when so far the American Railway Union has done little beyond ordering the withdrawal of switching crews, switch tenders, and towermen. By tomorrow, they promise that all conductors, engineers and firemen on freight and passenger trains will join in the strike and then, well, nobody can tell.

General Manager Ainsley of the Wisconsin Central notified his men that unless they go to work today he will supply their places with nonunion men. Then there may be trouble. . . .

The six o'clock train on the Great Western started out with two Pullman sleepers and one Pullman diner. It ran about two car lengths. The conductor rang the bell, the train stopped, the whole crew got down and cut off those three cars. This with a squad of policemen standing by and the company's officials looking on. The train pulled out without the Pullmans. It was the most decisive thing the boycotters have done yet.

SIXTH DAY OF THE NATIONAL RAILWAY BOYCOTT

9   *Chicago Tribune*, July 1, 1894, page 1

MOBS BENT ON RUIN

Debs' Strikers Begin a Work of Destruction

Men Who Attempt to Work Are Terrorized and Beaten

Dictator after the Managers

Continued and menacing lawlessness marked the progress yesterday of Dictator Debs and those who obey his orders in their efforts at coercing the railroads of the country into obeying the mandates of the American Railway Union. The Rock Island was the chief sufferer from the mob spirit which broke loose the moment its men struck. It was as much as a man's life was worth to endeavor to operate a train on that road to transact the business of the company, and at 6:20 o'clock the culmination was reached by the deliberate wrecking of a passenger train at Blue Island.[1] A striker named Murvin rushed to a switch over which an officer was standing guard, pushed him aside, threw the switch, and derailed the train. Strange to say, he was arrested. Fortunately, none of the passengers was hurt, but unfortunately for the road the cars were thrown across the track in such positions that they effectively blocked traffic. At 10 o'clock the officials threw up their hands and discontinued service for the night. At Blue Island, anarchy reigned. The Mayor and police force of that town could do nothing to repress the riotous strikers and they did their own sweet will. . . .

On the Illinois Central it was the same old story of destruction of the company's property without interference from the police. . . . Dictator Debs was as blatant as ever yesterday. He asserted . . . that the fight against Pullman was now a thing of the past. He is waging his warfare against the General Managers, who had committed the sin of combining against him.

[1] Blue Island was a close-knit community sixteen miles southwest of downtown Chicago. Many of the town's residents worked in local railway freight yards.

10   *Chicago Times,* July 1, 1894, page 1

ONE IS DERAILED

Rock Island Engine Runs Off at Blue Island

It Almost Brings on a Riot

Rock Island train No. 19 for Kansas City and St. Paul was partly derailed at Blue Island at 6:30 o'clock last night. The switch was thrown by James Mervin,[1] a switchman, and the heavy engine and tender left the rails and stuck fast in the mud, completely blocking the track. The train fortunately did not go over the embankment. It was well filled with passengers. . . .

Mervin was arrested by Deputy Sheriff Leibrandt and will be brought to Chicago for examination.

The train was a mixed train and was composed of three Pullmans . . . and ran along without interference until it reached the crossover switch at the west end of the Blue Island yard. There were some fifty strikers standing in the pouring rain on the right of the track just at the switch. The front wheels passed over them, there was a lurch, and the powerful engine careened to the left. . . . Several passengers who were standing on the platform were violently thrown to the ground, and some of them bruised besides being bespattered with mud. The wildest consternation ensued among them. . . . For a few minutes it looked as if a bloody conflict would follow. All was excitement, but added to the demand of the deputies for the crowd to stand back came a similar demand from several of the American Railway Union to let the law take its course. . . .

Mayor John Zacharias rushed down . . . in the drenching rain in his shirt sleeves. The prisoner shook him by the hand, and it was not until then that anyone seemed to know who the prisoner was. His name is James Mervin, aged 32 years, a switchman, and has been employed in the Rock Island yards at Blue Island. Mervin seemed to have hosts of friends [who] demanded bail, and the mayor fixed it at $5,000. . . . Scores of Mervin's friends proffered the small fortunes for the bond, but up to the latest hour they had not been able to subscribe the requisite amount. Mervin . . . denies, and his friends who were standing by him deny, that he touched the switch.

[1] The *Tribune* spelled the arrested man's name "Murvin"; the *Times* spelled it "Mervin."

FEDERAL TROOPS HAD BEEN IN CHICAGO FOR THREE DAYS

11   *Chicago Tribune,* July 7, 1894, page 1

YARDS FIRE SWEPT

Hundreds of Freight Cars, Loaded and Empty, Burn

Rioters Prevent Firemen from Saving the Property

From Brighton Park to Sixty-first street the yards of the Pan-Handle road were last night put to the torch by the rioters. Between 600 and 700 freight cars have been destroyed, many of them loaded. Miles and miles of costly track are in a snarled tangle of heat-twisted rails. Not less than $750,000—possibly a whole $1,000,000 of property—has been sacrificed to the caprice of a mob of drunken Anarchists and rebels. That is the record of the night's work by the Debs strikers in the Stock-Yards District.

They started early in the afternoon. . . . They were done by 10 o'clock; at that hour they had a roaring wall of fire down the tracks. . . . The flames of their kindling reddened the southwestern sky so that the whole city could know they were at work.

This work the rioters did calmly and systematically. They seemed to work with a deliberate plan. There was none of the wild howlings and ravings that marked their work of the night before.

12   *Chicago Times,* July 7, 1894, page 1

MEN NOT AWED BY SOLDIERS

Most of the Roads at a Standstill

Railway Union Is Confident of Winning against Armed Capital

Despite the presence of United States troops and the mobilization of five regiments of state militia, despite threats of martial law and total extermination of the strikers by bullet and bayonet, the great strike inaugurated by the American Railway Union holds three-fourths of the roads running out of Chicago in its strong fetters, and last night traffic was more fully paralyzed than at any time since the inception of the tie-up. . . . With the exception of an occasional car or two moved by the aid of the military, not a wheel is turning. . . .

In the southwest section of the city all railroad property is considered fair game for the attack of the mob. Apparently the police of this district think so, too, for they stand by and appear indifferent to the annihilation of property. Wholesale destruction by incendiarism yesterday succeeded to the train wrecking of the day previous. . . . Nothing pertaining to the railroads seems sacred to the crowd. A splendid new towerhouse, which operates the Pan-Handle's intricate inter-locking switches . . . was only spared yesterday through the efforts of a party of striking tower operators of the railroad. . . . The strikers saw there was danger of the fire spreading from a burning toolhouse nearby, a plank walk connecting the two. They tore this sidewalk up and thus saved the towerhouse. . . .

If the soldiers are sent to this district, bloodshed and perhaps death will follow today, for this is the most lawless element in the city, as is shown by their riotous work yesterday. . . . But the perpetrators are not American Railway Union men. The people engaged in this outrageous work of destruction are not strikers, most of them are not even grown men. The persons who set the fires yesterday on the authority of the firemen and police are young hoodlums. . . . The setting fire to the cars yesterday was done openly where anyone could see it and when the slightest effort would have resulted in the apprehension of the guilty ones, but no such effort was made. The firemen were overwhelmed with the work of attending to a dozen different fires and could not, and the police on the scene apparently didn't care to or would not make arrests. . . . At six o'clock, the police had not a single prisoner.

THE STRIKE DRAWS TO A CLOSE

On July 10, Debs and other ARU officers were arrested for violating the federal court injunction of July 2 constraining ARU activity. They were held for several hours until posting $10,000 bail.

13   *Chicago Tribune*, July 15, 1894, page 1

WITH A DULL THUD

The Strike Collapses with Wonderful Rapidity

DEBS' WILD ASSERTIONS

He Is Still Defiant While His "Union" Crumbles about Him

Like the last flicker of a candle that is almost burned out is the "war to the knife" defiance hurled yesterday by Eugene V. Debs in the face of the railroad managers of Chicago. Deserted by the men who answered his first calls for help, denounced by many who followed his banner of revolt only to lose their positions . . . with the very fabric of the American Railway Union falling upon his head and the support on which he stood slipping rapidly from under his feet, he declared that the strike was "on and would be fought to a successful issue."

The value of Mr. Debs' utterances at this stage of the game are shown con-clusively by comparing threats and assertions he made yesterday . . . with the condition of affairs last night. . . . "The Northwestern will not be turning a wheel tonight," said Mr. Debs. At midnight not a wheel on the Northwestern had failed to turn. The Northwestern people are inclined to look upon Mr. Debs' declaration as a huge joke. . . . And so it was on the Chicago, Milwaukee and St. Paul, which, according to Debs, was to suffer the same fate as the Northwestern. The officials of the road regard his threats with derision.

14 | *Chicago Times,* July 15, 1894, page 1

DEBS SURE HE CAN WIN

Says the Battle Is But Begun

More than 1,000 railroad men held an enthusiastic meeting at Uhlich's hall yesterday afternoon, the speakers being President Debs and Vice-President Howard.

President Debs then told the men that the situation was more favorable than it had been at any time since the men were called out. He said that telegrams from twenty-five points west of the Mississippi showed that the roads were completely tied up. . . . "I cannot stop now that defiance has been flung in our teeth by the General Managers' Association. I propose to work harder than ever and teach a lesson to those bigoted idiots. . . . The managers refuse to treat for peace. They say war to the end, and yet the law does not send them to jail. The law seems to be against us . . . but if the law makes it a crime to advise your men against the encroachments of capital by all the gods united I will rot in jail. . . .

"There are men who have returned to their work, but they are traitors. . . . We are better without them. Let them range themselves on the other side and we can then close up ranks and see where we stand. We must unite as strong as iron, but let us be peaceable in this contest. Bloodshed is unwarranted and will not win. It is not by blood that we want to win."

Analyzing Newspaper Articles

1. In comparing the factual claims in each newspaper's articles, do you find conflicting versions of the same event? Do you find that the papers reported on entirely different events on the same day?

2. How did the two papers differ in the way they reported on violent incidents?

3. What differences do you find in the way the two newspapers depicted Eugene V. Debs and George Pullman? What differences do you find in their depictions of the GMA, the Pullman workers, and the members of the ARU?

4. Based on the editorial bias you found in the articles, how would you describe the two newspapers' philosophical differences? Was each paper's bias more evident in the facts reported, or was it more evident in the language used to present the facts?

5. Based on these news articles, how would you describe the readers of the *Chicago Tribune*? What about the *Chicago Times* readers? What do you feel you know for sure about the regular subscribers to these newspapers?

6. Beyond subscription income, newspapers also made money by selling the daily issue on the city streets. Newsboys screamed out headlines to attract buyers. To what fears did the newspapers' headlines appeal? Which of these two papers would you say was more effective in inspiring fear with its headlines? What explains that difference?

7. After reading these articles, can you speculate on how the newspapers themselves may have influenced the strike? How would you test your theory?

8. Write your own news article, dated July 7, 1894, in which you use information from both the *Times* and the *Tribune* to tell a story that you regard as factually reliable even if you cannot be complete.

The Rest of the Story

In the aftermath of the Pullman strike, the *Times* and the *Tribune* offered predictably different coverage of the single most surprising outcome of the whole event: the report issued by the U.S. Strike Commission in mid-November 1894, just four months after the strike collapsed. The commission, which had been appointed by President Cleveland, was composed of three well-respected men from the country's business and political elite. Their detailed report was read with shock by both supporters and opponents of the strike because it was far more favorable to labor and far more critical of employers than anyone had expected.

Over the course of three hot weeks in August 1894, the commissioners took sworn testimony from 111 witnesses, including Pullman workers; representatives of the ARU, the GMA, and the Pullman company; newspaper reporters; police and politicians from Chicago; members of the U.S. Army; and various other interested parties. After listening to testimony that came to more than 650 pages, the three commissioners criticized the ARU for tying up the nation's rail system over a local factory dispute, but in general their report blamed the strike on George Pullman's stubborn refusal to negotiate with his workers. The report then praised the Pullman workers for their "dignified, manly and conservative conduct" throughout the strike. Finally, and most unexpectedly, the commissioners harshly condemned the GMA for its "arrogant and absurd" claim to the right to collectively set wages and working conditions across the railway industry while denying workers the right to organize as a competitive body.

The U.S. Strike Commission's most historically significant recommendations were that unions be legitimized by government policy and that the government set up a system for labor arbitration in order to avoid "barbarous" and costly strikes in the future. The prolabor *Times* claimed that such ideas "may serve organized labor for a charter and a creed." The probusiness *Tribune* agreed with the commissioners that George Pullman could have avoided the national mess by negotiating with his local workers, but it was silent on the commission's larger claims that Pullman should have distributed profits during the depression more fairly and that the GMA should allow unions. Instead, the *Tribune* reprinted an article from the fervently antiunion *Harper's Weekly* that fumed over the commissioners' "astonishing" radicalism, calling their recommendations "the first stage in a socialistic revolution" and the end of "civilized society."

Six months later, the *Chicago Tribune* took solace in the Supreme Court's judgment that Eugene Debs was guilty of violating a legitimate federal injunction, and the newspaper expressed pleasure that "Dictator Debs" would be spending six months in prison. As it turned out, however, Debs's sentence was less predictive of labor's future than the commission report was. It would take forty years, until the New Deal, before the government fully implemented the report's recommendations for labor arbitration, but the Pullman strike—and the report that emanated from it—marked a significant shift in public support for government as a strike mediator, not a strike breaker.

To Find Out More

Online Resources on the Pullman Strike

American Social History Project. *History Matters.* City University of New York and George Mason University. http://historymatters.gmu.edu. Search "Pullman Strike" to retrieve several significant documents.

Eugene V. Debs Foundation. http://debsfoundation.org. Offers photographs, a bibliography, and background information.

"The Origins of Labor Day." *Online NewsHour.* http://www.pbs.org/newshour/updates /business-july-dec01-labor_day_9-2/. An explanation of the link between the Pullman strike and Labor Day.

Historic Newspaper Repositories

National Digital Newspaper Program. National Endowment for the Humanities. http:// www.neh.gov/projects/ndnp.html. Digitizes "historically significant" U.S. newspapers published between 1836 and 1922.

United States Newspaper Program. National Endowment for the Humanities. http:// www.neh.gov/projects/usnp.html. A publicly funded project designed to "locate, catalog, and preserve on microfilm all newspapers published in the U.S. from the eighteenth century to the present."

Classic Secondary Sources on the Pullman Strike

Buder, Stanley. *Pullman: An Experiment in Industrial Order and Community Planning, 1880–1930*. New York: Oxford University Press, 1967. A balanced depiction of events.

Lindsey, Almont. *The Pullman Strike: The Story of a Unique Experiment and a Great Labor Upheaval*. Chicago: University of Chicago Press, 1942. An informative, but very partisan, defense of the Pullman workers and the American Railway Union.

Recent Secondary Sources on the Pullman Strike

Gilbert, James. *Perfect Cities*. Chicago: University of Chicago Press, 1991. Studies the Pullman strike in light of 1890s urban culture.

Papke, David Ray. *The Pullman Case: The Clash of Labor and Capital in Industrial America*. Lawrence: University Press of Kansas, 1999. Reviews the legal aspects of the strike.

Schneirov, Richard, Shelton Stromquist, and Nick Salvatore, eds. *The Pullman Strike and the Crisis of the 1890s*. Urbana: University of Illinois Press, 1999. A collection of essays on the topic.

Smith, Carl. *Urban Disorder and the Shape of Belief: The Great Chicago Fire, the Haymarket Bomb, and the Model Town of Pullman*. Chicago: University of Chicago Press, 1995. Examines connections between the Pullman strike and popular urban culture in the 1890s.

Secondary Sources on Historic Newspapers

Nord, David Paul. *Communities of Journalism: A History of American Newspapers and Their Readers*. Urbana: University of Illinois Press, 2001.

Nord, David Paul. *Newspapers and New Politics: Midwestern Municipal Reform, 1890–1900*. Ann Arbor: University of Michigan Press, 1979. Discusses newspapers and events related to the Pullman strike.

Schudson, Michael. *Discovering the News: A Social History of American Newspapers*. New York: Basic Books, 1978. Offers an interesting discussion of "objectivity" in news reporting.

CHAPTER 4

Settling into Our Memories

Three Immigrant Women's Autobiographies

Hilda Satt Polacheck, Rose Gollup Cohen, and Rosa Cassettari were only three of the 23.5 million immigrants who came to the United States in the years between 1880 and 1920, and only three of the hundreds of thousands of immigrants in that era whose lives were significantly shaped by contact with a social settlement house in their urban neighborhoods. We know this because we have these women's memoirs, their first-person recollections of their travel to the United States in the 1890s and their families' arduous struggles to survive the harsh conditions that so many immigrants faced at the turn of the twentieth century. Few immigrants from this era, even fewer female immigrants, left memoirs. So while historians have an abundance of materials testifying to the importance of social settlement houses to immigrant neighborhoods, and the importance of the middle-class, American-born women running those settlements, we have just a handful of memoirs that offer the immigrants' view of social settlements. The Polacheck, Cohen, and Cassettari memoirs are notable because they tell us about the challenges female immigrants faced and how women in the settlement houses helped them to meet those challenges.

Hilda Satt Polacheck moved with her middle-class family from Poland to Chicago in 1892 when she was ten years old. Rose Gollup left her peasant life in Russia in 1892 at age eleven and became a wage earner in New York City to help her father pay for her family's passage to America. Rosa Cassettari relocated to the Missouri minefields as a teenager in 1884 to join a brutal husband she had already learned to fear back home in Italy. These three women do not, of course, represent all those who emigrated to the United States in these years, but their compelling recollections humanize the staggering rows of immigration statistics from the U.S. census. In the 1880s alone, 5.2 million immigrants arrived in the

United States. This was more than the 3.7 million who came during the economic depression of the 1890s, but far less than the 8.8 million who landed between 1900 and 1910. Just the names of these three immigrants—Satt Polacheck, Gollup Cohen, and Cassettari—remind us that the nationalities of immigrants to the United States changed dramatically in these years. Up until 1890, the vast majority of immigrants had come from Germany, Ireland, England, Scotland, and the Scandinavian countries of Sweden, Norway, and Denmark. The expanded wave of immigrants who came after 1890, however, were from southern and eastern Europe, from Italy, Greece, Austria, Hungary, Bohemia, and from the territory between the Baltic Sea and the Black Sea known as the "Pale of Settlement," where the ruling Russian government confined 5 million Polish and Russian Jews. Changing economic conditions in Europe played a role in altering the composition of the emigrant flow to the United States, as did Russian government attacks on Jews. At the same time, expanding industrialization in the United States increased the demand for workers when northern race prejudice prevented the hiring of southern blacks. So at the very time that southern and eastern Europeans were feeling pushed out of their homes, American labor demand was pulling them across the Atlantic.

Certain citizens in the United States feared foreigners, even though their own parents or grandparents had been immigrants. They argued that the "new" immigrants from southern and eastern Europe were biologically and culturally inferior to the "old" immigrants from northern and western Europe and, therefore, would degrade the U.S. bloodstream and corrupt its democratic system of government. These "nativists" blamed immigrants' poverty on their supposedly innate stupidity and depravity; they dismissed as futile all civic efforts that tried to improve the living and working conditions in industrial American cities, where "new" immigrants comprised a sizeable share of the population. This *laissez faire*—leave it be—position served the interests of industrial capitalists who were happy to bring foreigners to the United States to work but did not want to pay the wages or create the working conditions that would enable immigrant families to move out of poverty. For nativists and many employers, immigrant poverty in isolated urban ghettos was just a fact of life; it was not something that called for civic intervention.

A number of middle-class and working-class Americans in these years put forth a competing view, which they defined as a "progressive" approach to social, cultural, economic, and political life in a diverse, industrializing democracy. Led by U.S. presidents Theodore Roosevelt and Woodrow Wilson, progressives appealed to Americans' belief that they could be the collective architects of their national fate by passing laws that shaped the human environment. For example, progressives advocated for legal restraints on corporate monopolies; minimum wage laws; regulations on the health conditions in factories; limits on child labor; compulsory education; and rules ensuring clean water, clean milk, clean meat, and uncorrupted medications. Although progressives disagreed among themselves about workers' right to unionize, women's right to vote, restrictions on the volume of immigrants, and blacks' claim to equal status, they shared the basic conviction that activist governments could encourage the everyday living

Figure 4.1 Lower East Side street *This photograph of children on the Lower East Side of New York City was taken in 1911, almost twenty years after Rose Cohen was a child laborer in that immigrant neighborhood. Even so, it offers us a lively, candid glimpse of the urban street life that would have been as familiar to Rosa Cassettari and Hilda Polacheck in Chicago as to Rose Cohen in New York. The horse cart in the background is a reminder that automobiles had not yet crowded children off the streets in working-class neighborhoods; with few public playgrounds available to them, such children typically played in the streets. But the spontaneous style of this photo was more common in the 1910s than in the 1890s as technological developments made it easier and cheaper for everyday folks to own cameras and take "snapshots" rather than stilted, posed photographs.* Source: Private Collection/J. T. Vintage/Bridgeman Images.

conditions needed for all individuals in the United States to make the most of their lives.

American women were more influential in the progressive era than they had been at any time in American political life (or would be again until the 1970s). Here, as with immigration, we find a coincidence of causes: a new population of college-educated women with ambitions beyond private domestic life was coming on the scene just when public debate was turning to the health and welfare of vulnerable immigrant families, especially the women and children in those families. Progressive women were imbued with the "maternalist" belief that every person deserved an opportunity to thrive and that all women shared a special talent for giving the care needed to create that opportunity. Progressive women were also determined to make caregiving a legitimate feature of public policy, and they created unique social programs to achieve their goals. Prominent among their innovations was the "social settlement house." Men like Dr. Graham Taylor of the Chicago Commons Settlement were active in the social settlement movement, but it was female leaders like Jane Addams of Chicago's Hull-House Settlement and Lillian Wald of New York City's Henry Street Settlement who gave the movement its tone, direction, and prominence.

Social settlement houses were distinctive in three ways. In the first place, they were, literally, homes located in industrial, immigrant neighborhoods where American-born, middle-class residents lived alongside foreign-born, working-class neighbors. They responded to their neighbors' immediate, practical needs on a daily basis by providing a wide variety of social, educational, cultural, health-related, legal, and civic services. At the same time, America's most prominent social settlement residents combined this direct, daily service with leadership in public policy debates. They advocated for broad civic reforms—from public playgrounds to minimum wage laws—and aggressively lobbied city, county, state, and federal officials to enact reform measures. Finally, social settlements were distinctive because the very act of "settling" among poor, mostly immigrant, industrial workers testified to residents' belief that democracy meant egalitarian mutuality between people from all walks of life. Rejecting the notion that they were doling out charity to helpless inferiors, settlement residents insisted that they and their neighbors were in a relationship of reciprocal respect, and that they all benefited equally from settlement activities. In an era of limited opportunities for educated women, settlement work offered women like Jane Addams and Lillian Wald a life of purpose and influence they could not have enjoyed anywhere else. They believed that their neighbors were saving their lives by welcoming them into their midst and supporting their endeavors.

The memoirs of Hilda Satt Polacheck, Rose Gollup Cohen, and Rosa Cassettari vividly illustrate the living and working conditions that progressive reformers sought to address through both direct service and legislation. Their stories also help us to understand the tangible ways that settlement house residents served their immigrant female neighbors. Immigrant wives and mothers had to cope with dirt and disease in unfamiliar urban settings alongside other immigrants who spoke different languages, cooked different foods, worshiped in different religions. They had to exercise authority over children who were more comfortable with the English language and American city life than they, and they had to keep hold of the pay envelopes of husbands whose only relaxation was in the local saloon. Further, their daughters, though less than 35 percent of the female population of the United States in 1900, comprised almost 50 percent of the female workforce. These young, unmarried female workers were crucial to American industry and to the survival of immigrant families, but immigrant mothers watched as the long hours, unsafe conditions, sexual harassment, and scanty wages made their daughters sick, depressed, or rebellious.

Reverence for motherhood offered common ground to immigrant mothers, daughters, and settlement residents, and residents' interest in the daily, domestic challenges of urban life made their endeavors directly relevant to their immigrant neighbors. But foreign-born mothers were not going to trust settlement residents to assist with their problems, and certainly not going to attend any settlement programs with women of different nationalities or enlist their children in any settlement classes, until they had complete trust that the settlement residents were not Protestant missionaries out to convert the Catholics and Jews or agents of the employer class seeking to brainwash workers into docility. Residents had to win over immigrant neighbors by demonstrating respect for different cultures, a willingness to listen and learn, and a genuine conviction that everyone who contributed to American prosperity deserved an opportunity to enjoy it.

Using the Source: Autobiographies

Autobiography, memoir, and *recollections* are all terms referring to life stories written by the people who lived them. For readers who want their history up close and personal, there is something very attractive about memoirs. They seem unfiltered, untouched by an expert, unmediated by authorities. Whether discovered as yellowed sheets of paper in a box hidden in the attic or cleanly bound between covers in a library, memoirs often appear to be the most authentic and transparent form of history. As the recollections by Hilda Satt Polacheck, Rose Cohen, and Rosa Cassettari demonstrate, however, there are complexities beneath the surface of these texts. Before we even open their covers, we must consider each memoir's origins: Polacheck handwrote eight different, incomplete versions of her life story in the 1950s, and her daughter turned those pages into a publishable book three decades later; Cohen published her memoir in 1918 shortly after writing it, but it went out of print for decades until discovered and republished in 1995; Cassettari was illiterate in English so her recollections were written down, not tape-recorded, by a settlement house resident in the 1920s but not published until 1970.

What Can Autobiographies Tell Us?

It is easy to understand why we are drawn to autobiographies. Life stories offer us unique access to the "feel" of a place and a time; they provide sounds, smells, tastes, attitudes, and emotions that only eyewitnesses can recall, and they give us a unique glimpse of human relationships in the past. For example, historians have long debated whether the native-born, middle-class residents of progressive era settlement houses were patronizing toward their immigrant, working-class neighbors. The eyewitness testimonies offered in the Polacheck, Cohen, and Cassettari memoirs do not end this debate, but they do offer support to those who argue that settlement houses successfully attracted thousands of visits from neighbors every week precisely because residents treated their neighbors with dignity and respect.

If we want to use the Polacheck, Cohen, and Cassettari memoirs as primary sources of information on the experiences of immigrant women as workers and settlement neighbors, we must keep three basic principles in mind: first, human memory is a fallible and biased tool for retrieval; no autobiography provides an objective, factually precise image of the past. Second, the overall emotional message conveyed by a memoir is often more reliable than the specific events recounted. Third, independent information about a memoirist's life is valuable for corroborating autobiographical claims but not always available or conclusive.

Cognitive psychologists tell us that our memories are not stored in our minds like neat reels of film. Instead, our minds hold, lose, regain, and reshape pieces to the incomplete puzzle that is our recollection of the past. Typically, autobiographers arrange the puzzle pieces of their memory (and imagine the missing pieces) according to their current beliefs about what happened in the past, and those current beliefs are shaped by intervening experiences. It is the mix of past experiences and current beliefs that shapes the message the autobiographer chooses to convey to the reader and shapes the stories she uses to convey that message. So when we read a memoir to access the past, we must keep in mind that memoir is never shaped out of pure, unadulterated memory. It is shaped by the memoirist's beliefs about herself and others at the time she is constructing her recollection.

When using memoirs as a source of historical information, we can draw on established knowledge and recorded information to figure out which claims in the memoir are accurate, which are plausible (if unprovable), and which are highly doubtful. The purpose of this exercise is not to expose memoir authors as liars. The purpose is to avoid confusing literary stories with historical fact, to feel confident when citing a memoir as a reliable illustration of historical conditions, and to discern where historical inaccuracy reveals a deeper emotional truth in the memoir.

Consider, for example, the questions and challenges a historian brings to this vignette that Hilda Satt Polacheck wrote about her first visit to the Hull-House Settlement:

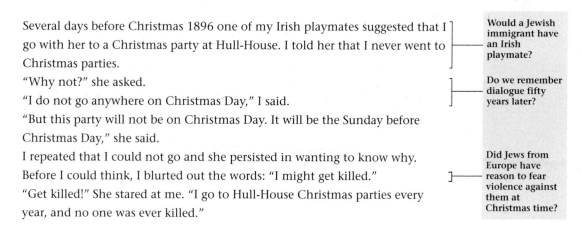

Several days before Christmas 1896 one of my Irish playmates suggested that I go with her to a Christmas party at Hull-House. I told her that I never went to Christmas parties.

Would a Jewish immigrant have an Irish playmate?

"Why not?" she asked.

"I do not go anywhere on Christmas Day," I said.

Do we remember dialogue fifty years later?

"But this party will not be on Christmas Day. It will be the Sunday before Christmas Day," she said.

I repeated that I could not go and she persisted in wanting to know why. Before I could think, I blurted out the words: "I might get killed."

Did Jews from Europe have reason to fear violence against them at Christmas time?

"Get killed!" She stared at me. "I go to Hull-House Christmas parties every year, and no one was ever killed."

I then asked her if there would be any Jewish children at the party. She assured me that there had been Jewish children at the parties every year and that no one was ever hurt. The thought began to percolate through my head that things might be different in America. In Poland it had not been safe for Jewish children to be on the streets on Christmas. I struggled with my conscience and finally decided to accompany my friend to the Hull-House Christmas party. . . .

What emotional memory is Hilda conveying here?

As I sat there, I am sure I felt myself being freed from a variety of century-old superstitions and inhibitions. There seemed to be nothing to be afraid of. . . .

What ideological point is she making about American democracy?

All feelings of religious intolerance and bigotry faded. I could not connect this beautiful party with any hatred or superstition that existed among the people of Poland.

Source: From *I Came a Stranger: The Story of a Hull-House Girl.* Copyright 1989 by the Board of Trustees of the University of Illinois. Used with permission of the University of Illinois Press.

There is no way to verify that this conversation at this particular party ever occurred. Hilda's daughter, Dena, conducted extensive research to document these stories but makes no mention of playmates, much less Irish playmates. For that reason, historians of immigration would not rely on Hilda's tale about an "Irish playmate" to challenge the wealth of solid data on Irish-Jewish animosity in all immigrant neighborhoods, including Chicago's. They could use this story, however, to say that, fifty years later, Hilda wanted to tell her readers that immigrant Jews were haunted by their well-documented European experiences with anti-Semitic violence, especially around Christmas, and Hilda had the literary sense to wrap that message in an engaging story about innocent children. So, too, historians could confidently quote Hilda's emotional memory of the safe, warm atmosphere at Hull-House because her personal recollection squares with dozens of sources from the 1890s testifying to the harmonious mixing of nationalities at the settlement's social gatherings. Indeed, even if there was no other evidence of democratic sociability at Hull-House, Hilda's story would still count as evidence that a Jewish woman carried into her old age positive emotions and political convictions about the settlement and wanted to record those feelings for posterity.

Every page of a seemingly simple autobiography raises questions about historical accuracy, literary license, and the ideological and emotional truths the author sought to convey. Do we believe, for example, Rose Cohen's story that Miss Mary Brewster refused to give her a copy of the New Testament because Brewster was protecting the reputation of the Henry Street Settlement? We believe it when we learn, from other sources, that the settlement's chief benefactor was Jacob Schiff, a wealthy Jewish banker and philanthropist who trusted Lillian Wald (herself a secular Jew) but kept close tabs on the settlement's operations and would have balked at any hint of efforts to convert Jewish immigrants to Christianity. What about Rosa Cassettari's story about yelling at a resident of the new Chicago Commons Settlement for displacing her from her apartment? Other versions of the Commons' first housing arrangements cast doubt on the specifics of this story, but skepticism about its veracity only underscores how important it was to Rosa to convey her emotional conviction that she gained a strong, independent voice only after moving to America.

The many questions we can raise about a memoir, and even the factual flaws our questions might reveal, do not invalidate memoirs as valuable sources of historical information. We simply have to read memoirs with our eyes wide open, fully aware that the personal emotions and ideological convictions expressed at the moment of recollection are often more reliable than the specific dates, people, and places we use to make sense of the scrambled pieces of our past. The checklist below will help you actively examine memoirs such as the three excerpted in this chapter.

CHECKLIST: Interrogating Autobiographies

☐ When was this autobiography written and under what circumstances?

☐ Who wrote this autobiography? What can I find out about the author from other sources?

☐ What was the author's purpose in writing this autobiography? What do outside sources tell me about the writer's agenda? What can I discern from "clues" in the autobiography?

☐ What aspects of this autobiographical story can be verified for objective accuracy?

☐ What aspects of this story convey the author's subjective emotions and convictions?

Source Analysis Table

The excerpts from the autobiographies included here focus on these women's encounters with settlement houses. The following table can help you compare examples of stories that you regard as factual and verifiable with examples of unverifiable stories that you see as more conveying the women's beliefs and values than accurately portraying all of the facts.

Autobiography Topics	Which Autobiographies Offer Evidence on Each Topic	Objective, Verifiable Claims	Subjective, Unverifiable Claims
Working conditions in 1890s urban United States			
Immigrant families' reliance on daughters' paid labor			
Tone of neighbors' interactions with settlement residents			
Programs at settlement houses			
Health services in immigrant neighborhoods			
Opportunities offered to neighbors by settlement houses			

The Source: Immigrant Women's Autobiographies

1   *I Came a Stranger: The Story of a Hull-House Girl*
by Hilda Satt Polacheck

> Hilda Satt Polacheck's father was a skilled artisan, so he was able to provide his family with a middle-class standard of living when they moved to Chicago from Poland in 1892. But her father died in March 1894, during the terrible economic depression of 1893–1894. She was twelve years old and still in school. Her mother set about trying to support the family by peddling staples like sugar, coffee, tea, and rice door-to-door and by sewing mittens in the evening. When that did not suffice to support Hilda, her mother, and her four siblings, Hilda's older sister left school to take a job in a knitting factory. Still, the family struggled to survive. In her memoir, Hilda recalled her response.

I started to brood over the condition of my family. What could I do to help? One bitter cold day, when the last bucket of coal had been put into the stove, I came to a decision. I would leave school and get a job. That night I confided in my sister and asked her if I could get a job at the knitting factory. She looked at me with great compassion. She wanted me to continue going to school but she knew the few dollars I could earn meant more food, which we all needed, and more coal with which the stove insisted on being fed. . . .

Mother shed many tears when I told her that I was going to work. But she realized that there was nothing else to do and agreed to the plan. . . . The first day that I left the house with my small bundle of lunch under my arm was a day of inner struggle for a little girl. . . . I was glad that I could help feed my family, but I could not forget that I would not go to school again. I did not realize at the time that it was possible to study away from school and that there were classes at Hull-House. . . .

The factory looked very large and imposing to me. It was a six-story brick building. We got into the elevator, my first elevator ride, and were taken to the fourth floor, I believe. There my name was taken and I presented my working permit. I had become an adult and a worker at the age of fourteen.[1]

---

[1] Dena Polacheck Epstein used other documents to conclude that her mother was probably thirteen when she started factory work, "making it necessary to lie about her age to secure working papers" because Illinois law said a worker had to be at least fourteen years old. Settlement house workers became very familiar with the problem of poor immigrant parents skirting the law by lying about children's ages in order to increase the number of wage earners in the family. Hilda may have concealed the truth in her autobiography in order to protect her mother's reputation.

Source: Hilda Satt Polacheck, *I Came a Stranger: The Story of a Hull-House Girl,* ed. Dena Polacheck Epstein (Urbana: University of Illinois Press, 1989), 51–52, 54–55, 56–57, 62–63, 68, 74–77.

Hilda recalled that she first encountered the Hull-House settlement and met its head resident, Jane Addams, when she was fourteen and working at the knitting factory.

Several days before Christmas 1896 one of my Irish playmates suggested that I go with her to a Christmas party at Hull-House. I told her that I never went to Christmas parties.

"Why not?" she asked.

"I do not go anywhere on Christmas Day," I said.

"But this party will not be on Christmas Day. It will be the Sunday before Christmas Day," she said.

I repeated that I could not go and she persisted in wanting to know why. Before I could think, I blurted out the words: "I might get killed."

"Get killed!" She stared at me. "I go to Hull-House Christmas parties every year, and no one was ever killed."

I then asked her if there would be any Jewish children at the party. She assured me that there had been Jewish children at the parties every year and that no one was ever hurt. The thought began to percolate through my head that things might be different in America. In Poland it had not been safe for Jewish children to be on the streets on Christmas. I struggled with my conscience and finally decided to accompany my friend to the Hull-House Christmas party. . . . It was the first time that I had sat in a room where there was a Christmas tree. In fact, there were two trees in the room: one on each side of the high brick fireplace. The trees looked as if they had just been brought in from a heavy snowstorm. The glistening glass icicles and asbestos snow looked very real. The trees were lighted with white candles and on each side stood a man with a pail of water and a mop, ready to put out any accidental fire.

People called to each other across the room. Then I noticed that I could not understand what they were saying. It dawned on me that the people in this room had come from other countries. Yet there was no tension. Everybody seemed to be having a good time. There were children and parents at this party from Russia, Poland, Italy, Germany, Ireland, England, and many other lands, but no one seemed to care where they had come from, or what religion they professed, or what clothes they wore, or what they thought. As I sat there, I am sure I felt myself being freed from a variety of century-old superstitions and inhibitions. There seemed to be nothing to be afraid of. . . . All feelings of religious intolerance and bigotry faded. I could not connect this beautiful party with any hatred or superstition that existed among the people of Poland.

As I look back, I know that I became a staunch American at this party. I was with children who had been brought here from all over the world. The fathers and mothers, like my father and mother, had come in search of a free and happy life. And we were all having a good time at a party, as the guests of an American, Jane Addams.

We were all poor. Some of us were underfed. Some of us had holes in our shoes. But we were not afraid of each other. What greater service can a human being give to her country than to banish fear from the heart of a child? Jane Addams did that for me at that party.

Hilda was fired from her job in the knitting factory when the employer found out that she attended a union organizing meeting and spoke up about the unsafe and inhumane conditions at her workplace. A friend got her a sewing job in a factory that produced women's blouses, called "shirtwaists." There, she was paid by the number of blouse pieces she made each day.

I was told that it was piecework and that I could not expect to earn any money until I had learned how to operate an electric sewing machine. . . . While waiting for my first lesson in making shirtwaists, I overheard my fore-lady talking to a man: "I don't want any experienced girls. They are too smart and too fresh, and they want good wages. And they turn out less work. Give me the 'greenhorns'—Italian girls, Polish girls, Jewish girls who can't speak English. Girls who have just come from the Old Country don't know how much they can earn. I make them work hard like the devil. And they work for whatever wages they get."

I soon learned that the conditions described by the forelady prevailed in all factories before trade unions were organized.

The hours were from eight to six, with a half hour for lunch, five and a half days a week. We did not work Saturday afternoon. This was an improvement in working conditions [over the knitting factory], and I learned very quickly. I was determined to earn as much as possible to make up for lost time.

As I look back on the methods used in the factory at that time, I have a feeling that it was the beginning of the assembly line in industry. No one made a complete shirtwaist. My job consisted of making cuffs. So for ten hours a day I sewed cuffs. The deadly monotony of this work was worse than the actual work. . . .

One evening in 1900, after a particularly boring day at the factory, I decided to walk over to Hull-House, three blocks from where I lived. I had not been there since that eventful Christmas Party. This event marked the beginning of a new life for me. . . .

After a span of fifty years, I look back and realize how much of my leisure time was spent at Hull-House and how my life was molded by the influence of Jane Addams. I was not only hungry for books, music, and all the arts and crafts offered at Hull-House, but I was starved for the social stimulus of people my own age. All this was to be found at the house on Halsted and Polk streets. . . .

Jane Addams was never condescending to anyone. She never made one feel that she was a "lady bountiful." She never made one feel that she was doling out charity. When she did something for you, you felt she owed it to you or that she was making a loan that you could pay back. . . . Her presence was felt everywhere in the house. Whether we were reading Shakespeare, or working in the Labor Museum . . . or listening to a lecture or concert, whenever she appeared, the room became brighter. . . . I remember Miss Addams stopping me one day and asking me if I had joined the dancing class. She thought I worked too hard and needed some fun. So I joined the dancing class and learned the waltz, two-step, and schottische.[2] By this time I was able to pay the dollar that

---

[2] The schottische is a round dance resembling a slow polka.

paid for ten lessons.[3] . . .We danced once a week in this carefree class, all winter. In June, the class closed for the summer with a gay cotillion, every bit as gay, if not as elaborate, as the ones staged today to introduce debutantes to society. No matter where the members of the dancing class came from, dingy hovels, overcrowded tenements, for that one night we were all living in a fairyland.

> When Hilda was in her early twenties, Addams arranged for her to enroll in a short-term program at the University of Chicago, where she honed her writing skills (and, in the process, learned how to use a typewriter). With Addams's contacts, Hilda left factory work, got a white-collar job at a publishing house, and met her future husband, William Polacheck. Using a path that led through Hull-House, she regained the middle-class status her family had enjoyed back in Poland.

[3] Hull-House's policy was that if neighbors contributed to the cost of classes, they would gain a sense of their own partnership with the settlement. If neighbors could not pay for classes, they were subsidized by the settlement's middle-class supporters.

2 | *Out of the Shadow: A Russian Jewish Girlhood on the Lower East Side*
by Rose Cohen

> Rose Cohen was born into the pious, peasant Gollup family in a small village in a region that was controlled by the Russian government but is, today, Belarus. Her father purchased false papers to escape Russian military service, but the government caught up with him after thirteen years, forcing him to leave his wife, five children, and aging parents and flee to New York City in 1890. A year later, when Rose was eleven years old, her father sent for her to come help him earn the money needed to bring her mother and younger siblings over to America. Like so many family elders, Rose's grandparents did not even consider making the trans-Atlantic trip. Once settled with her father in a small tenement apartment on Cherry Street, on New York's Lower East Side, Rose faced the dual shocks of unremitting sweatshop work and her father's accommodation to anti-Semitism. She recalled, for example, seeing her father cut his beard and his earlocks, traditional symbols of Jewish men's piety.

I saw him sitting at the table before the little mirror resting against the wall, clipping his beard. I was so surprised and shocked to see him actually do this thing that I could neither speak nor move for some minutes. And I knew that he too felt embarrassed. After the first glance I kept my eyes steadily on the floor in front of me and began to talk quietly but with great earnestness.

Source: Rose Cohen, *Out of the Shadow: A Russian Jewish Girlhood on the Lower East Side* (New York: George H. Doran, 1918), 106–107, 112–113, 113–114, 196, 230–231, 246, 248, 248–249.

"You had been pious at home, father," I said "more pious than any one else in our whole neighborhood. And now you are cutting your beard. Grandmother would never have believed it. How she would weep!"

The snipping of the scissors still went on. . . . At last he laid it down and said in a tone that was bitter yet quiet:

"They do not like Jews on Cherry Street. And one with a long beard has to take his life into his own hands."

"But, father," I said, looking at him now, "must we live on Cherry Street?"

"Yes, we must," he said, turning to me quickly and speaking in a more passionate tone. "They want the Jews to come and settle here. And because it is so hard to live here they have lowered the rents. I save here at least two dollars a month. You don't understand. For mother's journey we need not only tickets and money for other expenses, we also need money for at least second-hand furniture. This is not like home. There our house was our own. And for the lot and garden we paid one dollar a year. There, too, we were among friends and relatives. While here, if we haven't rent for one month, we are thrown out on the street. Do you understand?"

I said I understood.

After a few weeks of apprenticeship in the sweatshop where her father sewed men's suits, Rose found her own job in another shop under a harsh boss.

From this hour a hard life began for me. He refused to employ me except by the week. He paid me three dollars and for this he hurried me from early until late. . . . Late at night when the people would stand up and begin to fold their work away . . . he would come over with still another coat.

"I need it first thing in the morning," he would give as an excuse. I understood that he was taking advantage of me because I was a child. And now that it was dark in the shop except for the low single gas jet over my table and the one over his at the other end of the room, and there was no one to see me, more tears fell on the sleeve lining as I bent over it than there were stitches in it.

Rose's father dismissed her complaints that the boss "is hurrying the life out of me." He was working even longer hours than Rose and was intent on bringing the family to America.

I myself did not want to leave the shop for fear of losing a day or even more perhaps in finding other work. To lose half a dollar meant that it would take so much longer before mother and the children would come. . . . I longed for my mother and a home where it would be light and warm and she would be waiting when we came from work. . . . Often as the hour for going home drew near I would sit stitching and making believe that mother and the children were home waiting. . . . I pictured myself walking into the house. There was a delicious warm smell of cooked food. Mother greeted me near the door and the children gathered about me. . . . Their little arms were about my neck, and their warm faces against my cold cheeks. . . . Soon mother called, "Supper is ready."

There was a scampering and a rush to the table, followed by a scraping of chairs and a clattering of dishes. Finally we were all seated. There was browned meat and potatoes for supper.

I used to keep up [these fantasies] until I turned the key in the door and opened it and stood facing the dark, cold, silent room.

> After two years of constant labor, Rose and her father were able to bring the rest of the family to America. But it was 1893, the start of the terrible depression, work was scarce, and poverty dashed Rose's dreams of happy family life once reunited. Like her father and her sister, Rose took whatever work she could find, including domestic service work, but by the time she was fifteen years old, her health was so broken that she was unable to hold a job.

For people in my parents' circumstances it was not a usual thing to keep a daughter at home. And so, inquisitive relatives and neighbors began to ask why? Why was I staying at home? What was the matter with me? Why was I so pale? My parents felt they must hide the truth even at the cost of lying, for I was growing up—and what man would marry a sick girl! . . . But now I did not care. I did not care about anything. All I wanted was to be left lying still. . . . One day as I lay so I felt a touch on my wrist. This touch had become familiar since I had been ill. It was a doctor's touch. I opened my eyes and saw a woman, a stranger, sitting beside the couch. Neither in looks nor in dress had I ever seen any one like her in our neighborhood. She was also beautiful and distinguished.

"How do you feel?" she asked me. Her lips smiled but her eyes remained almost sad. She spoke to mother in German, gave her a card and went away. I spelled out the printed name on the card, Lillian D. Wald, 265 Henry Street.

> When Rose's condition did not improve, her parents followed Lillian Wald's advice that she go into the hospital for rest, food, and care. Her three months in Presbyterian Hospital, where she learned to read English by reading the New Testament, were followed by decent jobs at settlement-connected tailor shops and vacations from work at the settlement's summer camp. These experiences altered Rose's identity and vision of her future.

In my own case, it was through the illness which had seemed such a misfortune that I had stirred out of Cherry Street. But now that I had had a glimpse of the New World, a revolution took place in my whole being. I was filled with the desire to get away from the whole old order of things. . . . The Settlement was, of course, included in my mind in that outside world of which I dreamed. . . . One day . . . when I was thinking of [reading] the New Testament, it occurred to me [to ask for a copy at the Settlement]. I found Miss Brewster[1] in the little basement and asked her for it timidly . . . [I]t was hard for a Jewish girl, brought up as I had been, even to utter the words, "I want to read the New

---

[1] Mary Brewster was the fellow nursing student with whom Lillian Wald partnered in establishing the Henry Street Settlement in 1893. If this incident occurred, it would have been sometime in the settlement's first five years.

Testament." The thought of becoming a Christian was nowhere in my mind, but this would be the first real step beyond the boundary.

Miss Brewster looked at me silently. . . . She finally said, "I am afraid, Ruth[2] dear, we can not give it to you. You see your father would think, 'True, the nurses have been kind to my daughter but they have led her away from our faith.' And that would never do for the Settlement. Do you see?" . . . [T]hen she knelt before the bookcase. She hummed cheerfully as she looked from shelf to shelf, and I sat and watched her. Her every motion to me was new and interesting and charming. She represented the people I wanted to know, the new life I desired. She finally held out to me a tiny volume. . . . [I]t filled me with joy, for, strange and stupid as it may seem, it had not occurred to me that now I could read anything [in English, not just the New Testament]. I felt so proud that I could read an English book that I carried it about with me in the street. I took it along to the shop. I became quite vain.

> In the last 50 pages of her 300-page memoir, Rose Cohen reported a conflict with her father over her nonworking, nonearning summers at the settlement camp, her reluctance to marry, and her preoccupation with secular literature. She did not, however, tell her readers about her life course after 1900, when she was in her twenties and thirties. The historian Thomas Dublin determined that Rose achieved some notoriety when she first published *Out of the Shadow* in 1918, at age thirty-eight, but she died in obscurity just seven years later in 1925. He found a *New York Times* story from 1922 reporting on a suicide attempt by a Rose Cohen, forty, of 25 Decatur Avenue, Brooklyn, who "jumped into the East River from a landing at the New York Yacht Club." Dublin concluded that "we cannot tell the story of Cohen's last years with any certainty.

[2] Rose was called "Ruth" when she was a child.

---

3   *Rosa: The Life of an Italian Immigrant*
as recounted by Marie Hall Ets

> Rosa Cassettari was a poor worker in the silk industry in her native Italian region of Lombardy. When just a teenager, her foster mother married her off to a man who proved to be cruel and violent. Raised for obedience, this pious young woman dutifully followed her husband to the mining region of Missouri, where she learned to survive through self-assertion. When her husband opened a brothel in the mining town, she secreted away spare change to fund her escape to Chicago with her baby, telling herself that disobedience to a husband was allowed if he was ordering the wife to violate God's laws. In Chicago, she gained dispensation from the Catholic Church to marry Gionin, a man who had helped her escape. The Cassettaris struggled, but in recounting

Source: From *Rosa: The Life of an Italian Immigrant*, by Marie Hall Ets, University of Wisconsin Press, 1999. Used by permission of the University of Wisconsin Press.

her life to Marie Hall Ets in the mid-1920s, Rosa recalled the depression of 1893–1894 and a moment when they lucked into a good apartment.

Those new rooms we had in the big house with the Norwegian families, oh, I used to love them. They were so light and big with the high, high ceilings; I just loved them. But then one day a high-educated man came there, Dr. Taylor,[1] and he wanted to rent the whole building to make something. So the boss came and he told all the families we had to move. . . . Dr. Taylor, he told the boss that something good was coming. He said it was going to be a good home to teach the poor people good things. But whatever was coming, we had to get out anyway.

Me, I was sorry to leave that house, and I didn't know where to go. I couldn't find no more good rooms because nobody would rent to Italians. . . . I had to go in a basement about one block away next to a factory. That factory, I don't know what it was, but . . . they had so much fire in that factory that when the wind was one way, all the hot cinders came down on the sidewalk and the children scalded their feet. . . . I was sorry that I had to live in that basement! I used to take my children and go back and watch those carpenters working on our old home. I thought maybe we could get our old rooms back again. But even before the carpenters got through the work, the people started to move into that building. They were all high-up people, dressed up nice. Me, I was even mad with them that they made us poor people get out. . . .

Then one night after a while it rained hard. My poor rooms had one foot of water in. The baby's cradle was swimming around, and that basket of clothes I used to wash, it was swimming around too. We were up all night from the scare. My husband was throwing the water out with a shovel and sweeping it out with a broom. When morning came I went by our old house and I was standing by the door crying and angry. A nice lady, a nice young girl, came out and said, "Why are you here, lady? Why are you crying?"

I said, "It's you people—on account of you people I had to get out from this home! And now come and see where I live! Last night I was drowned with the water, me and my children!"

That young lady felt so sorry. She came along and saw my house. And still my husband was shoveling the water out. She said, "Oh, I'm very sorry! Very sorry! I'm going to go right away and look for a house for you."

And she did. She went and found a house and paid the rent and sent the wagon. She had to pay the rent ahead of time because it was such a poor time nobody had any money. Before six o'clock in the evening I was in the new home. It was three nice rooms in the front on the first floor of a wooden home. . . . And as soon as I could I collected all the little money I had and paid back the lady all the rent and the express she had to pay for me.

That lady—she wore a nice red blouse—she got a little work for me in [The Commons], the new settlement house. I started to wash the clothes for the

---

[1] Dr. Graham Taylor was the Congregational minister who founded the Chicago Commons after observing the operations at Hull-House for several months.

residents and cleaned around the building and helped the cook—anything they told me. . . .

In that time us poor women, we didn't have any pleasures—no movies, no shows, no this, no that. And so many drunken men there were! . . . After not long, one lady from the settlement house—she was American but she could talk German too—she asked me if I wanted to go round the neighborhood with her and ask all the women to come and start the woman's club. . . . In the first beginning we always came in the club and we made two circles in the room. One circle was for those ladies who could talk English and the other circle was for the ladies who talked German. . . . They used to tell us that it's not nice to drink the beer, and we must not let the baby do this and this. Me, I was the only Italian woman—where were they going to put me? I couldn't talk German so I went in the English circle. So after we had an hour . . . of the preaching, they would pull up the circle and we'd play the games together . . . the Norwegian, the German, the English, and me. Then we'd have some cake and coffee and the goodnight song. . . .

Pretty soon they started the classes to teach us poor people to talk and write in English. The talk of the people in the settlement was different entirely than what I used to hear. I used to love those American people, and I was listening and listening how they talked. That's how I learned enough English to go by the priest of the Irish church and confess myself and make the priest understand what was the sin! But I never learned to do the writing in English. I all the time used to come to that class so tired and so sleepy after scrubbing and washing the whole day—I went to sleep when they started the writing. I couldn't learn it. They had the clubs for the children too; my little girls loved to go. And after a few years when they started the kindergarten, my Luie was one of the first children to go in. . . .

> Rosa's husband, Gionin, was sent away for a year to recover from tuberculosis when Rosa was pregnant. She gave birth one cold night while her three small children tried, ineffectually, to feed their stove with coal and wood. By chance, two residents of the Commons settlement were visiting another family in the building.

Oh, that Miss Mildred and Miss May were angels to come and help me like that! Four nights Miss May stayed there and kept the fire going. They were high-up educated girls—they were used to sleeping in the warm house with the plumbing—and there they came and slept in my wooden house in the alley, and for a toilet they had to go down to that shed under the sidewalk. . . . That winter my Leo died . . . . All my walls were thick with frosting from the cold, and I got the bronchitis on the lungs, with blood coming up. So one of those good ladies from the Commons, she arranged and sent me to a kind of home in the country where people go to get well. They had nice nurses in that place and they cured me up good. I had a good time there too—I was all the time telling stories to entertain the other sick ladies. . . .

Me, I was always one that liked to entertain the people. So every noon I used to tell a story to the other cleaning women in the Commons when we were eating our lunch in the kitchen. In that time I didn't talk much English but I acted those stories so good that they understood anyway. . . . Then Dr. Taylor found me one night and said, "Come in the parlor, Mis' Cavalleri, and tell the story to the residents. . . . After then I all the time had to tell the stories to everybody—to the Woman's Club, to the man's meeting, to the boys' party, to the girls' party, to everybody. Sometimes when they had the big meetings in Hull House they would tell me to come there. One time that university in Evanston[2] made me come there and tell stories to those teachers who were going to school to learn the storytelling. I went everywhere. But always some resident . . . from the Commons had to go with me because I didn't know how to go alone. I loved to tell the stories. I never said no.

Gionin, oh he was glad when I told the stories. So for practice I used to test them on him first. If he listened good—if I made him laugh or made his tears fall, then I knew I said them good. Sometimes he went with me to those parties in the settlement; but when I went up to tell the story, he went out of the room. . . . He was so afraid I'd make a mistake. . . .

Ten summers I took my children and I went to the Commons summer camp to cook for the boys. . . . One summer Dr. Taylor let some Jew boys come to camp with the Italian boys. In the first beginning those boys were like the Devil and the Holy Ghost together! And such a war they put up! They pushed out the clothes to each other from the tents. But in the end they were worse than sweethearts. When it came to the end of two weeks they would even kiss each other—Jacob and Luigi, Tony and Sam. But whether they were Jews or Italians they all begged me to tell them the stories. And they all busted out laughing. . . .

I keep my little job in the settlement house, so I have that money extra and I can go to the picture-show and see the good story. I have it like heaven—I'm my own boss. . . . Only one wish more I have . . . I'd love to go in *Italia* again before I die. Now I speak English good like an American I could go anywhere. . . . I wouldn't be afraid now—not of anybody. . . . Me, that's why I love America. That's what I learned in America: not to be afraid.

> **Rosa was already a widow in the mid-1920s when she orally recounted her life story to Marie Hall Ets, who was a resident at the Chicago Commons Settlement. She was emphatic about continuing to work at the Commons because her adult son and daughter, who contributed to her support, thought she should stop working. Rosa continued to help out at the Commons until her death in 1943.**

[2] She is referring to Northwestern University, which was affiliated with the Chicago Commons Settlement and Hull-House Settlement through its own university settlement house, founded in 1891.

Analyzing Autobiographies

1. Looking over your Source Analysis Table, how would you use the autobiographers' objective claims to explain the popularity of settlement houses in immigrant neighborhoods in the progressive era? How would you use the subjective claims?

2. How did urban, industrial conditions give middle-class women an opportunity to claim that traditional female duty could be used to improve dirty, dangerous neighborhoods? How might this service have made female settlement residents less traditional in their womanhood?

3. Hilda Polacheck's memoir was published thirty years after she penned eight incomplete versions. Her daughter not only completed the editorial work needed to blend the versions into one book but also engaged in historical research to reveal which stories could be verified. Rose Cohen wrote and published her autobiography in 1918, shortly after writing it, and that same version was republished in 1995. Rosa Cassettari did not write a word of her memoir. A settlement house resident named Marie Hall Ets "took her stories down" as Rosa recounted them in the 1920s, when Rosa was in her sixties. When Ets first published Rosa's story in 1970, she explained that Rosa had let her put the stories "in order" and that she had "corrected" for Rosa's heavy Italian dialect to make her stories more accessible. Do the different paths to publication make you trust the reliability of one memoir more or less than the others?

4. The memoirs offer many examples of how contact with settlement houses helped immigrant neighbors. Using only Rose Cohen's story and Thomas Dublin's research on her later life, can you argue that contact with settlements could be emotionally harmful for some immigrants?

5. Select one objective, verifiable claim from each memoir and explain what historical sources you would consult to determine whether the three claims are accurate.

6. You read only excerpts from these autobiographies. If you were going to read these three life stories in their entirety, what questions would you bring to the texts? Write two questions for each memoir that you hope the complete memoirs would answer.

The Rest of the Story

Hilda Satt's memoir tells of her 1912 marriage to William Polacheck, an American-born German Jew whose business success in Milwaukee meant that Hilda did not work outside the home. Instead, she was active in Milwaukee's respectable Socialist Party and in the Women's International League for Peace and Freedom, an organization founded by Jane Addams. After she was widowed in 1938, Hilda supported her four children with a variety of government-funded social service jobs.

When Thomas Dublin sought details on Rose Gollop Cohen's life following the years she wrote about in *Out of the Shadow*, he learned that she did marry and have one daughter. He also learned that she honed her writing skills in classes at the Educational Alliance, a New York settlement house in downtown Manhattan that focused on serving eastern European Jews. The trail to Cohen's life went cold after the *New York Times* article reporting on a Rose Cohen's attempted suicide in 1922.

Marie Hall Ets had listened to and written down Rosa Cassettari's stories when Ets was a resident at the Chicago Commons settlement in the 1920s, but she did not consider turning those stories into a book until 1935, after publishing a successful children's storybook. According to Ets, "Rosa was excited. She wanted to help me publish other books and offered to tell me more of her stories."

The publication dates of these three memoirs tell their own story about public interest in immigrant lives over time. Cohen got a publisher for her memoir in 1918 when immigrants and their children comprised a significant share of the American reading public. Severe immigration restriction legislation passed in 1924, however, reflected the rising power of nativist politics and drastically reduced the number of immigrants to the United States until immigration laws were liberalized in 1965. When Hilda Polacheck was writing her recollections in the Cold War 1950s, she could find no publisher interested in the experiences of a Russian Jewish immigrant female who wrote proudly of being a Socialist. Similarly, Marie Hall Ets could find no publisher for Rosa Cassettari's stories in the years between 1935 and 1970. It was in the 1970s and 1980s that historians became very interested in the history of race and ethnicity, the history of women, and the history of workers. As a result, Rosa's story was published in 1970, Hilda Polacheck's was published in 1989, and Rose Cohen's was republished in 1995. If publishers do not think they will find buyers for memoirs, those life stories can languish in family attics or historical archives, awaiting a time when someone discovers them and convinces a publisher to make them widely available.

Hull-House was the nation's leading settlement in the progressive era and remained an active part of its Chicago neighborhood until 1963. Ironically, Hull-House did not survive the way other settlements have. Forced to close its thirteen-building operation in 1963 to make way for the urban campus of the University of Illinois, the original house now serves as a museum and meeting site on the UIC campus. Henry Street Settlement is still a vibrant part of New York City's culture and social services, operating seventeen program sites. So, too, the Chicago Commons continues to serve the urban community with early childhood education centers, academic programs for youth and adults, day services for seniors, and home care for seniors. Historic settlement houses like these work alongside other public and private community agencies all around the United States to meet the needs of their neighbors and lobby for public policies that will enhance the health, education, and welfare of working-class people in the twenty-first century.

To Find Out More

Immigrant Memoirs

Antin, Mary. *The Promised Land.* New York: Houghton Mifflin, 1912.

Bisno, Abraham. *Abraham Bisno, Union Pioneer.* Madison: University of Wisconsin Press, 1967.

Chotzinoff, Samuel. *A Lost Paradise: Early Reminiscences.* New York: Knopf, 1955.

Christowe, Stoyan. *This Is My Country.* New York: Carrick and Evans, 1938.

Davis, Philip. *And Crown Thy Good.* New York: Philosophical Library, 1952.

DiDonato, Pietro. *Three Circles of Light.* New York: Julian Messner, 1960.

Dublin, Thomas, ed. *Immigrant Voices: New Lives in America, 1773–1986*. Urbana: University of Illinois Press, 1993. A collection of excerpts from immigrant memoirs.

Galarza, Ernesto. *Barrio Boy*. South Bend, IN: University of Notre Dame Press, 1971.

Hasanovitz, Elizabeth. *One of Them: Chapters from a Passionate Autobiography*. New York: Houghton Mifflin, 1918.

Jastrow, Marie. *A Time to Remember: Growing Up in New York Before the Great War*. New York: Norton, 1986.

Lee, Mary Paik. *Quiet Odyssey: A Pioneer Korean Woman in America*. Seattle: University of Washington Press, 1990.

Nielsen, Thomas M. *How a Dane Became an American; or, Hits and Misses of My Life*. Cedar Rapids, IA: Torch Press, 1935.

Pesotta, Rose. *Bread upon the Waters*. New York: Dodd, Mead, 1944.

Roskolenko, Harry. *When I Was Last on Cherry Street*. New York: Stein and Day, 1965.

Yezierska, Anzia. *Bread Givers: A Novel*. New York: Persea, 1975. A classic American autobiographical novel in which a Jewish immigrant daughter traces her struggle to break free from her very traditional father.

Published and Online Sources on Settlement Houses

Addams, Jane. *Twenty Years at Hull-House with Autobiographical Notes*. Edited by Victoria Bissell Brown. Boston: Bedford Books, 1999.

Carson, Mina J. *Settlement Folk: Social Thought and the American Settlement Movement, 1885–1930*. Chicago: University of Chicago Press, 1990.

Chicago Commons. http://chicagocommons.org/.

Davis, Allen F. *Spearheads for Reform: The Social Settlements and the Progressive Movement, 1890–1914*. New York: Oxford University Press, 1967.

Henry Street Settlement. http://henrystreet.org/.

Urban Experience in Chicago: Hull-House and Its Neighborhoods, 1889–1963. http://uic .edu/jaddams/hull/urbanexp/contents.htm.

Wald, Lillian. *The House on Henry Street*. New York: Henry Holt, 1931.

Published and Online Sources on Immigration History

Bodnar, John. *The Transplanted: A History of Immigrants in Urban America*. Bloomington: Indiana University Press, 1985.

Daniels, Roger. *Coming to America: A History of Immigration and Ethnicity in American Life*. New York: HarperPerennial, 2002.

Immigration History Research Center (IHRC). University of Minnesota. http://ihrc .umn.edu.

Library of Congress. *American Memory*. http://memory.loc.gov. Browse "Immigration, American Expansion" for relevant documents.

Library of Congress. "Immigration and Ethnic Heritage." *American History*. http:// loc.gov/topics/content.php?subcat=16. A list of immigration-related documents from the Library of Congress collection.

New York City Tenement Museum. http://tenement.org. Virtual tour of the New York tenements occupied by immigrants in the early twentieth century.

Tichenor, Daniel J. *Dividing Lines: The Politics of Immigration Control in America*. Princeton, NJ: Princeton University Press, 2002.

Zolberg, Aristide R. *A Nation by Design: Immigration Policy in the Fashioning of America*. Cambridge, MA: Harvard University Press, 2006.

CHAPTER 5

Selling Respectability

Advertisements in the African American Press, 1910–1913

In July 1910, W. E. B. Du Bois — America's foremost black intellectual — resigned his secure position as a professor of economics and history at the all-black Atlanta University. Du Bois, the first African American to be granted a Ph.D. from Harvard University and a prolific author of articles and books exploring the injustices of the "color line" in modern America, gave up both salary and prestige for an obscure new enterprise. He moved to New York City to take on the role of director of publicity and research for the National Association for the Advancement of Colored People (NAACP), a new civil rights organization with little money and no reputation. Why would Du Bois take such a risk when even the organization's executive committee chair admitted that the fledgling NAACP was in no position to promise either "a financially promising or steady position"?

At age forty-two, Du Bois had witnessed the aggressive white denial of African American legal rights, political voice, and economic opportunities in his lifetime. When he was growing up in Massachusetts in the 1870s and 1880s, Du Bois shared the optimism of many other young blacks that progress toward racial equality was possible in postslavery America. By the time Du Bois and his generation of blacks reached adulthood in the 1890s and early 1900s, however, whites had closed off key avenues of progress. White legislators in every southern state disenfranchised black men through the use of such stratagems as the poll tax, the literacy test, and the grandfather clause. Those same southern legislators mandated the strict segregation of blacks from whites in all public facilities, from railway cars to drinking fountains, and in 1896 the United States Supreme Court approved these state actions in *Plessy v. Ferguson*, ruling that the Constitution allowed separate public facilities as long as they were equal. Such endorsement from the federal government was a reminder that whites' belief in their racial superiority was not confined to the South. Northern state legislators did not pass formal segregation laws, but informal customs presumed black inferiority: blacks could not obtain housing or professional work in integrated settings, could not shop or recreate in white areas, and faced danger if they challenged racial barriers.

Du Bois risked his career and his family's income to take the NAACP job because he shared the racially integrated organization's determination to fight the legal structures of racism and the extralegal violence that supported those structures. Du Bois was living in Atlanta in the summer of 1906 when ten thousand white rioters surged into the city's black neighborhoods over the course of four days, attacking people, homes, and businesses, and killing more than two dozen black citizens. And it was the brutal—northern—race riot in Springfield, Illinois, in the summer of 1908 that inspired a group of antiracist whites and blacks to form the NAACP. The two-day riot in Springfield was sparked when the local white sheriff refused to hand over two black men charged with violent crimes to an angry white crowd bent on enacting "lynch law," the common practice of hanging accused black men without the benefit of trial.

The founders of the NAACP, including Du Bois, were acutely aware that more than eighty black U.S. citizens were lynched every year in this era and that most lawmakers tolerated such vigilantism. The NAACP achieved one of its first victories in 1911 when it persuaded the U.S. Post Office to stop the mail transfer of "lynching postcards," gruesome photographs of dismembered blacks hanging from trees, which racists sent to each other as pieces of political entertainment.

While NAACP leaders mounted legal challenges to disenfranchisement, segregation, and violence, Du Bois took over publicity for the organization by launching a national monthly magazine titled *The Crisis*. His colleagues thought the magazine idea was doomed to failure because the organization was so new and unknown, and they authorized only $50 per month for its production. But Du Bois believed that the only way the NAACP would succeed was by clearly and constantly publicizing its challenge to white supremacy as well as its challenge to the dominant leader in the black community, Booker T. Washington.

Washington was the principal of the Tuskegee Industrial Institute in Alabama and had garnered substantial funding from liberal whites for advancing his well-publicized approach to racial "uplift." From his position as the unofficial leader of black America, Washington counseled African Americans to accept the white dictate to begin "at the bottom" and earn their way up. He discouraged blacks from seeking college degrees or pursuing professions, arguing instead for vocational training and employment as domestic servants, farmers, artisans, shopkeepers, and industrial laborers. Washington believed that if blacks made a solid contribution in the marketplace, working hard and earning a steady living, buying homes and starting small businesses, they would eventually be granted legal equality. He consistently pressed for this accommodationist economic strategy and for social separation of the races; he just as consistently opposed black agitation for voting rights or challenges to segregation of public facilities.

Du Bois used the pages of *The Crisis* to map an alternative route to racial equity. He argued that blacks would never make economic progress without the vote, access to all public facilities, collegiate as well as vocational education, and blunt renunciation of all racist theories. Du Bois did not oppose vocational training or dismiss the value of hard, daily labor, but he held that all such efforts were futile if not coupled with political agitation for the unmitigated rights and freedoms that the Constitution promised to all citizens.

African Americans and their white allies were more receptive to Du Bois's arguments in 1910 than they had been in the 1890s, when Washington's non-threatening approach seemed like a practical response to white hostility. But the creation of the NAACP testifies to rising doubts about Washington's strategy of accommodation in the early 1900s, as it became clear that black endeavors in the marketplace did not earn blacks the respect that Washington had predicted. On the contrary, black economic success increased racists' hatred because it fundamentally challenged their cherished belief in black laziness and stupidity. Well-dressed blacks were more vulnerable to verbal and physical abuse than those in humble clothing, blacks who owned their own businesses were disproportionately the targets of lynch mobs, and white rioters typically attacked black stores and rampaged through neighborhoods where blacks were homeowners.

The founders of the NAACP consciously challenged the racist demand that people of color stay in "their place," apart from and below whites, and challenged the companion view that any nonwhite person who was educated, economically successful, politically active, or culturally sophisticated was somehow unnatural, out of place, "uppity," and deserving of punishment. The organization's title referred to "colored people" instead of "Negroes" to mount this challenge on behalf of all nonwhites in the United States. The full title of Du Bois's magazine was *The Crisis: A Record of the Darker Races*, thus making the same point that all nonwhites labored to defeat American notions of white supremacy and racial segregation.

With Du Bois at the editorial helm, *The Crisis* was a hard-hitting political journal that ran sharp editorial critiques of racist policies and detailed reports on specific cases of racial discrimination. It denounced racist claims that black men were sexual predators who deserved lynching for their rape of white women. It also publicized the NAACP's legal and political campaigns against racism alongside proud stories of African Americans' professional, cultural, and business triumphs. The magazine thus reflected Du Bois's rejection of any sort of accommodation to white supremacy and defined the NAACP in contrast to Booker T. Washington. *The Crisis* also reflected attitudes that Du Bois shared with many of Washington's followers, in particular the belief that black citizens must counter negative stereotypes by being especially ambitious, hardworking, moral, upright, well read, well groomed, and well spoken—in short, respectable.

This set of prescriptions for black respectability can be viewed in several ways: as a daring resistance to racist images of bestial blacks, as blind obedience to the notion that blacks must earn their rights through good behavior, as a realistic strategy for making political and economic progress, and as a way for upwardly

***Figure 5.1 W. E. B Du Bois and the Publications Staff of* The Crisis** *W. E. B. Du Bois (standing, right) in the editorial offices of* The Crisis *at 70 Fifth Avenue in New York City. Du Bois had begun the magazine in two small offices of the* New York Evening Post *building, but he relocated it in 1913 after a political dispute with Oswald Garrison Villard, the* New York Post*'s editor and a cofounder of the NAACP. Du Bois dictated all magazine copy onto the reusable wax cylinders of a Dictaphone, an early sound recording device invented by Thomas Edison, and then staff members typed up his words.* Source: © Underwood & Underwood/ Underwood & Underwood/Corbis.

mobile blacks to set themselves above their more impoverished brothers and sisters. In fact, historians have employed every one of those interpretations when analyzing the attitudes evident in *The Crisis*. Such an array of arguments about blacks' values and motives is not a sign of historians' confusion. It is a testament to the complicated mix of resistance and accommodation that African Americans needed to survive in the early decades of the twentieth century.

Using the Source: Magazine Advertisements

In examining notions of respectability in the African American community, you will find advertisements to be particularly useful. The products, services, and opportunities that people sell and buy reveal a great deal about their values and aspirations. The ads in *The Crisis* reveal the segregated marketplace in which blacks operated and show how that marketplace served the magazine's main goal: to advance the status and dignity of African Americans.

From the first issue of *The Crisis* in November 1910, Du Bois included advertising in the journal's pages. "It is our purpose," he explained, "to make the advertising a means of real service to our readers as well as a source of income to us." The matter of income was not inconsequential. Given his colleagues' skepticism about the wisdom of publishing a monthly magazine, Du Bois had to make *The Crisis* an independent financial success. He also had to attract advertising despite the opposition of Booker T. Washington, who had the power to tell many black businesses not to advertise in the defiant new journal. So when *The Crisis* first began, a business owner's decision to take out an ad in the new magazine was as much a political statement as a commercial one. The advertiser both endorsed the NAACP's anti-accommodationist stance and calculated that the magazine's readers were an attractive market.

Confidence among the magazine's first advertisers was well rewarded. *The Crisis* was an immediate—and, to Du Bois, "phenomenal"—success. He had cautiously printed only 1,000 copies of the first issue, and it completely sold out at the modest price of ten cents per copy. In January 1911, *The Crisis* sold 3,000 copies; in February, 4,000; in March, 6,000. By 1913, the magazine had a circulation of 30,000 while membership in the NAACP was only 3,000. With those kinds of figures, Du Bois gained an independence within the organization that allowed him to defy those NAACP officers who feared that his uncompromising articles might offend potential white supporters.

The circulation figures also meant that *The Crisis* was an attractive place to advertise if your target audience was Americans who agreed with Du Bois's editorial stance on race. Analysis of the magazine's advertisements can help determine the early target audience for *The Crisis*. It seems logical to expect that the audience comprised those American blacks who had the education, income, and professional status to command equal treatment. In 1913, however, there were only a few thousand African Americans with college degrees, fewer than 3,000 black physicians, and not even 1,000 black lawyers. The 30,000 readers of *The Crisis* could not all have been members of the black elite. The audience must have extended further, but in what direction? By examining some of the advertisements that ran in *The Crisis,* we can find clues about the makeup of the magazine's readership.

What Can Magazine Advertisements Tell Us?

Because the whole purpose of advertising is to appeal to the needs and values of its audience, advertisements help historians determine what a group of people cares about and hopes to become. Using advertisements from a narrowly targeted publication such as *The Crisis* has some very particular advantages. We know that these ads were created by and for a black readership that aligned with Du Bois's vision of racial equality. We also know that the attitudes conveyed in the advertising were consistent with the political position of *The Crisis* because correspondence and records from the NAACP show that Du Bois exercised a strong editorial hand in accepting ads for the magazine.

The magazine certainly ran no ads for Cream of Wheat cereal or Aunt Jemima pancake mix, both produced by white-owned companies whose trademark images were African American figures in smiling, servile roles. But it is unlikely that those companies even tried to advertise in *The Crisis*. None of the era's popular, widely advertised products such as Ivory Soap, Gold Medal Flour, Pabst's Blue Ribbon Beer, or Coca-Cola ever appeared on the advertising pages of *The Crisis*. Those national, white-owned companies could reach black consumers through the pages of white-owned publications. They did not contribute advertising revenue to black daily newspapers and certainly not to a journal as outspoken as *The Crisis*.

The absence of such national advertising—and its revenue—in black publications is in itself evidence of economic segregation in the United States early in the twentieth century. Advertisements in *The Crisis* reveal the dimensions of the separate black economy, and they can be analyzed for signs of the strengths and the weaknesses in that economy. Du Bois agreed with Booker T. Washington that blacks must pursue economic independence and prosperity. The ads in *The Crisis* provide information on how African Americans were pursuing that goal. They offer us a taste of the variety of black economic pursuits and remind us that blacks could be found all along the class spectrum, from poor to working class to middle class to wealthy. By analyzing these advertisements, we can also explore the subtle ways in which black Americans asserted their economic and moral respectability in a segregated country.

Because we live in an advertising-drenched society and as consumers we "analyze" ads every day, we often find it easier to examine ads from the past than other sorts of historical documents. That familiarity can be a disadvantage, however, because it may lead us to exaggerate just how much ads can tell us. We can correct for such exaggeration by remembering that we don't buy every product we see advertised; we don't even "buy" all the claims advertisers make about the products we do purchase. Therefore, we do not want to jump to the conclusion that readers of *The Crisis* literally or figuratively bought everything in the magazine's ads. Advertising cannot tell us what people actually did buy; for that, we would need to see every company's sales figures. Because it is virtually impossible to ever find such figures, especially for small, black businesses, we must rely on ads, remembering they are only *indirect* evidence of economic activity.

The biggest mistake we can make in using advertisements as historical evidence is to pull one or two particularly funny or startling ads out of context and use them to represent the attitudes of an entire population of consumers. If all advertising is an indirect measure of a community's beliefs and behavior, then certainly no single ad can be used to represent an entire community's values. To guard against overgeneralization, historians analyze whole sets of ads over a period of time, looking at the ordinary alongside the unique, before making any claims about the target audience. To understand the need for caution when analyzing a single ad, consider the following example from the November 1911 issue of *The Crisis*. In most respects, it is typical of the magazine's ads, but in one respect it is very unusual.

Social class of
soap users?

Who is taking
the risk in this
deal?

Do You Want to Make Money?

CANVASSERS TO SELL SPHINX HANSOPE

Used in garage, machine shop, factory and home. Twenty-five boxes
for $1.25; you sell for $2.50. Whitens the skin, softens the hands, prevents
chapping, heals cracks and sores. The first aid in burns. Strictly antiseptic.

SPHINX LABOR-SAVING SOAP CO., Inc.

117 West Street, New York City

What is being
sold here?

Significance of
this claim?

Source: The Crisis, Volume 3, November 1911, 38.

This ad, like many in *The Crisis*, was not selling a product; it was selling a
job, an opportunity to make money. In the straightforward fashion that was
typical of *Crisis* ads, it listed the ostensible virtues of the product, gave the price
and profit, and described the potential market. In the sample of advertisements
included in this chapter, you will find several ads similar to this one and can
use them to theorize about the magazine's audience. You will, however, seldom
find references to skin whitening in ads from the magazine's early years. Other
press outlets for black advertisers carried many skin-whitening (and hair-
straightening) products, but *The Crisis* did not; the Sphinx Hansope ad is quite
unusual in that regard. This distinction reminds us that Du Bois's political views
shaped the magazine's advertising. It also reminds us that it would be a mistake
to use this one, atypical ad to argue that *Crisis* readers aspired to whiter skin, just
as it would be a mistake to base any generalization on a single ad.

The ads included in this chapter are a representative sample of those that
appeared in the first three years of *The Crisis*. The magazine grouped most of its
advertisements together at the back, in a six-page section called "The Advertiser," so readers not seeking jobs, products, or services could simply skip the
advertisements. You may want to consider that fact in your analysis, along with
other questions about African Americans' needs and aspirations at a time when
white racists sought to deny to blacks any measure of independence or respectability. The Checklist questions on page 107 will help you evaluate advertisements
as historical evidence.

CHECKLIST: Interrogating Advertisements

☐ When and in what historical context was the advertisement published? How did the historical context shape the ad?

☐ Who wrote the advertisement?

☐ What is the purpose of the ad? What strategies are used to make the ad most effective?

☐ Where did the advertisement appear, and who was the target audience?

☐ What inherent biases can you detect in the ad? What do these biases reveal about the time in which the ad was written? What do they reveal about the ad's creator?

Source Analysis Table

To aid your work, the advertisements in this chapter have been arranged by descriptive categories: housing, economic opportunities, education and race pride, and beauty and fashion. The following table allows you to categorize the ads in alternative ways for the purposes of historical analysis. As you peruse the ads, keep track of examples that illustrate these analytical categories, which move us beyond static description and toward detecting social patterns.

Analytical Categories	Examples in the Ads
The separate black economy resulting from segregation	
The Crisis **readers' access to economic opportunity and upward mobility**	
The use of religion, education, and gender to affirm black equality and respectability	

The Source: Advertisements from *The Crisis,* November 1910–March 1913

HOUSING

1 *Philip A. Payton, Jr., Company*

Source: *The Crisis*, Volume 1, January 1911, 35.

How to Elevate the Moral and Civic Tone of the Negro Community

Negroes—good, bad and indifferent—as long as they have lived in tenements, have had to live shamefully intermingled. Formerly they were forced to live in ramshackle tenements that had been abandoned by the whites, at exorbitant rents for wretched accommodations. But now, thanks to the thrift and enterprise of certain progressive Negro real estate agents, they may live in houses having the same conveniences and accommodations as the whites. While, happily, the physical surroundings of the Negro tenant have been radically altered, unhappily his moral surroundings remain unchanged. How, then, can we improve his moral surroundings? Co-operation is a *sine qua non* in the solution of this problem. Tenants MUST co-operate with their agents and agents MUST co-operate with one another in ameliorating the moral and civic condition of Negro communities.

Let the agent compel a prospective tenant to furnish references satisfying fair and reasonable requirements as imposed by, agreed upon and accepted *in toto* by all agents. The respectable tenant will be glad to do it. Any tenant not furnishing such references should be "jim-crowed," as it were, from decent neighborhoods.

This matter of bettering the moral and civic condition of Negro communities is a case of a wheel within a wheel. As has been emphasized before, the agent can do absolutely nothing without co-operation. Ministers wielding great influence over large congregations can lend a powerfully helping hand, if they will. We must all pull together. We cannot work resultfully in factions. It is unquestionably within our power to do it, if all others do their respective parts and the colored real estate agent does his.

Desirable Apartments for Desirable Tenants
Also Homes for Sale on Easy Terms

Philip A. Payton, Jr., Company

New York's Pioneer Negro Real Estate Agents
B R O K E R S ══════ A P P R A I S E R S

TELEPHONES
917 - 918 HARLEM   **67 West 134th St., New York City**

2   *White Rose Working Girls' Home*

Source: The Crisis, Volume 1, March 1911, 4.

'Phone 2877 Lenox

WHITE ROSE WORKING GIRLS' HOME

217 East 86th Street

Bet. Second and Third Avenues

Pleasant temporary lodgings for working girls, with privileges, at reasonable rates. The Home solicits orders for working dresses, aprons, etc.

Address:

MRS. FRANCES R. KEYSER, Supt.

3   *Hotel Dale*

Source: The Crisis, Volume 2, July 1911, 127.

NEW JERSEY

H O T E L   D A L E
C A P E   M A Y ,   N E W   J E R S E Y

This magnificent four-story structure, with every modern convenience, has just been completed at a cost of $50,000.

It is, without exception, the finest and most complete hostelry in the United States for the accommodation of our race.

The view from the hotel is magnificent: on the front, overlooking the celebrated golf links, the vista stretches away to take in the beautiful driveways and farms of the inland section of the Cape. The rear commands an extensive view of the harbor and sea. The invigorating ocean breezes reach every section of the hotel.

The Hotel Dale contains one hundred light, airy and luxuriously furnished rooms with every modern convenience. Electric lights throughout the entire house. Suites with bath and long distance telephone connections.

The open-air amusements available to the guests are numerous. The lawn of the hotel contains both croquet and tennis courts.

The sea bathing at Cape May is unsurpassed on the Atlantic Ocean. It is remarkable for its fine surf and is perfectly safe at all times for women and children. The hotel has its own private bath houses.

The sailing and fishing in the harbor and adjacent sounds are always attractive and boats may be had at all times.

The hotel is under the personal management of the owner, E. W. Dale, one of the most progressive and successful business men of our race. His experience as a hotel man has enabled him to use his very thorough knowledge of details in bringing the equipment of his hotel to perfection.

E. W. DALE, Owner and Proprietor

Mention THE CRISIS.

ECONOMIC OPPORTUNITIES

4   *Bussing-Wheaton Kitchen Supplies*

Source: The Crisis, Volume 4, April 1912, 266.

Agents—Big Money

Selling our seven-piece combination kitchen set, made up of articles absolutely needed in every household. They sell on sight. Mr. Jarvis sold fifty sets in one day. Send $1 for sample. Sent prepaid to any address in United States or Canada. Also our improved Slidewell Casters for chairs, which sell to everybody everywhere. Set of four sent postpaid for 15 cents.

BUSSING-WHEATON CO.
23 PARK ROW   DEPT. A   NEW YORK

5   *Jackson Specialty Company*

Source: The Crisis, Volume 5, November 1912, 46.

Don't Slave for Wages

Be your own boss. We show you how.
Particulars free.

JACKSON SPECIALTY CO.
Box 22A   East Lynn, Mass.

6 *N.Y. & N.J. Industrial Exchange*

Source: *The Crisis*, Volume 1, November 1910, 19.

7 *International Realty Corporation*

Source: *The Crisis*, Volume 2, October 1911, 262.

8   ## Cottman & Cottman Shipping

Source: The Crisis, Volume 1, December 1910, 32.

9   ## Nyanza Drug Company & Pharmacy

Source: The Crisis, Volume 1, December 1910, 32.

10   ## Blackdom, New Mexico

Source: The Crisis, Volume 3, February 1912, 170.

EDUCATION AND RACE PRIDE

11   *Wilberforce University*

Source: The Crisis, Volume 2, May 1911, 43.

FORWARD!

March Your Son Off to Wilberforce.

The only school for Negro Youth which has a Military Department equipped by the National Government and commanded by a detailed United States Army Officer.

DEPARTMENTS:

**MILITARY   CLASSICAL   THEOLOGICAL
NORMAL   SCIENTIFIC   MUSICAL
BUSINESS   TECHNICAL   PREPARATORY**

Banking taught by the actual operations in the Students' Savings Bank. Twelve Industries, 180 acres of beautiful campus, Ten Buildings. Healthful surroundings, exceptional community. Maintained in part by the State of Ohio.

W. S. SCARBOROUGH, President.

WM. A. JOINER, Superintendent, C. N. & I.

12   *Daytona Educational and Industrial School for Negro Girls*

The Daytona School became Bethune Cookman College in 1923. Mary McLeod Bethune founded the National Council of Negro Women in the 1930s and was a close advisor to First Lady Eleanor Roosevelt.

Source: The Crisis, Volume 4, September 1912, 213.

Daytona Educational and Industrial School for Negro Girls

Daytona, Florida

It reaches, by reason of its location, a large territory of Negro children deprived of educational privileges.

Its comfortable home life and Christian influences insure a certain individual attention and superior training impossible in larger institutions of its kind.

Mrs. Frances R. Keyser, formerly in charge of the White Rose Home for Working Girls, in New York City, has been elected Principal of the Academic Department. Write for catalog and detailed information.

MARY McLEOD BETHUNE
Founder and Principal

13

Knoxville College

Source: *The Crisis*, Volume 2, June 1911, 85.

Knoxville College

Beautiful Situation, Healthful Location
The Best Moral and Spiritual Environment
A Splendid Intellectual Atmosphere
Noted for Honest and Thorough Work
Offers full courses in the following departments: College, Normal, High School, Grammar School and Industrial.

Good water, steam heat, electric lights, good drainage. Expenses very reasonable. Opportunity for Self-help.

Fall Term Opened Sept. 27, 1911.
For information address

President R. W. McGranahan
KNOXVILLE, TENN.

14

Provident Hospital and Training School for Colored Nurses

Source: *The Crisis*, Volume 5, March 1913, 260.

Provident Hospital and Training School for Colored Nurses

Aim: To keep its technic equal to the best

Founded 1891

The first training school for colored nurses in this country, Freedman's excepted.

Comprises a training school for nurses, hospital, dispensary, and thoroughly equipped children's department; when funds are ample, post-graduate work may be undertaken.

The hospital is open to all. The races co-operate in the board of trustees, in the medical staff and in administration; the institution is the only one of its kind in which a colored man may act as interne.

Cost of buildings and equipment, $100,000; free from debt. Endowment, $50,000, contributed mostly by wills made by colored men. Additional endowment needed, $50,000.

The nurses' course covers three years; training and instruction given by both races, according to the highest modern standards.

15 Self-Published Books on the Race Question

Source: The Crisis, Volume 2,
March 1911, 32.

RACE ADJUSTMENT
By KELLY MILLER, Howard University, Washington, D. C.   A Standard Book on the Race Question.
PRICE $2.00

Social Equality ....5 cents
An Appeal to Reason, open letter
    to John Temple Graves.......10 cents
Roosevelt and the Negro.......10 cents
Forty Years of Negro Education.10 cents
Ultimate Race Problem........10 cents
The Political Capacity of the
    Negro ....10 cents
The Talented Tenth............10 cents

ADDRESS AUTHOR

The Curse of Race Prejudice
JAMES F. MORTON, JR., A.M., *Author and Publisher*
Forceful, rational, comprehensive. An arsenal of facts and unanswerable arguments. Invaluable for propaganda. Read the chapter on "The Bugbear of Social Equality," which is a veritable eye-opener. Thousands already sold. Agents wanted everywhere.
PRICE 25 CENTS
Address the Author at 244 West 143d Street, New York. N. Y.

16 Mary White Ovington on the Race Question

Mary White Ovington was one of the white founders of the NAACP and was the organization's executive secretary for more than thirty years.

Source: The Crisis, Volume 2, July 1911, 132.

"HALF A MAN"
The Status of the Negro in New York
By
MARY WHITE OVINGTON
With a foreword by Dr. Franz Boas of Columbia University

Chapter I. How the colored people won their civil and political rights.
Chapters II. and III. The Negro tenement and the life of the poor.
Chapters IV. and V. How the colored man earns his living, with a full description of the professions; the ministry, the stage.
Chapter VI. The colored woman, her discouragements and successes.
Chapter VII. A vivid description of the life of the well-to-do Negroes.
Chapter VIII. The Negro in politics in New York.
Chapter IX. The author's personal views on the race question.

Price $1.00; by mail, $1.12.

LONGMANS, GREEN & CO., Publishers, NEW YORK

This book is for sale in the Book Department of The Crisis, 26 Vesey St., N. Y.

17   *National Negro Doll Company*

Source: *The Crisis*, Volume 2, July 1911, 131.

Give the Child a Doll

The Most Beautiful of All the Toys on the Market Are the

NEGRO DOLLS

¶ YOUR child would be happy if it had a Negro doll such as are sent out by the National Negro Doll Company, Nashville, Tennessee. Every race is trying to teach their children an object lesson by giving them toys that will lead to higher intellectual heights. The Negro doll is calculated to help in the Christian development of our race. All dolls are sent by express, charges paid.

DOLLS FOR THE SEASON 1911-1912 NOW READY

Prices from **50c.** up to **$8.50**

For Illustrated Booklets, Prices and Other Information, Send Five Cents to the

National Negro Doll Company

519 Second Avenue N., Nashville, Tenn.

R. H. BOYD, President   H. A. BOYD, Manager

BEAUTY AND FASHION

18   *Solomon Garrett, Tonsorial Artist*

Source: *The Crisis*, Volume 1, December 1910, 33.

SOLOMON GARRETT

Tonsorial Artist

782 Fulton Street, near Adelphi Street

BROOKLYN, N. Y.

All Kinds of Workmanship
Cigars and Tobacco for Sale
Daily and Weekly Papers and Magazines

Brooklyn Agents for THE CRISIS

19   *Madame C. J. Walker Manufacturing Company*

Madame C. J. Walker was an enormously successful black entrepreneur who developed treatments for straightening women's hair. She did not market those treatments as hair straighteners. She donated large sums of money to the NAACP's antilynching campaign and to Mary McLeod Bethune's school (see Source 12 on p. 114).

Source: The Crisis, Volume 4, January 1912, 130.

Is Your Hair Falling Out?

Your Hair Will Not Be Beautiful Unless It Is Healthy

When the hair splits, breaks off, falls out, or you have an abnormal amount of dandruff, you need the attention of a hair specialist.

Have You Dandruff ?

MADAME WALKER'S ←PREPARATIONS→

Have You Eczema ?

will not only relieve these conditions and encourage a soft, healthy growth, but in using them you get the advice and personal attention of *Madame Walker*, who is regarded as an expert in the treatment of scalp diseases

——— ADDRESS ———

MADAME C. J. WALKER
640 N. WEST STREET   INDIANAPOLIS, IND., U. S. A.

20   *The Dunbar Company: Face Powder*

Source: The Crisis, Volume 5, December 1912, 104.

It Has Come at Last

It had to come and it was for us to introduce it.

A Face Powder for Colored Women

CRISIS-MAID
Perfect Face Powder

Whether the complexion is cream, olive or brown, we have a tint to match it.

It is *scientifically perfect*, embodying certain ingredients soothing to the most sensitive skin, while a soft breath of Oriental perfume enhances its cosmetic value.

It is the final touch to milady's toilette; adding a certain inexpressible charm to her appearance, which evokes words of admiration from friends and passersby.

Its quality is unsurpassed.

Miss Clough says:

"Its quality equals that of the most expensive imported powders."

Price 50c. postpaid

Send 2c. stamp for sample

Address:

The Dunbar Company

EXCLUSIVE DISTRIBUTORS

26 Vesey Street New York

MISS INEZ H. CLOUGH
Formerly of the Williams and Walker Company; now playing the "Big Circuit" in vaudeville.

Mention THE CRISIS.

Analyzing Magazine Advertisements

1. What evidence of economic segregation do you find in the ads?

2. Within that segregated economy, what sorts of job opportunities and business ventures were available to African Americans in the pages of *The Crisis*?

3. What can you infer about the magazine's readership based on the advertisements? What can you say about their experiences and values?

4. Did *The Crisis* advertisements conform to traditional notions of morality and gender roles? Did they radically challenge racist stereotypes? Could they do both at the same time?

5. African American history for the years between 1900 and 1915 often focuses on the differences between the "prove yourself" strategy of Booker T. Washington and the "demand your rights" approach of W. E. B. Du Bois. Can you use these ads to argue that readers of *The Crisis* drew on only one of these strategies in their daily lives?

6. In the face of racist segregation, African Americans advocated for integration while creating separate institutions, services, and businesses. Now that you have perused these advertisements, write a letter to the editor of *The Crisis* in which you argue for either economic integration or racial separatism as the best pathway to African American rights and respectability.

The Rest of the Story

W. E. B. Du Bois served continuously as editor of *The Crisis* from 1910 until he resigned in 1934 in a heated and somewhat ironic disagreement with the NAACP board of directors over the issue of segregation. Du Bois had begun his political career fiercely opposed to any black cooperation with white-imposed, legally enforced racial segregation. During the 1920s, however, he became persuaded that black nationalism, rooted in strong, separate black communities, was the key to black advancement. He came to regard the NAACP's legal campaigns for racial integration as futile and threatening to black autonomy, and he increasingly looked for socialist solutions to economic inequalities in the United States.

Du Bois's belief in socialistic black nationalism foreshadowed the radical black politics of the late 1960s and early 1970s, but for young African Americans in the 1920s, Du Bois seemed hopelessly out of date. Despite his enthusiasm for black pride and autonomy, he was too intellectual and too traditional in his gender attitudes to fully embrace the cultural experiments of the Harlem Renaissance. And despite his embrace of socialism, he was also too elitist to approve of Marcus Garvey's mass movement of working-class blacks in support of black nationalism. In fact, the advertising in *The Crisis* during the 1920s and early 1930s became more elitist; promotions for small businesses and get-rich-quick sales opportunities disappeared, while ads for private schools and colleges, beauty products, and books about famous African Americans increased.

Du Bois's independent stance, combined with the economic depression that began in 1929, caused the circulation of *The Crisis* to decline considerably by 1934. At that point, the NAACP board asserted its authority, insisting that the magazine's editorial policy conform to the organization's integrationist goals. So Du Bois—at age sixty-six—quit.

For the next twenty-nine years, until his death at age ninety-five, Du Bois continued to evolve intellectually and politically. He produced several major scholarly works that are still read and admired today. During the anticommunist era of the 1950s, he was arrested and tried as a foreign agent but was acquitted. Nonetheless, the federal government deprived him of his passport and freedom to travel for several years. In 1960, when he was finally allowed to leave the United States, Du Bois moved to the west African nation of Ghana and began work on the *Encyclopedia Africana*. He died in Ghana on August 27, 1963. News of Du Bois's death was announced the next day from the speakers' platform at the march on Washington, D.C., where Martin Luther King Jr. delivered his "I Have a Dream" speech.

Throughout the twentieth century, the NAACP persisted in challenging the "separate but equal" principle that the Supreme Court had endorsed in 1896. The organization funded lawsuit after lawsuit and in 1954 was finally victorious in *Brown v. Board of Education*, when the Supreme Court overruled *Plessy v. Ferguson* and ruled that legislated separation can never be equal and is, therefore, unconstitutional. In the decades since the *Brown* decision, the NAACP has continued to work against racial discrimination in legal, political, cultural, and educational arenas. *The Crisis* continues to be the official publication of the NAACP, although it is a for-profit operation that is legally separate from the NAACP. The magazine's Web site (http://www.thecrisismagazine.com) prominently features a photograph of W. E. B. Du Bois and declares that it "seeks to educate and challenge its readers about issues that continue to plague African Americans and other communities of color." In these ways, the magazine stands as a legacy of W. E. B. Du Bois.

To Find Out More

Resources on The Crisis

The Crisis. http://thecrisismagazine.com. Web site includes current issues and information. Bound volumes containing past issues are available in many libraries and through interlibrary loan.

Wilson, Sondra Kathryn, ed. *The* Crisis *Reader: Stories, Poetry, and Essays from the N.A.A.C.P's* Crisis *Magazine.* New York: Modern Library, 1999.

Secondary Sources on the NAACP

Berg, Manfred, and John David Smith. *The Ticket to Freedom: The NAACP and the Struggle for Black Political Integration.* Gainesville: University Press of Florida, 2005.

Lewis, David Levering. *W. E. B. Du Bois: Biography of a Race, 1868–1919.* New York: Henry Holt, 1993.

Sullivan, Patricia. *Lift Every Voice: The NAACP and the Making of the Civil Rights Movement.* New York: New Press, 2009.

Verney, Kevern, and Lee Sartain, eds. *Long Is the Way and Hard: One Hundred Years of the NAACP.* Fayetteville: University of Arkansas Press, 2009.

Secondary Sources on Race, 1880–1919

Brundage, W. Fitzhugh. *Under Sentence of Death: Lynching in the South.* Chapel Hill: University of North Carolina Press, 1997.

Franklin, John Hope, and August Meier. *Black Leaders of the Twentieth Century.* Urbana: University of Illinois Press, 1982.

Gaines, Kevin K. *Uplifting the Race: Black Leadership, Politics, and Culture in the Twentieth Century.* Chapel Hill: University of North Carolina Press, 1996.

Harlan, Louis R. *Booker T. Washington: The Making of a Black Leader, 1856–1901.* New York: Oxford University Press, 1972.

Harlan, Louis R. *Booker T. Washington: The Wizard of Tuskegee, 1901–1915.* New York: Oxford University Press, 1983.

NAACP. *Thirty Years of Lynching in the United States, 1889–1918.* New York: NAACP, 1919.

Tolnay, Steward E. *A Festival of Violence: An Analysis of Southern Lynchings, 1882–1930.* Urbana: University of Illinois Press, 1995.

Waldrep, Christopher, ed. *Lynching in America: A History in Documents.* New York: New York University Press, 2006.

White, Deborah Gray. *Too Heavy a Load: Black Women in Defense of Themselves.* New York: Norton, 1999.

Resources on the History of Advertising

Kern-Foxworth, Marilyn. *Aunt Jemima, Uncle Ben, and Rastus: Blacks in Advertising, Yesterday, Today, and Tomorrow.* Westport, CT: Praeger, 1994.

Manring, M. M. *Slave in a Box: The Strange Career of Aunt Jemima.* Charlottesville: University of Virginia Press, 1998.

Marchand, Roland. *Advertising the American Dream: Making Way for Modernity, 1920–1940.* Berkeley: University of California Press, 1985.

Norris, James D. *Advertising and the Transformation of American Society, 1865–1920.* New York: Greenwood, 1990.

Pope, Daniel. "Making Sense of Advertisements." *History Matters: The U.S. Survey Course on the Web.* City University of New York and George Mason University. http://historymatters.gmu.edu/mse/ads/. Discussion of how to use advertisements as historical evidence and links to Web sites that feature ads from the past.

Sivulka, Juliann. *Soap, Sex, and Cigarettes: A Cultural History of American Advertising.* Belmont, CA: Wadsworth, 1997.

CHAPTER 6

Living under Fire

World War I Soldiers' Diaries

Sergeant Elmer Straub was sound asleep in his tent on the northeastern edge of the western front at 3:30 a.m. on November 1, 1918. Suddenly, "one of the fiercest barrages that I have ever heard in my life started off. The machine guns in the rear of us started to chatter and above all of the big guns they could be heard spitting their indirect fire over the German lines." According to the entry that Straub made in his diary the next morning, "Our tent is only twenty feet directly in front of the third piece[1] and every time it shoots we rise about two inches from the jar of it all. The night had turned into day from the light of the guns firing. . . . I got up and gave the scene the once over and then I crawled under my blankets and went to sleep." Straub then thought to add, "Probably it seems impossible to one not knowing the conditions to believe that one could sleep during such a time, but in a few minutes I was asleep, and there I stayed until 6:30 this morning."

Elmer Straub, a college-student-turned-artillery-man from Indianapolis, Indiana, had managed to sleep through the opening shots of the last great Allied offensive that would, in just over a week, put an end to World War I. By the time he wrote this entry in his daily war-front diary, Straub was quite familiar with "the conditions." Having been in France for more than a year, he was among the most experienced U.S. soldiers at the battlefront that day. As an enlisted

---

[1] "Piece" was a term for a particular piece of artillery, a large gun mounted on wheels. In all likelihood, Straub was sleeping next to the French-made "75." This gun was popular because it fired fifteen rounds per minute from its 8.8-foot long barrel, sending high explosives or shrapnel up to five miles. It was called a "75" because the diameter of the barrel's bore was 75 millimeters.

member of the 150th Field Artillery battalion of the Forty-second "Rainbow" Division[2] of the American Expeditionary Force (AEF) in France, Straub had already been in several major battles and had witnessed the dramatic expansion of U.S. forces throughout the summer. By August, 10,000 raw U.S. recruits were arriving daily by transport ship; by September, there were three million Americans in country; and by the end of that month, more than one million of them were amassed between the Argonne Forest and the Meuse River in northeastern France, ready to join with their French and British allies for a final, all-out offensive against the German army.

World War I raged in Europe for four years, from 1914 to 1918. Treaties had drawn the Allied powers (Britain, France, and Russia) into a war alongside Serbia against the Central powers (Austria, Germany, and Turkey). The United States under President Woodrow Wilson stayed out of this war between imperial powers until 1917, when political and economic interests dictated the country's entry on the Allied side. The Wilson administration's reluctance to join the fray meant that the U.S. military was not a decisive player in the European action until the last six months of the war. What, exactly, did the U.S. forces contribute in those six months to help bring an end to this seemingly endless war? And what survival strategies did men at the front adopt to do the jobs they were assigned, get through the day, and sleep through the night?

What the Americans contributed was men: 3.9 million of them were mobilized for the fight overseas; 2.6 million actually served in combat. Those men coped with the war's intense battle conditions by focusing on the immediate, the everyday, the small details of life they could control. The war sped up in its closing months, and its momentum overwhelmed any U.S. effort to create a smooth-running, well-oiled military machine. So the men at the front focused on finding food any way they could, getting sleep any way they could, hoping for a relief order that would move them away from the front lines and the incessant pounding of the artillery, and figuring out how, each day, they could possibly transport themselves, their guns, their gear, and their wounded from one location to another. At the same battle and on the same day when Sergeant Straub wrote about sleeping through the artillery barrage, Corporal Eugene Kennedy noted in his diary that, given only fifteen minutes to "strike tents, roll packs and march," he managed to grab "a loaf of bread and shove it in the breast of my overcoat." And Captain John Trible, writing in his diary on that same day in the same battle, noted that his medical unit had moved to a "pretty civilized" village, had "secured a billet" with a local family, and had "slept in beds for the first time in two months." These tales mark small victories over tangible problems. The solutions offered quick doses of instant gratification and could block out the larger, more terrifying questions of whether they would live or die and whether the Allies would win or lose.

Immediately upon entering the war in April 1917, the United States faced a logistical nightmare. In the spring of 1917, the United States had a standing

---

[2] The Forty-second "Rainbow" Division comprised National Guard units from all over the United States.

army of just 128,000 and only 164,000 National Guard reserves. The exhausted Allies were calling for a quick infusion of four million fresh soldiers to turn the tide against Germany. To meet that need, the federal government instituted a draft. For the first time in U.S. history, the vast majority of the American men who served in the wartime military were conscripts, not volunteers; since being drafted was the norm, conscripts were not accused of any cowardly reluctance to serve. Sergeant Straub volunteered after spring classes ended at Indiana University, but both Corporal Kennedy and Captain Trible waited to be called up.

Straub's first night in the army at Fort Benjamin Harrison in Indiana illustrated the U.S. military's growing pains: Straub had no cot to sleep on. So he got a pass, walked into town, and bought his own cot. To recruit, house, feed, train, supply, and then ship a whole new fighting force across the Atlantic Ocean, the slow-moving, bureaucracy-bound, tradition-heavy peacetime U.S. Army had to shift into high gear. Once trained and deployed, each division of 28,000 men would need twenty tons of food, ammunition, and other supplies every single day. Much of that material, along with the men, had to be carried in British ships because the U.S. shipbuilding effort was inadequate.

Newly invented munitions with the capacity to automatically fire a dozen or more rounds of bullets, shrapnel, or explosives a significant distance made World War I the first "modern" war. But even though the United States supplied rifles and ammunition to the Allies from the start of the hostilities, it was not a leader in new weapons development. Indeed, once it joined the war, the AEF was utterly dependent on French and British artillery, airplanes, ships, and tanks. In the nineteen months between declaring war and celebrating the armistice, the United States never manufactured more than 20 percent of the artillery and aircraft that it used in France.

At the start of 1918, when the United States was still organizing its army back home, Europe was stuck in a two-year stalemate that had mired millions of European soldiers in muddy trenches running from Belgium to Switzerland. French and British military leaders, arguing for efficiency, wanted to integrate the U.S. recruits into the existing Allied army, under European generals. But General John J. Pershing, U.S. commander of the AEF in Europe, believed that only an energetic, independent U.S. Army fighting out in the open on its own terms could break the European stalemate, and the general assumed he had until 1919 to build such an army.

So Pershing was surprised in March 1918 when Germany broke the stalemate with a powerful offensive that brought the German line to within thirty miles of Paris. A separate peace treaty signed with the new Soviet government in Moscow in March 1918 had freed the Germans to shift all their resources to the western front, and they hoped that an early spring campaign would destroy the war-weary Allies at a moment when there were only 300,000 U.S. soldiers in France.

The Germans did not win the war that spring, but they did shape the Allies' timetable. Speed was now essential. Fresh, eager, and wholly inexperienced U.S. troops began to pour into France. They joined the French and British in bloody

Figure 6.1 Mired in the Mud, 1918 More than one million American soldiers moved toward the Argonne Forest and the war's final battle in September 1918, and congestion along the supply lines continued to plague the military's strategy. Here we see a wartime traffic jam in the French village of Esnes, which had been devastated in the Battle of Verdun two years earlier. Muddy roads meant that men, trucks, and horses crawled along at a pace of two miles per hour. Source: Library of Congress Prints and Photographs Division.

summertime battles that pushed the Germans back along the River Marne, where Sergeant Straub manned artillery posts and Captain Trible, a physician attached to the Medical Corps of the Third Infantry Division, patched up a never-ending stream of wounded men. Even as they were winning battles, U.S. soldiers were mowed down alongside their French and British comrades by German machine guns. By mid-July, the Allies had the Germans on the defensive, but the pace of this reignited war outran U.S. efforts to coordinate troop numbers with supplies and transport. Tons of food rotted on the docks in the French port of Calais because there were not enough trucks to move it to the front, and the trucks that were available sank in the mud on roads too narrow and bombed out to carry the battle traffic.

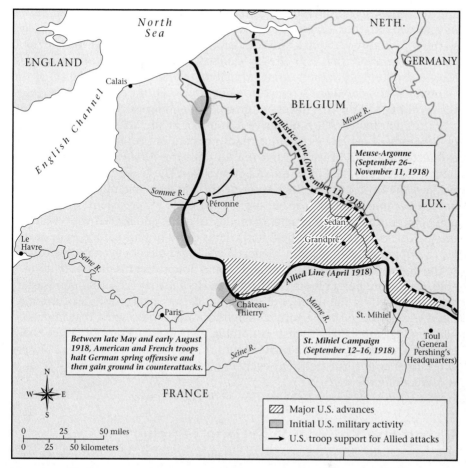

Map 6.1 Allied Military Offensive, 1918 *This map shows the locations of the battle at the St. Mihiel bulge in September 1918 and the Meuse-Argonne campaign, which raged from late September until the armistice on November 11, 1918. Notice the distance the Allied troops covered as they pressed northeast from Chateau-Thierry in May to beyond Sedan by the end of the war in November.*

By September, the European Allied Command was certain that a concerted offensive in the Meuse-Argonne region could win the war. (See Map 6.1.) General Pershing negotiated for an independent U.S. command in the Argonne sector of the battle, starting on September 26. First, though, he wanted to fight an independent battle that he had been planning for a year: he wanted to strike at St. Mihiel, where earlier French losses had given the Germans control over a bulge in the western front. So on September 11, 1918, just two weeks before Pershing was supposed to amass 1.2 million Americans in the Argonne Forest, he was sixty miles south with 600,000 of those men—including Straub, Trible, and Kennedy—staging an independent U.S. assault on the Germans at St. Mihiel. As it turned out, the Germans were already retreating from the St. Mihiel bulge, so the U.S. victory was quick and comparatively painless, incurring only 7,000 casualties in a war that had already claimed millions of lives on both sides. More a psychological than a strategic victory, the St. Mihiel battle secured the Germans'—and the Allies'—respect for Americans' fighting energy and increased the confidence of the U.S. forces on the eve of their biggest challenge.

The coordinated Allied offensive that began in the Meuse-Argonne region on September 26, 1918, was neither quick nor painless. For forty-seven days, an exhausted German army resisted the unremitting Allied advance in which fresh U.S. recruits died at a rate of 550 per day. The logistical woes that had plagued the United States since entering the war were magnified in this huge battle over uneven terrain made more impassable by persistent rain, narrow and bomb-rutted roads, and acres of muddy trenches and barbed-wire entanglements. Trucks stuck in battlefield traffic jams could not bring food in or evacuate the wounded. At one point, General Pershing could not even get his vehicle to the front of the line, and he certainly could not protect his men from hunger, cold, mud, rain, bugs, blood, death, or fear. His gallant visions of open warfare were frustrated by the realities on the ground, but still Pershing's young men faced the horrors of battle with a straightforward, can-do spirit that impressed allies and enemies alike. There was nothing particularly elegant or clever about the U.S. contribution to the final six months of World War I; the AEF simply threw itself against the front line every day, grabbing as much food and sleep as it could along the way.

Using the Source: Wartime Diaries

"Diaries are forbidden to be kept near the front," wrote Major General James G. Harbord in *his* diary on September 4, 1918. "They are likely to fall into hostile hands," claimed Harbord, "as diaries by German soldiers are found to be one of the prolific sources of information obtained from prisoners of war. Every Boche[3] seems to keep one."

Not every U.S. soldier kept a war-front diary, but many did ignore the ban on diaries at the front. Some of those diaries may have informed the Germans about supplies and morale in the AEF, although it is unlikely the musings of a lowly soldier revealed any secrets about troop movements or battle strategies.

World War I diaries do not lay out the grand panorama of "the Great War." Daily entries from sergeants and corporals do not serve us if we want to grasp the debates over strategy between General Pershing and his European counterparts, nor do they help us grasp the worldwide effect of the war's economic and political outcome. Diaries are, however, a superb source if we want to

---

[3] Harbord was using a derogatory French term for "German." In French, *alboche* means simply "German," whereas *caboche* means "blockhead" or "head of a small nail."

understand how it felt, on the ground, to be a small actor in this momentous historical event.

What Can Wartime Diaries Tell Us?

The most obvious advantage to wartime diaries as a source is that, unlike letters, they were not subject to the scrutiny of the military censor. Soldiers could write things in diaries that they could not, or perhaps would not, tell the folks back home. Wartime diaries often have a quality of casual immediacy and private candor that cannot always be found in letters from the front. In addition, a diary offers the historian a running record over a period of time, whereas letters are episodic, offering only snapshots of an unfolding story that the diary tracks from day to day. Indeed, one of the striking features of the three diaries excerpted in this chapter is that the diarists made entries—some very brief, others quite detailed—virtually every day while they were overseas in the AEF, no matter how difficult the battlefield circumstances. Their regular entries give us a unique picture of daily life in wartime and reveal the surreal mix of danger, duty, and daily needs that confronted every enlisted man in World War I. Corporal Eugene Kennedy's diary entry from the Argonne Forest on October 17 reminds us of the risks a soldier faced when foraging for food or building a bridge at the western front:

Hungry soldiers at the Meuse-Argonne front were not about to hand over a lucky catch to the mess sergeant

We get a sense of the speed required when Kennedy writes that he had to "throw" a bridge across a river

An explosion due to a mine planted by the "bosche" had blown 2 men (French), two horses and a wagon into fragments. [The wagon] was full of grub. We each loaded a burlap bag with cans of condensed milk, peas, lobster, salmon and bread. I started back . . . but was nabbed by a "Frenchy" and had to give up the chow. Quinn was behind me when suddenly another mine exploded. The biggest I ever saw. Rocks and dirt flew sky high. Quinn was hit in knee and had to go to hospital. . . . At 6:00 p.m. each of our four platoons left camp in units to go up front and throw . . . an artillery bridge across the Aire River. . . . We were heavily shelled and gassed causing much confusion.

This "Frenchy" must have outranked Kennedy, but it is the man's nationality, not his rank, that Kennedy chooses to record

Danger lurked in the most mundane places

Source: Corporal Eugene Kennedy, untitled diary, June 5, 1917–June 19, 1919, Hoover Institution on War, Revolution, and Peace archives, Stanford University.

It is quite possible that wartime diarists were writing for a particular reader and not simply for themselves. Perhaps a soldier wanted his parents or his wife to know what the experience was like but thought it best not to share the details until after the war was over and his fate known. Thus, we cannot presume that wartime diaries were written unself-consciously, with no audience in mind. Although rich in daily details, they may not reveal a soldier's innermost thoughts and fears.

Moreover, the diary that was written at the front may not be the version that we read in archives or in published form. All three diaries excerpted here, for example, have been copied from their original versions. Were they altered at the same time?

Corporal Eugene Kennedy's diary was painstakingly transcribed in a precise hand onto engineers' graph paper. Kennedy probably made the copy himself. Did he edit out some remarks? We know that he added a few. For example, in his November 1 entry, he wrote, "This date marked the opening of the last big drive." Although that is a historically accurate statement, it is not something he could possibly have known on November 1, 1918.

After typing up his wartime diary in 1920, Dr. John Trible spoke directly to his imagined reader, explaining that the original diary was "written on any available piece of paper and tied together" and that the entries were "copied exactly as they were written." Rather than eliminate comments, Trible added pages of very frank annotations to his typically brief wartime entries, making his 219-page document part diary and part memoir.

When Sergeant Elmer Straub allowed the Indiana Historical Commission to publish his diary in 1922, he included an introductory paragraph assuring his reader that "in recopying this diary I have tried to keep, throughout the whole work, just what was in the original." Straub apologized for misspellings and inconsistent verb tenses by explaining that "I had no special set time each day when I could sit down and write what was going on. I wrote . . . sometimes under very trying conditions, when it took all I had to keep from throwing it away." Did Straub, the university student, keep his diary out of a sense of duty to record history? Can that account for his unusual aside to the reader on November 1, 1918, that someone "not knowing the conditions" might find it "impossible . . . to believe that one could sleep during" an artillery barrage? Or did he add this note later, for the published version?

The stories behind each of these documents bring to mind yet another cautionary note about wartime diaries as evidence of soldiers' experiences: those who kept diaries during World War I were probably not representative members of the AEF. All three diarists included here were white, native-born, and educated. Moreover, none were in the infantry that marched directly onto the field with rifles and bayonets during a battle; Straub manned artillery from whatever heights he could find, Kennedy built roads and bridges, and Trible provided medical care. These men were culturally equipped and militarily situated to be able to keep diaries. By contrast, the vast majority of the white men who served in the AEF were rifle-carrying infantrymen, 18 percent were foreign-born, and almost one-fourth were functionally illiterate. Occasional racist remarks in these diaries indicate that these three men shared the disdain that many whites had for the 520,000 blacks who made up 13 percent of the AEF. African Americans always served in segregated units, typically as supply-carrying laborers, not rifle-bearing soldiers. Almost half the AEF's black recruits were illiterate, and fewer than 700 were allowed to serve as officers; few black soldiers had the skills to keep a diary.

Although the soldiers who kept diaries came from the more comfortable, educated ranks of American society, their reports of hunger, cold, bugs, mud, and ever-present danger offer good evidence that the war was a great leveler and none were spared the harsh conditions at the front. As you read through the diary excerpts in this chapter, keep in mind the following Checklist questions, which will help you evaluate any diary as historical evidence.

CHECKLIST: Interrogating Diaries

☐ When and under what circumstances was the diary written? How did the circumstances affect the content and tone of the diary?

☐ Who wrote the diary? What clues do the entries provide about the diarist's race, ethnicity, social class, education, and values?

☐ What appears to be the diarist's purpose? Does the author of the diary seem to have been keeping a private record of memories, or was the author writing for some imagined audience?

☐ Did the author use the diary primarily to record emotions, fears, and hopes or to record events, opinions, and achievements? Is it an introspective diary, a narrative diary, or a mix of both?

☐ Can you corroborate events in the diary by using other historical sources? How factually accurate is it?

☐ How representative is the diarist of others in his or her situation? Are there particular biases in the diary that you must acknowledge in using the diary as a historical source?

Source Analysis Table

Use the following table to keep track of each diarist's attention to immediate and more distant concerns. To help compare the diaries, you may track the frequency of comments on each topic by using tally marks or page numbers, or you may add notes on the date and tone of each comment.

Source	Food and Sleep	Rain and Mud	Roads and Transport	Combat and Danger	Germans	Politics of War and Peace
1. Kennedy						
2. Trible						
3. Straub						

The Source: World War I Diaries from the St. Mihiel and Meuse-Argonne Battles, September 17, 1918–November 11, 1918

The daily entries from the Kennedy, Trible, and Straub diaries were taken from two moments at the end of the war: the St. Mihiel offensive in September 1918 and the Meuse-Argonne offensive in October and November 1918. In these entries, the soldiers talk about their daily experience at the front, what matters occupy their attention, and how men manage the normal business of life (eating, sleeping, staying clean, and keeping dry and warm) while also fighting a war.

1   *Corporal Eugene Kennedy, Company "E," 303rd Engineers, Seventy-eighth Division, AEF*

Corporal Kennedy lived in upstate New York and turned thirty-one years old, the top age limit for military draft eligibility, in February 1918. Two months later, he received his draft notice, and by June 1918 he was serving in Europe.

THUR., SEPT. 12, 1918 Hiked through dark woods. No lights allowed, guided by holding on the pack of the man ahead. Stumbled through underbrush for about half mile into an open field where we waited in soaking rain until about 10:00 P.M. We then started on our hike to the St. Mihiel front, arriving on the crest of a hill at 1:00 A.M. I saw a sight which I shall never forget. It was the zero hour and in one instant the entire front as far as the eye could reach in either direction was a sheet of flame, while the heavy artillery made the earth quake. . . . We waded through pools and mud across open lots into woods on a hill and had to pitch tents in mud. Blankets all wet and we are soaked to the skin. Have carried full pack from 10 P.M. to 2 A.M. without a rest and I wouldn't mind a "blighty."[1] Despite the cannonading I slept until 8:00 A.M. and awoke to find every discharge of 14″ artillery shaking our tent like a leaf. Remarkable how we could sleep. No breakfast. . . . Cautioned to be ready to move at a moment's notice. Firing is incessant so is rain. See an air battle just before turning in.

[1] A "full pack" contained the items needed for daily life and weighed close to ninety pounds; "Blighty" is a slang term for England. If a nonfatal wound were serious, the soldier would be shipped to England for recovery.

Source: Corporal Eugene Kennedy, untitled diary, June 5, 1917–June 19, 1919, Hoover Institution on War, Revolution, and Peace archives, Stanford University. (Bracketed text within the selections has been added by the editors to help fill in gaps and clarify unfamiliar terminology.)

FRI., SEPT. 13, 1918 Called at 3:00 A.M. Struck tents and started to hike at 5:00 A.M. with full packs and a pick. Put gas mask at alert position and hiked about 5 miles to St. Jean. . . . Passed several batteries and saw many dead horses who gave out at start of push. Our doughboys are still shoving and "Jerry"[2] is dropping so many shells on road into no man's land that we stayed back in field and made no effort to repair shell-torn road. Plenty of German prisoners being brought back. . . . Pitched tent in shrubbery. At last a night's rest. Guns booming all the time.

SAT., SEPT. 14, 1918 Hiked up to same road again with rifle, belt, helmet, gas mask and pick. Shells are not falling fast today. We are just in rear of support lines. First time under shell fire. Major Judge's horse killed. R.G. Gibbs has a finger knocked off each hand while burying some of our men killed in opening drive. Clothing, bandages, equipment of all sorts, dead horses and every kind of debris strewn all over. . . . Big pit fall in road about 50' across and 30' deep. Worked hard all day. Terribly congested traffic.

MON., SEPT. 16, 1918 Nice day. Worked on road. Jerry drops shells over occasionally. Saw three of our doughboys dead along side of road. Traffic in good shape now. . . . Never saw such litter. Reports coming back that our division is being badly cut up.

TUE., SEPT. 17, 1918 Worked near town that is reduced to a heap of stone (Regneville).[3] Trenches are 20' deep and in some places 15' across. The wire entanglement is beyond description.[4] Several traps left by Germans. Man in our division had his arm blown off picking up a crucifix. . . . Wonder how it was possible to advance over such ground. . . . Camped in woods just vacated by Germans.

THUR., SEPT. 19, 1918 More rain. Camp in awful shape. Taking stone from Regneville homes to repair road. . . . Hard work. . . . More gas alarms at night. Many dead soldiers in woods, half mile up road.

SUN., SEPT. 22, 1918 Worked all day on road. They are in good shape now. Germans shell our area. . . . Never saw such mud.

MON., SEPT. 23, 1918 Rain and cold. Worked on road. . . . Pres. Poincare[5] and wife visit restored territory.

[On October 3, Kennedy's division moved sixty miles northwest to join the Meuse-Argonne offensive, which had begun on September 26.—Eds.]

---

[2] British slang for a German.

[3] The cemetery near Regneville has graves of 4,153 of the Americans killed in the St. Mihiel offensive. In all, 7,000 U.S. casualties, both killed and wounded, resulted from this four-day battle.

[4] Wire entanglements were elaborate fences of wood and barbed wire that troops on both sides erected in fields to make it difficult for opponents to advance in either direction.

[5] Raymond Poincaré (1860–1934), president of the Republic of France (1913–1920).

Mon., Oct. 7, 1918 Hiked until 3 A.M. Raining. Pitched tent in mud. Got up in time to eat. Very cold. Laid around 'till 5:30 P.M. Loaded on lorries. 18 men to an auto, 8 would fit. Raining hard. Rode about 3 hrs. Unloaded near Clermont. . . . Hiked four miles and pitched tents in Argonne forest.

Tues., Oct. 8, 1918 Nothing to eat. Detailed in evening to go after rations. Hike 4 miles each way. Nearly frozen. Greene brought jam from commissary so we had hard tack[6] and jam before going to bed. Some feast.

Wed., Oct. 9, 1918 Detailed again to go after rations. Tough trip but got half a loaf of bread from Negro in box car.

Sun., Oct. 13, 1918 Found a fine German garden. Onions, carrots, cabbage, celery, and potatoes. Got some bread from a "froggy"[7] for a pack of Bull Durham.[8] Good feed. Territory all plowed up with shells. Germans had a fine home here and abandoned a lot of supplies.

Wed., Oct. 16, 1918 Took bath at Apremont in a tent. Freezing weather but bath feels fine. First in 7 weeks.

Thur., Oct. 17, 1918 Struck tents at 8:00 A.M. and moved about 4 miles to Chatel. Pitched tents on a side hill so steep that we had to cut steps to ascend. . . . An explosion due to a mine planted by the "bosche" had blown 2 men (French), two horses and a wagon into fragments. . . . Arriving on the scene we found Quinn ransacking the wagon. It was full of grub. We each loaded a burlap bag with cans of condensed milk, peas, lobster, salmon and bread. I started back . . . but was nabbed by a "Frenchy" and had to give up the chow. Quinn was behind me when suddenly another mine exploded. The biggest I ever saw. Rocks and dirt flew sky high. Quinn was hit in knee and had to go to hospital. . . . At 6:00 P.M. each of our four platoons left camp in units to go up front and throw . . . an artillery bridge across the Aire River.[9] . . . We were heavily shelled and gassed causing much confusion. . . . I went back and collected platoon, took some quick flops,[10] and ducked some close ones. We put a bridge across 75' span, constructed entirely from old blown bridge. Job finished and back at camp at 11:30 P.M. No casualties. . . . The toughest job we had so far.

Fri., Oct. 18, 1918 Nothing doing all day, waiting for night to work under cover of darkness. Started up front at 6:00 P.M. . . . Put bridge in highway that had been blown out. Worked one half hour when "Jerry" shelled us so strong that we had to leave job. We could hear snipers' bullets sing past us and had to make our way back carefully along R.R. track bank, dodging shells every few steps. Gas so thick that masks had to be kept on, adding to the burden of carrying

---

[6] Hard, saltless biscuit that did not get stale too fast.

[7] Slang for a Frenchman.

[8] A U.S. brand of cigarette.

[9] As an engineer assigned to building roads and bridges, Kennedy was often exposed to combat. In this case, his job was to quickly construct a bridge on which artillery could perch.

[10] Kennedy and his men had to flop on the ground to avoid being hit by artillery shell fragments.

a rifle, pick, shovel, and hand saw. Had to run from one dug-out to another until it let up somewhat when we made a break for road and hiked to camp about 3 kilos. Gas masks on most of the way, shells bursting both sides of road. Arriving in camp Mac had hot coffee for us.

FRI., Nov. 1, 1918 Started out at 4:00 P.M. The drive is on. Fritz[11] is coming back at us. Machine guns cracking . . . artillery from both sides. A real war and we are walking right into the zone. Ducking shells all the way. The artillery is nerve racking and we don't know from which angle "Jerry" will fire next. Halted behind shelter of R.R. track just outside of Grandpre after being forced back off main road by shell fire. Jerry is shelling Grandpre all the time. Trees splintered like toothpicks. Machine gunners on top of R.R. bank. Breakfast served to us in a protected gully along road. Pushed into Grandpre at 10:00 A.M. to clear streets for the artillery to advance. . . . Sniper's bullets . . . wounded Sgt. Adams, Louderback, Harrison, Koerner, and Greaetehouse.

SUN., Nov. 3, 1918 Plenty of evidence of Hun[12] evacuation. All culverts and innumerable spots in R.R. blown out. . . . Many dead Germans along the road. One heap on a manure pile. Started to fill in shell holes when I was selected with Bill Harvey, Frank Gilberg and Jos Ewell to make reconnaissance of roads in vicinity. Interesting job. Devastation everywhere. Our barrage had rooted up the entire territory like a ploughed field. Dead horses galore, many of them have a hind quarter cut off. The Huns need food. Dead men here and there. The sight I enjoy better than a dead German is to see heaps of them.

SAT., Nov. 9, 1918 Moved out with full packs at 8 A.M. Hiked to Les Islettes about 20 kilos. Hard tack and "corn willie"[13] for lunch. YMCA, K of C,[14] Salvation Army here and we picked up "beaucoup" eats, especially chocolate.[15] Bunked in a fine big chateau.

SUN., Nov. 10, 1918 First day off in over two months. Went to church where an American chaplain read Mass and an American soldier choir sang. Seemed good. Co. took a bath and we were issued new underwear but the "cooties"[16] got there first. . . . The papers show a picture of the Kaiser entitled "William the Lost" and say that he had abdicated. Had a good dinner. Rumor at night that armistice was signed. Some fellows discharged their arms in the courtyard but most of us were too well pleased with dry bunk to get up.

---

[11] Slang for a German.

[12] A derogatory term for a German, implying that he was like the barbarous warriors who served under Attila in the fifth century C.E.

[13] Soldiers' slang term for canned corned beef, which they were served regularly and complained about regularly.

[14] Knights of Columbus is a Catholic men's service organization.

[15] In French, *beaucoup* means "many," "much," or "in abundance." Chocolate was Kennedy's favorite food; earlier diary entries indicate that while other men scouted for liquor, Kennedy always sought chocolate.

[16] Slang for lice.

2   *Captain John M. Trible, Medical Corps, Sanitary Train, Third Infantry Division, AEF*

Captain Trible was drafted to serve as a lieutenant in the infantry, but he applied to serve as an officer in the Medical Corps instead and was appointed to that branch of the service in July 1917. He went to France in February 1918. At the time he entered the service, Trible was thirty-three years old, married, the father of a young son, and working as a physician in Cuero, Texas.

THUR., SEPT. 12, 1918 Left Uruffe at 8 P.M. last night, arrived in woods north of Borcq at 7 A.M. in the morning after a fierce night of rain and mud and inky darkness. It has rained all day and eight of us are in a tent resting up. Information as to the action in front of us is mighty good. Hun prisoners are passing here now. We are in front of the St. Mihiel salient or spur,[1] and not far from Metz in Germany. *Post-war annotation: During this night we passed one truck train that was all lighted up, which was very unusual to say the least, and we learned afterwards that these trucks were loaded with German prisoners, carrying them to the rear, for it made no difference to the French if the lights on this train should attract hun shells, for that would mean just so many less German prisoners to feed and care for. The drivers on all of these trucks were Indo-Chinamen, who did not value their lives any more than did the French.*

TUES., SEPT. 17, 1918 Another moonlit night with the usual bombardment. Some of our Division is moving this morning, and we expect to follow during the day. *Post-war annotation: The St. Mihiel drive was over and our Division was being withdrawn, after having so few casualties that it had not been necessary for any of our four hospitals to even unpack their equipment. . . . Our casualties did not number over three men killed and seven or eight wounded. . . . When the infantry units went over the top after the barrage, they met with little or no resistance to speak of.*

[Captain Trible and his medical unit began making their way northwest toward the Meuse-Argonne front as soon as the St. Mihiel battle was over, but he had duties along the way.—Eds.]

WED., SEPT. 18, 1918 Had a most miserable night last night. Left Borcq at 2 P.M. and traveled in a long truck train that stopped every ten minutes, reached Julvecourt at 2 P.M. today, nothing to eat, nor no water to drink while en route.

[1] The bulge in the battlefront that made St. Mihiel vulnerable from three sides.
Source: The Diary of John Trible, Captain M.C., U.S. Army, February 26, 1918–May 18, 1919, Tulane University Manuscripts Division, Joseph Merrick Jones Hall Tulane University Libraries, 1–219. (Bracketed text within the selections has been added by the editors to help fill in gaps and clarify unfamiliar terminology.)

Fri., Sept. 20, 1918 Rained most of the day. Went to Julvecourt and interviewed the prisoner I had been appointed to defend.[2]

Sat., Sept. 21, 1918 Trial of the attempted rape case in which I am to act as counsel for the defendant was deferred on account of difficulty getting witnesses. Very chilly and cold and rained all morning.

Mon., Sept. 23, 1918 The country hereabouts is packed with American troops. It is cold, damp, and gloomy. We anticipate that there will be a big fight on in a few days.

Tues., Sept. 24, 1918 The sun came out and it is drying up a little and is also a little warmer. . . . Had a successful courtmartial case this afternoon as my client . . . won out and was acquitted. *Post-war annotation: I secured his acquittal with considerable difficulty as Midgely [the prosecuting officer] was determined he should be convicted, which probably was what should have happened. Midgely was sore at me about the management of the case for some time for I won his acquittal on technicalities.*

Wed., Sept. 25, 1918 Rec'd ten letters from my girl today; they had some very clear pictures of the man crying and on a donkey hitched to a cart.[3] . . . This morning before daybreak, a barrage north of us started, and we believe the American offensive has been launched, though no one knows.

Thurs., Sept. 26, 1918 Left the woods where we were at two A.M. this day and came north of Verdun. The real American attack—battle of the Argonne—started at eleven o'clock last night, the barrage was fierce. We slept all morning in the woods and have been watching prisoners being brought in. All reports are favorable for this, the apparently greatest of all battles.

Mon., Sept. 30, 1918 We understand that we are to relieve the 79th Division on the line at once, but the congested roads will make it slow going. We understand that the huns are vigorously counterattacking our troops, it is said with no other results than heavy loss of life. *Post-war annotation: It is probable that we owed the length of our stay here to the bad roads and the terrible congestion on them, for in a way we were shut off from the world and couldn't get out. . . . Through the firing and the heavy traffic worked thousands of men of the Engineers with picks and shovels, and little sacks filled with rocks from shell holes. They were literally building up the road under our feet. . . . There was no living thing in all this sector but soldiers. All vegetation was dead, most of the trees were shattered, and the others had been killed with gas.*

Sun., Oct. 6, 1918 Had an awful day of it as we have been flooded with wounded, many of whom died on our hands and the others were desperately wounded. There has been terrific artillery action today. . . . I am about all in as my nerves are shot to pieces. It is very damp and chilly. *Post-war annotation: These desperately*

[2] With lawyers in short supply at the front, any professionally trained officer could be asked to serve as a soldier's legal counsel.

[3] Trible's "girl" is his wife, Ottie Belle Trible; "the man" is his four-year-old son, John Bowles Trible.

wounded were a wonderful bunch, they did not whimper or complain, all they wanted was something to smoke, and we had plenty of tobacco for all of them, also we had a generous supply of morphine, which we used freely. . . . We also had plenty of whiskey which we also used freely to get them warmed up.

SAT., OCT. 12, 1918 Many wounded again during the night. . . . Our evacuation service is absolutely rotten, many men thus lose their only chance of life. Today is quieter. . . . Still we know very little of what is happening, except that it seems to be favorable, though at a high cost. We have many wounded in our ward.

THURS., OCT. 17, 1918 This is our sixth anniversary. May the next be spent with her whom I love. . . . Very few patients and very poor evacuation. Only lost six men yesterday. We are being relieved today by the 90th Division.

FRI., OCT. 18, 1918 There seems to be a doubt as to whether our division is being relieved or not.

SUN., OCT. 20, 1918 Rec'd orders last night to move at daybreak this morning to a point near Septsarges, 8 kilometers north of here. . . . We are acting as a shock hospital and are located on a road on the top of a high hill. It has simply poured all day and is very cold. We had to pitch and equip our tents in a sea of mud and water. My hands are so cold that it is with difficulty that I write this.

SAT., OCT. 26, 1918 We have now been in for twenty-seven days without rest or relief.

[Trible's division was finally relieved of duty on October 28, and Trible was ordered to Velaines, Belgium, to serve in a hospital there.—Eds.]

THURS., NOV. 7, 1918 From the news of today the huns are on the run everywhere, as all armies have made big advances. . . . The usual rumors are afloat that peace has been declared. We are hopeful but not assured.

SUN., NOV. 10, 1918 Was in luck today . . . letters from my girl. . . . The news therein is not good for it is as I feared, both she and J.B. were sick with the influenza, but they have a good doctor, Dr. Peck of Dallas, and apparently both are doing well. Everything is rumor and everyone has at least one story to tell. . . . Retribution is now coming very rapidly to [the Germans] to pay them for their violation of international law and the laws of humanity. It has been quite cold today. I wrote and thanked Dr. Peck for his great kindness to my loved ones.

MON., NOV. 11, 1918 Eleven in the morning—orders cancelled—the French flag appears on passing cars and there is great enthusiasm, for it is announced that the armistice was signed at five this morning, to take effect at eleven A.M. on the eleventh day of the eleventh month of the year 1918. . . .

Everywhere the Huns are retreating in great disorder, leaving supplies and guns. This surely is one of the great days in history.

<table>
<tr><td>3</td><td></td></tr>
</table>

3 *Sergeant Elmer F. Straub, 150th Field Artillery, Forty-second "Rainbow" Division*

> Sergeant Straub had been a student at Indiana University before the war. He registered for the draft but must have been a member of the National Guard because his Forty-second "Rainbow" Division comprised National Guard units. Upon enlisting in late July 1917, Straub joined an artillery unit.

SAT., SEPT. 7, 1918 It is just one year today since we left Indianapolis.

SUN., SEPT. 8, 1918 In an old half-shot-down building near here, in this village of Mandres, there is a branch of the Salvation Army and this morning nearly all of the boys slipped away and got two pancakes, syrup and a cup of coffee for nothing; they certainly treat the boys right. The commissaries and the Red Cross also gave out raincoats, underwear, sox and towels but the Y.M.C.A. are regular robbers. . . . We will be spending our time peering over 'No Man's Land' in the St. Mihiel sector. For noon mess we had fried potatoes, hard tack and coffee and we are expected to keep alive on that, for I suppose we will get nothing but that from now on until we get off the front. . . . Swell food for men who get as little sleep and do as much work as we do! After mess Hoover and I went over to the Salvation Army where we bought some soap and safety razor blades and then the old man in charge gave us some great big California grapes and they surely went good. . . . At 8:00 we took the horses out to graze as they do not get half the food they ought to.

MON., SEPT. 9, 1918 We got up to the O.P. [observation post] about 9:45 A.M. . . . It is right in the front lines and about four kilometers in front of our guns. There is more artillery stationed between our guns and the O.P. than I have ever seen before. The 'big party' is to start sometime between the 15th and the 20th of this month and the first day's objective is the village of Pannes. We can see the lay out of both the American and German infantries; the Americans are in the valley directly in front of our O.P. and the Germans are on the high ground just beyond. During the morning we located about fifteen villages that are now in German hands and also got the terrain pretty well in mind. . . . During the afternoon . . . I went out in the big woods right in back of the O.P. and picked several hats of great big blackberries.

THURS., SEPT. 12, 1918 At 1:05 A.M. the party started off; only the heavy artillery started the thing and according to all dope it was a big surprise to the Germans. There was so little retaliation fire that they used only about half the artillery they had up here. . . . At 10 A.M. [we] started forward . . . into Pannes. The road was certainly a sight, there were three columns of troops going forward

Source: Sergeant Elmer Straub, *A Sergeant's Diary in the World War*, volume 3, Indiana World War Records (Indianapolis: Indiana Historical Commission, 1923), 11–343.

on this one narrow little road. The road itself was in an awful condition, full of shell holes, bridges out and all torn up. The Engineers were working on the bridges and filling up the shell holes, wounded were being brought back this way. . . . We could overlook the whole valley that not twelve hours before was 'No Man's Land' and now it is crowded with human bodies, both dead and alive. . . . The Germans . . . left everything behind in their hurry to get out, and considering all of it, American casualties were very small. . . . In the villages that we passed through we saw many, many French civilians who had lived in their old homes under German military rule ever since the start of the war. When our officers would pass them they would all come to attention showing that the Germans had made them live and regard them as "THE RULERS" of the land, and when our men and officers treated them well they would do anything for our convenience.

[At 4:30 a.m. on Friday, October 4, Straub and his artillery regiment, with horses, trucks, and wagons, began their sixty-mile march northwest to the Argonne sector. — Eds.]

MON., OCT. 7, 1918 This morning . . . when we got to the edge of Mont-faucon, the Colonel stopped and we all dismounted. . . . The Colonel showed us a big valley where he said we could put our gun positions. . . . This is the Argonne Woods.

TUES., OCT. 15, 1918 Maxwell had been out last night stealing food and when he got up this morning we started to eat again. We made three batches of fudge and had toast, butter, pancakes, fried potatoes and sugar. . . . We found out that our doughboys gained their objective but had to drop back. . . . [They] have had about 1500 casualties since they have been up here and they are in pretty bad shape.

WED., OCT. 16, 1918 The battery is lower now on horses than it ever has been, we have only 131 left and my single mount looks like a real skeleton because of lack of food.

FRI., OCT. 18, 1918 We went . . . on up toward the front. We saw very, very many American and German dead lying around and the whole country is terribly devastated. Mud is no name for it. . . . I hope and pray that all of our horses fall dead or something happens to prevent us from taking up our new gun position; our first piece will be put 100 feet from 12 German dead and more than twenty dead horses. . . . This life is certainly one h --- and I surely hope that something very unusual happens to break the spell of mud, rain, work, monotony, and dissatisfaction that we are under.

SAT., OCT. 19, 1918 The country around is practically the same as that we saw a few days ago, all torn up, full of shell holes, dead lying wherever one looks and the whole country dead except for the American soldiers. We tied our horses at the base of a very steep hill and then took our instruments and climbed to the top, where we could see all over the surrounding country, our lines and the German lines. We immediately . . . put on the phone and then Lieut. Knaff started to adjust the battery on a German O.P. that was located in the top of a tree near the edge of the woods. . . . It took about 40 rounds and the tree was no more. . . . All thru this valley one can see American dead lying about and it seems as if the first aid men who are supposed to litter these men off do not do their work properly because . . . it is certainly a gruesome looking place. On our way back I took a short cut and got into some sneezing gas. I was afraid to run my horse as he is so poor that I thought he would drop dead; I have been sneezing ever since.

SAT., OCT. 26, 1918 This morning while I was eating, Lieut. Knaff told me that the position we had located was not far enough in advance. . . . By the time I arrived at the [new] position it was clear and there was a deal of aerial activity. . . . About 2:00 the Germans began to . . . fire both H.E. and shrapnel;[1] each H.E. shell contains a little mustard gas so I inhaled weak gas all the rest of the day. . . . While the gun squads were putting the guns in place I tried to help Coleman and some of our detail boys with our instrument wagon which had gotten stuck in a shell hole on account of a balky horse they had pulling it. Shells were coming thick and fast, both H.E. and gas, so all of the work was very slow. . . . It was 12:30 before the pieces were in place and laid ready to fire, and then when I looked the place over I found that the third piece was in a ditch.

MON., OCT. 28, 1918 This morning we all got up happy as there had been no one killed during the night. . . . The gas was very strong during the night. . . . Two of our horses had been killed during the night and one of our men was sent to the hospital with gas. . . . After I had finished my breakfast and watered and fed my horse, I again started to work on our hole—making it deeper . . . and now I think we are pretty safe.

FRI., NOV. 1, 1918 After I had taken my shave this A.M. . . . I decided I ought to have a few trinkets so I started out to meet one of the columns of prisoners. . . . I asked one fellow whether he had a watch and he said yes; so I made him give it to me and then I went to one of the others who gave me another watch, and the third gave me a knife, so I figured that I had enough. I did not like the idea of taking their things from them but some one else would have, so I suppose it was all right. There were many wounded being brought in, both German and American; the German prisoners who were not injured always carried the wounded men in, whether German or American. Three German medics were captured and they were put to work taking care of wounded. . . . They were certainly good workers and did the work right. . . . The nerve that the boys display when they come in wounded is certainly remarkable. They don't even whimper. . . . I held one American "Doughboy's" hand as he died. . . . It was sure a mess of blood at the first aid station and it finally 'got to' Perry and me,

---

[1] High explosives (H.E.) destroy property, whereas shrapnel and mustard gas kill people.

so we stopped and went to tend our horses. . . . I talked to many of [the German prisoners] and they were all anxious to go to America and were overly glad that they were thru with the whole thing. . . . The Germans certainly praise the Americans and say that they have never seen such wonderful artillery work. As I was talking to one he looked at my name . . . and he asked me whether or not I was German. I told him that I was, and then he told me that he lived beside an old shoemaker named Straub in Strassburg. Before I could say much more to him he was rushed on and I lost him in the crowd, everything was one big, mad whirl. We are now firing at a range that requires a number 00 charge, the heaviest charge we have. . . . As a whole the day has been rather exciting and I have smoked so many cigarettes that my tongue burns like fire. I have just taken the cotton out of my ears.

SAT., NOV. 2, 1918 I could not go to sleep immediately so I sat up until 11:30 and read until I got sleepy. One would at least think that one would have a few unpleasant dreams after a day such as the one yesterday, but after I got to sleep, I slept thru until 8:00 this morning without a whimper. After breakfast . . . we started forward to locate a new gun position.

WED., NOV. 6, 1918 There is an awful lot of "snow" going around about peace talk and the latest dope we have is that the "doughboys" are about 30 kilometers in front of us and are still going toward the rear. Things are quiet and they say the war is over for them.

THURS., NOV. 7, 1918 Well the night was about as quiet as we have had for the past four or five months. . . . This morning I saw an American Y.W.C.A. girl. . . . She is the first woman I have seen for about four months.

FRI., NOV., 8, 1918 During the night I had an awful coughing spell and short breath and I think it is the effects of the gas that we were in there. . . . We hear that peace is practically at hand.

MON., NOV. 11, 1918 Of course all morning the boys were waiting for news of peace. Battery had their wireless up and at 9:30 received word that Germany had accepted our peace terms and that at 11:45 there would be no more firing on any of the fronts. Of course the fellows had a smile on their faces but there was not any rejoicing to amount to anything. . . . The "snow" is already out as to what we are going to do next, and I'll say that it is not very pleasing news. We are either to go to Austria or Germany for M.P. duty.

Analyzing Wartime Diaries

1. Looking over your source analysis table on page 132, what differences do you find in the Kennedy, Trible, and Straub comments on food and sleep, rain and mud, roads and transport, and combat and danger? How do you explain any differences you see?

2. The entries you read are from the same weeks in the war. How were these three soldiers' combat experiences similar? How were they different? What accounts for the differences?

3. What differences do you find in the ways the three diarists spoke about, and seemed to feel about, the German soldiers? How do you explain these differences?

4. Compare Captain Trible's comments on the armistice on November 10 and 11 with Corporal Kennedy's on November 10 and Sergeant Straub's on November 11. Why do you think the reactions of the thirty-four-year-old physician from Texas were different from those of the young soldiers from New York and Indiana?

5. How informed were these soldiers about the overall strategy and success of the Allied war effort? If one of these diaries had fallen into German hands, how could the Germans have used the diary entries to gain a military advantage?

6. How could these diary entries be used in writing a history of World War I? What biases in the diarists' perspective would you have to take into account when using these sources? In what ways are you confident that they reflect the experiences of most soldiers?

7. The technology of war has changed dramatically since World War I. Make a list of the ways in which soldiers' daily experiences today differ from those recorded in these diaries. Make a second list of the ways in which they are similar. Based on these lists, would you argue that soldiers' daily experiences have essentially changed or remained largely the same since World War I?

The Rest of the Story

Sergeant Elmer Straub's prediction that he would be sent to Germany after the war proved accurate. He and his artillery battery were stationed in Bad Neuenahr, near the Rhine River, from December 1918 through March 1919. Straub's thirty pages of diary entries from this period do not say much about the nature of his duties, apart from taking care of his horses and serving as a military presence, but the entries are thick with descriptions of the good food, comfortable beds, hours of sleep, and friendly German people. Straub then spent four months at the University of Edinburgh, under U.S. Army auspices, before returning to the states, where he was discharged on August 5, 1919. He walked into his parents' home in Indianapolis at 7:30 a.m. on August 7.

After the war, Corporal Eugene Kennedy stayed in France, where his engineering company worked on reconnaissance maps. His fifty pages of postarmistice entries, like Straub's, said more about his meals (including his "first ice cream in fourteen months") and his sightseeing trips around France than about his military work. But, like Straub, Kennedy continued to keep the daily diary until he reached his home near Albany, New York, in June 1919. His final entry stated, "Peg and I . . . ordered announcement cards. We then called on Father Looney and made arrangements to be married July 9th."

Captain John Trible continued to serve as an army physician for six months after the war. He wrote in his diary about his postarmistice duty caring for U.S. soldiers, in both France and Germany, who were suffering from influenza. Entries in November and December made frequent mention of the hundreds of flu cases he was treating and the number of men dying each day.

Neither Trible, Straub, nor Kennedy wrote about the flu before the war ended, but this pandemic, which killed twenty million individuals worldwide in 1918–1919, was taking its toll on the U.S. military in the last weeks of the war. Indeed, the crowded conditions in training camps and troop ships in the summer of 1918 encouraged the spread of the deadly epidemic. Between September and November, 23,000 enlisted men in training in the United States died of flu-induced pneumonia; another 9,000 soldiers died of the flu in France. Overall, an estimated one-fourth of the U.S. Army suffered from the flu during the war, and in the unrelenting final weeks of battle, almost 100,000 members of the AEF (including General Pershing) suffered from it. Of the 126,000 U.S. soldiers who died in the war, 66,000 soldiers died from the flu.

All historians of World War I acknowledge the contributions and sacrifices of U.S. soldiers during the war, but no one pretends that their sacrifices can compare with those made by the Allied forces with whom the United States fought. The 60,000 Americans who died in combat represent a small fraction of the five million Allied deaths and the three million deaths on the German side. The U.S. casualty rate—dead and wounded combined—was about 206,000, or 8 percent of the 2.6 million Americans who served in combat, whereas the British casualty rate was 35 percent, the French casualty rate was 76 percent, and the Austro-Hungarian casualty rate was a staggering 90 percent.

All three diarists profiled in this chapter survived the war, making them quite representative of the U.S. soldiers who served. Thousands came home without a limb, without their sight, or without their sanity, but the vast majority, including Kennedy, Trible, and Straub, returned home and resumed their lives as workers and family members in their communities. In the coming decades, the American veterans of World War I would become a forceful lobby for government benefits to those who had served the nation under fire. After World War II, political leaders who had been World War I veterans, including President Harry Truman, helped enact the GI Bill, providing returning soldiers with aid that had not been available after World War I.

To Find Out More

World War I Diaries, Letters, and Memoirs

Baker, Chester E. *A Doughboy's Diary*. Shippensburg, PA: Burd Street Press, 1998. A post-war memoir.

Holt, W. Stull. *The Great War at Home and Abroad: The World War I Diaries and Letters of W. Stull Holt*. Edited by Maclyn P. Burg and Thomas J. Pressly. Manhattan, KS: Sunflower University Press, 1998.

Kennedy, Corporal Eugene. Diary. Hoover Institution on War, Revolution, and Peace, Stanford University.

Pfennig, Clair F. *All for Heaven, Hell, or Hoboken: The World War I Diary and Letters of Clair F. Pfennig, Flash Ranger, Company D, 29 Engineers, A.E.F.* Edited by Anthony G. Finan. St. Louis: Crimson Shamrock Press, 1999.

Rogers, Bogart. *A Yankee Ace in the RAF: The World War I Letters of Captain Bogart Rogers*. Edited by John H. Morrow Jr. and Earl Rogers. Lawrence: University Press of Kansas, 1996.

Rowe, Josiah P., Jr. *Letters from a World War I Aviator*. Boston: Sinclaire Press, 1986.

Saltonstall, Nora. *Out Here at the Front: The World War I Letters of Nora Saltonstall*. Edited by Judith S. Graham. Boston: Northeastern University Press, 2004. Offers the viewpoint of an army nurse in a mobile unit at the western front.

Springs, Elliot White. *War Birds: Diary of an Unknown Aviator*. New York: George H. Doran Company, 1926. This work is actually a novel, but it does not announce itself as fiction.

Straub, Sergeant Elmer. *A Sergeant's Diary in the World War*. Indiana World War Records, vol. 3. Indianapolis: Indiana Historical Commission, 1923.

Trible, Captain John. Diary with annotations. Special Collections, Howard-Tilton Memorial Library, Tulane University, New Orleans.

U.S. Army Military History Institute. World War I diaries. Carlisle, Pennsylvania.

Virginia War History Commission. World War I diaries. Virginia State Archives, Richmond, Virginia.

Secondary Sources on World War I

Barbeau, Arthur E., and Henri Florette. *The Unknown Soldier: African-American Troops in World War I*. Philadelphia: Temple University Press, 1974.

Byerly, Carol. *Fever of War: The Influenza Epidemic in the U.S. Army during World War I*. New York: New York University Press, 2005.

Ford, Nancy Gentile. *Americans All: Foreign-Born Soldiers in World War I*. College Station: Texas A&M University Press, 2001.

Freidel, Frank. *Over There: The Story of America's First Great Overseas Crusade*. Boston: Little, Brown, 1965. Uses many excerpts from diaries and letters as well as splendid photographs.

Gilbert, Martin. *The First World War: A Complete History*. New York: Owl Books, 2004.

Keegan, John. *The First World War*. New York: Knopf, 1999.

Keene, Jennifer. *Doughboys, the Great War, and the Remaking of Modern America*. Baltimore: Johns Hopkins University Press, 2001.

Keene, Jennifer. *World War I.* Daily Life through History Series. Westport, CT: Greenwood, 2006.

Strachan, Hew. *The First World War.* New York: Penguin Non-Classics, 2005.

Zieger, Robert H. *America's Great War: World War I and the American Experience.* New York: Rowman and Littlefield, 2000.

Multimedia Resources on World War I

"The Great War 1918." *American Experience.* DVD. Directed by Tom Weidlinger. Boston: WGBH Boston Video, 2005. A one-hour program focused on soldiers' experiences, using interviews with World War I veterans.

The Great War and the Shaping of the 20th Century. DVD. Executive Producer: Blaine Bagett. Los Angeles: KCET; London: BBC, 1996. An eight-part series tracing the chronological progression of the war. For more information on each segment go to http://www.pbs.org/greatwar/chapters/index.html.

The Great War Society. http://www.thegreatwarsociety.com. Includes memoirs and diaries.

Library of Congress. "World War I: The Great War." *Veterans History Project.* http://www.loc.gov/vets/stories/ex-war-wwi.html. Archive of World War I documents.

CHAPTER 7

Singing of Struggle

Mexican Workers' Folk Songs from the American Southwest

M exican workers rose with the dawn in Los Angeles in the 1920s and turned on their radios to KELW to hear Pedro Gonzalez host his Spanish-language program of both live and recorded musical favorites. From 4 a.m. until 7 a.m. every morning, Gonzalez broadcast from a local Burbank studio thanks to his sponsor, Folger's coffee. With the largest concentration of ethnic Mexicans anywhere outside of Mexico City in the 1920s, Los Angeles was an ideal market for radio stations and advertisers looking to reach the burgeoning population of Mexican consumers in the United States. And since U.S. law forbade the importation of Mexican phonograph records, Los Angeles was also the hub of the Mexican recording business in the United States. Los Angeles was not alone in developing and broadcasting the culture of the Mexican American *barrio*, however. From the border towns of Texas, west through New Mexico and Arizona, on up the coast of California and over into the midwestern cities of Chicago and Detroit, performers, entrepreneurs, and advertisers combined the commercial spirit of the 1920s with the ethnic energy of the day. It was a moment of creative expression that captured the struggles of Mexicans who crossed the border for work in the first decades of the twentieth century.

Among the most popular musical forms in the Mexican community was the *corrido*, a style of folk song characterized by storytelling about both heroic figures and everyday folks. Musicians sang *corridos* in local clubs, meeting halls, storefronts, and family gatherings, as well as recorded them in makeshift studios for phonograph records and radio broadcasts. The boom in Mexican migration between 1900 and 1930 sparked a corollary boom in the creation of *corridos* about the migrant experience. Indeed, folklorists regard these decades as the golden age of the *corrido*; migrants to the United States were full of stories about loss

148

and gain, personal love and political anger, national loyalty and cultural change, ethnic pride and racial insult. Since Anglo Americans paid scant attention to non-English cultural productions, Mexicans in the United States were free to say whatever they wanted in their *corridos*. As Manuel H. Peña put it, the *corrido* "functioned as a 'collective diary' expressing symbolically the people's reactions to events vital to their self-interests."

At the very time Mexican culture, commerce, and community life in the U.S. Southwest was being rejuvenated by infusions of new immigrants, U.S. employers were frantically resisting political pressures to restrict Mexican immigration. Those pressures had begun in the decade before World War I and became more intense in the postwar 1920s when American nativists defined foreigners as a threat to the nation's economic prosperity, political liberties, and racial purity. Mexicans were not the only targets of nativists' prorestriction campaign; newcomers from southern and eastern Europe, from South Asia, and from Japan were also cited as candidates for the same sort of exclusionary laws enacted to keep out the Chinese in the 1880s and 1890s.

The particular charges leveled against Mexican immigrants built on a history of nativist hostility to Catholics and to nonwhites. During the 1920s, the American Protective Association and the Ku Klux Klan harkened back to mid-nineteenth century fears about the Irish by arguing that Catholics were too deferential to hierarchy and too loyal to a foreign pope to ever succeed as independent citizens in America's democracy. Twentieth-century nativists coupled that cultural fear with a racial one. Although the U.S. Bureau of the Census classified Mexicans as "white," nativists relied on the modern pseudo-science of eugenics to argue that Mexicans were a "mongrel" race of *mestizo* Indians, "diseased of body, subnormal intellectually, and moral morons of the most hopeless type." Mexican presence in the United States, said these nativists, threatened "a race problem that will dwarf the negro problem of the South; and the practical destruction, at least for centuries, of all that is worthwhile in our white civilization."

These attacks not only threatened new Mexican immigrants and Mexican American citizens with centuries-long roots in southwestern soil, they also threatened the southwestern employers whose enormous profits depended on Mexican labor. By the 1920s, Mexicans constituted three-fourths of the workers in the Texas cotton fields and three-fourths of those employed in the Texas construction industry. Mexicans also made up three-fourths of California's farm labor force, two-thirds of those employed in mining in the southwest, and between 60 and 90 percent of the track crews on the region's railways. Employers and economists agreed that the rapid expansion of agriculture, mining, railroads, and construction in Texas, Arizona, New Mexico, and California was made possible by economic and political forces that sent Mexican workers northward after 1890.

Just as the spread of commercial agriculture had pushed millions of peasants off traditional lands in Europe, so, too, in Mexico, under the dictatorial rule of Porfirio Diaz, elite landowners drove small farmers off of their self-sufficient *ejidos* (villages) to create huge coffee and sugar estates. The construction of railways in Mexico made this commercialization of agriculture possible while also making it possible for displaced peasants to travel north for jobs in the United States. In the years before World War I, crossing the border was easy, and although jobs north of the border paid low wages by U.S. standards, they paid a great deal better than jobs in the depressed and overcrowded Mexican market. The push from the Mexican economy and the pull of the U.S. economy were further stimulated by the activities of labor agents in the United States who ignored U.S. laws against recruiting "contract labor" in foreign countries. Labor agents profited from fees paid by U.S. employers for supplying work crews and from fees paid by Mexicans for the transportation north. As if the economic logic of Mexican migration north were not enough, the eruption of the decade-long Mexican Revolution against Diaz, starting in 1910, sent tens of thousands of Mexicans to the United States, fleeing the violence and chaos of civil war.

Estimates of the Mexican population in the United States in this pre–World War I era are inevitably imprecise because there was no U.S. Border Patrol until 1924 and only slight enforcement, at urban checkpoints, of the few immigration laws then on the books. Mexicans crossed and recrossed the border with regularity, further complicating any attempt to count the number of foreign-born Mexicans in the United States at any point in time. According to scholars' best estimates, however, about 78,000 Mexican nationals were living in the United States in 1890; by 1900, that figure had risen to 103,000. Over the next decade, the immigrant population more than doubled, to 222,000, in 1910; it more than doubled again, to 478,000, by 1920. Understanding that these figures likely underestimate the overall flow northward, scholars typically agree that between a million and a million and a half Mexican immigrants entered the United States between 1890 and 1929. Although Mexicans probably comprised less than 5 percent of the twenty-two million immigrants who entered the United States between 1890 and 1930, they inspired as much fear in the hearts of nativists as did the more numerous Italians, Russian Jews, Hungarians, and Slavs arriving in those years.

Proponents of immigration restriction scored two significant legislative victories after 1915, despite the strong opposition of employers who profited from cheap immigrant labor. In 1917, after thirty years of effort, a bill requiring that immigrants be literate in their native language, along with a rule that each immigrant pay an $8 "head tax" to fund the nation's emerging immigration bureaucracy, finally overrode presidential veto. More dramatically, in 1924, Congress fixed numerical quotas on the number of each nationality eligible to enter the United States in any year, and it tied those quotas to the number of each nationality in the United States in 1890, before southern and eastern Europeans began to dominate the immigrant stream.

Employers in the U.S. Southwest responded to these new laws by applying political pressure to protect their economic interests in Mexican labor. Taking advantage of the World War I labor shortage in 1918 and 1919, they gained exemptions from the literacy bill and head tax for Mexican workers. Although the southwestern lobby failed to convince Congress to extend these exemptions

Figure 7.1 Mexican Musicians, 1918 In this rare photo, guitarist Florencio Estrada poses with accordion player Frumencio Estrada, presumably his brother. We do not know the names of the other men pictured here, who may be friends, relatives, or fellow musicians. In the early twentieth century, Mexican folksingers, or corridistas, sang and entertained audiences with songs about human rights, the Mexican government, the plight of migrant workers, and immigrant life in the United States. Source: Courtesy of the Arhoolie Foundation.

into the 1920s, it was notably successful in its fight to exempt Mexico (along with the entire Western Hemisphere) from the quota restrictions imposed in 1924. Legal border crossing from Mexico was more difficult after the 1924 law passed—immigrants now had to pay $10 to secure a visa, pass the Spanish literacy test, and pay the $8 head tax—but there was no annual quota on the number of Mexicans legally allowed in. Moreover, with only 450 border patrol agents assigned to cover both the Canadian and Mexican borders, illegal entry into the United States was not difficult for those who could not pass the literacy test or afford the fees. Spared the constraint of a quota, employers soon learned the value of hiring undocumented workers who could be threatened with deportation if they did not work long hours at low pay.

How did employers in the Southwest convince Congress to ease restrictions on their Mexican labor pool? They did so by lobbying with a blend of truth and fiction that served their economic interests. Employers, accurately noting that both white and black U.S. workers were leaving low-paid agricultural work for better-paid urban jobs, then proposed Mexican workers as the solution to the labor problem by inaccurately depicting them as "an inferior race of people" who could "live on less than any people in the world and are seemingly happy."

Employers testifying before the House of Representative's Committee on Immigration and Naturalization in early 1920 claimed that the adult Mexican worker was "a 13-year-old child in a grown body" who could be "led most anywhere," was "specially fitted for the burdensome task of bending his back to pick the cotton," did not "think of yesterday . . . never thinks of tomorrow," and was "ignorant" about politics and economics. According to this testimony, the Mexican worker cared little about "where he is born" but, conveniently, was a "bird of passage" who flew back to Mexico as soon as the job was done and so did not establish the sort of ethnic communities that nativists found so threatening to American civilization. One spokesman for the California Farm Bureau Federation sought to protect his state's labor pool by claiming that there was "no such thing" as a permanent Mexican community in the United States, while Congressman Carl Hayden of Arizona described the border between Arizona and Sonora, Mexico, as an "arbitrary boundary line, with the people on the American side needing the assistance" of those on the Mexican side.

In defending their access to Mexican labor, employers and their advocates chose to deny that Mexicans were actively creating new communities and institutions in the United States, establishing their own businesses and consumer demands, and creating their own cultural adaptations, including the use of radio stations and phonograph records to transmit their original *corrido* commentaries on modern immigrant life. Instead, they constructed the Mexican worker as a docile, dim-witted beast of burden, obediently coming and going, grateful for low wages, impervious to insult, blind to wider horizons, and untroubled by the need to leave home to survive. *Corridos* tell a different story.

Using the Source: Folk Music

Folk music is music from the bottom up. It is created by people without wealth or power, without commercial intent, and usually without a single, identified author. Like the poetry and stories produced through the oral folk process, folk songs morph and evolve as they pass from one singer to another, from one town to the next. But the purpose of folk songs persists: to share stories, emotions, values, and attitudes among people with common experiences and a common culture. Folk songs are not written to be sold to strangers; they are internal memos—a "collective diary"—to be passed among those who share a history and worldview.

The Mexican *corrido* is a Spanish-language folk song with distinctive characteristics of form and content. Typically, the *corrido* is structured in eight-syllable lines arranged in four- or six-line stanzas. The rhyme is usually based on vowel sounds, and either the first and fourth lines and the second and third lines rhyme or the first and third lines and second and fourth lines rhyme. The melody, sung by the male *corridista* (balladeer) who accompanies himself on the guitar, relies on the text to shape the pitch and rhythm of the song. The melody is repeated with each stanza, but if the *corrido* has a refrain, it may be sung in a different rhythm.

The key feature of the *corrido* is its narrative structure. It always reports on particular events in a particular time and place, but its central purpose is to use narrative to make an editorial comment about the social or political meaning of the events recounted. The *corrido* can be used to tell a very personal story, but it is best known as a type of folk song that talks about national identity, cultural pride, and community life.

Although folklorists have been able to find roots of the *corrido* style in Spanish romance ballads of the sixteenth century, they generally agree that the folk song we now recognize as a *corrido* emerged in Mexico in the second half of the nineteenth century as a vehicle for peasant commentary on the injustices of the Porfirio Diaz dictatorship. Folklorists define the golden age of the *corrido* as the years between 1900 and 1930 because at that time, in the border region encompassing northern Mexico and southern Texas and New Mexico, the *corrido* emerged as the dominant form of Mexican folk music. The combination of the Mexican Revolution and Mexican immigration to the United States produced multiple, often competing tensions in the lives of working-class Mexicans and Mexican Americans. The *corrido* proved to be a highly adaptable form for communicating about Mexican nationalism and the cultural, economic, and political tensions that went along with loyalty to Mexico.

It does not appear that either the U.S. recording industry or radio programmers imposed any censorship over the content of *corridos* that were recorded in the 1920s, even though these folk songs often commented critically on American culture and on the treatment of Mexicans in the United States. The commercial interests that recorded and broadcast this folk music were not trying to sell it beyond the borders of the *barrio*; they sought to profit from the sale of music that appealed to working-class consumers in the Mexican community, so they had no motive to limit that appeal by diluting the authenticity of the music. Moreover, U.S. music companies and radio stations were not sufficiently interested in, or threatened by, Mexican opinions of American culture to silence those opinions. Ironically, then, Mexicans' marginal status in the United States meant that *corridos* became a popular commodity, but they were not commodified in ways that corrupted their grass-roots messages.

What Can Folk Music Tell Us?

Music created by ordinary people to report and reflect on their personal experience gives us a historical source that has some similarities to newspaper stories and some similarities to diaries or letters. The immediacy of the stories in the *corridos* makes them a less filtered, less distorted version of events than we can find in a memoir. But the artistic and editorial nature of the song—and the fact that folk singers are free to revise songs to heighten the meaning—remind us that the *corrido* narrative is less devoted to detailed accuracy than to interpretation. Thus, it is an imperfect news report but an excellent window into the emotional, cultural, and political sentiments of the community that produced it.

Historians who study the *corrido* find that, early in the twentieth century, popular *corridos* like "The Ballad of Gregorio Cortez" celebrated the proud Mexican nationalism of heroes who stood up to enemies, such as the Diaz dictatorship or the Texas Rangers. By the end of the 1920s, however, the *corrido* had become a folk art form that captured the complex collision of national pride, cultural loyalty, grinding poverty, and economic opportunity that mark U.S.-Mexican border history. At their emotional core, these *corridos* reveal a tortured debate within the border community: who was the hero, the Mexican who stayed at home or the Mexican who went north? Contrary to the Anglo image of the Mexican as a backward peon making a simple and temporary economic choice to work in the United States, the lyrics of the *corrido* reveal a more complicated and conflicted set of calculations:

Mucha gente así lo ha dicho: *dizque* no somos patriotas porque les vamos a servir a los infames patotas.	Many people have said that we are not patriotic because we go to serve the accursed big-footed ones.	There are costs to your reputation in the community if you take U.S. jobs There are costs to personal dignity in working for foreigners you disrespect and who disrespect you
Pero que se abran trabajos y que paguen buen dinero y no queda un Mexicano que se vaya al extranjero.	But let them give us jobs and pay us decent wages; not one Mexican then will go to foreign lands.	Your national dignity is hurt if you are angry at your own leaders for not creating jobs Love of country goes beyond wealth; it is rooted in home and family and culture
Ansia tenemos de volver a nuestra patria idolatrada, pero qué le hemos de hacer si está la patria arruinada.	We're anxious to return again to our adored country; but what can we do about it if the country is ruined?	The revolution has not brought the changes we had hoped; we must find ways for our families and communities to survive

Source: From "*Defensa de los norteños*" ("Defense of the Emigrants"), original author unknown, trans. María Herrera-Sobek. In María Herrera-Sobek, *Northward Bound: The Mexican Immigrant Experience in Ballad and Song* (Bloomington: Indiana University Press, 1993), 80–83.

Those of us who do not understand Spanish cannot fully enjoy the rhymes and poetics of the original *corrido*, although we can see how the rhyming patterns shift from stanza to stanza. Because the essence of the *corrido* is the story and the commentary on the story, however, an English translation can still convey the messages about patriotism, loyalty, economic struggle, and cultural identity that are rich with historical meaning. Even in English, for example, it is evident that the *corridista*—the singer of the *corrido*—always operates as the authoritative voice in the story. Some *corridos* are sung from the standpoint of the person who ventured across the border for work, some from the standpoint of the person who chose not to make that journey, and some from the standpoint of a person who is proud of having immigrated to the United States; some are even sung from the standpoint of a person who regrets that decision. Occasionally, the *corridista*'s voice changes standpoint within one *corrido*, thereby reflecting the debate within the Mexicano community, and within the hearts and minds of individual Mexicans, over the question of emigration.

Among Americans in the 1900–1930 period, debate about Mexican immigration was cast in stark terms between those seeking to profit from Mexican labor and those who feared that Mexicans would corrupt Anglo-American civilization. Those engaged in that debate depicted the Mexican in one of two ways: as a simpleton who came temporarily for wages and made no imprint on American culture or as schemer who threatened to pollute American culture.

The *corridos* included here offer the Mexican side of the emigration debate in these decades, revealing the cultural and political tensions that Mexicans themselves experienced as witnesses to and participants in the migration northward for jobs. They give us access to Mexicans' own worries about national integrity, community cohesion, and cultural identity, mirroring the debate about how to navigate the 2,000-mile border separating Mexico and the United States.

The table on pages 156–57 will help you organize your own thoughts about the *corridos* presented in this chapter. In addition, the following Checklist questions will help you actively examine lyrics in general.

CHECKLIST: Interrogating Song Lyrics

☐ When and under what circumstances was the song produced?

☐ Who wrote or produced the song?

☐ For what purpose was the song written or produced? (Commercial? Political? Some combination?)

☐ Who was the song's intended audience? What effect was the song intended to have?

☐ What main theme does the song explore? What is its central point of view? What conflicting attitudes are evident in the lyrics?

☐ What biases can you detect in the lyrics?

Source Analysis Table

The ten *corridos* included here are representative of those produced along the border between Mexico and the United States in the years between 1910 and 1930. They allow you to analyze the multiple viewpoints on migration that Mexicans shared with one another in these years. By keeping track of exactly what *corridistas* said about Mexico, about the United States, and about migrants, you can trace the terms of the migration debate within the Mexican community and discover the multiple positions that just one *corrido* could express.

Corrido Title	Praise for Mexico	Criticism of Mexico	Praise for United States	Criticism of United States	Praise for Migrants	Criticism of Migrants
1. "An Emigrant's Farewell" / "Despedida de un norteño"						
2. "Advice to the Northerners" / "Consejos a los norteños"						
3. "The Northerners" / "Los norteños"						
4. "Defense of the Emigrants" / "Defensa de los norteños"						
5. "Ballad of Pennsylvania" / "Corrido de Pensilvania"						

Corrido Title	Praise for Mexico	Criticism of Mexico	Praise for United States	Criticism of United States	Praise for Migrants	Criticism of Migrants
6. "Verses of the Beet-Field Workers" / "Versos de los betabeleros"						
7. "Mexicans Who Speak English" / "Los Mexicanos que hablan ingles"						
8. "Radios and Chicanos" / "Radios y chicanos"						
9. "The Ranch" / "El rancho"						
10. "Red Bandannas" / "Los paños colorados"						

The Source: Mexican *Corridos,* 1910–1930

1   *An Emigrant's Farewell*
(Despedida de un norteño)

Despedida de un norteño

¡Adiós! mi Patria querida;
yo ya me voy á ausentar,
me voy para Estados Unidos,
donde pienso trabajar.

¡Adiós! mi madre querida,
la Virgen Guadalupana,
adios mi patria amorosa,
República Mexicana!

Pues, en fin, yo ya me voy,
te llevo en mi corazón,
Madre mía de Guadalupe,
échame tu bendición.

Me voy triste y pesaroso
á sufrir y á padecer
Madre *mía* de Guadalape,
tu me concedes volver. . . .

Me voy a Estado Unidos
á buscar *manutención,*
¡adiós, mi patria querida,
te llevo en mi corazón!

Pues yo no tengo la culpa
que abandone así a mi tierra
la culpta es de la pobreza
que nos tiene en la miseria. . . .

Adiós, Guanajuato hermoso,
mi Estado donde nací,
me voy para Estado Unidos,
lejos, muy lejos de tí. . . .

Al llegar á Aguascalientes
con mucho gusto y esmero,
no arreglé mi pasaporte
por la falta de dinero.

An Emigrant's Farewell

Good-bye, my beloved country,
Now I am going away;
I go to the United States,
where I intend to work.

Good-bye, my beloved mother,
the Virgin of Guadalupe;
good-bye, my beloved land,
my Mexican Republic!

At last I'm going,
I bear you in my heart;
my Mother Guadalupe,
give me your benediction.

I go sad and heavy-hearted
to suffer and endure;
my Mother Guadalupe,
grant my safe return. . . .

I go to the United States
to seek to earn a living.
Good-bye, my beloved land;
I bear you in my heart.

For I am not to blame
that I leave my country thus;
the fault lies in the poverty,
which keeps us all in want. . . .

Good-bye, fair Guanajuato,
the state where I was born;
I'm going to the United States
far, far from you. . . .

I reached Aguascalientes
with much pleasure and gaiety;
I didn't arrange my passport
for lack of any more money.

Source: "Despedida de un Norteño/An Emigrant's Farewell" from Paul S. Taylor, "Songs of the Mexican Migration." *Puro Mexicano,* J. Frank Dobie, ed. Publications of the Texas Folklore Society, no. 22. Austin: Texas Folk- Lore Society, 1935. 222–24.

Luego pasé Zacatecas con muchísima atención en el tren de pasajeros se me partió el corazón. . . .	Then I passed Zacatecas, giving it much attention, but in the passenger train my heart was breaking. . . .
Ya llegamos á Chihuahua, pues ya de aquí me despido, ¡adiós, mi Patria querida! ¡adiós, todos mis amigos!	Now we've reached Chihuahua, so here I bid you farewell; good-bye, beloved country, good-bye, all my friends!
Ya con ésta me despido de mi Patria Mexicana he llegado á Ciudid Juárez ¡oh Virgen Guadalupana!	And so I take my leave of my country, Mexico. I have reached Ciudad Juarez. Oh, Virgin of Guadalupe!

2 *Advice to the Northerners*
(Consejos a los norteños)

Consejos a los norteños	*Advice to the Northerners*
Ahora sí no llorarán, vayan juntando el transporte, muchachos aficionados, esos que les gusta el Norte.	Now you can cease your crying, start saving money for your ticket, all of you young men, who love the North.
Arreglen su maletita, ya váyanse preparando cepillen bien la gorrita para entrar de contrabando.	Get your luggage ready, start preparing yourselves, brush well your hat so you can cross illegally.
Porque si entran por el puente les han de tronar los huesos ahora no entran de gollete les cobran dieciseis pesos.	'Cause if you cross the bridge, your bones will creak you can't cross free no more the fee is sixteen pesos.
Báñense hasta con legía pa' quitarse lo mugroso, ya no den en qué decir con el gringo pretencioso.	Bathe well even with lye to get the dirt off. Don't get a bad reputation with those pretentious gringos.[1]
Ahora sí van a lonchar y a comer buenos jamones porque aquí en nuestro terreno no compran ni pantalones	Now you will be lunching and eating good ham, 'cause here in our country you can't even buy pants.

[1] According to María Herrera-Sobek, a scholar of *corridos,* this lyric represents one of the first times the derogatory term *gringo* appears in a Mexican immigrant song. Previously, the term "americanos" was used. After the 1914 U.S. naval invasion of Mexico at Vera Cruz, designed to affect the outcome of the Mexican Revolution, Mexicans adopted this more negative term.

Source: Advice to the Northerners (Consejos a los norteños). María Herrera-Sobek.

Vamos a Estado Unidos a ganar guenos salaries, que los señores patones necesitan operarios.	Let's go to the United States to earn good money, 'cause the big-footed ones need [machine] operators.
Porque los ricos de aquí no mueven ningún quehacer, con el reparto de tierras me los pusieron a leer.	Because the rich here don't stimulate employment with the new land distribution they've been put to reading.[2]
La cosa está del demonio, ya no hay ni revolución, nomás lo que esta aumentando son ladrones de a montón. . . .	Things are like hell here, the Revolution is over, what is increasing here now are thieves by the bushel. . . .
Vamos a portar chaqueta, la que nunca hemos usado, camisas de pura seda como también buen calzado.	Let's go wear jackets which we've never worn before, pure silk shirts and good quality shoes.
Aquí si nos afanamos siempre andamos encuerados, por allá en el extranjero parecemos diputados.	Here even if we work hard we are always naked. Over there in a foreign land we'll look like senators.
Ahora sí, amigos, nos fuimos a atravesar las fronteras, no le hace que luego digan que somos chuchas cuereras.	Now's the time to go to cross the border. It doesn't matter if they say we are stray dogs.
Ese no vió que el país está peor que los infiernos, todos son bullas y habladas y de domer solo cuernos . . .	That dude didn't see that our country is worse off than hell. Everything is noise and talk and food is nowhere found. . . .
Me duele hasta el corazón dejar mi patria querida, adios, mi padre y mi madre, ya les doy la despedida.	My heart aches so to leave my beloved country. Good-bye, my father and mother, I bid you farewell.
Adiós, México lucido, con su Hermosa Capital, ya me voy, ya me despido, no te volveré a mirar.	Good-bye, my illustrous Mexico, with its beautiful capital, I am leaving, farewell, I shall never see you again.
Adiós, muchachas hermosas, adiós, todos mis amigos, regresaré de Fifí portando muy buen abrigo.	Good-bye, beautiful girls, good-bye to all my friends. I shall return a dandy wearing a fine coat.

[2] Herrera-Sobek explains that this term is a sarcastic reference to the revolution's promise that big estates will be broken up and the land returned to the peasants. The implication here is that the rich were busy studying their land grants to find a way to maintain control of their estates.

3   *The Northerners* (Los norteños)

Los norteños	*The Northerners*
Voy a cantarles señores estos versos divertidos de todos los mexicanos que van a Estado Unidos.	I am going to sing to you sirs these funny verses; about all the Mexicans who go to the United States.
Por conocer muchas tierras Y ganar harto dinero se enrolan en lost enganches a tierras del extranjero.	Because they want to know many lands and to earn lots of money, they enroll and contract themselves to go to foreign lands.
Los que no pueden lograr su tarjeta de bracer se pasan de contrabando por El Paso o por Laredo.	Those that cannot obtain their bracero[1] card go across illegally through El Paso or Laredo.
Si su mujer es legal sufre y tiene que esperar pero si es de pocas pulgas lo tiene que coronar.	If his wife is faithful, she suffers and has to wait; but if she has no scruples she cuckolds him.
En ranchos y en ciudades encuentran luego que hacer en el traque o en los plantíos y corte de betabel.	On the ranches and in the cities, they find work to do; on the railroad tracks or in agriculture, or in the beet-cutting business.
En Waco y en Corpus Christi en Houston y Nuevo Orleans conocen lo que es avena los sanquequis y los flans.	In Waco and Corpus Christi, in Houston and New Orleans, they get a taste for oatmeal, pancakes and custard pudding.
Cuando regresan del norte muchos no quieren ni hablar porque traen muy buena ropa y harto dolár que gastar.	When they return from the North many do not even want to speak because they bring good clothing and plenty of dollars to spend.
Al llegar a una estación dicen al despachador (hablando): *Camo vegier, guime guan tiquete* *Mr., tenquio may fren*	Upon arriving at the station they tell the clerk (speaking): *Come over here, give me a ticket,* *Mr., thank you my friend*

[1] "Bracero" means worker. This lyric is a reminder that the U.S. Border Patrol had the authority to deny entry to those considered "likely to become a public charge," which meant someone who could not earn a living. Although U.S. law proscribed employers from giving jobs to foreign workers before they entered the country, having a card showing that you had a job in the United States was a guarantee of legal passage across the border. During World War II, Congress created the Bracero Program to bring in needed Mexican workers.

Source: The Northerners (Los norteños). María Herrera-Sobek.

orray, beri gut, gut bay
mascando el inglés le piden
un billete por favor.

Hábleme usted castellano
les contesta el boletero
y dígame lo que quiere
ya no me hable como perro.

La verdad que causa risa
con esos recien llegados
que porque vienen del norte
la quieren dar de ilustrados.

Si te subes en el tren
luego los oirás hablar
vengo a ver a mi familia
y me vuelvo a regresar.

Los gringos pagan muy bien
y son muy considerados
yo no vuelvo a trabajar
a los ricos mexicanos.

Otros resuelven quedarse
en la tierra do Tío Sam
porque dicen q'en su patria
no se consigue ni pan.

Pero en verdad les diré
para no ir a aventurar
no se necesita el norte
si aqui hay en que trabajar. . . .

Ya con ésta me despido
aquí se acabó el recorte
de los famosos citrines
de esos que llegan del norte.

all right, very good, good-bye.
In broken English, they ask him
for a ticket, please.

Speak to me in Spanish,
the clerk answers them;
And tell me what you want,
Don't speak to me like a dog.

To tell the truth, it's really funny,
those recent arrivals;
because they're coming from the North,
they pretend they are learned.

If you get on the train
You can hear them talking:
"I came to see my family,
but I am returning."

"The gringos pay us well
And they are very considerate;
I shall never work again
for the rich Mexicans."

Others decide to stay
in the land of Uncle Sam
because they say in their country
You can't even find bread.

But in truth I'll tell you,
One need not go on adventures;
we don't need the North,
there is work here. . . .

Now I take my farewell,
I have finished cutting down
those famous dandies,
those coming back from the North.

4   *Defense of the Emigrants* (Defensa de los norteños)

Defensa de los norteños

Lo que dicen de nosotros
casi todo es reqalidad;
más salimos del terreno
por pura necesidad.

Defense of the Emigrants

What they say about us
is mostly the truth,
but we left the country
from sheer necessity.

Source: Defense of the Emigrants (Defensa de los norteños). María Herrera-Sobek.

Que muchos vienen facetos
yo también se los dijera;
por eso la prensa chica
tuvo donde echar tijera.

So many come back boasting,
I too can tell you that;
that is why the local press
speaks harshly about them.

Pero la culpa la tienen
esos ingrates patrones
que no les dan a su gente
ni aun cuando porte chaqueta.

But those who are to blame
are those unkind employers
who don't give their people [work]
even when they wear a jacket.

No es porque hable del país
pero claro se los digo
que muchos trabajadores
enseñan hasta el ombligo. . . .

I'm not criticizing the country,
but I frankly will tell you
that many of the laborers
are naked to their navels. . . .

Yo no digo que en el norte
se va uno a estar muy sentado,
ni aun cuando porte chaqueta
Lo hacen a uno diputado.

I don't say that in the North
one is going to be taking it easy
even though one wears a jacket
one is not made a congressman.

Allí se va a trabajar
macizo, a lo Americano,
pero alcanza uno a ganar
más que cualesquier paisano. . . .

One has to work there,
hard, in the American fashion,
but one succeeds in earning
more than any of our countrymen. . . .

Mucha gente así lo ha dicho:
dizque no somos patriotas
porque les vamos a server
a los infames patotas.

Many people have said
that we are not patriotic
because we go to serve
the accursed big-footed ones.

Pero que se abran trabajos
y que paguen buen dinero,
y no queda un Mexicano
que se vaya al extranjero.

But let them give us jobs
and pay us decent wages;
not one Mexican then
will go to foreign lands.

Ansia tenemos de volver
a nuestra patria idolatrada,
pero qué le hemos de hacer
si está la patria arruinada.

We're anxious to return again
to our adored country;
but what can we do about it
if the country is ruined?

Si han hablado de nosotros
es por muchos fanfarrones
que andan sonando los pesos
cual si trajeran millones. . . .

If they've talked about us,
it is because of all the braggarts
who go jingling their dollars
as if they brought back millions. . . .

Que no vengan de facetos
les digo a mis companeros;
amigos, yo no presume
porque soy de los rancheros. . . .

"Don't come back boasting,"
I say to my companions;
"Friends, I don't put on airs
because I am just a ranchero." . . .

Yo ya me voy para el norte
amigos, no se los niego;
ahí les dejo a sus requitos
a que los toree Juan Diego.

Now I am leaving for the North;
friends, I do not deny it;
I leave you with your rich fellows—
let who will be bothered with them.

Muchachos, yo los convido
a la Nación extranjera;
no le hace que algunos digan
que somos chucha cuerera.

Boys, I invite you
to the foreign nation;
don't be bothered if they say
that we are mercenary.

5 *Ballad of Pennsylvania*
(Corrido de Pensilvania)

Corrido de Pensilvania

El día veintiséis de abril
a las séis de la mañana,
salimos en un enganche
para el Estado de Pensilvania.

Mi chinita me decía:
yo me voy en esa agencia,
para lavarles la ropa
y pa' darles su asistencia.

El reenganchista me dijo:
No lleves a tu familia,
para no pasar trabajos
al Estado de Pensilvania. . . .

Adiós, Estado de Texas,
con toda su plantación,
ya me voy pa' Pensilvania
por no pizcar algodon.

Adiós, Fort West, de Jara
puebla de mucha importancia,
ya me voy pa' Pensilvania
por no andar en la vagancia. . . .

Cuando llegamos allá
que del tren ya nos bajamos,
preguntan las italianas,
¿de dónde vienen, mexicanos?

Responden los mexicanos
los que ya sabían inglés:
Venimos en un enganche
del Estado de Fort West.

Estos versos los compuse
cuando ya venía en camino,
son poesías de un mexicano
nombrado por Constantino.

Ballad of Pennsylvania

The 26th of April
at six o'clock in the morning
we left as a work crew
for the state of Pennsylvania.

My little lady said to me:
"I'm going as part of that group
to wash your clothes
and help you."

The crew leader told me:
"Don't bring your family
so you won't lose jobs
in the state of Pennsylvania." . . .

Good-bye, state of Texas,
with all your planted fields,
I'm headed to Pennsylvania
so as not to pick cotton.

Good-bye, Fort West, Dallas,
a town of great importance,
I'm headed to Pennsylvania
so I won't be idle anymore. . . .

When we arrived over there
we'd just gotten off the train,
and the Italian girls asked,
"Where do you come from, Mexicans?"

The Mexicans answered back,
those that already knew English:
"We come as a work crew
from the state of Fort West."

I composed these verses
while already on the way,
they are the poetry of a Mexican man
Called Constantino.

Source: "Ballad of Pennsylvania" (Corrido de Pensilvania). Benjamin J. Galina.

Ya con esta me despido,	And with this I depart,
con mi sombrero en las manos;	with my hat in my hands;
y mis fieles compañeros	and my loyal comrades
son trescientos mexicanos.	Are three hundred Mexican men.

6   *Verses of the Beet-Field Workers*
(Versos de los betabeleros)

Versos de los betabeleros

Verses of the Beet-Field Workers

Año de mil novecientos	In the year 1923
veinte y tres en el actual,	of the present time,
fueron los betabeleros	the beet farmers went
a ese Michiga a llorar.	to Michigan, to cry.
Aquí vienen y nos cuentan	Here they come and they tell us
que nos vayamos para allá,	that we should head up there
porque allá no tienen todo	because here they don't have anything
y no vamos a batallar.	and we won't have a hard time up there.
Pero son puras mentiras.	But it's all lies.
Cuando ya estamos allá,	When we get up there,
empiezan a regañarnos,	they start to scold us,
ye queremos regresar.	and then we want to return.
Cuando llegamos a Jiusto	When we got to Houston
no hallábamos qué hacer.	we couldn't find anything to do.
El tiempo estaba muy duro.	The weather was bad
No se quería componer.	and didn't get any better.
Cuando llegamos a Jiusto	When we got to Houston,
trabajando noche y día	working night and day,
no nos daban de comer	they didn't feed us
no más que pura sandía.	nothing but watermelon.
Al pasar de Estado de Tejas	On crossing out of the state of Texas
a las dos de la mañana,	at two in the morning,
le pregunté al enganchista	I asked the crew leader
que si íbamos a Luisaiana.	If, perhaps, we were headed to Louisiana.
Gritaba Juan el Coyote,	Juan el Coyote shouted,
con su sombrero de lado:	with his hat at his side:
—Yo no volveré a Kansas	"I won't go back to Kansas
a trabajarle al condado.	to work for the county."
Gritaba Juan el Coyote	Juan el Coyote shouted
con esa boca de infierno:	with that infernal mouth:
—Yo no volveré a Kansas	"I won't go back to Kansas
a trabajarle al gobierno.	to work for the government."

Source: "Verses of the Beet-Field Workers" (Versos de los betabeleros). Benjamin J. Galina.

Despedida no la doy
porque no la tengo aquí.
La dejé en el Estado de Tejas
para que se acuerden de mí.

I won't sing my farewell
Because I don't have it here.
I left it in the state of Texas
so that they may remember me.

7   *Mexicans Who Speak English*
(Los Mexicanos que hablan ingles)

Los Mexicanos que hablan ingles

Mexicans Who Speak English

En Texas es terrible
por la revoltura que hay,
no hay quién diga "hasta mañana,"
nomás puro *good-bye.*

In Texas it is terrible
the way things are all out of order;
no one says "hasta mañana,"
nothing but pure "good-bye."

Y jau-didi-dú mai fren,
en ayl sí you tumora,
para decir "diez reales"
dicen *dola yene cuora.*

And "howdy-dee-do my frien',
an' I'll see you tomorro'."
In order to say "diez reales"
they say "dollah an' a quarter."

Yo enamoré una tejana,
y de esas de sombrilla,
le dije:—¿Te vas conmigo?—
y me dijo:—¡Lunque jail!—

I won the heart of a Tejana girl,
one of those with a parasol;
I said to her, "¿*Te vas conmigo?*"
And she said to me, "Looky heah!"

Enamoré otra catrina,

d'esas de garsolé
le dije:—¿Te vas conmigo?—
y me dijo:—¿Huachu sei?— . . .

I won the heart of another fashionable
    lady,
one of those with a garsolé;[1]
I said to her, "¿*Te vas conmigo?*"
And she said to me, "What you say?" . . .

Todos queremos hablar
la lengua americana,
sin poder comprender
la nuestra castellana.

All of us want to speak
the American language,
without understanding
our own Spanish speech.

Y en Texas es terrible
por la revoltura que hay,
no hay quién diga "hasta mañana,"
nomás puro *good-bye.*

And in Texas it is terrible
the way things are all out of order;
No one says "*hasta mañana,*"
nothing but pure "good-bye."

[1] A cap with a brim to keep out the sun.

Source: Mexicans Who Speak English" (Los Mexicanos que hablan ingles). Benjamin J. Galina.

8 *Radios and Chicanos* (Radios y chicanos)

Radios y chicanos	*Radios and Chicanos*
En estos tiempos modernos de electrizar el sonido me entretengo buenos ratos componiendo este corrido.	In these modern times of electrified sound I entertain myself by writing this *corrido*.
Ver a un buen amigo mío que al dejar mi pueblo grato, creyó que al cruzar el río se le iría lo zurumato.	I saw a good friend of mine leave my charming hometown, thinking that by crossing the river he would no longer be a hick.
Sí será, sí será, parece mentira que siendo chicano, tan hombre y tan sano, se vino de allá.	It's true, it's true; seems like a lie that a chicano, So manly and so healthy, Would come from over there.
Y al llegar a la frontera, le dicen que el emigrado necesita regardera para pasar a este lado.	And upon arriving at the border they tell him that an immigrant has to take a shower in order to cross to this side.
Llega al fín a este condado y alquila un apartamento, sin saber que en este estado se termina en el cement. . . .	He finally gets to this county And he rents an apartment, without knowing that in this state all ends up in cement. . . .
Y al sentirse con tostones se va haciendo de confianza y al comprar trajes rabones se siente casi Carranza.	Finding himself with fifty-cent pieces he gets more and more confident and after buying tight, tail-less suits he feels almost like Carranza.[1]
Se compra caja de fierro especial para itacates, ya no piensa en el destierro ni en ninguno de sus cuates. . . .	He buys a metal box meant to carry his lunch, he doesn't think anymore about his exile nor about his old friends. . . .
Se alquila un radio victrola con foquitos y botones, pues su casa está muy sola sin música ni canciones.	He rents a radio-victrola[2] with bulbs and buttons because his house is too lonely without music or songs.

[1] Venustiano Carranza was president of Mexico from 1914 to 1920. He came into power after overthrowing one revolutionary leader and was himself overthrown by another.

[2] A brand of record player manufactured by the Victor Talking Machine Company in the 1920s.

Source: "Radios and Chicanos" (Radios y chicanos). Benjamin J. Galina.

Y a la hora que le transmiten
los conciertos al chicano,
resulta que anuncian puercos
y el major mole poblano.

Sí será, sí sera
parece mentira
que en vez de canciones
anuncien melons
los de la cíudad. . . .

Al fín de tres curators de hora
nos cantan algún mariachi
luego anuncian la señora
que fabrica buen tepache.

Siguen luego otros asuntos
demonstrando las rebajas,
que le hacen a los difuntos
si les compran buenas cajas. . . .

Sí será, sí será
parece mentira
que nos hagan majes
en estos parajes
los de la ciudad.

But when they broadcast
concerts for the chicano
they wind up advertising hogs
And the best *mole poblano*.[3]

It's true, it's true;
seems like a lie
that instead of songs
they advertise melons,
these city people. . . .

After forty-five minutes
they sing us some *mariachi*[4]
then they advertise the woman
who makes the best *tepache*.[5]

Other advertisements follow
showing off the discounts
that they give for the deceased
if you buy them a good casket. . . .

It's true, it's true;
seems like a lie
that they treat us like suckers
in these places,
these city people.

[3] Mole from Pueblo, popularly known as *mole poblano*, is a sauce made with chili peppers, ground nuts, spices, and Mexican chocolate.

[4] A genre of music from Jalisco, Mexico, that combines string and brass instruments.

[5] A drink made from pineapple, brown sugar, cinnamon, and beer.

9 · *The Ranch* (El rancho)

El rancho

A cantar vamos unos cuantos versos
de lo que ahora se usa por aquí,
¡dónde más valiera que se usara todo
como en el rancho donde yo nací.

Por aquí todos con el automóvil
matando gente pasan por ahí,
¡cuánto más valiera carreta con bueyes
como en el rancho donde yo nací!

The Ranch

Let's sing a few verses

about what they do now around here,
though it is more worthy to do things

like on the ranch where I was born.

Around here everyone with a car
is killing people who pass by.
How much better was the ox-cart

like on the ranch where I was born!

Source: "The Ranch" (El rancho). Benjamin J. Galina.

Por aquí todas con crema y colores	Around here the women use creams and blushes
se ponen bellas como un maniquí!	doll themselves up like mannequins!
¡cuánto más valiera muy bien bañaditas	How much better were they washed clean
como en el rancho donde yo nací! . . .	like on the ranch where I was born!
Por aquí todas al estilo mula	Around here the women, dance-hall style,
andan tusadas hasta por aquí	go around with hair clipped up to here.
¡cuánto mas valiera con chica trenzota	How much better was the braided girl
como en el rancho donde yo nací! . . .	like on the ranch where I was born!
Por aquí todas faldas muy rabonas	Around here the camp-followers in short skirts
van enseñando hasta por aquí	go around showing off all the way up to here.
¡cuánto más valiera para no ver cosas	How much better not to see such things.
volverme al rancho donde yo nací!	Take me back to the ranch where I was born!
Adiós paisanos, ya nos despedimos,	Good-bye countrymen, we say good-bye,
este corrido se termina aquí,	this *corrido* ends here
no volveremos a cantar canciones	We won't return to singing songs
como en el rancho donde yo nací.	Like on the ranch where I was born.

10   *Red Bandannas* (Los paños colorados)

Los paños colorados

Red Bandannas

Los paños colorados	Red bandannas
Los tengo aborrecidos	I detest,
y ahora las pelonas	and now the flappers
los usan de vestidos.	use them for their dress.
Las muchachas de S. Antonio	The girls of San Antonio
son flojas pa'l metate	are lazy at the *metate*[1]
quieren andar pelonas	They want to go bobbed,
con sombreros de petate.	with straw hats on.

[1] A traditional kitchen tool for grinding corn.

Source: "Red Bandannas (Los paños colorados)." "Los paños colorados/Red Bandannas (Los paños colorados)" from Mario Gamio, *Mexican Immigration to the United States: A Study in Human Migration and Adjustment* (New York: Dover, 1971).

Se acabaron las pizcas	The harvesting is finished,
se acabó el algodón	so is the cotton.
Ya andan las pelonas	The flappers stroll out now
de puro vacilón.	For a good time.

Analyzing Folk Songs

1. What aspects of Mexican life are praised in these *corridos*? What aspects of life in the United States are praised?

2. How are criticisms of life in Mexico different from criticisms of life in the United States?

3. How is the Mexican migrant depicted in each of these *corridos*? Is the migrant a man or a woman? A hero? A villain? A success? A failure? What is the image of the migrant that emerges, for you, from this set of folk songs?

4. In which of these folk songs does the narrator adopt one definite stance toward migration north? In which does the narrator express more than one viewpoint on migration?

5. How do the stories and the attitudes in these folk songs challenge the assumptions about Mexicans made by U.S. employers or nativists in the United States? How do the songs support American assumptions about Mexicans?

6. A century has passed since the *corridos* included in this chapter were written. Write a one-page essay in which you argue *either* that these folk songs reflect a bygone era or that they are still relevant to the experience of modern migration. Make sure you include specific lyrics to illustrate your position.

The Rest of the Story

Mexicans and Mexican Americans continued to produce *corridos* throughout the twentieth century even as other musical forms gained popularity in the border region and the work of song writing itself was professionalized. Historians, though, can track the ups and downs of the Mexican migration story through the lyrics of the *corridos*. In good times and bad, the *corridistas* continued to sing of the struggle between material and cultural survival, between opportunities in the United States and Mexican traditions.

Many of the *corridos* of the 1930s told the bitter tale of repatriation of Mexican nationals and deportation of Mexican Americans during the Great Depression. When high unemployment and declining wages created an economic crisis in the Anglo population, policymakers chose a variety of strategies to remove Mexican nationals and U.S.-born Mexicans from both the labor pool and the pool of welfare recipients. Government officials in the Southwest encouraged voluntary repatriation by sponsoring train transport back to Mexico. Officials also coerced migration southward by refusing public or private relief aid to unemployed members of the Mexican American community and by staging police raids intended to frighten community members into leaving, regardless of their legal status in the United States. Overall, it is estimated that 500,000 residents of the United States moved to Mexico, voluntarily or involuntarily, during this depression decade. The Mexican government assisted these efforts because it viewed the postrevolutionary migration northward as an insult to national pride and a drain on the Mexican economy. Mexican leaders hoped to spark economic development in Mexico with the aid of U.S.-trained workers and hoped to avoid the embarrassment of mass deportations from the United States by voluntarily bringing Mexicans home. As *The Immigration Corrido* from the 1930s noted:

Hay que salir de este país	We must leave this country
toditos a nuestra tierra,	all must return to our homeland,
para no prestart lugar	so that they don't have the excuse
a que nos echen pa' fuera	to kick us out of their country.

As soon as World War II began and urban demand for U.S. agricultural products returned, however, employers in the Southwest again lobbied the government for easy access to Mexican labor. In response, Congress established the Mexican Farm Labor Program, popularly known as the Bracero Program, which contracted to bring in 220,000 workers during the war. The Mexican government, having failed to revive its own economy, supported the Bracero Program because it promised a minimum wage level and humane living conditions for contract workers from Mexico.

Support from U.S. employers and Mexican politicians kept the Bracero Program alive for two decades following World War II, sponsoring 4.5 million legal border crossings, but, ironically, encouraging illegal Mexican employment in the United States as well. Workers either slipped away from their officially approved jobs before their bracero contract expired so that they would not be sent back to Mexico or they slipped into the United States without papers because the official bracero quota was full but U.S. jobs still beckoned. Undocumented Mexican workers were very attractive to employers in the United States because their labor conditions were not protected by any U.S. laws or agreements with the Mexican government. In fact, as labor unions in the United States argued throughout the 1950s, working conditions for even legal braceros seldom met the standards set by U.S. law. *Corridos* were not a prominent form of musical expression in the 1940s and 1950s, perhaps because this was not an era of great social protest, but we can see dissatisfaction with the Bracero Program in *The Corrido of the Uprooted Ones* from 1942:

Nos trabajan como esclavos	They work us like slaves
y nos tartan como perros.	And treat us like dogs.
No mas falta que nos monten	All we need is for them to ride us
y que nos pongan el freno.	and put the bridle on us.
Si alguno lo toma a mal	If someone doesn't like what I say
es que no lo ha conocido.	it's because he wasn't there.
Que se vaya a contratar	Let him go as a bracero
a los Estados Unidos.	to the United States.

In the United States, the Cold War and the civil rights movement created pressure for reform of immigration law. The quota system enacted in 1924 was based on racist distinctions that insulted the eastern European and Asian people who the United States hoped to win over in the global contest with communism. The Immigration and Nationality Act of 1965 replaced the 1924 quotas with an across-the-board annual limit of 170,000 visas for immigrants from the Eastern Hemisphere, with no more than 20,000 allowed in from any one country.

Just as significantly, the 1965 reform act also instituted, for the first time in U.S. history, a limit on the overall number of immigrants allowed in from the Western Hemisphere, granting just 120,000 visas per year to the country's neighbors. Although the new law also established a system for granting visas beyond these quotas to family members of legal residents and naturalized citizens, the family-reunification visa program could not meet the needs of Mexican workers and their U.S. employers. The immediate, if unintended, effect of the 1965 law was to increase the number of undocumented workers coming to the United States from Mexico. The supply of U.S. visas had shrunk, but the supply of U.S. jobs had not. A renaissance in *corrido* creation during the 1970s, inspired by César Chávez's United Farm Workers union movement, reflected the era's pride in organizing workers to advocate for their rights and their ethnic culture. In one *corrido* from that decade, "The Ballad of Sespe Ranch," the narrator, Don Jesús Toledo, declared:

Ahora que ya les ganamos	Now that we have won
con honor las votaciones,	with honor the referendum
lucharemos por contraltos	we will fight for contracts
que nos dan más protecciones.	that will afford us protection.

Since passage of the 1965 reform act, Americans and Mexicans have struggled with the tension between employer demand for agricultural and service workers, Mexican desire for employment, and social and political opposition to the undocumented, unregulated labor market. Even policymakers who share citizens' concerns over the corruption of the immigration process have feared the economic consequences of shutting off access to Mexican labor, assuming a shut-off mechanism could be found. None of the economic recessions since 1965, including the most recent period of sustained unemployment since late 2008, has produced any demand by U.S. workers for agricultural jobs; in 2010, with national unemployment rates nearing 10 percent, federal labor officials estimated that more than 60 percent of farm workers in the United States were undocumented. If legal workers could be attracted to agricultural labor through a substantial increase in wages, the effect on food prices in the United States would produce a whole new set of economic and political problems. And the dilemma in agricultural work is only one of various conundrums that policymakers face when trying to develop what has come to be called "comprehensive immigration reform."

The search for reasonable, effective reforms in Mexican immigration policy remains clouded in political controversy, yet recalling that Congressman Carl

Hayden of Arizona referred to the border between Arizona and Mexico as "arbitrary" in 1920, we can better appreciate the shifting rules and fluctuating attitudes that characterize U.S. immigration history. Throughout this history of change, Mexicans have persistently created an American identity that blends the culture of the homeland with the perceived opportunities of the north. As Rumel Fuentes's 1977 *corrido* titled *Mexican American* stated:

Por mi madre yo soy mexicano	Mexican by parentage
por destino soy americano	American by destiny
yo soy de la raza de oro	I am of the golden race
yo soy méxico americano.	I am Mexican American.

To Find Out More

Collections of Corridos Lyrics

Gamio, Manuel. "The Songs of Immigrants." Chap. 7 in *Mexican Immigration to the United States: A Study of Human Migration and Adjustment.* Chicago: University of Chicago Press, 1930.

Guerrero, Eduardo. *Canciones y corridos populares.* 2 vols. Mexico City: Publicados por Eduardo Guerrero, Collection of *hojas sueltas* in Biblioteca Nacional, 1924.

Guerrero, Eduardo. *Corridos mexicanos.* Mexico City: Publicados por Eduardo Guerrero, Collection of *hojas sueltas* in Biblioteca Nacional, 1924.

Herrera-Sobek, María. *Northward Bound: The Mexican Immigrant Experience in Ballad and Song.* Bloomington: Indiana University Press, 1993.

Mendoza, Vincente T. *50 corridos mexicanos.* Mexico City: Ediciones de la Secretaría Pública, 1944.

Paredes, Americo. *A Texas-Mexican "Cancionero": Folksongs of the Lower Border.* Urbana: University of Illinois Press, 1976.

Taylor, Paul S. "Songs of the Mexican Migration." In *Puro Mexicano*, edited by J. Frank Dobie. Publications of the Texas Folklore Society, no. 22. Austin: Texas Folk-Lore Society, 1935.

Audio Sources for Corridos

American Folklife Center. "Southern Mosaic: The John and Ruby Lomax 1939 Southern States Recording Trip." *American Memory.* Library of Congress. http://memory.loc.gov/ammem/lohtml/lohome.html. Browse by "Audio Recordings" and then choose "Corridos" from the list.

Ayala, Ramón. "30 Corridos-Historias Nortenas." Corpus Christie, TX: Freddie Records, 2007.

"Mexican Corridos." Smithsonian Center for Folklife and Cultural Heritage. Washington, DC: Smithsonian Folkways Recordings, 1956.

"Musica de la Frontera." *The Strachwitz Frontera Collection of Mexican and Mexican American "Corrido Music." Music of the Southwest.* University of Arizona. http://parentseyes.arizona.edu/msw/corrido/index.html. Includes MP3 downloads from 1980s corridos competitions.

Secondary Sources on Corridos

Dickey, Dan W. "Corridos." *The Handbook of Texas Online*. Texas State Historical Association. http://www.tshaonline.org/handbook/online/articles/lhc01.

Flores, Richard R. "The Corrido and the Emergence of Texas-Mexican Social Identity." *Journal of American Folklore* 105 (1992): 166–82.

Herrera-Sobek, María. *Northward Bound: The Mexican Immigrant Experience in Ballad and Song*. Bloomington: Indiana University Press, 1993.

Limón, José E. "The Rise, Fall, and 'Revival' of the Mexican-American Corrido: A Review Essay." *Studies in Latin American Popular Culture* 2 (1983): 202–7.

McDowell, John Holmes. "The *Corrido* of Greater Mexico as Discourse, Music, and Event." In *"And Other Neighborly Names": Social Process and Cultural Image in Texas Folklore*, edited by Richard Bauman and Roger D. Abrahams. Austin: University of Texas Press, 1981.

Paredes, Americo. "The Ancestry of Mexico's *Corridos*: A Matter of Definitions." *Journal of American Folklore* 76 (1963): 231–35.

Paredes, Americo. "The Mexican *Corrido*: Its Rise and Fall." Chap. 6 in *Folklore and Culture on the Texas-Mexican Border*, edited by Richard Bauman. Austin: University of Texas, 1993.

Paredes, Americo. *"With a Pistol in His Hand": A Border Ballad and Its Hero*. Austin: University of Texas Press, 1978.

Peña, Manuel H. "Folksong and Social Change: Two Corridos as Interpretive Sources." *Aztlan* 13 (Fall 1982): 13–40.

Peña, Manuel H. "The Dawning of a New Age: Musical Developments, 1910–1940." Chap. 2 in *The Mexican American Orquesta: Music, Culture, and the Dialectic of Conflict*. Austin: University of Texas Press, 1999.

Peña, Manuel H. "Vocal Music of the Twentieth Century." Chap. 2 in *Música Tejana: The Cultural Economy of Artistic Transformation*. College Station: Texas A&M University Press, 1999.

Simmons, Merle E. "The Ancestry of Mexico's *Corridos*." *Journal of American Folklore* 76 (1963): 1–15.

Secondary Sources on Mexican Immigration

Camarillo, Albert. *Chicanos in a Changing Society: From Mexican Pueblos to American Barrios in Santa Barbara and Southern California, 1848–1930*. Cambridge, MA: Harvard University Press, 1979.

Galarza, Ernesto. *Merchants of Labor: The Mexican Bracero Story*. Santa Barbara, CA: McNally and Loftin, 1964.

Ngai, Mae. *Impossible Subjects: Illegal Aliens and the Making of Modern America*. Princeton, NJ: Princeton University Press, 2004.

Reisler, Mark. *By the Sweat of Their Brow: Mexican Immigrant Labor in the United States, 1900–1940*. Westport, CT: Greenwood, 1976.

Sanchez, George. *Becoming Mexican American: Ethnicity, Culture, and Identity in Chicano Los Angeles, 1900–1945*. New York: Oxford University Press, 1993.

CHAPTER 8

Painting a New Deal

U.S. Post Office Murals from the Great Depression

In the spring of 1941, Gustaf Dalstrom was hard at work painting a mural on the wall of the post office in St. Joseph, Missouri. On the eve of World War II, the federal government's New Deal was in its ninth year of struggle against economic depression, but recovery was elusive and unemployment still widespread. Dalstrom had a job thanks to one of the New Deal's public arts programs, and citizens of St. Joseph came to watch him work, equipped with lists of questions prepared by the local schools' art director. Dalstrom willingly paused in his labors to give brief talks about art in general and mural painting in particular.

As an artist employed by the U.S. government and engaged in conversation with local citizens about the imagery on their post office wall, Dalstrom represented a "new deal" in the relationship among the government, the arts, and the American public. Amid the Great Depression of the 1930s, this artistic new deal was just one of the array of economic stimulus and reform programs that President Franklin Delano Roosevelt had created within his "New Deal" administration. Some of these programs were aimed at providing direct *relief* to the millions of Americans who were without any income in the 1930s. Other programs were intended to bring about *recovery* from the economic depression, while still others sought to institute *reforms* that would prevent future economic and social catastrophe on the scale of the Great Depression. Roosevelt did not view the arts as a luxury the nation could afford only in prosperous times. Instead, he and his allies regarded economic support for artists and public funding for the arts as a natural part of the New Deal's relief, recovery, and reform effort.

Before the New Deal, the federal government had played a very small role in sponsoring the visual arts in the United States. Tax funds were invested in the architecture of public buildings, but these structures were not a site for aesthetic innovation, and few officials at any level of government felt called to campaign for more public funding for the arts. Wealthy art patrons enjoyed the private control they exercised over the art world and the status that control signified; they had no desire to encourage public investment in the arts. Citizens who could not afford to purchase original artwork regarded it as an elite luxury; they did not demand that their taxes go to support the visual arts, and they did not often think of artists as fellow workers. Artists, meanwhile, debated whether public funding for the arts would enliven American art or invite government control over artistic expression.

The New Deal altered this history in three ways. Through its relief programs, it recognized artists as workers who, when faced with unemployment, deserved as much state assistance as any other category of workers. Through its recovery programs, the New Deal defined the arts as a vital tool for uplifting citizens' spirits, focusing them on their individual and collective capacities, and encouraging them to draw from good times in the past to plan for better times in the future. And through its reform programs, the New Deal created mechanisms for public funding of the arts that would allow for communication between federal officials and local citizens about what constituted "good" art for a particular community.

The New Deal's effort to provide relief to working artists is most famously evident in the Federal Arts Program (FAP). Men and women who could demonstrate that they had made a living from their artistic endeavors before the Depression were eligible for federal support of their work during the Depression. Between 1935 and 1943, the FAP subsidized 10,000 artists who, in exchange for a federal paycheck, produced tens of thousands of works of art—posters, sculptures, tapestries, murals—that were displayed in federal, state, county, and municipal buildings for decades to come. Members of Congress had questioned the wisdom of giving money to artists, who did not look, sound, or operate like typical American workers. New Deal lobbyists, however, argued that it made more economic sense to pay artists $1,200 a year to continue creating art, and then put that art in government buildings, than to hand out welfare checks to scruffy bohemians and get no product in return.

Meanwhile, artists feared that an FAP relief check meant that the government would dictate what FAP artists produced. They had to be assured that the Roosevelt administration would not interfere with artistic freedom. While some FAP art was not approved for display in public buildings, no needy artists were denied FAP funds simply because the government disliked their artwork. The Federal Arts Program, then, was both a direct relief effort for artists and a reform program that used tax monies to visually enliven public spaces and, according to New Deal publicity, provide "art for the millions."

The arts figured into the New Deal's recovery and reform programs in other tangible and spiritual ways. As part of its effort to provide construction work for unemployed Americans, the Roosevelt administration built 1,100 new post office buildings in cities and towns across the nation. The Fine Arts Section of the U.S. Treasury Department then sponsored a series of competitions among artists to see whose proposals would win commissions to paint murals in each of the new post offices. These competitions launched an unprecedented public process that brought federal officials, artists, and local citizens together in sometimes heated debate over which proposals should be commissioned and how a commissioned artist's vision for the mural should be altered to suit local citizens' tastes.

For example, Gustaf Dalstrom won the commission to paint the mural in the St. Joseph, Missouri, post office because the federal and local officials who judged the competition liked his proposal to paint a scene titled *Negro River Music*. Dalstrom's vision was inspired by the music of Stephen Foster, a white American songwriter who idealized nineteenth-century African American life. When the local newspaper published news of Dalstrom's plan to depict a group of blacks happily gathered in song and dance, a delegation from St. Joseph's African American community met with the committee of civic leaders who had approved the design to complain that the mural would portray blacks as "lazy people with no other thoughts but singing, dancing, and clowning." This particular local protest by a group of African American citizens was not successful; Dalstrom's mural was painted as he designed it and as the local officials had approved it. In other instances, though, especially in those communities where the mural critics had more power than the blacks of St. Joseph, Missouri, local protests were successful and led to alteration in the mural design.

The Treasury Department's post office mural project was both hailed and damned for its approach to recovery and reform. Supporters applauded the project for providing uplifting images to a citizenry in need of spiritual recovery from the hard times. Some of those images, such as Dalstrom's *Negro River Music*, harkened back to idealized moments of imagined ease and harmony, but those who led the Treasury Department's Fine Arts Section actually favored mural proposals that displayed Americans' capacity for hard work and extolled their ability to solve problems through cooperation and innovation. Advocates of the post office mural project believed that public art that conveyed a message of faith and confidence in the working people of America would energize the government's recovery efforts. They also believed that government efforts to organize and finance public discussions of art, which the competitions for post office murals certainly did, were an appropriate expansion of the state's role as a sponsor of the arts in the United States.

Critics of the New Deal's post office murals saw the program as a disturbing case of state-sponsored political propaganda rather than as public sponsorship of the arts. Those critics who feared the size and power of the New Deal apparatus argued that government-commissioned and locally approved artwork might uplift the citizenry but also served to generate goodwill toward the federal government. An upbeat, colorful, mural-size reminder of the best in American life, painted on the wall of the local post office, could restore local confidence while at the same time persuading voters that a big, strong federal government provided valuable goods, including postal service and public art.

Other critics, who worried about artists' creative independence, criticized the post office mural project because the artists who won commissions in the mural competitions were not free to make their own aesthetic choices. Unlike the FAP, which allowed artists to produce whatever art they liked, the Treasury

Figure 8.1 Post Office Mural, Silver Spring, Maryland *This post office mural celebrated the town of Silver Spring's "Old Tavern" from the Civil War era. Nicolai Cikovsky, the Russian immigrant who painted the mural, depicted Union soldiers reading their mail outside the Eagle Inn on Silver Spring's Georgia Avenue, where the new post office was built during the New Deal. The oil-on-canvas mural, measuring six feet by sixteen feet, was painted in Cikovsky's studio. Here it is being installed on the post office wall. Restored in 1997, the mural is on display at the Silver Spring Public Library.* Source: Courtesy National Archives.

Department's Fine Arts Section exercised strong control over the style and content of the post office murals. In its effort to please the eye of the average American citizen standing in line at the post office, the government avoided abstract modern art, with its fractured forms and destabilized shapes. Instead, the Treasury-sponsored works reflected a particular movement in the artistic world known as

American Scene painting, which shared the general public's disdain for abstract modern art.

Like the New Deal itself, American Scene painting fostered a coalition between rural conservatives, represented by "Regionalists" in the art world, and urban radicals, who were the "Social Realists" among artists. Regionalists produced paintings that idealized traditional rural life, whereas Social Realists used gritty images to protest the social injustices of the urban, industrial world. Artists in both groups saw themselves as the creators of a uniquely American vision, and artists in both groups were by far the most successful at winning post office mural commissions.

Local committees typically approved of proposals for American Scene murals that celebrated everyday people engaged in familiar activities. Those committees included businessmen, club women, teachers, clergy, librarians, and the postmaster, and they were drawn to visual art that used an accessible style to celebrate local scenery and distinct regional histories. Some local citizens complained if a Social Realist went too far in showing the underside of American life, just as others complained when a sentimental Regionalist like Gustaf Dalstrom produced an image of "clowning" African Americans. On the whole, though, local responses were generally quite positive, producing just the sort of enthusiasm for accessible, community-approved public art that supporters praised and critics feared.

The persistence of unemployment in 1941, when Dalstrom was painting in Missouri, testifies to the weaknesses in Roosevelt's economic recovery efforts. But the popularity of the post office murals testifies to the New Deal's success at encouraging local communities to confront hard times with a mix of tradition, reform, and artistry.

Using the Source: Public Art

Visual images, like written texts, are best understood when we have a sense of the specific context in which the artist or author was working. When studying post office murals, for example, it is useful to remember that the supervising officials in the Fine Arts Section of the Treasury Department, along with the local committees approving the murals, preferred American Scene paintings over other styles. Artists who wished to win a commission for a "Section" mural quickly learned to "paint Section," which meant toning down tendencies toward modern, abstract imagery and emphasizing the positive qualities of common Americans. It is also useful to know that although the Treasury Department never stated its preference for the American Scene style, it did very explicitly state that the content of all post office mural art had to fit into one of three categories: the history of the U.S. Postal Service itself, the history of the local community, or the community's everyday life.

The post office murals that were produced under these circumstances are dismissed by most art historians today as mere "embellishments." Because the original vision of every artist was typically altered, corrected, and revised by government officials and local committees, art historians claim that the resulting works do not qualify as authentic artistic expression. So predictable was the representational style of the murals that emerging modern artists of the day, such as Jackson Pollock, refused to even submit sketches to the Treasury Department's "Section" competitions. Ironically, it is precisely this feature of post office mural art—that it conformed to the aesthetic tastes of a broad swath of Americans—that makes it particularly useful for social and political historians who want to grasp the national mood of the 1930s and the Roosevelt administration's talent for harnessing that mood to its goals.

What Can Public Art Tell Us?

When we use visual art for insight into social attitudes, it does not matter whether the experts regard that visual art as "good" art. Popular art, whatever its quality, is valuable for revealing national sentiments and tastes. When we know that the popular American Scene school of painting rejected modern art on the grounds that it was a European expression ill-suited to capturing authentic American culture, we enrich our sense of the United States' proud isolation from Europe in the years preceding World War II. When we see how often and how delicately the post office murals balanced the Social Realists' tribute to industrial workers with the Regionalists' idealizing of rural life, we get a visual glimpse of the internal conflict that Americans faced when their modern economy collapsed under them: even as they cheered for factory workers, they longed for a simpler past on the farm. And when we remember that the post office murals were meant to inspire citizens to believe in their own productive capacities and that community members influenced the murals' content, we can treat the murals as the common ground that artists, citizens, and government officials shared when defining American traditions and aspirations.

Political historians and art historians study visual images for different purposes and make different contributions to our understanding of visual art. For example, art historians see the Social Realists who painted American Scene post office murals as "conservative" because they rejected the innovations of abstract modernism. Political historians, however, see the Social Realists as radical for making social and economic injustice their artistic subject in the 1920s and 1930s, when abstract modernists seemed unconcerned with the world's problems. Similarly, it is political history, not art history, that explains why Roosevelt's New Deal administration wanted to combine sentimental Regionalism and defiant Social Realism under the patriotic tent of American Scene painting. The voter base for the Democratic Party's New Deal was a volatile coalition of urban, northern, unionizing workers and rural, southern white farmers and sharecroppers. Just as Roosevelt's speeches and public policies sought to appeal to each of those groups, so, too, the New Deal's public art tried to appeal to its competing constituencies.

Thus, when Detroit's Northwestern Branch Postal Station wanted to represent everyday life in the 1930s, a clear choice of subject matter was the auto industry. William Gropper—who would go on to become a major figure in Social Realist art after World War II—won the commission with his design for *Automobile Industry*:

Is labor individual or collective?

Significance of out-size bodies?

A strictly realistic rendering of an auto plant?

Source: Smithsonian American Art Museum, Washington DC/Art Resource, NY.

Scale of the men to their machines?

Gropper's blending of realism, romanticism, and abstraction in this mural can help us grasp the ways in which Americans in the 1930s, and especially supporters of the New Deal, mixed together their sense that workers were dwarfed by industrial capitalism with their belief that workers were the real engine that kept society progressing. The slight abstractions we see in this mural also illustrate the subtle ways in which modernism influenced popular culture in the 1930s, even among those who thought they were resisting modern abstraction.

The ten post office murals included in the next section all evoke the theme of work because that was such an important focus of the government's campaign to renew the depressed spirit of the American people. These murals come from different regions of the United States and from all three of the Treasury Department's thematic categories: postal history, local history, and everyday life. They give you an opportunity to examine images of industrial and agricultural workers that local citizens and the federal government found unifying and uplifting.

The table on page 183 will help you organize your own thoughts about the murals presented in this chapter. In addition, the Checklist questions on page 182 will help you actively examine public art in general.

CHECKLIST: Interrogating Public Art

☐ When was the public art produced? Who commissioned it?

☐ What is the subject matter of the public art, and how does it represent the surrounding community?

☐ Who produced the public art? What inspired the artist's vision?

☐ What was the purpose of this public art? What do nonartistic sources reveal about the goals of this art? What does the art itself reveal about the goals?

☐ Who was the audience for this art? How was it meant to serve or influence the audience?

☐ What is the common message in this public art? What point of view is conveyed in these images?

Source Analysis Table

The ten post office murals included in this chapter represent many of the geographic regions, types of labor, and political messages that were depicted in the post office murals sponsored by the New Deal. In regard to race and gender, however, this sample overstates the frequency with which nonwhite men and women appeared in the total set of post office murals. Although nonwhites comprised 10 percent of the workforce in 1930 and women comprised 22 percent, neither group appeared with such frequency in the murals of workers. White men were overrepresented in the murals because of the era's social attitudes, particularly regarding paid labor. We made a special effort to select some murals that show women and nonwhite men so that you could analyze the murals' depictions of gender and race as well as their artistic style and overall view of American workers.

Mural	Artistic Style: Social Realism or Regionalism?	Work Style: Individualistic or Collective?	Gender: Men's Jobs? Women's Jobs?	Race: White Jobs? Nonwhite Jobs?
1. The Riveter				
2. Development of the Land				
3. Postman in a Storm				
4. Legend of James Edward Hamilton				
5. Tennessee Valley Authority				
6. Plowshare Manufacturing				
7. Sorting the Mail				
8. Mining				
9. Orange Picking				
10. Tobacco Industry				

The Source: Post Office Murals Depicting "Work" in Local Communities, 1936–1942

1 *The Riveter* by Ben Shahn
Bronx, New York, 1938

Shahn, a Lithuanian immigrant, was one of the best-known and most politically active artists to paint Section art. *The Riveter* was one of several panels that made up the mural *Resources of America*, which Shahn and his wife, Bernarda Bryson, painted for the Bronx post office.

Source: Smithsonian American Art Museum, Washington DC/Art Resource, NY.

Development of the Land by Elsa Jemne, Ladysmith, Wisconsin, 1938

Jemne, a native of St. Paul, Minnesota, had studied in Europe before World War I. She was criticized by both Treasury officials and the citizens of Ladysmith for inaccurately rendering the size and scale of the farmer and his corn in conveying her celebratory message.

Source: Smithsonian American Art Museum, Washington DC/Art Resource, NY.

3   *Postman in a Storm* by Robert Tabor
Independence, Iowa, 1938

Tabor was born in Independence, Iowa, and lived most of his life there. When he lost his traveling sales job during the Depression, he began to paint. He was funded by the Federal Arts Program before winning a Treasury Section commission for this mural.

Source: Smithsonian American Art Museum, Washington DC/Art Resource, NY.

4 | *Legend of James Edward Hamilton—Barefoot Mailman* by **Stevan Dohanos,** West Palm Beach, Florida, 1940

Dohanos painted six scenes evoking the life of this Florida mail carrier, who died in 1887 "in the line of duty." Dohanos said in an interview in 1982 that "there is a difference of opinion as to whether sharks or alligators" caused Hamilton's demise.

Source: Smithsonian American Art Museum, Washington DC/Art Resource, NY.

Tennessee Valley Authority by Xavier Gonzalez
Huntsville, Alabama, 1937

President Roosevelt regarded creation of the Tennessee Valley Authority (TVA) in 1933 as one of the great achievements of the New Deal. Through the TVA, which covers more than 40,000 square miles, the federal government built dams that brought electricity to the rural Southeast, and it became actively involved in planning the region's resource conservation, agricultural, and industrial policies.

Source: Tennessee Valley Authority, 1937, Xavier Gonzalez, mural for U.S. Post Office in Huntsville, Alabama. Commissioned through the New Deal art projects. Courtesy of the U.S. General Services Administration, Public Buildings Service, Fine Arts Collection.

6 | *Plowshare Manufacturing* by Edward Millman
Moline, Illinois, 1937

John Deere started building steel plows for prairie farming in Moline, Illinois, in 1837. Despite the Depression, the Deere Company celebrated its centennial in 1937 as the leading employer in Moline with a record $100 million in gross sales. The image below is reproduced from one of the drawings Millman created before painting the mural in the Moline post office.

Source: Edward Millman, American, 1907–1964, *Study for Manufacture of Plowshares in Moline*, 1935, Gouache with colored pencils, watercolor, and graphite on cream illustration board, 613 x 763 mm, The Art Institute of Chicago, Obj: 116148, The Art Institute of Chicago.

7

Sorting the Mail by Reginald Marsh, Washington, D.C., 1936

There is no record of citizen complaints in Washington, D.C., about Marsh's nonliteral depiction of mailroom labor.

Source: Sorting the Mail, 1936, mural for William Jefferson Clinton Federal Building, Washington, D.C. Commissioned through the Section of Fine Arts, 1934–1943. Courtesy of the U.S. General Services Administration, Public Buildings Service, Fine Arts Collection.

8

Mining by Michael Lenson, Mount Hope, West Virginia, 1942

The United Mine Workers of America (UMW) was founded in 1890, but the union struggled for legitimacy until the passage of the National Labor Relations Act of 1935 during the New Deal. The act established federal mechanisms for union formation and bargaining with employers. Mine workers in 1942 were led by John L. Lewis, the charismatic UMW president who gave his union a high profile on the national labor scene in the New Deal years.

Source: Smithsonian American Art Museum, Washington, DC/Art Resource, NY.

9 | *Orange Picking* by Paul Hull Julian
Fullerton, California, 1942

The "second gold rush" to California occurred in the early 1900s, when families from the Midwest moved westward in hope of making it rich in citrus farming. By 1942, family farming had largely been replaced by agribusiness, which hired migrant labor from Mexico.

Source: Smithsonian American Art Museum, Washington DC/Art Resource, NY.

10 | *Tobacco Industry* by Lee Gatch
Mullins, South Carolina, 1939

For murals in southern post offices, the Treasury Section and its artists sought a balance between deference to the local power structure and a desire to depict African American life. So, while supervisors were seldom depicted in industrial or agricultural murals outside the South, they were included in southern murals about work. At the same time, local southern committees asked that murals not show the poor whites who actually worked alongside blacks in the cotton and tobacco fields.

Source: Tobacco Industry, 1939, Lee Gatch, oil sketch for U.S. Post Office mural in Mullins, South Carolina. Courtesy of the U.S. General Services Administration, Public Buildings Service, Fine Arts Collection.

Analyzing Public Art

1. When comparing the industrial murals with the agricultural murals, do you find any difference in the artistic style or in the makeup of the workforce? Do you find differences in the depiction of work itself?

2. What message do you find in these post office murals about the virtues of the American worker? Which two murals would you select from this group to illustrate this message, and why would you choose those two?

3. How did artists' emphasis on the power of collective work serve to advance the New Deal's political agenda? How did depictions of individual workers in these murals foster citizens' confidence in the government?

4. As noted, this sample of murals overrepresents the number of white women and nonwhite women and men depicted in the entire collection of murals. How are gender roles and racial roles depicted in this sample?

5. In actuality, white men were overrepresented in the nation's post office murals. What political and emotional purposes were served by emphasizing the productive role of white men in the United States in these Depression years?

6. When the United States joined the Allied fight against Germany and Japan in World War II, the government faced hard budgetary choices about New Deal programs, including the post office mural program. Write a one-page editorial, from a citizen's standpoint in 1942, stating why you think the government should continue to fund the program during wartime or should end the program. Is your position based on practical reasons, or is it based on a philosophical viewpoint?

The Rest of the Story

Many of the Treasury-sponsored murals painted during the New Deal still survive in post offices throughout the United States or in buildings that once were post offices. Some survive only in photographs because their buildings were torn down. Still others have not survived at all. What has most definitely survived is the debate over public funding for the arts that the New Deal ignited.

Federal spending on the arts dried up by 1942, when the U.S. government turned all its resources toward fighting World War II. In the years following the war, however, political debate over the role of the arts in society resumed. Many artists from the Social Realist school, such as William Gropper, became targets of the anticommunist McCarthy investigations in the 1950s because they criticized capitalism. At the same time, anticommunists also expressed hostility to the modern, abstract art movement, which now seemed to have subversive qualities of its own. One postwar newspaper editorial claimed, "Modern art is communistic because it is distorted and ugly. . . . Art which does not glorify our beautiful country in plain, simple terms that everyone can understand breeds dissatisfaction. . . . Those who create and promote it are our enemies."

World War II had changed the position of the United States in the world, however, and many Americans embraced the modern art movement as a sign of this nation's closer ties to Europe and its more sophisticated status as a global power. In addition, cold warriors like President John F. Kennedy argued that the country's modern, innovative art was a global advertisement for the authenticity of American freedom and predicted that government support of artists' unshackled experimentation would prove that the United States, unlike the Soviet Union, was a free, truly civilized society. Like Franklin Roosevelt, Kennedy combined genuine idealism about the uplifting power of art with a political opinion that government support of the arts was in the nation's self-interest.

In late 1965, two years after Kennedy's assassination, President Lyndon B. Johnson was able to turn Kennedy's dream into reality by incorporating the National Endowment for the Arts (NEA) into his Great Society program. In doing so, Johnson endorsed Kennedy's view that a truly great nation demonstrated its respect for freedom and civilization by generously funding artists' unpredictable search for self-expression. In their enthusiasm for this ideal, NEA supporters did not address the possibility that artists might use their public funding to create art that expressed unpopular criticisms of American life. No one set up mechanisms for resolving conflicts between government-funded artists and taxpayers who disagreed with those artists' views.

The NEA program to provide grants on the order of $5,000 to individual artists was only one of a variety of NEA programs operating between 1967 and 1995. During that time, thousands of young, experimental artists were selected to receive financial aid by a "peer panel" of artists who reviewed applications for NEA grants. At the same time, the NEA gave more substantial grants to local arts organizations, museums, and art schools. Coincident with, and likely related to, the creation of the NEA, arts flourished in the United States in these years, and artists found many more opportunities for creating, displaying, and selling their art than ever before.

The success of the arts in the United States intersected with the end of the Cold War to produce a new kind of cultural collision. The political debate shifted away from freedom and communism and toward sexuality and race. In that context, many conservative activists combined their concerns over large government with their fears of artistic expression by homosexuals and nonwhites who seemed to challenge traditional values. The debate came to a head in 1989, when news emerged that the NEA had given a $30,000 grant to the Institute of Contemporary Art in Philadelphia, which had in turn exhibited Robert Mapplethorpe's nude photos of multiracial sex acts within the sadomasochistic gay subculture. Conservatives were enraged at this use of taxpayer dollars. Mapplethorpe's death from AIDS that year only confirmed his status as a dangerous outsider whose work threatened, as one opponent put it, to "pollute" the body politic.

The ironic result of this incident was that Congress voted in 1995 to abolish all NEA grants to individual artists, even though funding for the Mapplethorpe exhibit had come through a grant to an organization. Today, the NEA funnels all its now-reduced funds through local arts organizations, which are on notice not to support individual artists who might threaten the organization's future funding. The debate over whether taxpayer support for artistic freedom should require citizens to fund images they find repugnant has not ceased. But, as with the New Deal, the government's support for the NEA has stimulated lively public debate over the place of the arts in a democratic society.

To Find Out More

Collections of Mural Images

National Archives. "Online Exhibits." http://www.archives.gov/exhibits. A search for "post office murals" produces a variety of images from the mural project. This Web site also offers images of artistic works produced under the Federal Arts Program.

Park, Marlene, and Gerald E. Markowitz. *Democratic Vistas: Post Office and Public Art in the New Deal*. Philadelphia: Temple University Press, 1984.

Secondary Sources on New Deal and Other Federal Arts Programs

Brenson, Michael. *Visionaries and Outcasts: The NEA, Congress, and the Place of the Visual Artist in America*. New York: New Press, 2001.

Contreras, Belisario R. *Tradition and Innovation in New Deal Art*. London: Associated University Presses, 1983.

Levy, Alan Howard. *Government and the Arts: Debates over Federal Support of the Arts in America from George Washington to Jesse Helms*. Lanham, MD: University Press of America, 1997.

Marling, Karal Ann. *Wall-to-Wall America: A Cultural History of Post Office Murals in the Great Depression*. Minneapolis: University of Minnesota Press, 1982.

McKinzie, Richard D. *The New Deal for Artists*. Princeton, NJ: Princeton University Press, 1973.

Melosh, Barbara. *Engendering Culture: Manhood and Womanhood in New Deal Public Art and Theater*. Washington, DC: Smithsonian Institution Press, 1991.

National Endowment for the Arts. http://arts.gov. Official Web site of the NEA.

Secondary Sources on the New Deal

Dickstein, Morris. *Dancing in the Dark: A Cultural History of the Great Depression*. New York: Norton, 2009.

Hamby, Alonzo. *For the Survival of Democracy: Franklin Roosevelt and the World Crisis of the 1930s*. New York: Free Press, 2004.

Hamby, Alonzo. *Liberalism and Its Challengers: FDR to Reagan*. Oxford: Oxford University Press, 1985.

Kennedy, David. *Freedom from Fear: The American People in Depression and War, 1929–1945*. New York: Oxford University Press, 1999.

McElvaine, Robert S. *The Great Depression: America, 1929–1941*. New York: Times Books, 1984.

Watkins, T. H. *The Hungry Years: A Narrative History of the Great Depression in America*. New York: Henry Holt, 1999.

CHAPTER 9

Challenging Wartime Internment

Supreme Court Records from Korematsu v. United States

O n Friday afternoon, May 30, 1942—almost six months after the bombing of Pearl Harbor in Hawaii—Fred Korematsu was arrested while standing outside a drugstore in San Leandro, California, smoking a cigarette and waiting for his girlfriend, Ida Boitano. The police charged Korematsu with violating a military order directed at residents of California, Oregon, and Washington who were "enemy aliens" born in Japan or U.S. citizens of Japanese descent. West Coast residents were supposed to evacuate their homes and report to an "assembly center" with just one suitcase in hand. The U.S. Army planned to distribute these 112,000 individuals among ten "relocation centers," or internment camps, that the government had constructed in isolated areas of eastern California, Idaho, Utah, Arizona, Wyoming, Colorado, and Arkansas. Fred Korematsu's Japanese-born parents and U.S.-born brothers had reported, as ordered, to the Tanforan assembly center south of San Francisco by May 9, 1942. Indeed, virtually all who fell under the military order obeyed it. But Fred chose to disobey the order, and from that individual act arose one of the most famous Supreme Court cases in U.S. history.

Fred Korematsu did not set out, at age twenty-two, to place his name at the center of the U.S. debate over civil liberties in wartime. He was a U.S.-born, working-class Californian, a trained welder, a graduate of Castlemont High School in Oakland, and a registered voter, but not at all a political activist. He had tried to enlist in the army six months before Pearl Harbor. If gastric ulcers had not made Korematsu ineligible, he would have joined 5,000 other Americans of Japanese descent already serving in the U.S. armed forces. Once war broke out in December 1941, Korematsu's personal goal was to move to the Midwest with his white girlfriend and stay out of all the anti-Japanese trouble brewing on the

West Coast in the wake of Japan's attack on Pearl Harbor. Long-time opponents of Japanese settlement on the West Coast were using the crisis of war with Japan as an opportunity to stir up fears and hostilities. Because the bombing in Hawaii had left West Coast residents feeling vulnerable, and because 88 percent of the U.S. residents of Japanese descent lived on the West Coast, the anti-Japanese campaign was concentrated in that region.

For Japanese living in the United States, trouble began immediately after Pearl Harbor with implementation of a U.S. war plan to arrest all suspicious "enemy aliens" who might be involved in espionage. The Japanese attack had thrust the United States into a world war with European allies against Japan, Germany, and Italy. But German and Italian "enemy aliens" living in the United States were questioned only if they were affiliated with profascist organizations, and only half of the 10,000 questioned were interned during the war for their political beliefs. Government policy toward Japanese on the Pacific coast was entirely different. There, the U.S. government moved to evacuate all 40,000 immigrants born in Japan, who were known as issei. None of those immigrants was a U.S. citizen because the U.S. naturalization law in force since 1790 stipulated that an immigrant had to be "white" to be eligible for citizenship. Nativists convinced their allies in the military and Congress that anger over this race-based naturalization rule, along with anger at the 1924 law excluding all future Japanese immigrants, would cause the issei population to be loyal to Japan during the war.

In the first two months following the attack on Pearl Harbor, key members of the army's command staff in San Francisco and key members of the California congressional delegation expanded the evacuation plan to include all nisei, the U.S.-born children of Japanese immigrants. The plan to evacuate these 72,000 Japanese American citizens was based on the belief that they, too, posed a security threat to the West Coast. Advocates of the plan argued, without proof, that Japanese espionage in Hawaii had facilitated the Pearl Harbor attack. Interestingly, no one ever proposed evacuating Hawaii's residents of Japanese descent, who constituted one third of the Hawaiian population and were a vital part of the Hawaiian workforce. Evacuation of all West Coast Japanese, who constituted only 1 percent of the region's population, did not hurt the general economy; it did, however, help those associations of California growers that had for decades sought to eliminate direct competition from successful Japanese American farmers. Those with economic interests thus joined forces with anti-Japanese nativists during wartime to support the exclusion of all Japanese without regard for citizenship status and without individual questioning about political loyalties.

The debate within the government over treatment of Japanese Americans reflected a conflict between military necessity and constitutional rights. Advocates of military necessity won the debate by arguing that Japanese Americans on the West Coast constituted an espionage threat for three racial reasons: first, because "their racial characteristics are such that we cannot understand or trust even the citizen Japanese"; second, because their bitterness over U.S. racism would make them disloyal; and third, because effective surveillance of suspicious individuals would be impossible since "the Occidental[1] eye cannot readily distinguish one Japanese resident from another." Thus, internment advocates pointed to the fact of racist treatment to presume Japanese American bitterness and disloyalty. They also relied on American racism to explain why government officials could not distinguish loyal Japanese from the disloyal through the process of individual interrogation being used with German and Italian aliens in the United States.

In the weeks and months following Pearl Harbor, a series of governmental orders led up to the final internment order. On February 4, 1942, an 8:00 p.m. curfew was imposed on all people of Japanese ancestry living in the Pacific states. On February 19, President Franklin D. Roosevelt issued Executive Order 9066, which gave the U.S. military independent authority to designate sensitive areas during wartime, including the authority to determine which persons were to be excluded from those areas, and to provide transportation, food, and shelter for anyone evacuated. A month later, Congress endorsed the president's action with Public Law 503. The very broad wording of both the executive order and the new law allowed Lieutenant General John DeWitt, commander of the western region of the United States, maximum latitude to take whatever protective measures he thought necessary in wartime. Aware of the bitter claims that lax security had been to blame for Pearl Harbor and politically sympathetic to the anti-Japanese activists, DeWitt was determined that no sabotage or espionage would take place while the West Coast was under his command.

Like all Japanese Americans, Fred Korematsu paid close attention to the public debate over evacuation in the winter and spring of 1942. By the time the president issued Executive Order 9066, Fred had already been expelled from his local labor union for his Japanese heritage, and he was planning to take advantage of the government suggestion that Japanese Americans voluntarily relocate inland before any official evacuation proceedings began. But Fred, like many others, waited too long to relocate. On March 27, 1942, the government issued a "freeze" order, which meant that Japanese Americans could no longer voluntarily move inland. Three days later, General DeWitt announced that an evacuation "was in prospect for practically all Japanese." Korematsu then knew that if he stayed on the West Coast, he would be evacuated to a camp. So he quickly underwent plastic surgery to disguise his ethnicity and acquired a fake ID, thinking he could evade the authorities and escape inland with his girlfriend. The ruse did not work; at the end of May, the San Leandro police picked him up, probably on a tip from his girlfriend.

The American Civil Liberties Union (ACLU), established during World War I to challenge wartime violations of the Bill of Rights, faced a serious dilemma in World War II. Members of its national board were closely aligned with President Roosevelt and hesitated to criticize his wartime policies, but ACLU activists on the West Coast were anxious to challenge the constitutionality of Japanese internment. Despite opposition from the ACLU leadership in Washington, D.C., ACLU lawyers in San Francisco and Seattle sought out Japanese American citizens

---

[1] The Occident refers to Europe and the Western world, as opposed to the Orient (Asia).

Figure 9.1 Fred Korematsu with His Family *Fred Korematsu (third from the left) is shown here with his family in their Oakland, California, nursery. Fred refused to comply with the wartime internment orders and did not join his family when they were taken in 1942 to Tanforan, a former racetrack south of San Francisco. He later spent two years in an internment camp in Utah.* Source: National Portrait Gallery, Smithsonian Institution/Art Resource, NY.

who had been arrested for violating military orders and tried to convince them to become a "test case." Korematsu was one of only four Japanese Americans among the relatively few who had violated orders in the first place to agree to challenge the order instead of paying the fine and quietly entering an internment camp. All four cases were complicated along the way by legalistic machinations, judicial technicalities, divisions within the ACLU and among the lawyers for the Japanese Americans, and serious disagreement between the War Department and the Justice Department over how to defend the federal government's internment policy.

It took two and a half years for Fred Korematsu's case to reach the Supreme Court. In those years, he was interned at a relocation camp in Topaz, Utah, where he witnessed the dry, dusty, and desolate conditions under which tens of thousands of Japanese Americans lived for up to three years. While in the camp, he met with some hostility from those issei and nisei who believed that he was unwise to challenge the government's policies. Because his loyalty was never in question, Korematsu, like many other nisei, was allowed out of the camp on a work furlough, so he worked in Salt Lake City and later in Detroit. Indeed, by the time his case reached the Supreme Court in October 1944, tens of thousands of nisei had been released from camps on work furloughs or to enroll in U.S.

universities and colleges and were living in the Midwest and on the East Coast, away from the anti-Japanese hysteria in the Pacific states. Others were distinguishing themselves in wartime battle. The 442nd Regimental Combat Team, composed entirely of nisei from the internment camps, was the most decorated unit in the U.S. Army.

In the months before the *Korematsu* decision was handed down, members of the Roosevelt administration were arguing for the end of Japanese American internment, and the general who had replaced DeWitt on the West Coast had declared that evacuation was no longer a military necessity. Organized protests by some Japanese Americans in the internment camps had raised the hackles of anti-Asian activists, however, so Roosevelt postponed the end of the detention policy until after the November 1944 election. On December 17, 1944, the U.S. government announced that those Japanese Americans certified as loyal would not be detained or excluded from the West Coast after January 2, 1945. The next day, the Supreme Court announced its decision in Korematsu's case: his conviction for violating the evacuation order was upheld; the military order itself was judged to be constitutional.

At first glance, the Supreme Court's ruling in *Korematsu v. United States* appears to establish the principle that the federal government has the constitutional authority to select a group of citizens, based on their national origin, and evacuate them from their homes for the purpose of indefinite detention. However, when we read the actual records from the case, including the Supreme Court justices' opinions in the case, we find that the ruling defined the government's authority in very narrow terms, saying nothing about detention. We also find that the most precedent-setting statement in the Court's ruling turned out to be the claim that "all legal restrictions which curtail the civil rights of a single racial group are immediately suspect. . . . Courts must subject them to the most rigid scrutiny." Even as it was allowing discrimination based on race, the Court was setting a broad, new legal rule for later courts to follow. Henceforth, all cases of racial discrimination in the United States would be judged according to this new principle, which came to be called "strict scrutiny."

Using the Source: Supreme Court Records

The records of the Supreme Court in the *Korematsu* case can help us extend our understanding beyond the specifics of Japanese internment and grasp the larger legal precedents that were established by this wartime incident. The frenzy of war is short-lived, but Supreme Court judgments can last for decades. When we say that the Court's decisions set "precedent," we mean that each decision from the highest court in the land establishes a governing rule or principle that guides lower court rulings in future, related cases or until the Supreme Court chooses to look at the issue again and possibly overturn the established precedent. So, the records surrounding the Court's decision in the *Korematsu* case not only reflect the wartime debate over internment, they also reveal the legal precedents set in this case, precedents that have not, to this day, been overturned.

The Supreme Court did not have to take the *Korematsu* case. The Court is empowered to take any case it chooses from the 5,000 cases that petition for a hearing each year. The nine justices who sit on the Supreme Court actually consider only about 150 cases annually. The cases they choose are those that raise significant constitutional questions about the rights of the individual and the powers of the government; they are the cases that seem to demand a high court precedent for lower courts to follow. During World War II, the Supreme Court agreed to hear four cases related to treatment of Japanese Americans on the West Coast. Fred Korematsu's case and the case of Mitsuye Endo were both decided in December 1944. In *Korematsu v. United States*, the court ruled that wartime evacuation was legal, but in the Endo case, the court said that the government could not continue to detain a citizen whose loyalty had been officially certified. The distinction the court made was between "evacuation" and "detention." A year before these two rulings, in 1943, the Supreme Court had established a precedent in the cases of Minoru Yasui and Gordon Hirabayashi that it was legal for the government, in wartime, to impose an evening curfew on a group of people defined by their ethnicity. Prosecutors in Korematsu's case relied on the precedent set in *Hirabayashi v. United States* to defend the legality of wartime evacuation.

What Can Supreme Court Records Tell Us?

The relative permanence of Supreme Court records is an obvious advantage in studying history; the precedents set down by the Court do not quickly shift with the winds of popular opinion. This means, however, that we cannot use the records from a case like *Korematsu v. United States* as a measure of popular opinion. The decisions rendered by the Supreme Court do not derive from a poll, nor are they the result of a democratic election, so we must not presume that the arguments in the records represent the views of average Americans. Maybe they do, maybe they don't; the court records themselves cannot tell us. The Constitution, though, tells us that whether or not the majority of the American public agreed with the majority on the Supreme Court in a case like *Korematsu*, it was the Court's majority opinion that became the law of the land for the indeterminate future.

A great advantage to using Supreme Court records as a historical source is that they offer concise, generally well-written summaries of both the facts under dispute in the case and the constitutional principles and established precedents that shaped the justices' ruling on those facts. Indeed, the written arguments that the lawyers on both sides of the case present to the justices are called briefs because they are supposed to be concise statements of both the factual and legal issues in the case. In addition, justices' opinions can be quite brilliant summaries of both the facts in the case and the constitutional principles bearing on the case.

This virtue in Supreme Court briefs and opinions is also a disadvantage for those of us who are interested in history but have not studied the law. Court records are full of legal terminology and references to previous cases that the lawyers or justices use to support their positions. Another disadvantage of court records for those who simply want to know more about the history of a case is that lawyers and justices do not reveal all the background factors, emotional issues, political considerations, private relationships, and personal beliefs that informed a particular argument or decision. Despite these disadvantages, we can still get the gist of a legal argument without knowing the details of every reference, and a careful reading of court records can give us clues about where to dig into the background of a case.

Consider these excerpts from an amicus curiae (friend of the court) brief filed by the attorneys general of the states of California, Oregon, and Washington in *Korematsu v. United States*. These particular friends were speaking on the side of the government, offering the Supreme Court their views on why the military evacuation of Japanese Americans was justified in wartime. Like most briefs, this one offered claims of fact, statements of opinion, constitutional principle, and legal precedent to support its position:

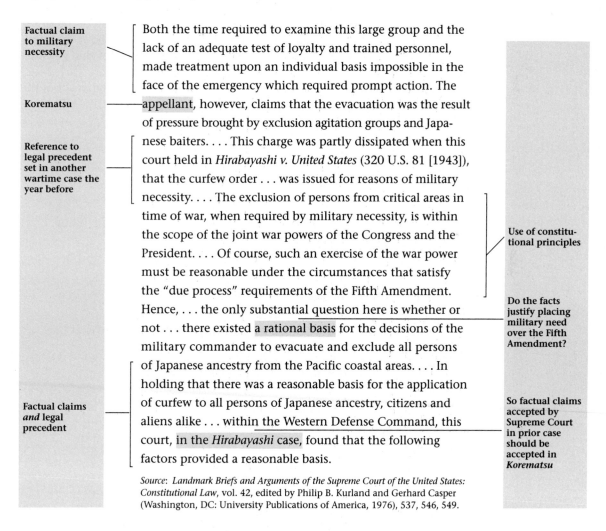

Factual claim to military necessity

Korematsu

Reference to legal precedent set in another wartime case the year before

Use of constitutional principles

Do the facts justify placing military need over the Fifth Amendment?

Factual claims *and* legal precedent

So factual claims accepted by Supreme Court in prior case should be accepted in *Korematsu*

Both the time required to examine this large group and the lack of an adequate test of loyalty and trained personnel, made treatment upon an individual basis impossible in the face of the emergency which required prompt action. The appellant, however, claims that the evacuation was the result of pressure brought by exclusion agitation groups and Japanese baiters. . . . This charge was partly dissipated when this court held in *Hirabayashi v. United States* (320 U.S. 81 [1943]), that the curfew order . . . was issued for reasons of military necessity. . . . The exclusion of persons from critical areas in time of war, when required by military necessity, is within the scope of the joint war powers of the Congress and the President. . . . Of course, such an exercise of the war power must be reasonable under the circumstances that satisfy the "due process" requirements of the Fifth Amendment. Hence, . . . the only substantial question here is whether or not . . . there existed a rational basis for the decisions of the military commander to evacuate and exclude all persons of Japanese ancestry from the Pacific coastal areas. . . . In holding that there was a reasonable basis for the application of curfew to all persons of Japanese ancestry, citizens and aliens alike . . . within the Western Defense Command, this court, in the *Hirabayashi* case, found that the following factors provided a reasonable basis.

Source: *Landmark Briefs and Arguments of the Supreme Court of the United States: Constitutional Law*, vol. 42, edited by Philip B. Kurland and Gerhard Casper (Washington, DC: University Publications of America, 1976), 537, 546, 549.

The amicus curiae brief then listed thirteen factors that supposedly made evacuation of Japanese Americans reasonable under the wartime circumstances. Among the reasons offered were the following: the attack on Pearl Harbor put the Pacific coast in danger; war production facilities on the Pacific coast were in danger; the majority of Japanese Americans lived on the Pacific coast; white hostility had increased Japanese solidarity; Japanese American children attended Japanese-language schools; in 1927, the vast majority of U.S.-born children of Japanese descent held dual citizenship; and the Japanese consulate was influential with Japanese community elders in the United States.

In the end, six of the Supreme Court's nine justices rendered a decision stating that the evacuation of West Coast residents of Japanese descent was constitutional. The other three justices dissented from the majority opinion and wrote their own opinions on why the majority was wrong. The judicial opinions from *Korematsu* illuminate both the case-specific arguments heard in the courtroom and the larger constitutional issues debated among the justices themselves. In the lawyers' briefs and justices' opinions that follow, you will see again most of the points raised in the amicus curiae brief on page 203. In "The Rest of the Story" (pp. 215–17), you will see what research in the 1980s revealed about the validity of the "factual claims" on military necessity and the effect of that research on Fred Korematsu.

The table on page 205 will help you organize your own thoughts about the documents presented in this chapter. In addition, the following Checklist questions will help you actively examine court documents in general.

CHECKLIST: Interrogating Court Documents

- ☐ When was the court document produced, and what was the nature of the case being heard?
- ☐ Who wrote the document? What can I find out about the author from other sources?
- ☐ What is the main argument (or arguments) presented in the document? What evidence is used to support the argument?
- ☐ What was the author's purpose in writing the document? What bias is inherent in the document?
- ☐ Who was the audience for this court document? How was the document meant to affect that audience?
- ☐ What appear to be objective facts in this document, and what appear to be subjective opinions?
- ☐ What does the language used in the document reveal about its purpose, audience, and bias?

Source Analysis Table

The records included here give you a sense of the arguments presented to the Supreme Court by the Justice Department, Fred Korematsu's lawyer, the ACLU, and the Japanese American Citizens' League (JACL). There are also excerpts from the majority and minority opinions issued by the Court at the conclusion of the case. The following table lets you keep track of the debates over factual claims, references to broad constitutional issues, claims to legal precedent, and statements of unsubstantiated opinion.

	Argument made by:	Argument for:	Argument against:
Factual claims about military necessity			
Constitutional issues of due process and war powers			
Legal claims to precedents in prior cases			
Statements of unsubstantiated opinion			

The Source: Briefs and Supreme Court Opinions in *Korematsu v. United States,* October Term, 1944

1 | *Part Three of the Brief Submitted by the Solicitor General of the United States and the Department of Justice Supporting Korematsu's Conviction*

In this section of its three-part brief, the Justice Department spoke directly to the question of "whether the evacuation from the local region of persons of Japanese ancestry . . . was a valid exercise of the war power under the circumstances." The footnotes in this section were part of the Justice Department's brief and constituted an important part of its claim to factual evidence.

The situation leading to the determination to exclude all persons of Japanese ancestry from Military Area No. 1 and the California portion of Military Area No. 2 was stated in detail in the Government's brief in this Court in *Hirabayashi v. United States.* . . . That statement need not be repeated here.[1] In brief, the facts which were generally known in the early months of 1942 or have since been disclosed indicate that there was ample ground to believe that imminent danger then existed of an attack by Japan upon the West Coast. This area contained a large concentration of war production and war facilities. Of the 126,947 persons of Japanese descent in the United States, 111,938 lived in Military Areas No. 1 and No. 2, of whom approximately two-thirds were United States citizens. Social, economic, and political conditions . . . were such that the assimilation of many of them by the white community had been prevented. There was evidence indicating the existence of media through which Japan could have attempted, and had attempted, to secure the attachment of many of these persons to the Japanese Government and to arouse their sympathy and enthusiasm for war aims. There was a basis for concluding that some persons of Japanese ancestry, although American citizens, had formed an attachment to, and

[1] The *Final Report* of General DeWitt (which is dated June 5, 1943, but which was not made public until January, 1944) . . . is relied on in this brief for statistics and other details concerning the actual evacuation. . . . We have specifically recited in this brief the facts relating to the justification for the evacuation, of which we ask the Court to take judicial notice, and we rely upon the *Final Report* only to the extent that it relates to such facts.

Source: Landmark Briefs and Arguments of the Supreme Court of the United States: Constitutional Law, vol. 42, ed. Philip B. Kurland and Gerhard Casper (Washington, DC: University Publications of America, 1976), 213–15.

sympathy and enthusiasm for, Japan.[2] It was also evident that it would be impossible quickly and accurately to distinguish these persons from other citizens of Japanese ancestry. The presence in the Military Areas Nos. 1 and 2 of persons who might aid Japan was peculiarly and particularly dangerous. . . . The persons affected were at first encouraged and assisted to migrate under their own arrangements, but this method of securing their removal . . . was terminated by Public Proclamation No. 4. . . . It was necessary to restrict and regulate the migration from the Area in order to insure the orderly evacuation and resettlement of the persons affected. . . . The rate of self-arranged migration was inadequate, partly because of growing indications that persons of Japanese ancestry were likely to meet with hostility and even violence.

[2] In addition to the authorities cited in the *Hirabayashi* brief, see Anonymous (An Intelligence Officer), "The Japanese in America, the Problem and the Solution," *Harper's Magazine,* October, 1942. . . . See also "Issei, Nisei, Kibei," *Fortune Magazine,* April, 1944.

2   *Brief Submitted by Wayne M. Collins, Counsel for Appellant*

Collins's impassioned, ninety-eight-page (not so) brief made a variety of arguments against the military necessity for and constitutionality of evacuation and internment. The excerpts below, including the footnote, indicate the tone of Collins's brief and his arguments regarding General DeWitt's motives in interpreting Executive Order 9066 as an evacuation and internment order.

If [General DeWitt] really believed these people to be spies and saboteurs . . . why did he delay from December 7, 1941, to March 30, 1942, before removing the first contingent to assembly centers? . . . Was General DeWitt so blind that he didn't realize that in the interval between December 7, 1941, and the date of his unprecedented orders . . . boards of investigation could have examined the loyalty of each of the prospective deportees. . . . They could have been examined in less time than it took to build the shacks that were to house them.[1] The inconvenience and cost of examining would have been trifling. The cost of housing, evacuation and administration of his program has cost this country many

[1] The General issued several hundred individual civilian exclusion orders against "white" naturalized citizens of prior German and Italian allegiance whom he deemed dangerous. These were given individual hearings on the question of their loyalty. . . . If the General had time to provide examinations for these individuals can he be heard to deny he had time to examine Japanese descended citizens before evacuating them? His special treatment of these whites proves his bias against the native-born yellow citizen.

Source: Landmark Briefs and Arguments of the Supreme Court of the United States, 119, 152, 161, 163, 165, 196. (Bracketed text within the selections has been added by the editors to help fill in gaps and clarify unfamiliar terminology.)

millions. . . . Why did he keep secret the reasons he insisted upon this frenzied evacuation? How could this nation abide the secret reasons he carried in his head when we had neither evidence nor ground to believe him to have been the wisest man in the nation? What are the facts upon which he would justify the outrage he perpetrated? . . .

What one day will be celebrated as a masterpiece of illogic . . . appears in General DeWitt's letter of February 14, 1942, one month before the evacuation commenced. (*Final Report*, p. 34). He characterizes all our Japanese as subversive. . . . He states . . . that "the Japanese race is an enemy race" and the native-born citizens are "Americanized" but their "racial strains are undiluted" and being "barred from assimilation by convention" may "turn against this nation." . . . The very fact that no sabotage has taken place to date is a disturbing and confirming indication that such action will be taken." . . .

Who is this DeWitt to say who is and who is not an American and who shall and who shall not enjoy the rights of citizenship? . . . General DeWitt let Terror out to plague these citizens but closed the lid on the Pandora's box and left Hope to smother. It is your duty to raise the lid and revive Hope for these, our people, who have suffered at the hands of one of our servants.

3   *Amicus Curiae Briefs Submitted by the American Civil Liberties Union*

> Due to conflict within the ACLU, that organization was not Korematsu's attorney of record, but it did submit a "friend of the court" brief to persuade the Supreme Court to hear the *Korematsu* case and submitted another at the time of the hearing. These excerpts are taken from both briefs, as is footnote 1.

October 1943 Brief Asking the Supreme Court to Review the Judgment of the Ninth Circuit Court of Appeals

We believe that this case presents the question of the power of the military to detain citizens against whom no charges have been preferred. We contend that no such power has been granted by Congress, or could be constitutionally granted.

The issue is presented because the evacuation orders . . . made it quite plain that not evacuation only was required, but indefinite detention as well. . . . That the evacuation and detention were part of a single integrated program is made clear in a recently published report by the War Department. . . .

We submit that the Congress gave neither to the President nor to military authorities any power so far reaching, and that in the absence of legislation the President has no such power even in time of war. . . . It is only when martial law

Source: Landmark Briefs and Arguments of the Supreme Court of the United States, 81–83, 302–4.

has been declared that executive authority may be exercised over citizens. . . . Finally, we submit that even the President and the Congress, acting together, may not detain citizens of the United States against whom no charges have been preferred. . . . The framers [of the Constitution] permitted the suspension of the writ of habeas corpus,* by which unlawful detention was normally challenged, but permitted such suspension only in time of invasion or insurrection . . . only at a time of direst immediate emergency, not at all as a precautionary measure.

October 1944 Brief Asking the Supreme Court to Overturn Fred Korematsu's Conviction

General DeWitt does try to show military necessity by reference to reported illegal radio signals which could not be located, lights on the shore, and the like. . . . The Government's brief . . . contains no reference . . . to illicit radio signals, signal lights . . . or to . . . hidden caches of contraband. . . . Moreover, in several respects the recital in the DeWitt Report is wholly inconsistent with the facts of public knowledge. It is well known, of course, that radio detection equipment is unbelievably accurate. . . . Secondly, the fact that no person of Japanese ancestry has been arraigned for any sabotage or espionage since December 7, 1941, certainly suggests, in view of the unquestionable efficiency of the F.B.I., that no such acts were committed. . . . Nowhere in [DeWitt's *Final Report*] is there a line, a word, about the reports of other security officers. General DeWitt does not tell us whether he consulted either the Director of the Federal Bureau of Investigation or the Director of the Office of Naval Intelligence. . . . Since no recommendation from either the Office of Naval Intelligence or the F.B.I. are referred to, one can only assume either that they were not sought or that they were opposed to mass evacuation.[1]

---

* A writ of habeas corpus is an order that a prison official bring a prisoner before a court to show that the prisoner has been arrested and detained for actual legal cause. — Eds.

[1] There is a fair indication that, whether or not its recommendations were asked, the Office of Naval Intelligence would have stated that mass evacuation was wholly unnecessary. In *Harper's Magazine* for October, 1942, there is an article by an anonymous officer . . . [which] is almost certainly from the Office of Naval Intelligence, which has always been understood as primarily concerned with Japanese intelligence work. The concluding paragraph states: "To sum up: the entire 'Japanese Problem' has been magnified out of its true proportion, largely because of the physical characteristics of the people. It should be handled on the basis of the *individual*, regardless of citizenship, and *not* on a racial basis."

4 **Amicus Curiae Brief Submitted by the Japanese American Citizens' League on Behalf of Fred Korematsu**

The JACL submitted a 200-page "friend of the court" brief that emphasized Japanese American assimilation and loyalty to the U.S. government. In response to the charge that Japanese American loyalty was in doubt because many Japanese Americans held dual citizenship, the JACL brief explained that, prior to 1924, Japanese law automatically conferred Japanese citizenship on any child born of Japanese parents anywhere in the world. After Japanese Americans persuaded the Japanese government to change that law, the percentage of U.S.-born children of Japanese descent holding dual citizenship plummeted by 85 percent.

It has been necessary to present the evidence concerning the assimilation, loyalty and contributions of Americans of Japanese ancestry because . . . [in] all the loose talk about "lack of assimilation" and "close-knit racial groups" there is no hint that the trained investigators who have pursued the subject for years were even consulted. . . . Dr. Robert E. Park, chairman of the Department of Sociology of the University of Chicago, directed a large-scale study of resident Orientals . . . [and] determined that the American of Japanese ancestry "born in America and educated in our western schools is culturally an Occidental, even though he be racially an Oriental." . . .

The civilians who, because they were influenced by Pearl Harbor sabotage rumors, became panic-stricken and requested evacuation . . . did not know the facts. Perhaps the politicians . . . too, were ignorant. But General DeWitt, who ordered the evacuation, certainly must have been aware of the truth and must have been cognizant of the grounds on which his fellow officer, General Delos C. Emmons, refused to order mass internment of the persons of Japanese descent in Hawaii.

Why then did General DeWitt, in spite of what he knew or could easily have learned, act upon the advice of racists and mean-spirited economic rivals? We contend that General DeWitt accepted the views of racists instead of the principles of democracy because he is himself a confessed racist. . . . On April 13, 1943, in testifying before the House Naval Affairs Committee in San Francisco, General DeWitt . . . said:

> A Jap's a Jap. . . . I don't want any of them. We got them out. . . . They are a dangerous element, whether loyal or not. It makes no difference whether he is an American citizen. Theoretically, he is still a Japanese and you can't change him.

Source: Landmark Briefs and Arguments of the Supreme Court of the United States, 504–6, 527–28.

5   *The Opinion of the Supreme Court*
Issued December 18, 1944

> Justice Hugo L. Black issued the eight-page majority opinion of six of the Court's nine judges. Chief Justice Harlan Stone and Justices Stanley Reed, Felix Frankfurter, Wiley Rutledge, and William O. Douglas concurred. All of those justices, except for Chief Justice Stone were appointed to the Supreme Court by President Franklin Delano Roosevelt.

It should be noted, to begin with, that all legal restrictions which curtail the civil rights of a single racial group are immediately suspect. That is not to say that all such restrictions are unconstitutional. It is to say that courts must subject them to the most rigid scrutiny. Pressing public necessity may sometime justify the existence of such restrictions; racial antagonism never can. . . . Executive Order 9066 . . . declared that "the successful prosecution of the war requires every possible protection against espionage and against sabotage." . . . In *Hirabayashi v. United States* . . . we sustained a conviction obtained for violation of the curfew order. . . . It was because we could not reject the finding of the military authorities that it was impossible to bring about an immediate segregation of the disloyal from the loyal that we sustained the validity of the curfew order as applying to the whole group. In the instant case, temporary exclusion of the entire group was rested by the military on the same ground. . . .

We uphold the exclusion order as of the time it was made and when the petitioner violated it. In doing so, we are not unmindful of the hardships imposed by it upon a large group of American citizens. But hardships are part of war, and war is an aggregation of hardships. . . . Citizenship has its responsibilities as well as its privileges, and in time of war the burden is always heavier. . . . The contention is that we must treat these separate orders [for exclusion and for detention] as one and inseparable; that, for this reason, if detention in an assembly or relocation center would have illegally deprived the petitioner of his liberty, the exclusion order and his conviction under it cannot stand. . . . We cannot say . . . that his presence in that [assembly] center would have resulted in his detention in a relocation center. . . . It is sufficient here to pass upon the [exclusion] order which petitioner violated. To do more would be to go beyond the issues raised, and to decide momentous questions not contained within the framework of the pleadings or the evidence in this case. . . . To cast this case in the outlines of racial prejudice, without reference to real military dangers which were presented, merely confuses the issue.

Source: United States Reports, vol. 323, Cases Adjudged in the Supreme Court at October Term, 1944, 214–24.

Justice Owen J. Roberts, Dissenting from the Majority

Justice Roberts was one of only two justices on the Supreme Court in 1944 who had not been appointed by President Roosevelt. In his five-page dissent, Justice Roberts criticized the majority's reliance on the *Hirabayashi* precedent and its claim that it was valid to rule narrowly on evacuation and not address the question of detention without trial.

The predicament in which the petitioner thus found himself was this: he was forbidden, by Military Order, to leave the zone in which he lived; he was forbidden, by Military Order, after a date fixed, to be found within that zone unless he were in an Assembly Center located in that zone. General DeWitt's report to the Secretary of War concerning the program of evacuation and relocation of Japanese makes it entirely clear . . . that an Assembly Center was a euphemism for a prison. No person within such a center was permitted to leave except by Military Order. . . . The civil authorities must often resort to the expedient of excluding citizens temporarily from a locality. . . . If the exclusion . . . were of that nature the *Hirabayashi* case would be an authority for sustaining it. But the facts above recited . . . show that the exclusion was part of an overall plan for forcible detention. . . . The two conflicting orders, one which commanded him to stay and the other which commanded him to go, were nothing but a cleverly devised trap to accomplish the real purpose of the military authority, which was to lock him up in a concentration camp. . . . We know that is the fact. Why should we set up a figmentary and artificial situation instead of addressing ourselves to the actualities of the case?

Source: United States Reports, vol. 323, Cases Adjudged in the Supreme Court at October Term, 1944, 225–30.

 ## Justice Frank Murphy, Dissenting from the Majority

Justice Murphy had voted with all the other justices in the 1943 *Hirabayashi* case, upholding a curfew for West Coast residents of Japanese descent. His written opinion in that case stated that such a curfew for one ethnic group bore "a melancholy resemblance to the treatment accorded to members of the Jewish race in Germany" and "goes to the very brink of constitutional power." In his ten-page dissent from the majority's decision in *Korematsu*, Justice Murphy focused on balancing military necessity and citizens' constitutional rights.

In dealing with matters relating to the prosecution and progress of a war, we must accord great respect and consideration to the judgements of the military

Source: United States Reports, vol. 323, Cases Adjudged in the Supreme Court at October Term, 1944, 233–42.

authorities. . . . Their judgements ought not to be overruled lightly by those whose training and duties ill-equip them to deal intelligently with matters so vital to the security of the nation. At the same time, however, it is essential that there be definite limits to military discretion, especially where martial law has not been declared. Individuals must not be impoverished of their constitutional rights on a plea of military necessity that has neither substance nor support. . . . The military claim must subject itself to the judicial process of having its reasonableness determined. . . . The action [must] have some reasonable relation to the removal of dangers of invasion, sabotage, and espionage. But the exclusion of all persons with Japanese blood in their veins has no such reasonable relation . . . because [it] must necessarily rely for its reasonableness on the assumption that *all* persons of Japanese ancestry may have a dangerous tendency to commit sabotage and espionage. . . . It is difficult to believe that reason, logic or experience could be marshalled in support of . . . this erroneous assumption of racial guilt. In [General DeWitt's] *Final Report* . . . he refers to all individuals of Japanese descent as "subversive," as belonging to an "enemy race" whose "racial strains are undiluted." . . . Justification for the exclusion is sought . . . mainly upon questionable racial and sociological grounds not ordinarily within the realm of expert military judgement. . . . A military judgement based upon such racial and sociological considerations is not entitled to the great weight ordinarily given the judgements based upon strict military considerations. . . . I dissent, therefore, from this legalization of racism.

8

Justice Robert Jackson, Dissenting from the Majority

In his six-page dissent, Justice Jackson challenged the relevance of *Hirabayashi* as a precedent and distinguished between the immediate decisions of the military and the precedent-setting decisions of the Supreme Court.

It is said that if the military commander had reasonable military grounds for promulgating the orders, they are constitutional and become law and the Court is required to enforce them. There are several reasons why I cannot subscribe to this doctrine.

It would be impracticable and dangerous idealism to expect or insist that each specific military command in an area of probable operations will conform to conventional tests of constitutionality. . . . But if we cannot confine military expedients by the Constitution, neither would I distort the Constitution to approve all that the military may deem expedient. That is what the Court appears to be doing, whether consciously or not. I cannot say, from any evidence before me, that the orders of General DeWitt were not reasonably expedient military

Source: United States Reports, vol. 323, Cases Adjudged in the Supreme Court at October Term, 1944, 242–48.

precautions, nor could I say that they were. But even if they were permissible military procedures, I deny that it follows that they were constitutional. . . .

Much is made of the danger to liberty from the Army program of deporting and detaining these citizens of Japanese extraction. But a judicial construction of the due process clause that will sustain this order is a far more subtle blow to liberty than the promulgation of the order itself. A military order, however constitutional, is not apt to last longer than the military emergency. . . . But once a judicial opinion rationalizes such an order to show that it conforms to the Constitution . . . the Court for all time has validated the principle of racial discrimination. . . . The principle then lies about like a loaded weapon ready for the hand of any authority that can bring forward a plausible claim of an urgent need. Every repetition imbeds that principle more deeply in our law and thinking and expands it to new purposes. . . . A military commander may overstep the bounds of constitutionality, and it is an incident. But if we review and approve, that passing incident becomes the doctrine of the Constitution. There it has a generative power of its own. . . . Nothing better illustrates this danger than does the Court's opinion in this case. It argues that we are bound to uphold the conviction of Korematsu because we upheld one in *Hirabayashi v. United States*, when we sustained these orders in so far as they applied a curfew requirement to a citizen of Japanese ancestry. . . . Now the principle of racial discrimination is pushed from support of mild measures to very harsh ones, from temporary deprivations to indeterminate ones. And the precedent which it is said requires us to do so is *Hirabayashi*. . . . Because we said that these citizens could be made to stay in their homes during the hours of dark, it is said we must require them to leave home entirely; and if that, we are told they may also be taken into custody for deportation; and if that, it is argued they may also be held for some undetermined time in detention camps. How far the principle of this case would be extended before plausible reasons would play out, I do not know.

Analyzing Supreme Court Records

1. What factual claims about the military necessity of Japanese American evacuation were in dispute in this case? Did any of the justices rely on the factual claims to support their judicial opinion? Did any of the justices question the military's claims?

2. How did Justice Black apply the precedent set in the *Hirabayashi* curfew case to his majority opinion in the *Korematsu* evacuation case? In his dissent, why did Justice Jackson reject the use of *Hirabayashi* as a precedent in this case?

3. According to Justice Black, why is an evacuation order not the same as a detention order? What did Justice Roberts say in disagreeing with Justice Black on this point?

4. The majority opinion established the principle of strict scrutiny in reviewing all laws that "curtail the civil rights of a single racial group," but held that "real military dangers" meant that the evacuation of 1942 passed the

test of strict scrutiny. On what grounds did Justice Murphy dissent from this reasoning?

5. Fred Korematsu's conviction was overturned in 1984 (see "The Rest of the Story"), but the Supreme Court ruling in this case still stands. What was the role of "factual claims" in overturning the conviction? How did the constitutional principle of "strict scrutiny," as set forth in the original *Korematsu* decision, help overturn the conviction?

6. After the terrorist attacks of September 11, 2001, and the passage of the USA PATRIOT Act (Public Law 107-56), legal scholars debated whether the Supreme Court's opinion in *Korematsu v. United States* might be used as a legal precedent for the categorical evacuation of Arab Americans as a military necessity in the war on terrorism. Imagine that it is just a few months after the September 11 attacks. Drawing on the logic in the Supreme Court documents in the *Korematsu* case, write a one-page argument for or against evacuation and detention of all Americans of Arab descent in the name of national security.

The Rest of the Story

In April 1984, forty years after the Supreme Court declared Fred Korematsu guilty of disobeying a military order to evacuate his home, his case was reconsidered in the U.S. District Court for Northern California, and his conviction was overturned. This extraordinary turn of events was unprecedented in U.S. legal history, and it occurred because a lawyer and legal historian, Peter Irons, conducted historical research and found evidence he never even dreamed existed.

Irons set out in 1981 to write a book about Japanese American cases involving curfew, evacuation, and internment during World War II. While digging through the unexamined records of the Justice Department, Irons happened upon written evidence that the Justice Department and the War Department knew that General John DeWitt had falsified data about Japanese subversive activity on the West Coast when he submitted his *Final Report* to officials of the federal government in June 1943. The Supreme Court justices had read the *Final Report* and had relied on it as the factual basis for allowing curfews in the *Hirabayashi* decision. In 1944, however, Edward Ennis, the Justice Department lawyer charged with preparing the government's defense in *Korematsu v. United States*, questioned the *Final Report*'s claims that Japanese Americans had used signaling equipment and radio transmissions to engage in acts of espionage. Ennis quickly learned that the Federal Bureau of Investigation, the Office of Naval Intelligence, and the Federal Communications Commission had all told General DeWitt that every rumor of such espionage had been thoroughly investigated and found false; all signals from the coast and all radio transmissions had been accounted for. By including the rumors of subversion but excluding the agencies' findings in his *Final Report*, DeWitt had knowingly fabricated claims to a "military necessity" for the evacuation of all Japanese Americans.

When he realized that the *Hirabayashi* decision was based on disproved rumors, Ennis alerted Solicitor General Charles Fahy and Assistant Secretary of

War John McCloy that the Justice Department would be engaged in a suppression of evidence if it did not report these findings to the Supreme Court. Fahy and McCloy refused to inform the Supreme Court that the *Final Report* was falsified, but they did refrain from using that phony evidence in the written brief in the *Korematsu* case and did agree to include the footnote, which you read on page 206 subtly indicating limited confidence in DeWitt's report. A surviving outline of Fahy's oral argument indicates that he planned to quote from the *Final Report*'s espionage rumors in addressing the Supreme Court, but the Justice Department has lost the transcript of Fahy's presentation, so there is no proof that Fahy knowingly misled the Court on the matter of Japanese American espionage. In retrospect, Ennis regretted not resigning from his Justice Department position over this issue, but at the time he thought he could do more good on the inside. Indeed, he slipped his information to the lawyers for the ACLU, and you can see in their amicus curiae brief an effort to alert the Supreme Court to flaws in the *Final Report*.

In 1982, when Peter Irons told sixty-two-year-old Fred Korematsu that the "military necessity" evidence used in his case had been falsified and that he had legal grounds to seek a reversal, Korematsu told Irons to go ahead with the case. Irons worked with a team of Japanese American lawyers, all children of citizens who had been interned during the war. The Justice Department offered to "pardon" Korematsu rather than face exposure of falsified evidence in open court. Korematsu replied that the Justice Department should instead seek a pardon from him.

Korematsu's lawyers decided to take their case to the federal district court rather than the United States Supreme Court. This less-risky strategy offered the best chance that Korematsu would be personally exonerated, but it meant that the precedent set at the Supreme Court level would not be altered. In 1984, after reviewing the evidence, U.S. District Court Judge Marilyn Hall Patel overturned Korematsu's conviction on the grounds that a "fundamental error" had occurred in the original trial. With Fred Korematsu sitting before her in court, Judge Patel said:

> *Korematsu* remains on the pages of our legal and political history. As a legal precedent it is now recognized as having very limited application. As a historical precedent it stands as a constant caution that in times of war or declared military necessity our institutions must be vigilant in protecting constitutional guarantees . . . and national security must not be used to protect governmental actions from close scrutiny and accountability. It stands as a caution that in times of international hostility and antagonisms our institutions, legislative, executive, and judicial, must be prepared to protect all citizens from the petty fears and prejudices that are so easily aroused.[2]

Between 1949 and 1980, very slow progress was made in the effort to compensate Japanese Americans for the financial losses resulting from relocation and

---

[2] *Korematsu v. United States*, 584 F. Supp. 1406 (N.D. Cal. 1984).

detention. In 1980, due to pressure from the Japanese American Citizens League and Japanese American elected officials, Congress established the Commission on Wartime Relocation and Internment of Civilians to review the facts surrounding implementation of Executive Order 9066 and to "recommend appropriate remedies." Peter Irons's research findings were among the facts available to this government commission. In 1988, four years after Fred Korematsu was exonerated, President Ronald Reagan signed the Civil Liberties Act, which provided for a $20,000 redress payment to each of the 60,000 surviving internees, including Fred Korematsu.

Before his conviction was overturned, Korematsu had not even told his children that he was a convicted criminal. After it was overturned, he welcomed opportunities to speak about his case. In an interview for the film *Of Civil Wrongs and Rights: The Fred Korematsu Story*, he said, "In order for things like this to never happen, we have to protest. Protest but not with violence, otherwise they won't listen to you, but you have to let them know, otherwise they're not going to hear you. So, don't be afraid to speak up." In 1998, when he was seventy-eight years old, Fred Korematsu was awarded the Presidential Medal of Freedom, the nation's highest civilian honor. He died of respiratory failure in 2005. Today, his daughter, Karen Korematsu-Haigh, serves on the Board of the Directors of the Korematsu Institute for Civil Rights and Education, which is affiliated with the Asian Law Caucus, the California-based legal center that succeeded in its suit to overturn Fred Korematsu's conviction.

To Find Out More

Korematsu v. United States *Court Documents*[3]

"*Korematsu v. United States.*" http://caselaw.lp.findlaw.com/scripts/getcase.pl?court=us&vol=323&invol=214. Includes the unabridged texts of the Supreme Court justices' majority opinion and three dissenting opinions.

Kurland, Philip B., and Gerhard Casper, eds. *Landmark Briefs and Arguments of the Supreme Court of the United States: Constitutional Law*. Vol. 42. Washington, DC: University Publications of America, 1976. The full text of the lawyers' briefs and the amicus curiae briefs submitted to the Supreme Court in *Korematsu v. United States* are on pages 3–563.

Resources on Japanese American Internment

"Japanese American Exhibit and Access Project." University of Washington. http://lib.washington.edu/exhibits/harmony.

---

[3] There are no transcripts of the lawyers' oral arguments before the Supreme Court in the *Korematsu* case. The Court did not provide for the recording and transcription of oral arguments until 1955.

"Japanese Relocation and Internment during World War II." *Archives Library Information Center*. National Archives. http://www.archives.gov/research/alic /reference/military/japanese-internment.html.

Kikuchi, Charles. *The Kikuchi Diary: Chronicles of an American Concentration Camp*. Urbana: University of Illinois Press, 1973.

Kikumura, Akemi. *Through Harsh Winters: The Life of a Japanese Immigrant Woman*. Novato, CA: Chandler and Sharp, 1981.

Tateishi, John. *And Justice for All: An Oral History of the Japanese American Detention Camps*. New York: Random House, 1984.

Secondary Sources on Korematsu v. United States and Japanese American Internment

Daniels, Roger. *Prisoners without Trial: Japanese Americans in World War II*. New York: Hill and Wang, 1993.

Hatamiya, Leslie T. *Righting a Wrong: Japanese Americans and the Passage of the Civil Liberties Act of 1988*. Palo Alto, CA: Stanford University Press, 1993.

Irons, Peter. *Justice at War*. New York: Oxford University Press, 1983.

Irons, Peter. *Justice Delayed: The Record of the Japanese American Internment Cases*. Middletown, CT: Wesleyan University Press, 1989.

Ng, Wendy. *Japanese American Internment during World War II: A History and Reference Guide*. Westport, CT: Greenwood, 2002.

Personal Justice Denied. Report of the Commission on Wartime Relocation and Internment of Civilians. Washington, DC: Civil Liberties Education Fund; Seattle: University of Washington Press, 1997.

Film Documentaries on Japanese Internment

Of Civil Wrongs and Rights: The Fred Korematsu Story. Eric Paul Fournier, writer/ director/producer. San Francisco: NAATA, 2000.

The Rabbit in the Moon. Emiko Omori, writer/director/producer. Ho-Ho-Kus, NJ: Wabi-Sabi Productions, 1999.

CHAPTER 10

The Cold War Heats Up

Presidential Recordings from the Cuban Missile Crisis

President John Kennedy was still in his bathrobe and slippers when his National Security advisor, McGeorge Bundy, brought him the photographs showing construction of nuclear missile sites on the island of Cuba, just ninety miles off the Florida coast. It was Tuesday, October 16, 1962, Day One of the thirteen-day ordeal known as the Cuban missile crisis. Kennedy told Bundy to call a meeting that morning with fifteen of his trusted advisors, and he called his brother Robert, the attorney general. "We have some big trouble," announced the president. "I want you over here."

Kennedy was a liberal Democrat from Massachusetts, a World War II veteran, and a dedicated cold warrior who had promised in his inaugural address that the United States would "pay any price, bear any burden" and "oppose any foe to assure the survival and success of liberty." As a Cold War candidate, Kennedy had charged the Republicans with allowing an unfavorable "missile gap" to grow between U.S. and Soviet nuclear capacity and for failing to stand tough against Soviet-sponsored communism in satellite states such as Cuba. Once he came into office, Kennedy learned that there was no missile gap; the United States had many times more nuclear weapons than the Soviets. He learned, too, that nations like Cuba could not be controlled as easily as pawns on a chess board.

Fidel Castro had seized power in Cuba during the socialist revolution of 1959, just two years before Kennedy was sworn in as president in January 1961, and Cuba had been a thorn in Kennedy's side since the start of his administration. In April 1961, Kennedy had approved a plan by the Central Intelligence Agency (CIA) to secretly fund an invasion of Cuba by 1,500 Cuban exiles. They were to land by boat at the Bay of Pigs, incite a general uprising among the Cuban people, and overthrow Castro and his Soviet-friendly regime. The plan, however, was doomed by biased information and poor planning: 51,000 of Castro's militia met the invaders, killing 115 and capturing 1,200. President Kennedy walked away from the humiliating incident determined to base future decisions on accurate information, thorough discussion, and candid advice from advisors he could trust.

Like many Americans during the Cold War, President Kennedy was Eurocentric in his view of the world; he thought that the U.S.-Soviet contest over control of Europe was the real story and that contests elsewhere in the world were subplots. In Kennedy's judgment, Soviet actions in places like Cuba were merely tactical moves. He believed that the Soviet Union, led by Nikita Khrushchev, would risk nuclear war for control of the German city of Berlin but would not risk war over Cuba. Indeed, in the eighteen months between the Bay of Pigs and the Cuban missile crisis, the Kennedy administration developed Operation Mongoose, which included military plans to invade Cuba and assassinate Castro. When the Cubans and Soviets charged the United States with creating such covert plans, the Kennedy administration denied the charge but did not cancel Operation Mongoose, apparently not fearing Soviet retaliation for any U.S. aggression against Cuba.

In the weeks leading up to the Cuban missile crisis, Kennedy vigorously rejected Republican claims that the Soviets were pouring offensive weapons into Cuba. All of the CIA data supported the Soviets' public insistence that the weapons they were shipping to Cuba were purely "defensive," and Khrushchev's private assurances to Kennedy reinforced the president's view that the Soviets would not take unnecessary risks in the Western Hemisphere. Still, September polling data showed that although 80 percent of U.S. respondents generally approved of Kennedy's foreign policy performance, 63 percent doubted that he was standing firm enough on the weapons situation in Cuba. Kennedy answered his critics and asserted his cold warrior credentials by publicly announcing that "if Cuba should possess the capacity to carry out offensive actions against the United States, then the United States would act." Confident that the Soviet Union would not be provocative in Cuba, Kennedy did not imagine that he would ever have to match his warning with military action. A month later, he learned that just as his government had lied when denying subversive activity in Cuba, so had the Soviet government lied when denying the shipment of nuclear weapons to Cuba.

Between October 16, when the U.S. government acquired evidence of nuclear weapons in Cuba, and October 28, when the Soviets agreed to remove those weapons, the world came as close as it has ever come to full-scale nuclear war. If the United States had chosen to abide by its word and "act" to remove the nuclear missiles on Cuba, the Soviets might have launched those missiles or its own missiles against U.S. cities, or the Soviets might have attacked Berlin or some other European capital. In either case, the United States might then have launched its nuclear missiles against the Soviets. As Kennedy noted at the time, any misstep could result in "the final failure"; Kennedy and Khrushchev would have presided over the end of the world.

The president's first decision in the crisis was to develop U.S. strategy in close consultation with the fifteen advisors he summoned to the White House on Day One. This group, called "ExComm"—the Executive Committee of the National Security Council—met every day, sometimes more than once a day, for the next twelve days. Determined not to repeat the mistakes of the Bay of Pigs invasion, Kennedy sought a decision-making process that would provide him with candid debate on all possible options and outcomes using the most accurate data available. Kennedy participated fully in that debate, often pointing out how U.S. actions might appear to allies in Europe, who faced Soviet missiles every day and would think it a "mad act" to risk European security in order to remove a few missiles in Cuba. Kennedy never suggested that the Soviet Union might be viewing covert U.S. action against Cuba as a sufficient threat to install missiles; he continued to think Berlin was the real issue. But he did coldly calculate that the placement of intercontinental ballistic missiles in Cuba represented no real change in the military balance of power. As the president put it, "It doesn't make any difference if you get blown up by an ICBM flying from the Soviet Union or one that was 90 miles away."

Still, Kennedy knew that the United States could not simply ignore the missiles. He had publicly stated that the United States would act if offensive weapons appeared in Cuba, so he either had to act or had to face a serious decline in U.S. prestige and power. In the entire debate over how to act, however, Kennedy was the person in the room most intent on eliminating the missiles from Cuba without sparking any armed conflict. Unlike his military advisors and, initially, his brother Robert, President Kennedy did not seek to use the crisis—and risk nuclear annihilation—to settle the score on Cuba. He took the Cold War very seriously, but he took the nuclear threat even more seriously; destruction of the human race was a burden Kennedy was not willing to bear.

For the first seven days of the crisis, the American people did not know about the missiles, and the Soviets and Cubans did not know that U.S. surveillance had detected them. Secrecy gave Kennedy a full week to deliberate with his advisors. They debated a range of responses, from a letter of protest to Khrushchev to an all-out surprise air strike and invasion. At the end of that clandestine week, the president went on national television to reveal the existence of Soviet missiles in Cuba and announce a measured response: the United States would "quarantine" Cuba through a naval blockade so that no more offensive weapons could be shipped in, and it would ask for a United Nations resolution demanding immediate elimination of all nuclear weapons on the island. In laying out this response, Kennedy made clear to the American public and to Khrushchev that the United States was prepared to take more aggressive action if necessary.

For the next four days, the world held its breath. The Soviets insisted that the weapons were a defensive deterrent against the constant threat of U.S. invasion, and United Nations diplomats shuttled between the U.S. and Soviet delegations. Meanwhile, some Cuba-bound Soviet ships seemed to be bowing to the blockade by turning around at sea, but construction on the nuclear missile sites in Cuba continued at an alarming pace. U.S. military maneuvers made clear to the Soviets that the White House was preparing for an attack on Cuba—and

Figure 10.1 The Executive Committee of the National Security Council, 1962 This photo, taken during the Cuban missile crisis, shows the members of the Executive Committee. Seated to the president's left are Secretary of Defense Robert S. McNamara, Deputy Secretary of Defense Roswell Gilpatric, Chairman of the Joint Chiefs of Staff General Maxwell Taylor, Assistant Secretary of Defense Paul Nitze, Deputy United States Information Agency Director Donald Wilson, Special Counsel Theodore Sorensen, Special Assistant McGeorge Bundy, Secretary of the Treasury Douglas Dillon, Vice President Lyndon B. Johnson (hidden from view), Attorney General Robert F. Kennedy, Ambassador Llewellyn "Tommy" Thompson, Arms Control and Disarmament Agency Director William C. Foster, CIA Director John McCone (hidden from view), Under Secretary of State George Ball, and Secretary of State Dean Rusk. Source: Cecil Stoughton. White House Photographs. John F. Kennedy Presidential Library and Museum, Boston.

the Soviet Union. Kennedy was briefed on the limited civil defense aid available for citizens in urban areas in the event of a nuclear attack and told that there was no aid for rural citizens. Defense officials also told the president that the Cuban missiles could reach as far as central Washington State, even though a 1962 map in the National Security Archives shows that the missiles' range fell within an arc from between Dallas and Oklahoma City, over to Cincinnati and on to Washington, D.C. Regardless of the reach of the missiles, the president faced a terrible choice.

Finally, late on Friday night, October 26, the eleventh day of the crisis, Kennedy received a thirteen-page private letter from Khrushchev offering to remove the missiles in exchange for a U.S. promise not to invade Cuba. The next morning, when Kennedy and his advisors were discussing how to respond to this offer, the news reported a public statement from Khrushchev offering to remove the Cuban missiles if the United States would remove fifteen Jupiter nuclear missiles stationed at the Turkish-Soviet border. To the men debating strategy in the

White House, it appeared as if the fate of the planet rested on the response they fashioned to these mysteriously different offers. Saturday, October 27, Day Twelve, was the longest and most difficult day of the crisis.

In popular culture treatments of the Cuban missile crisis—such as the Hollywood film *Thirteen Days*—a clever U.S. government finessed the crisis by simply ignoring Khrushchev's public demand for the trade of protective missiles in Turkey and responding only to the private request that the United States pledge not to invade Cuba. In real life, the resolution was more complicated.

President Kennedy advocated for acceptance of the Turkish missile deal, arguing that the United States planned to dismantle the outdated Jupiter missiles anyway and use newer missiles on Polaris submarines to protect Turkey. ExComm members disagreed with the president; they disliked the political appearance of a Turkish-Cuban missile trade and pressed for acceptance only of Khrushchev's private demand that the United States vow not to invade Cuba.

While ExComm debated, Khrushchev became convinced that both the U.S. military and Fidel Castro were itching to go to war, even nuclear war. His alarm mounted with the Saturday afternoon news that his own Soviet officers in Cuba had violated no-shoot orders and had killed a U.S. Air Force surveillance pilot, thereby increasing pressure on the Kennedy administration to attack Cuba.

In the end, Kennedy and Khrushchev avoided war by agreeing to both of Khrushchev's offers. In a secret Saturday night meeting with the Soviet ambassador to the United States, Robert Kennedy followed up that day's public offer not to invade Cuba with private assurance that the United States would, in four or five months, remove the Jupiter missiles. Khrushchev publicly accepted the no-invasion offer on Sunday morning, even before he knew about the Jupiter missile offer. In April, the missiles were removed from the Turkish border. The United States never signed a noninvasion agreement, however, because Castro would not allow the United Nations to verify the absence of offensive weapons on his island.

On Monday, October 29, President Kennedy ordered the creation of a commemorative gift for his advisors; his secretary, Evelyn Lincoln; and his wife, Jacqueline. He asked for a small silver plaque simply displaying the month of October with a line highlighting the dates October 16 through October 28. For the moment, the Cold War had cooled down.

Using the Source: Presidential Tapes

The genuine threat of nuclear war in October 1962 provides ample reason for our continued interest in the Cuban missile crisis. But a companion reason is that the United States managed its side of this world crisis through a unique decision-making process: an ad hoc "ExComm" led by the president for a discrete period of time. Fortunately for those who study decision making, crucial portions of that process were preserved on tape recordings made in the Cabinet Room and the Oval Office. Presidential tape recordings became famous during Richard Nixon's Watergate scandal in the 1970s, but presidents had actually been taping selected Oval Office conversations since Franklin Roosevelt was in office in the 1930s.

President Kennedy had a taping system installed in the summer before the missile crisis, probably to assist him in later writing his memoirs. To operate this simple system in either the Oval Office or the Cabinet Room, he flipped switches hidden under his office desk or at his seat at the Cabinet Room table. Concealed microphones would then transmit conversations to the reel-to-reel tape recorder in the White House basement. The only people who knew about the system were the president, his brother Robert, Evelyn Lincoln, and the two Secret Service agents who had installed the system and who changed the reels of tape when they ran out.

Over the course of the thirteen-day Cuban missile crisis, President Kennedy recorded close to forty hours of discussion with his ExComm. This group came together in seventeen tape-recorded meetings that lasted from thirty minutes to four hours each. Between meetings, the president attempted to attend to other business, but ExComm members worked virtually around the clock on the missile crisis, consulting with military and diplomatic experts to gather information and explore alternatives, punctuating their days and nights with catnaps in their offices and constantly preparing for their meetings with the president.

The Kennedy tapes, whose existence became public in 1973 during the Watergate scandal, have allowed scholars to explore the decision-making process used in the White House to avert nuclear war in 1962. The tapes support Kennedy's own claim that, as a chief executive, "the last thing I want around here is a mutual admiration society." Following the Bay of Pigs debacle, which Kennedy blamed on inadequate interrogation of the plan, the president encouraged debate among his aides, explaining, "I want all the input, but when they don't give it to me, I've got to dig in their minds." According to Robert Lovett, who had served as secretary of defense under Harry Truman, "President Kennedy had a quality which I have rarely seen in the holder of the chief executive office; that is, a willingness to have the person whose advice he sought answer with complete frankness and, if necessary, bluntness."

The tape recordings from the Cuban missile crisis reveal Kennedy presiding over meetings that lacked a rigid agenda; discussion often shifted rapidly from one issue to another, and participation was nonhierarchical. The president frequently pulled the discussion back to the topic of most immediate concern to him, but older ExComm members accustomed to a more structured approach worried that the seminar-like discussions of an impending nuclear holocaust were dangerously inefficient. Because the crisis ended peacefully, however, Kennedy's method earned respect as a way to air creative alternatives and devise solutions that best integrate different ideas.

What Can Presidential Tapes Tell Us?

The most obvious advantages of presidential tapes are that they are unscripted, candid, and in the moment. They capture as no other document could the actual process President Kennedy employed to elicit an array of strategic options from his very expert, but very scared, advisors. Any effort to label some of Kennedy's debating advisors as warmongering "hawks" and others as conflict-averse "doves" is challenged by the evidence on the tapes, which show that different individuals took different stances at different times. The tapes show plans evolving in response to specific developments and reveal participants revising their positions in the face of new evidence or arguments. They also show the mounting fatigue and anxiety as the days wore on; sentence structure suffered, ExComm members increasingly interrupted one another, and shorthand references to previous discussions were more frequent. These qualities give the tapes an immediacy and authenticity missing from carefully written recollections.

Consider, for example, this set of exchanges on Saturday, October 27, the most stressful day of the crisis, when ExComm members were debating the merits of Khrushchev's two offers: either that the United States pledge not to invade Cuba or that the United States remove missiles from Turkey.

President Kennedy knows he is repeating his position

Before the crisis and in the first two days of the crisis, Robert Kennedy was a staunch advocate for invading Cuba. Has he forgotten the invasion plans he helped design? Has he changed his mind?

What is happening to the free give-and-take of ideas?

PRESIDENT KENNEDY: I think it would be better . . . to get clarification from the Soviet Union of what they're talking about. . . . As I say, you're going to find a lot of people think this [Turkish missile offer] is a rather reasonable position. . . .

ROBERT KENNEDY: . . . I haven't refined this at all—but he's [privately] offered us this arrangement in Cuba—that he will withdraw the bases in Cuba for assurances that we don't intend to invade Cuba. We've always given those assurances. We'd be glad to give them again. . . . The question of the Turkish bases . . . has nothing to do with the security of the Western Hemisphere . . . [but] we will withdraw the bases from Turkey if . . . you withdraw your invasion bases in the Soviet Union. . . .

BUNDY: I think it's too complicated, Bobby.

ROBERT KENNEDY [sharply]: Well, I don't think it is.

PRESIDENT KENNEDY: . . . The first thing that you want to emphasize before you go into details is that the [unclear] 24 hours, that work's going to stop today before we talk about anything. . . . The other thing is not to have the Turks make any statement so that this thing— Khrushchev puts it out, and the next thing the Turks say they won't accept it. . . . Now, how long will it take for us to get in touch with the Turks?

Attorney General Robert Kennedy admits he is just working out the argument in his head

Is the president's brother trying to expand U.S. gains by reducing the number of Soviet bases?

How does this comment convey the president's response to his brother's proposal?

Source: The Kennedy Tapes: Inside the White House during the Cuban Missile Crisis, ed. Philip Zelikow, Timothy Naftali, and Ernest R. May (Cambridge, MA: Belknap Press, 2001).

These unstructured and wide-ranging discussions offer a fascinating case of actual decision making but have a real disadvantage as a source of information: they are disorganized and repetitive. ExComm members might be exploring the air strike option one moment and then asking whether every ship's crew patrolling the quarantine zone included a Russian speaker and then speculating on developments at the United Nations. Sometimes, ExComm members discuss two or three things at once; often, they repeat points that have been made before and will be made again. As a result, it is difficult to track isolated topics through the 700-page written transcript of the missile crisis tapes.

Another disadvantage to these voluminous recordings is that they offer an incomplete record in at least two ways. First, not everything that transpired in the U.S. government during the crisis was taped: important meetings were held outside the Oval Office and the Cabinet Room, President Kennedy did not flip on the tape recorder for every meeting in the Oval Office (although he did record all Cabinet Room meetings), and some discussions end abruptly because the Secret Service agents did not realize that a tape had run out. The tapes are also an incomplete record of the crisis because they cannot tell us what was going on in Moscow or in Havana; to get the Soviet and Cuban sides of the story, we must turn to the notes and recollections of non-American participants.

A final disadvantage of the tapes as a historical source is that the poor quality of the original recordings makes it difficult to decipher exact phrasings. This has caused considerable dispute among historians who use the tapes. Everyone agrees that mistakes are inevitable, even with our modern capacity to digitize and amplify, but there are legitimate disputes over the words spoken in particularly fuzzy sections and equally legitimate disputes over whether isolated transcription problems affect the overall record. In the last crunch of the crisis, for example, did Secretary McNamara suggest "an eye for an eye" or "half an eye for an eye?" Does it matter? Historians are still debating that moment on the tapes as well as others.

In the excerpts from the tapes provided here, you can see the Kennedy decision-making process that still fascinates students of leadership style. You can also engage with two of the main issues that occupied ExComm's attention during the crisis: What course of immediate action will be strong and threatening but not ignite nuclear war? What response to Khrushchev's two offers is most likely to resolve the crisis in a way favorable to the United States and its European allies?

The table on pages 228–29 will help you organize your own thoughts about the tapes presented in this chapter. In addition, the Checklist questions on the facing page will help you actively examine presidential recordings in general.

CHECKLIST: Interrogating Presidential Tapes

- ☐ When, exactly, and under what circumstances were these tapes recorded?
- ☐ Who is responsible for recording the tapes?
- ☐ Whose voices were recorded on the tapes? Did those being recorded know they were being taped?
- ☐ What was the purpose of these tapes? Were the meetings held in order to record the participants, or were the tapes a by-product of meetings held for another purpose?
- ☐ How might the quality of the audio recording affect the tape's usefulness as historical evidence? Could the recording be incomplete or altered?
- ☐ Who was the intended audience for these tape recordings? Who was meant to listen to them and use them?
- ☐ What are the viewpoints of those recorded on the tapes, and what biases can you detect from their statements? What can you learn from other sources about biases that the individuals in the tapes may hold?

Source Analysis Table

The following table allows you to keep track of selected participants' views on the key debate in two early meetings (October 16 and October 18) and two of the last ExComm meetings (October 27). Not all fifteen ExComm members are included in these excerpts.

ExComm Member	October 16 Should U.S. react to Cuban missiles? If so, how?	October 18 Should U.S. conduct air strikes? If not, what alternatives?	October 27 Should U.S. ignore second Khrushchev communication? Why? How?
President John Kennedy			
Robert McNamara, Secretary of Defense			
Dean Rusk, Secretary of State			
McGeorge Bundy, National Security Advisor			
Edwin Martin, Assistant Secretary of State for Inter-American Affairs			
General Maxwell Taylor, Chair, Joint Chiefs of Staff			

ExComm Member	October 16 Should U.S. react to Cuban missiles? If so, how?	October 18 Should U.S. conduct air strikes? If not, what alternatives?	October 27 Should U.S. ignore second Khrushchev communication? Why? How?
Llewellyn "Tommy" Thompson, U.S. Ambassador-at-Large			
Robert F. Kennedy, Attorney General			
George W. Ball, Under Secretary of State			
Paul H. Nitze, Assistant Secretary of Defense for International Security Affairs			
Ted Sorensen, Kennedy aide and speechwriter			

The Source: Presidential Tape Recordings from the Cuban Missile Crisis, 1962

The portions of the ExComm meetings included here have been excerpted from much broader, more lengthy discussions so that you can focus on particular topics and arguments.

1   *Tuesday, October 16, 6:30 p.m.* (Day One of the crisis; second ExComm meeting of the day)

ExComm is trying to determine if the intelligence on the missiles in Cuba is accurate and what action, if any, should be taken. General Marshall "Pat" Carter (deputy director of the CIA) is briefing ExComm on the reconnaissance photos taken of the missile sites the night before.

PRESIDENT KENNEDY: General, how long would you say we had before these, at least to the best of your ability for the ones we now know, will be ready to fire?

GENERAL CARTER: Well, our people estimate that they could be fully operational within two weeks. . . .[1]

ROBERT MCNAMARA [Secretary of Defense]: That wouldn't rule out the possibility that one of them might be operational very much sooner.

[President Kennedy queries Carter on plans for more surveillance flights the next day. —Eds.]

PRESIDENT KENNEDY: There isn't any question in your mind, however, that it is a medium-range [ballistic] missile [MRBM]?

CARTER: No. There's no question in our minds at all. . . .

MCGEORGE BUNDY [National Security Advisor]: How do we really know what these missiles are, and what their range is, Pat? I don't mean to go behind your judgment here, except that there's one thing that would be really catastrophic, [which] would be to make a judgment here on a bad guess as to whether these things are—We mustn't do that. . . .

---

[1] In these excerpts, ellipses (i.e., . . .) tell you that words from the transcript have been deleted in order to condense the material for this chapter. Dashes (i.e.,—) tell you that the speaker simply trailed off. Where the transcribers could not tell what the speaker was saying, you'll see [unclear]. Bracketed text has been added by the editors to help fill in gaps and clarify unfamiliar terminology.

Source: The Kennedy Tapes: Inside the White House during the Cuban Missile Crisis, ed. Philip Zelikow, Timothy Naftali, and Ernest R. May (Cambridge, MA: Belknap Press, 2001).

McNamara: I tried to prove today . . . that these were *not* MRBM's. And I worked long on it. I got our experts out, and I could not find evidence that would support any conclusion *other* than that they are MRBM's. . . .

[Discussion turns to the options for dealing with these new missile installations, including the possibility of a surprise air strike.—Eds.]

Dean Rusk [Secretary of State]: I would not think they would use a nuclear weapon [in response to an air strike by the United States] unless they're prepared to generate a nuclear war. I don't think, I just don't see that possibility . . . we could be just utterly wrong—but we've never really believed that Khrushchev would take on a general nuclear war over Cuba.

Bundy: May I ask a question in that context?

Kennedy: We certainly have been wrong about what he [Khrushchev] is trying to do in Cuba. There isn't any doubt about that. Not many of us thought that he was going to put MRBM's on Cuba. . . .

Bundy: But the question I would like to ask is . . . what is the strategic impact on the position of the United States of MRBM's in Cuba? How gravely does this change the strategic balance?

McNamara: Mac, I asked the Chiefs that this afternoon, in effect. And they said "substantially." My own personal view is: Not at all. . . .

Kennedy: . . . It doesn't make any difference if you get blown up by an ICBM flying from the Soviet Union or one that was 90 miles away. Geography doesn't mean that much. . . .

Edwin Martin [Assistant Secretary of State for Inter-American Affairs]: It's the psychological factor. . . .

Kennedy: What's that again, Ed? What are you saying?

Martin: Well, it's the psychological factor that we have sat back and let them do it to us. That is more important than the direct threat. . . .

Kennedy: Last month I said we weren't going to [allow Soviet missiles in Cuba]. Last month I *should* have said that we don't care. But when I said we're *not* going to [allow it], and then they go ahead and do it, and then we do nothing, then I would think that our risks increase. . . . What difference does it make? They've got enough to blow us up now anyway. I think it's just a question of—After all, this is a political struggle as much as military. Well, so where are we now? . . .

McNamara: Mr. President, we need to do two things, it seems to me. First we need to develop a specific [air] strike plan limited to the missiles and the nuclear storage sites. . . . Since you have indicated some interest in that possibility, we ought to provide you that option. . . . But that's an easy job to do. The second thing we ought to do, it seems to me, as a government, is to consider the consequences. I don't believe we have considered the consequences of any of these actions satisfactorily. And because we haven't considered the consequences, I'm not sure we're taking all the action we ought to take now to minimize those. I don't know quite what kind of a world we live in after we've struck Cuba, and we've started it. . . . How do we stop at that point? I don't know the answer to this. . . .

GENERAL MAXWELL TAYLOR [Chairman of the Joint Chiefs of Staff]: Mr. President, I should say that the Chiefs and the commanders feel so strongly about the dangers inherent in a limited strike that they would prefer taking *no* military action rather than take a limited strike. . . . My inclination is all against the invasion, but nonetheless trying to eliminate as effectively as possible every weapon that can strike the United States. . . .

ROBERT KENNEDY [arguing for invasion]: Assume we go in and knock these [missile] sites out. . . . Where are we six months from now? . . . If you're going to get into it at all . . . we should just get into it and get it over with, and take our losses. And if he wants to get into a war over this. . . .

MCNAMARA: Mr. President, that is why we ought to put on paper the alternative plans and the probable, possible consequences. . . . Even if we disagree, then put in both views. Because the consequences of these actions have not been thought through clearly. The one that the Attorney General just mentioned is illustrative of that. . . .

TAYLOR: Mr. President, I personally would just urge you not to set a schedule . . . until all the intelligence that could be—

KENNEDY: That's right. I just wanted, I thought, we ought to be moving. I don't want to waste any time. . . . I just think we ought to be ready to do something, even if we decide not to do it.

2 | *Thursday, October 18, 11:10 a.m.* (Day Three of the crisis; first ExComm meeting of the day)

ExComm is considering the military's advice to proceed with a massive air strike and debating whether this attack should be a surprise "first strike" or one preceded by a clear warning to Khrushchev.

RUSK: . . . I think the American people will willingly undertake great danger and, if necessary, great suffering, if they have the deep feeling that we've done everything that was reasonably possible to determine whether this trip was necessary . . . [all of which] will militate in favor of a consultation with Khrushchev. . . . There is the possibility, only a possibility, that Khrushchev might realize that he's got to back down on this. We can't be—I have no reason to expect that. This looks like a very serious and major commitment on his part. But at least it will take that point out of the way for the historical record, and just might have in it the seeds of prevention of a great conflict. . . .

LLEWELLYN E. "TOMMY" THOMPSON [U.S. Ambassador-at-Large]: . . . If you do give him [Khrushchev] notice, the thing I would fear the most is a threat to

Turkey and Italy to take action, which would cause us considerable difficulty [unclear] . . .

BUNDY: What is your preference, Tommy?

THOMPSON: My preference is this blockade plan. . . . I think it's highly doubtful the Russians would resist a blockade against military weapons, particularly offensive ones, if that's the way we pitched it to the world.

PRESIDENT KENNEDY: What do you do with the weapons already there?

THOMPSON: Demand they're dismantled, and say that we're going to maintain constant surveillance, and if they are armed, we would then take them out. . . .

PRESIDENT KENNEDY: Of course then he would say: "Well, if you do that, then we will—"

THOMPSON: I think [Khrushchev] would make a lot of threatening language but in very vague terms. . . .

PRESIDENT KENNEDY: Yeah. I think it more likely he would just grab Berlin. . . .

THOMPSON: I think that or, if we just made the first strike, then I think his answer would be, very probably, to take out one of our bases in Turkey, and make it quick too and then say that: "Now I want to talk." I think the whole purpose of this exercise is to build up to talks with you, in which we try to negotiate out the bases. There are a lot of things that point to that. One that struck me very much is, if it's so easy to camouflage these things or to hide them in the woods, why didn't they do it in the first place? They surely expected us to see them at some stage. That, it seems to me would point to the fact their purpose was for preparation of negotiations.

PRESIDENT KENNEDY: The only offer we could make, it seems to me, that would have any sense, according to him, would be the—giving him some out, would be our Turkey missiles. . . .

MCNAMARA: If there is a strike without preliminary discussion with Khrushchev . . . I think we must assume we'll kill several hundred Soviet citizens [working at the missile sites]. Having killed several hundred Soviet citizens, what kind of response does Khrushchev have open to him?

GEORGE W. BALL [Under Secretary of State]: . . . [If we take] a course of action where we strike without warning, that's like Pearl Harbor. It's the kind of conduct that one might expect of the Soviet Union. It is not conduct that one expects of the United States. And I have a feeling that this 24 hours [warning] to Khrushchev is really indispensable.

PRESIDENT KENNEDY: Then if he says, "Well, if you do that, we're going to grab Berlin." The point is, he's probably going to grab Berlin anyway.

BALL: Sure. Go ahead.

PRESIDENT KENNEDY: He's going to take Berlin anyway. . . .

MCNAMARA: Well, when you're talking about taking Berlin, what do you mean exactly? Does he take it with Soviet troops?

PRESIDENT KENNEDY: That's what it would seem to me.

MCNAMARA: . . . We have U.S. troops there. What do they do?

TAYLOR: They fight.

MCNAMARA: They fight. I think that's perfectly clear.

PRESIDENT KENNEDY: And they get overrun.

MCNAMARA: Yes, they get overrun, exactly.

UNIDENTIFIED: Well, you have a direct confrontation.

ROBERT KENNEDY: Then what do you do? . . .

UNIDENTIFIED: It's then general war. Consider the use of—

PRESIDENT KENNEDY: You mean a nuclear exchange?

GENERAL TAYLOR: Guess you have to. . . .

KENNEDY: Now, the question really is what action we take which lessens the chances of a nuclear exchange, which obviously is the final failure. . . . Let's just think. We do the message to Khrushchev and tell him that if work continues, et cetera, et cetera. At the same time, launch the blockade. If the work continues, that we go in and take them out. . . .

3 | *Saturday, October 27, 10:00 a.m.* (Day Twelve of the crisis; first ExComm meeting of the day)

> The naval quarantine of Cuba has been in effect since October 24. ExComm is meeting to discuss Khrushchev's Friday night proposal that the Soviets remove the missiles from Cuba in exchange for a U.S. promise not to invade Cuba. Suddenly, the president is handed a news release that has just come over the wire.

PRESIDENT KENNEDY [reading from the news release]: "President Khrushchev told President Kennedy yesterday he would withdraw offensive weapons from Cuba if the United States withdrew rockets from Turkey."

BUNDY: No he didn't. . . .

TED SORENSEN [Kennedy aide and speechwriter]: He didn't really say that, did he?

PRESIDENT KENNEDY: That may not be—He may be putting out another letter. . . . Pierre, that wasn't the letter we received was it?

PIERRE SALINGER [Press Secretary]: No. I read it pretty carefully. It doesn't read that way to me either. . . .

RUSK: I really think we ought to talk about the political part of this thing. . . . The Turkish thing hasn't been injected into the conversation [at the United Nations], and it wasn't in the letter last night. It thus appears to be something quite new.

MCNAMARA: This is what worries me about the whole deal. If you go through that letter, to a layman it looks to be full of holes. I think my proposal would be to keep—

BUNDY: Keeping the heat on. . . .

MCNAMARA: Keep the heat on. This is why I would recommend the 2 daylight and one night [surveillance] mission. . . .

PRESIDENT KENNEDY: I think what I'd like to do is—I think we ought to go ahead, so it's all right with me. I think we might have one more conversation about [the nighttime mission] however, at about 6:00, just in case during the day we get something more. . . .

In case this [newly reported Khrushchev proposal] *is* an accurate statement, where are we with our conversations with the Turks about the withdrawal of these—

PAUL H. NITZE [Assistant Secretary of Defense for International Security Affairs]: [The Turks] say this is absolutely anathema and is a matter of prestige and politics. . . . I would suggest that what you do is to say that we're prepared only to discuss *Cuba* at this time. After the Cuban thing is settled we can be prepared to discuss anything. . . .

BUNDY: It's very odd, Mr. President. If he's changed his terms from a long letter to you . . . only last night, set in the purely Cuban context . . . there's nothing wrong with our posture in sticking to that line.

PRESIDENT KENNEDY: But let's wait, and let's assume that this is an accurate report of what he's now proposing this morning. There may have been some changes over there.

BUNDY: I still think he's in a difficult position to change it overnight, having sent you a personal communication on the other line.

PRESIDENT KENNEDY: Well, now, let's say he has changed it. This is his latest position.

BUNDY: Well, I would answer back saying that, "I would prefer to deal with your—your interesting proposals of last night."

PRESIDENT KENNEDY: Well now. . . . We're going to be in an unsupportable position on this matter if this becomes his proposal. In the first place, last year we tried to get the missiles out of there because they're not militarily useful, number one. Number two, it's going to be—to any man at the United Nations or any other rational man, it will look like a very fair trade.

NITZE: I don't think so. . . . I think you would get support from the United Nations on the proposition: "Deal with this Cuban thing. We'll talk about other things later." I think everybody else is worried that they'll be included in this great big trade if it goes beyond Cuba. . . .

PRESIDENT KENNEDY: Well, have we gone to the Turkish government before this came out this week? I've talked about it now for a week. Have we had any conversations in Turkey, with the Turks?

RUSK: . . . We've not actually talked to the Turks.

BALL: . . . If we talked to the Turks, I mean, this would be an extremely unsettling business.

PRESIDENT KENNEDY: Well, *this* is unsettling *now*, George, because he's got us in a pretty good spot here. Because most people would regard this as not an unreasonable proposal. I'll just tell you that. In fact, in many ways—

BUNDY: But what *most* people, Mr. President?

PRESIDENT KENNEDY: I think you're going to find it very difficult to explain why we are going to take hostile military action in Cuba, against these sites . . . [when] he's saying: "If you'll get yours out of Turkey, we'll get ours out of Cuba." I think we've got a very touchy point here.

BUNDY: I don't see why we pick that track when he's offered us the other track within the last 24 hours. You think the public one is serious?

PRESIDENT KENNEDY: I think you have to assume this is their new and latest positions, and it's a public one. . . . I think we have to be thinking about what our position is going to be on *this* one, because this is the one that's before us, and before the world.

SORENSEN: As between the two, I think it's clear that practically everyone here would favor the private proposal.

RUSK: We're not being offered a choice. . . .

PRESIDENT KENNEDY: But seriously, there are disadvantages to the private one, which is this guarantee of Cuba. But in any case, this is now his official one. . . .

NITZE: Isn't it possible that they are going on a dual track, one a public track and the other a private track? The private track is related to the Soviets and Cuba, and the public track is one that's in order to confuse the public scene with additional pressures.

PRESIDENT KENNEDY: It's possible.

THOMPSON: I think, personally, that [the public] statement is the one the Soviets take seriously.

NITZE: Fight the Turkish one with the best arguments we can. I'd handle this thing so we can continue on the real track, which is to try to get the missiles out of Cuba pursuant to the private negotiation. . . .

PRESIDENT KENNEDY: I think it would be better . . . to get clarification from the Soviet Union of what they're talking about. . . . As I say, you're going to find a lot of people think this is a rather reasonable position. . . .

ROBERT KENNEDY: . . . I haven't refined this at all—but he's [privately] offered us this arrangement in Cuba—that he will withdraw the bases in Cuba for assurances that we don't intend to invade Cuba. We've always given those assurances. We'd be glad to give them again. . . . The question of the Turkish bases . . . has nothing to do with the security of the Western Hemisphere . . . [but] we will withdraw the bases from Turkey if . . . you withdraw your invasion bases in the Soviet Union. . . .

BUNDY: I think it's too complicated, Bobby.

ROBERT KENNEDY [sharply]: Well, I don't think it is.

PRESIDENT KENNEDY: . . . The first thing that you want to emphasize before you go into details is that the [unclear] 24 hours, that work's going to stop today before we talk about anything. . . . The other thing is not to have the Turks make any statement so that this thing—Khrushchev puts it out, and the next thing the Turks say they won't accept it. . . . Now, how long will it take for us to get in touch with the Turks?

UNIDENTIFIED: I'll find out [unclear], Mr. President. We'll see.

BALL: I think it's going to be awfully hard to get the Turks not to say [that the Soviet offer is unacceptable].

PRESIDENT KENNEDY: No, but we can give them some guidance. . . .

BUNDY: I think it will be very important to say at least that the current threat to peace is not in Turkey; it is in Cuba. There's no pain in saying that, even if you're going to make a trade later on. Then I think we *should* say that the public . . . message is at variance with other proposals which have been put forward within the last 12 hours. . . .

PRESIDENT KENNEDY: Let's not kid ourselves. They've got a very good proposal, which is the reason they made it public—

BUNDY: . . . Last night's message was Khrushchev's. And this [public] one is his own hard-nosed people overruling him. They didn't like what he said to you last night. Nor would I, if I were a Soviet hard-nose. . . .

PRESIDENT KENNEDY: They've got a good product. This one is going to be very tough. . . . If we are forced to take action, this will be, in my opinion, not a blank check, but a pretty good check [for the Soviets] to take action in Berlin on the grounds that we are only unreasonable, emotional people, that this is a reasonable trade, and we ought to take advantage of it. . . .

4 — *Saturday, October 27, 4:00 p.m.* (Day Twelve of the crisis; second ExComm meeting of the day)

In this four-hour meeting, ExComm members are working on the wording of a letter to Khrushchev. They are still debating whether the United States should address only the Soviets' private offer to remove missiles in Cuba in return for a U.S. noninvasion pledge or address the Soviets' public offer to remove missiles in Cuba in return for the U.S. removal of missiles in Turkey.

THOMPSON: Mr. President, if we go on the basis of a trade, which I gather is somewhat in your mind, we end up, it seems to me, with the Soviets still in Cuba with planes and technicians and so on, even though the missiles are out. And that would surely be unacceptable. . . .

PRESIDENT KENNEDY: Yeah, but . . . I'm just thinking about what we're going to have to do in a day or so, which is 500 [air] sorties . . . and possibly an invasion, all because we wouldn't take the missiles out of Turkey. We all know how quickly everybody's courage goes when the blood starts to flow, and that's what's going to happen . . . when we start these things and they grab Berlin. . . . Let's not kid ourselves. . . . Today it sounds great to reject [the Turkey deal], but it's not going to after we do something. . . .

THOMPSON: I don't agree Mr. President. I think there's still a chance that we can get this [noninvasion of Cuba] line going.

PRESIDENT KENNEDY: That he'll back down? . . . [But] this other [Turkish] one, it seems to me, has become their public position, hasn't it?

THOMPSON: This may be just pressure on us. I meant to accept the other . . . noninvasion of Cuba. . . . The important thing for Khrushchev, it seems to me, is to be able to say: "I saved Cuba. I stopped an invasion." And he can get away with that if he wants to, and he's had a go at this Turkey thing, and we'll discuss that later. . . .

SORENSEN: In other words, Mr. President, your position is that once he meets this condition of the halting work and the inoperability, you're then prepared to go ahead on either the specific Cuban track or what we call a general détente [Turkish missile] track?

PRESIDENT KENNEDY: Yeah, now it all comes down [to] . . . whether we have to agree to his position of tying [Cuba to Turkey]. Tommy doesn't think we do. I think that, having made it public, how can he take these missiles out of Cuba if we do nothing about Turkey?

BALL: You give him something else. . . . And the promise that when this is all over there can be a larger [unclear].

PRESIDENT KENNEDY: He's going to want to have that spelled out a little.

THOMPSON: His position, even in the public statement, is that this all started by our threat to Cuba. Now he's [able to say he] removed that threat. . . .

ROBERT KENNEDY: Well, the only thing is, we are proposing here the abandonment [unclear].

PRESIDENT KENNEDY: What? What? What are we proposing?

ROBERT KENNEDY: The abandonment of Cuba.

SORENSEN: No, we're just promising not to invade. . . .

> [They continue to discuss the specific language of the letter to Khrushchev. They are working from a draft letter written by Adlai Stevenson, U.S. ambassador to the United Nations, and a draft they have been developing in the meeting. At this exhausted moment, a younger brother's teasing of his older brother breaks the tension.—Eds.]

BALL: I tell you Mr. President . . . I think if we could take our letter, introduce some of the elements of Adlai's letter in the last part of it, that might do it. I'm not sure how yet.

ROBERT KENNEDY: Why do we bother you [President Kennedy] with it? Why don't you guys work it out?

PRESIDENT KENNEDY: . . . There's no question [of] bothering me. I just think we're going to have to decide which letter to send.

ROBERT KENNEDY: Why don't we try to work it out without you being able to pick it apart.

[*Prolonged laughter*] . . .

PRESIDENT KENNEDY: The one you're going to have to worry about is Adlai, so you might as well work it out with him.

[*Louder laughter*]

SORENSEN: Actually, I think Bobby's formula is a good one. . . .

BUNDY: That's right, Mr. President. I think Bobby's notion of a concrete acceptance on our part of how we read last night's telegram is very important. . . .

TAYLOR: Mr. President, the [Joint Chiefs of Staff] have been in session during the afternoon. . . . The recommendation they give is as follows: That the big [air] strike, Oplan [Operations Plan] 312, be executed no later than Monday morning, the 29th, unless there is irrefutable evidence in the meantime that offensive weapons are being dismantled and rendered inoperable. That the execution of the strike plan be followed by the execution of 316, the invasion plan, 7 days later. . . .

PRESIDENT KENNEDY: Well that's the next place to go. But let's get this letter [sent to Khrushchev].

[The final letter focuses on immediate cessation of missile construction and elimination of the missiles in exchange for a U.S. promise not to invade. It says that discussion of "other armaments" must involve U.S. allies in the North Atlantic Treaty Organization and can be discussed once the Cuban missile crisis is settled. In private, that evening, Attorney General Robert Kennedy assures Soviet ambassador Anatoly Dobrynin that the United States will remove the Jupiter missiles from Turkey in a few months.—Eds.]

Analyzing Presidential Tapes

1. On October 16, what were the arguments for and against a U.S. military reaction to the installation of Cuban missiles?

2. On October 18, what were the arguments for and against an unannounced U.S. air strike? What alternatives did ExComm members propose?

3. Why did ExComm members not want to respond publicly to Khrushchev's second communication?

4. Some say that these tapes reveal an egalitarian decision-making style. Do you find President Kennedy operating as one among equals, as first among equals, or in a more hierarchical relationship with ExComm members? What is your evidence for your position?

5. Based on the transcripts you read, would you argue that ExComm and President Kennedy were making decisions based on rational calculations or on fear and insecurity? What are the benefits and costs of their approach to decision making in this situation?

6. Ask older friends or relatives what they remember about the Cuban missile crisis. Did the family stock up on food? Did they have a bomb shelter? Were there more bomb drills at school? Do they recall President Kennedy's televised address? Do they recall feeling afraid? Write a brief summary of what you learned from your interviews.

The Rest of the Story

In November 2002, Cuban missile crisis participants from the United States, Russia, and Cuba marked the fortieth anniversary of the event with a conference in Havana, Cuba. These government officials gathered for three days, as they had gathered five times before, since 1987, to compare their memories of the event and to test their memories against newly released government documents. The conference proceedings, combined with documents from the time and participants' written recollections, have produced a rich record of the Cuban missile crisis, along with three main conclusions. First and foremost, the world was even closer to a nuclear holocaust in October 1962 than anybody knew at the time. Second, the Kennedy decision-making process, although valuable for its caution, was not as rational as some political scientists once claimed. Third, ExComm's caution was not the sole reason that disaster was averted. Caution on Khrushchev's part was equally important. Although risky, aggressive action by both the U.S. government and the Soviets had caused the crisis, the leaders of both countries recognized the danger in the moment and took bold, sober action to avert it.

We now know that Cuba possessed missiles equipped with nuclear warheads before the crisis began and that those weapons were positioned to fire at the United States in the event of an invasion. We also now know that there were forty-two concealed nuclear warheads in Cuba and that U.S. surveillance had not been able to locate them all, so an air strike would not have eliminated the threat. Finally, we know now, but did not know at the time, that the Cubans possessed tactical nuclear weapons that could be used in battle against an invading U.S. military and that U.S. estimates of 5,000 Soviet military personnel in Cuba was low, by a factor of ten. Khrushchev knew all of this in October 1962 and knew how close the United States was to taking military action. Indeed, unbeknownst to President Kennedy, the U.S. military was engaged in covert action on the ground in Cuba during the last weekend of the crisis.

Was ExComm's response to the information it did possess entirely rational? Was the decision-making process as cool and calculated as some have argued? James G. Blight, of Brown University, says no. Blight, a key organizer of the conferences for missile crisis participants, has concluded from those conference discussions, his own study of the ExComm tape transcripts, and government documents that the nonrational emotion of fear operated during the crisis in a beneficial way. Rather than causing the U.S. government to take rash action, genuine fear for the survival of the planet caused the members of ExComm to exercise more caution than they had in their precrisis calculations about how to maneuver in the Cold War's global chess game. Cold logic could have caused the United States to follow the established military protocol in this situation and quickly attack. Logic could also have led to the conclusion that the Soviet Union would not risk war for Cuba. It was fear of others' irrationality and fear of the known outcome of nuclear war that caused ExComm to take a cautious approach.

Throughout the crisis, President Kennedy knew better than anyone that his decision-making process would be praised only if the human race survived to tell the tale. Afterward, he knew how important it was that Khrushchev had proved equally afraid of nuclear annihilation and was willing, at the crucial moment, to give up the Cuban missiles. If Khrushchev was not willing to defend those missiles, however, why had he sent them to Cuba in the first place? Here, rationality and irrationality apparently cooperated. The Soviet leader rationally wanted to aid Castro, who had solid evidence of U.S. plans to invade; he wanted to use Cuba as a pawn in the Berlin chess game (just as Kennedy had assumed); and he wanted to compensate for the deterrence gap between the Soviets' fifty intercontinental nuclear missiles and America's five hundred comparable missiles by placing forty-two less-expensive medium-range nuclear missiles near the U.S. coastline. Khrushchev's irrational belief that he could secretly install those missiles in Cuba without causing conflict with the United States derived from his reliance on false intelligence reports, his failure to carefully analyze probable U.S. reactions, and his unwillingness to expose his plan to debate among his advisors. Fortunately, the irrationality that ExComm members feared did not carry Khrushchev beyond the brink.

Popular culture treatments of the Cuban missile crisis perpetuate the myth that the United States was an innocent victim in this story, rather than a mature combatant in global Cold War politics, and obscure the importance of the Soviet Union in cutting the public and private deals that averted disaster. Exposure to the complex conversations on the ExComm tape recordings helps correct these errors and reminds us that open communication and decent humility are valuable weapons in a nation's arsenal.

To Find Out More

Primary Sources on the Cuban Missile Crisis

Chang, Laurence, and Peter Kornbluh, eds. *The Cuban Missile Crisis, 1962*. New York: New Press, 1992. Includes some tape transcripts along with dozens of memos, cables, meeting notes, letters, and briefing papers.

"The Cuban Missile Crisis, 1962: A Political Perspective after 40 Years." National Security Archive. http://nsarchive.gwu.edu/nsa/cuba_mis_cri/. Includes recently declassified documents, audio clips from the ExComm meetings, and some of the photographs taken by reconnaissance aircraft of the missile installations in Cuba.

Doyle, William. *Inside the Oval Office: The White House Tapes from FDR to Clinton*. New York: Kodansha America, 1999.

Foreign Relations of the United States 1961–1963. Vol. 11, *Cuban Missile Crisis and Aftermath*. U.S. Department of State. http://history.state.gov/historicaldocuments/frus1961-63v11. Includes declassified documents.

Kennedy, Robert F. *Thirteen Days*. New York: Norton, 1968. A compelling memoir, although tape transcripts call into question a number of the author's claims.

The Presidential Recordings: John F. Kennedy. Vols. 1–3, *The Great Crises*. New York: Norton, 2001. Published with a CD, this work is currently the most complete and accurate transcription of the ExComm tapes.

The World on the Brink: John F. Kennedy and the Cuban Missile Crisis. John F. Kennedy Presidential Library and Museum online exhibit. http://www.jfklibrary.org/Historical+Resources/JFK+in+History/Cuban+Missile+Crisis.htm. Includes three audio clips, JFK's national broadcast address, a slide show, and declassified documents linked to each day of the crisis.

Zelikow, Philip, Timothy Naftali, and Ernest R. May, eds. *The Kennedy Tapes: Inside the White House during the Cuban Missile Crisis*. Cambridge, MA: Belknap Press, 2001. Concise edition of *The Presidential Recordings*.[1]

Secondary Sources on the Cuban Missile Crisis

Blight, James G. *The Shattered Crystal Ball*. Savage, MD: Rowman and Littlefield, 1990.

Blight, James G., Bruce J. Allyn, and David A. Welch. *Cuba on the Brink: Castro, the Missile Crisis, and the Soviet Collapse*. Lanham, MD: Rowman and Littlefield, 2002.

Brenner, James G., Philip Blight, James G. Blight, and Philip Brenner. *Sad and Luminous Days: Cuba's Secret Struggle with the Superpower after the Missile Crisis*. Lanham, MD: Rowman and Littlefield, 2002.

Dobbs, Michael. *One Minute to Midnight: Kennedy, Khrushchev, and Castro on the Brink of Nuclear War*. New York: Knopf, 2008.

Freedman, Lawrence. *Kennedy's Wars: Berlin, Cuba, Laos, and Vietnam*. New York: Oxford University Press, 2000.

Fursenko, Aleksandr, and Timothy Naftali. *"One Hell of a Gamble": Khrushchev, Castro, and Kennedy, 1958–1964*. New York: Norton, 1997.

George, Alice L. *Awaiting Armageddon: How Americans Faced the Cuban Missile Crisis*. Chapel Hill: University of North Carolina Press, 2003.

Reeves, Richard. *President Kennedy: Profile of Power*. New York: Simon and Schuster, 1993.

Stern, Sheldon M. *The Week the World Stood Still: Inside the Secret Cuban Missile Crisis*. Stanford, CA: Stanford University Press, 2005.

Film Documentary Related to the Cuban Missile Crisis

Virtual JFK: Vietnam If Kennedy Had Lived. Koji Masutani, director. New York: New Video Group, 2009. Explores key diplomatic confrontations during the Kennedy administration, including close attention to the Cuban missile crisis.

[1] Both *The Kennedy Tapes* and *The Presidential Recordings* were published under the auspices of the Presidential Recordings Program of the Miller Center of Public Affairs at the University of Virginia. Both correct transcription errors in the 1997 edition of *The Kennedy Tapes: Inside the White House during the Cuban Missile Crisis*, edited by Philip Zelikow and Ernest R. May. For more information on this program, go to http://millercenter.org. You can find audiotapes from the crisis days by entering "Cuban Missile Crisis" into the search engine on this Web site.

CHAPTER 11

Speaking of Equality

The Senate Debate on the Civil Rights Act of 1964

On Sunday, March 8, 1964, Senator Hubert Humphrey, a Minnesota Democrat, appeared on the NBC news program *Meet the Press* to discuss the civil rights bill that had been approved in the House of Representatives and was about to be debated in the Senate. Humphrey took the opportunity to lavish praise on Illinois senator Everett Dirksen, the leader of the Republican minority in the Senate. "He is a man who thinks of his country before he thinks of his party," declared Humphrey. "He is one who understands the legislative process intimately and fully, and I sincerely believe that when Senator Dirksen has to face that moment of decision where his influence and where his leadership will be required in order to give us the votes that are necessary to pass this bill, he will not be found wanting."

Moments after the show ended, President Lyndon B. Johnson was on the phone to Humphrey, who Johnson had designated the "floor manager" for the civil rights bill. "Boy, that was right," the president told the senior senator from Minnesota. "You just keep at that. Don't let those bomb throwers, now, talk you out of seeing Dirksen. You get in there to see Dirksen! You drink with Dirksen! You talk to Dirksen! You listen to Dirksen!"

President Johnson did not micromanage the Senate strategy for passing the Civil Rights Act of 1964, and on those occasions when he tried to impose his ideas, the Senate Democratic leadership did not always go along. On this one point, though, there was agreement all around: partnership between pro–civil rights Democrats and pro–civil rights Republicans was absolutely key to passage of this 1964 legislation, and Dirksen was central to that partnership. "It is not Hubert Humphrey that can pass this bill," Humphrey regularly reminded Dirksen. "Ultimately, it boils down to what you do."

For decades, African Americans and their white allies had been demanding federal legislation to prohibit racial segregation and racial discrimination. The expansion of the civil rights movement in the 1950s had caused Congress to pass two civil rights bills, in 1957 and 1960, which established the U.S. Civil Rights Commission and made mild efforts to protect voting rights. Those bills, however, did nothing about segregation of public spaces or discrimination in employment because Democrats from the nation's southern states blocked all legislation on these matters. Since 1937, Southern senators had prevented eleven civil rights bills from even coming up for a vote in the Senate. This minority of the one hundred senators was able to kill civil rights legislation because of a peculiarity in the customs of the Senate; unlike the House of Representatives, which had rules limiting the length of debate on any bill, the Senate imposes no limit on debate. If a bill reaches the full Senate for a vote, a handful of senators can choose to "filibuster," a term derived from the Spanish word for pirate or hijacker. Senators can hijack a bill by simply continuing the debate, stalling all other Senate business, and exhausting their opponents. According to the rules in place in 1964, the only way to end a filibuster was for two thirds of the Senate—sixty-seven senators—to vote for "cloture," end the filibuster, and thereby bring the bill to a vote.

In 1964, the Senate comprised sixty-seven Democrats and thirty-three Republicans, the majority of whom were in favor of ending state-mandated segregation in the United States. Of the sixty-seven Democrats, however, eighteen were prosegregation, anti–civil rights Southerners, and they would filibuster any civil rights bill. All the rhetorical and political and moral energy of Martin Luther King Jr., Lyndon Johnson, Hubert Humphrey and the entire civil rights movement could not produce a civil rights law if Republican senator Everett Dirksen did not lead at least eighteen Republicans into a partnership with Northern Democrats to defeat the Southern filibuster. With a Democrat in the White House and Democrats dominating both houses of Congress, would the Republicans be willing to assist the opposition party in gaining that sort of victory, or was there political advantage in staying out of the civil rights fight and letting the split Democratic Party simply defeat itself?

Dirksen and a critical number of his Republican colleagues chose partnership with Northern Democrats in 1964. They were responding to a whole set of circumstances that made 1964 different from any previous moment in civil rights history. There was, to begin with, the moral and organizational strength of the grass-roots civil rights movement. Every month black and white citizens alike protested segregation and discrimination in hundreds of public demonstrations, and national polls showed that 62 percent of Americans supported civil rights legislation. President John F. Kennedy had responded with the current, far-reaching bill in a televised speech in June 1963 when, for the first time since Abraham Lincoln, a U.S. president told the citizens that the nation was

> confronted primarily with a moral issue. It is as old as the Scripture and is as clear as the American Constitution. The heart of the question is whether all Americans are to be afforded equal rights and equal opportunities; whether we are going to treat our fellow Americans as we want to be treated.

Figure 11.1 Bus Station in Durham, North Carolina, May 1940 *This photograph depicts everyday life in the segregated South before U.S. entry into World War II. Wherever they went in the segregated region, African Americans faced an unrelenting array of signs designating "white" and "colored" spaces that reminded them that whites drew the lines that most blacks did not dare cross. One wonders if the photographer meant to capture the ironic ad for an article on "Hitler's Love Life." In the coming years, the U.S. fight against Nazi racism would cast segregation as un-American.* Source: Library of Congress, Prints and Photographs Division.

Two months later, in August 1963, Martin Luther King delivered his "I Have a Dream" speech before a quarter of a million people at the march on Washington, and President Kennedy was assassinated that November. Lyndon Johnson consciously built on that momentum in his first address as president to Congress, six days after assuming the office. Speaking in his distinctive, slow southern accent, the former senator from Texas declared that "no memorial oration or eulogy could more eloquently honor President Kennedy's memory than the earliest possible passage of the civil rights bill." To the surprise of many who did not know that Johnson had privately pressured Kennedy to support civil rights, this new, Southern president made it very clear that he expected serious action on civil rights legislation.

In the wake of Johnson's speech, the House of Representatives passed the civil rights bill, known as H.R. 7152, in February 1964, by a vote of 290 to 130. This progress was due to the leadership of Representative Emmanuel Celler of New York, Democratic chair of the Judiciary Committee, and Representative William McCulloch of Ohio, a senior Republican on the Judiciary Committee. It was McCulloch who insisted that the Senate, meaning Dirksen, not make any substantive changes in the strong antisegregation, antidiscrimination provisions of H.R. 7152. Had Dirksen and other Senate Republicans chosen to align with the

Southern Democrats against the civil rights bill in 1964, they would have been defeating the efforts of House Republicans as well as ignoring the mood of the country and their own consciences. Time moves slowly in the Senate, however. It took four months, from February to June, and fifty-seven days of continuous debate, between March 30 and June 19, before the bipartisan team in favor of H.R. 7152 could persuade more than sixty-seven senators to vote for cloture and, for the first time in history, break the Southerners' filibuster and bring a civil rights bill to a vote. Once that happened, victory was assured since only a majority vote was needed to pass the bill. But victory was not assured in February or March or April or May when Humphrey, the bill's floor manager, was fighting ideological and organizational battles to win enough votes for cloture.

Humphrey worked closely and steadily to assuage Dirksen's ideological concerns, knowing that if Dirksen came around, he brought along crucial votes. Dirksen demonstrated his early cooperation with the civil rights bill by the simple act of assigning Republican senator Thomas Kuchel of California to partner with Humphrey on organizing the floor debate. Dirksen himself did not endorse the bill until mid-May, however. In Dirksen, Humphrey faced a conservative, probusiness, small-government Republican who was philosophically in favor of equal rights across race but feared the practical tools that the civil rights bill proposed for achieving those rights. Dirksen did not agree with Georgia senator Richard Russell, who believed that H.R. 7152 was a socialist takeover of private property, but he did worry that the "public accommodations" section required private business owners to serve any legitimate customer and feared that the "equal employment" provisions transferred too much authority from the states to the federal government.

For weeks, Humphrey and his allies worked patiently through the seventy amendments that Dirksen proposed to H.R. 7152, reminding those who opposed negotiating with Dirksen that the bill was dead without his support. At the same time, Humphrey asked President Johnson to meet with Dirksen and make clear that no weakening compromise on public accommodations or employment discrimination was possible; the American people would not stand for it, and McCulloch, Dirksen's colleague in the House, would not stand for it. In the end, Dirksen negotiated some increases in state authority for enforcement of the law, but he conceded that public businesses could not handpick their customers based on personal preference.

While Humphrey and his colleagues were working to convince Dirksen and other undecided senators of the merits of the legislation so that they would vote to end the filibuster, he and Kuchel were also managing the tactical challenges of the filibuster itself. Against President Johnson's wishes, the majority leader, Montana senator Mike Mansfield, decided not to physically exhaust the Southern filibusterers by holding round-the-clock floor sessions. "This is not a circus or a sideshow," declared the reserved senator. "We are not operating a pit with spectators coming into the galleries late at night to see senators of the Republic come out in bedroom slippers without neckties, with their hair uncombed, and pajama tops sticking out of their necks." So, throughout the 1964 civil rights filibuster—the longest in Senate history—Mansfield convened the Senate at 10:00 a.m. and sent the members home by midnight.

As civilized as it was, this scheduling decision did not solve all the organizational challenges that the Senate's peculiar operating procedures created for Senators Humphrey and Kuchel. Consider this trio of rules they had to work around. (1) Unlike the House of Representatives, which adjourned at the end of each workday, the Senate merely called a "recess" at the end of the day; it did not formally adjourn until the matter before it had been settled, so a "legislative day" in the Senate could last for days, weeks, or months. (2) A single senator could deliver only two speeches on a topic in one "legislative day"; but (3) a new "legislative day" could be declared if a member "called a quorum" and there were not fifty-one senators on the floor. "Calling a quorum" simply meant asking that the president of the Senate take attendance to find out if fifty-one senators, the number required to conduct business, were actually present in the Senate chamber.

These rules meant that Southern filibusterers benefited if they could manufacture a new "legislative day." They tried to do this by calling a quorum at random points in the day; that action was the equivalent of calling a time-out while senators not on the floor scurried to get there and be counted in attendance. If the quorum was met because sufficient senators got to the floor within the agreed-upon period of time, the filibusterers at least got a rest. If the quorum was not met, those senators opposing the filibuster looked uncommitted and disorganized, a new "legislative day" began, and every senator had a new allocation of two speeches on the topic, so no single filibusterer was forced to speak for hours and hours.

Hubert Humphrey's triumph in 1964 was due, in part, to the tactics he employed to meet the quorum calls and show that the pro–civil rights senators were disciplined and determined to defeat the filibuster and bring the bill to a vote. This demonstration of strength was crucial for convincing some senators that a vote for cloture in this instance was not a futile or impolitic gesture. So, for example, Humphrey and Kuchel created "platoons" whose members knew to quickly answer quorum calls when they were on duty; they published a daily newsletter that included a "Quorum Scoreboard," reporting that the previous day's quorum calls had been met in, say, nineteen minutes or twenty minutes or a record fifteen minutes. When Humphrey, Dirksen, Mansfield—and their civil rights opponent, Georgia senator Richard Russell—went to a Washington Senators' baseball game together, an announcement over the public-address system said, "Attention please, there has been a quorum call in the United States Senate. All U.S senators are requested to return to the Senate chamber immediately." Only the Georgia senator stayed in his seat.

It took four months of ideological debate, backroom arm-twisting, and tactical maneuvering, but by June 10, Humphrey had gathered more than the sixty-seven votes needed for cloture. Before a packed gallery in the Senate, forty-four Democrats and twenty-seven Republicans, a total of seventy-one senators, invoked cloture. In the subsequent week, Southern Democrats introduced 106 amendments and lost virtually every vote. Finally, on June 19, seventy-three senators (two more than had supported cloture) voted for H.R. 7152. The House quickly approved the slightly amended bill and sent it to the White House, where President Johnson signed it into law on July 2, 1964.

Using the Source: Senate Speeches

The issue of racial segregation in public places was one of the most tangible—and deliberately humiliating—aspects of racial discrimination in the United States between 1900 and 1964. Black protest alone could not end this undemocratic practice; only legislative action on the part of the U.S. Congress could end it nationally. For that reason, Senate speeches about Title II of the Civil Rights Act, which barred racial segregation in all "public accommodations," is a significant feature of civil rights history. Debate over federal prohibition of segregation in private businesses and local municipalities forced senators to make a difficult moral and political choice: Which is more important, private citizens' right to control their businesses and to avoid people they don't like, or private citizens' right to equal access to public services? Which is more vital to the life of the democracy?

All the senators' recorded discussion of this issue occurred on the floor of the Senate; none of it occurred in committee hearings because H.R. 7152 was never vetted in the Senate Judiciary Committee, as it normally would have been. For years, Senator James O. Eastland of Mississippi, chair of the Judiciary Committee, had protected his region's racial segregation by killing all civil rights legislation before it could reach the Senate floor. For that reason, a majority of senators voted to invoke a Senate rule that allowed H.R. 7152 to move directly from the House of Representatives to the floor of the Senate without hearings. You will see comments about that parliamentary maneuver in the speeches included here.

The absence of Senate committee hearings meant that any argument any senator wanted to make for or against the legislation had to be introduced by that senator personally during the filibuster on the Senate floor. A senator could not rely on testimony from constitutional lawyers, civil rights activists, prosegregation citizens, or the hundreds of Protestant, Catholic, and Jewish clergy who lobbied in favor of the Civil Rights Act during the filibuster.

In some filibusters in the past, senators had dragged out debate and exhausted their opponents by simply reading from the newspaper or the telephone book, but that did not occur in this instance. Because there was no committee testimony, because the filibuster was conducted during regular business hours, and because Humphrey chose to mount a serious challenge to the filibuster, senators on both sides delivered relevant, substantive speeches about the bill's faults and virtues, its danger and its necessity. For fifty-seven days, all senators who participated in the debate spoke directly to the racial and constitutional questions raised by H.R. 7152. Deep historic differences divided members of the Senate on this issue, but at this moment in history the American people forced their senators to work together as participants in one of the greatest debates in U.S. history.

What Can Senate Speeches Tell Us?

Like all political speeches, Senate speeches are designed to persuade. Rhetoric is the art of verbal persuasion; the goal is always to convince the listener to agree with the speaker. The great advantage of all political speeches is that no matter how many lies or distortions are uttered, speeches always reveal what the speaker truly believes to be the most persuasive approach to winning support from a particular audience. In the case of Senate speeches, every senator has two audiences to consider: voters back home and colleagues in the Senate.

There is a particular advantage to Senate speeches in the high-profile 1964 civil rights debate: every senator knew that the words uttered in the nation's capital were being quoted in home state newspapers and could directly affect the next election. A speech in this debate had to appeal to popular opinion back home and had to be one the senator could defend on the stump. On this bill, no senator could casually trade a vote in exchange for a new bridge or highway; the stakes were too high. The result is that the speeches in this debate provide us with an unusually reliable record of the public positions senators were willing to take on these questions in 1964. That does not mean that we can assume the speeches necessarily reveal what every senator "really" believed about race. In some cases, the speeches were personally sincere; in other cases, they were not. Insight into every senator's heart is not what these public, political speeches offer us. Instead, they tell us what every senator in 1964 regarded as winning arguments.

Consider, for example, this excerpt from a speech by Senator Sam Ervin, a prosegregation Democrat from North Carolina who opposed H.R. 7152. Ervin's comments were made on March 18, 1964, during the debate over whether to bypass the Judiciary Committee. At this point, opponents like Ervin were trying to convince their colleagues that this bill needed a full committee investigation.

Raises the issue of states' loss of power under this federal legislation

This reference to a jurist from the early twentieth century highlights Ervin's expertise as a constitutional lawyer

This argument is meant to appeal to senators sympathetic to racial justice but worried about overextending federal powers

If Congress enacts the bill it will say that a part of the legislative power is to be vested in the Department of Health, Education, and Welfare, that a part of the legislative power is to be vested in the Housing Administration, and that a part of the legislative power is to be vested in the Department of Commerce. . . . Is that what we wish to do with the legislative power of the United States? . . . Suffice it to say, Mr. President, that the bill undertakes to centralize in the Federal Government powers over the lives of the people, which the Constitution vests in the States or reserves to the people themselves. . . . As Chief Justice White declared, in substance, in *McCray v. United States*, 195 U.S. 27, 55, the safety of our institutions depends upon its strict observance by all those who hold offices created by the Constitution. That statement by Chief Justice White is something which Senators should take to heart.

Source: Senator Sam Ervin, March 18, 1964, H.R. 7152, 88th Cong., 2nd sess., *Congressional Record* 110, pt. 4 (1964), 5610.

Predicts that H.R. 7152 would endow agencies of the executive branch with powers that belong to Congress

Typically, refers to the president of the Senate, who is the vice president of the United States. At this time, however, there was no vice president, so the reference is to the president pro tem of the Senate, the senator presiding "at the time" (pro tempore)

Ervin's focus on the bill's threat to congressional power and its threat to states' powers does not give us dramatic prosegregationist rhetoric. In that sense, a disadvantage of Senate speeches is that they can appear legalistic and indirect. Ervin's legalistic argument does tell us, however, what a smart, politically savvy segregationist regarded as the best rhetorical strategy for winning his argument.

The twenty-seven opponents of H.R. 7152 did not have to convince a majority of their colleagues that racial discrimination was a good thing. They just needed to convince enough colleagues that H.R. 7152 was a bad piece of legislation that should not be brought to a vote; they just needed to prevent a cloture vote. The Senate speeches can tell us what arguments some senators used to discredit H.R. 7152 and what arguments others used to insist that the Senate could not abandon the bill at this historic moment. Because there were no African Americans in the U.S. Senate in 1964, these speeches cannot give us an African American perspective on racial segregation in the United States. The speeches can, however, reveal how privileged white Americans were grappling with the issue of racism in the United States and what principles and priorities they chose to emphasize in the debate over H.R. 7152.

The table on pages 252–53 will help you organize your own thoughts about the speeches presented in this chapter. In addition, the following Checklist questions will help you actively examine congressional speeches in general.

CHECKLIST: Interrogating Congressional Speeches

☐ When and under what circumstances was the speech delivered?

☐ Who delivered the speech? What can be learned about the speaker from other sources?

☐ What was the main argument of the speech? What evidence is used to support that argument?

☐ Who was the audience for the speech? Were there multiple audiences? In what ways was the speech designed to appeal to its audience(s)?

☐ What biases can you detect from the language used in the speech? What do these biases reveal about the time in which the speech was delivered? What do they reveal about the speaker?

Source Analysis Table

The selection of speeches that follow were delivered on the floor of the Senate either during the filibuster or right before, when senators debated the proposal to bypass the Judiciary Committee. Most of the selections focus on the "public accommodations" aspect of H.R. 7152 (often referred to as Title II), which prohibited racial discrimination in privately owned businesses that were open to the general public. Some of the speeches focus on the issue of racial segregation, whereas others focus on the constitutional or legislative issues implicit in the bill. The following table allows you to note and compare the racial and legislative arguments put forth in each speech.

Speaker	Position on H.R. 7152	Arguments Regarding Racial Discrimination	Arguments Regarding This Particular Bill
1. Senator Mike Mansfield			
2. Senator Richard Russell			
3. Senator John Stennis			
4. Senator Hubert Humphrey			
5. Senator Thomas Kuchel			

Speaker	Position on H.R. 7152	Arguments Regarding Racial Discrimination	Arguments Regarding This Particular Bill
6. Senator Sam Ervin			
7. Senator Strom Thurmond			
8. Senator James O. Eastland			
9. Senator Everett Dirksen			
10. Senator Barry Goldwater			

The Source: Speeches from the Senate Debate on the Civil Rights Act of 1964

1 | *Majority Leader Mike Mansfield (D-Montana),* February 17, 1964

Senator Mansfield was the elected leader of the Democratic majority in the Senate. It was his job to shepherd the civil rights bill through the Senate to victory. In his opening address to the Senate on H.R. 7152, he named Senator Hubert Humphrey (D-Minnesota) and Senator Thomas Kuchel (R-California) as the senators with "direct responsibility" for handling the bill, and he defended his decision to procedurally bypass Senator Eastland's Judiciary Committee.

The civil rights bill has now arrived from the House. In the near future, the leadership will propose to the Senate that this measure be placed on the calendar, without referral to committee, and that, subsequently, the Senate as a body proceed to its consideration.

The procedures which the leadership will follow are not usual, but neither are they unprecedented. And the reasons for unusual procedures are too well known to require elaboration.

The substance of the bill has been discussed and debated, not for a week or a month, but for years. President Johnson has prescribed for civil rights legislation an urgency second to none. . . . Mr. President, speaking for myself, let me say at the outset that I should have preferred it had the civil rights issue been resolved before my time as a Senator or had it not come to the floor until afterward. The Senator from Montana has no lust for conflict in connection with this matter. . . . But, Mr. President, great public issues are not subject to our personal timetables; they do not accommodate themselves to our individual preference or convenience. They emerge in their own way in their own time. . . . We hope in vain if we hope that this issue can be put over safely to another tomorrow, to be dealt with by another generation of Senators.

The time is now. The crossroads is here in the Senate. . . . If the Senate were to choose the course of evasion and denial, we would leave this body a less significant and less respected factor in the Government of the United States than it was when we entered it. I implore the Senate, therefore, to consider deeply the consequences of such a course. . . . The Senate's role [ought to be that of] a leading participant, an essential and active participant, in shaping the continuing process

Source: Senator Mike Mansfield, opening address to the Senate, on February 17, 1964, H.R. 7152, 88th Cong., 2nd sess., *Congressional Record* 110, pt. 3 (1964), 2882–84. (Bracketed text within the selections has been added by the editors to help fill in gaps and clarify unfamiliar terminology.)

of equalizing opportunities, that all Americans may share fully in the promise of the Constitution. . . . Senators would be well advised to search, not in the Senate rules book, but in the Golden Rule for the semblance of an adequate answer on this issue.

2   *Senator Richard Russell (D-Georgia),*
February 25, 1964

Senator Russell opposed Senator Mansfield's motion to move H.R. 7152 past the Judiciary Committee. President Kennedy's regard for the Georgia senator as a friend and mentor had been one factor stalling the president's initiative on civil rights legislation.

I can understand the concern with the anticipated legislative situation on the so-called civil rights bill; but I hope, in this time of great pressure, that the Senators will not lose completely their sense of perspective. I hope Senators will look into the parliamentary question that would be involved, as to whether one member of the Senate . . . has the right by a single objection to bypass the committees of the Senate and bring a bill to the calendar. That is the issue that will be before the Senate from a parliamentary standpoint. . . . I hope Senators will not consider this a dilatory action on my part. It is not part of a filibuster. I am seeking only to remind the Senate of its responsibilities and of the desirability of not throwing its rules out the window when a certain type of legislation comes along. We should apply the same rule whether we are enthusiastically in favor of a piece of legislation or whether we are against it.

Source: Senator Richard Russell, February 25, 1964, H.R. 7152, 88th Cong., 2nd sess., *Congressional Record* 110, pt. 3 (1964), 3498.

3   *Senator John Stennis (D-Mississippi),*
March 10, 1964

The Senate did not vote to bypass hearings in the Judiciary Committee until March 26, more than a month after Senator Mansfield's opening remarks. But even before that procedural matter was settled, senators began debating the merits of the bill itself. In this speech, Senator Stennis was arguing against Title II of H.R. 7152, which prohibited racial segregation in public accommodations.

Source: Senator John Stennis, March 10, 1964, H.R. 7152, 88th Cong., 2nd sess., *Congressional Record* 110, pt. 4 (1964), 4818.

I recognize that Congress has great power in many fields but it should not—and I trust the Senate will not—attempt to use this power to wipe out and eradicate inherent and basic individual rights which are clearly beyond the reach of governmental control. Included in this is the right to acquire and own property and to use, or to restrict the use of it, as one sees fit; the right of an independent proprietor to operate his business as he sees fit; and the right of an individual to choose his own associates and customers.

I submit, Mr. President, that the basic constitutional issues involved in Title II of H.R. 7152 are of much greater significance and importance than our personal feelings and convictions about racial matters and the merits of integration.

Let us look at what Title II proposes to do. . . . Under the terms of the bill, the heavy hand of Federal control will extend to private business establishments. . . . The owners and operators of [these] establishments . . . will be divested of their long-recognized right to enjoy and utilize their property as they see fit. . . . These rights are fundamental and they cannot be impaired by the Federal Government under the guise of protecting the real or fancied rights of other individuals.

4   *Senator Hubert Humphrey (D-Minnesota),*
March 30, 1964

Senator Humphrey presented, as Democratic floor leader for H.R. 7152, a sixty-eight-page overview of the entire bill. He spoke for more than three hours in his opening remarks on the legislation for which he had been advocating for fifteen years.

I have been privileged to initiate this debate, and I issue this friendly challenge [to the bill's opponents]: we will join with you in debating the bill; will you join with us in voting on H.R. 7152 after the debate has been concluded? Will you permit the Senate and, in a sense, the Nation, to come to grips with these issues and decide them, one way or another? This is our respectful challenge. I devoutly hope it will be accepted. . . .

Mr. President, I turn now to Title II, one of the most important, significant, and necessary parts of the bill. This title deals with discrimination in places of public accommodation, a practice which vexes and torments our Negro citizens perhaps more than any other of the injustices they encounter. . . . It is difficult for most of us to fully comprehend the monstrous humiliations and inconveniences that racial discrimination imposes on our Negro fellow citizens. . . . He can never count on using a restroom, on getting a decent place to stay, on buying a good meal. These are trivial matters in the life of a white person, but for some 20 million American Negroes, they . . . must draw up travel plans much as

Source: Senator Hubert Humphrey, March 30, 1964, H.R. 7152, 88th Cong., 2nd sess., *Congressional Record* 110, pt. 5 (1964), 6528, 6531–32.

a general advancing across hostile territory. . . . The Committee on Commerce has heard testimony from travel experts that if a Negro family wants to drive from Washington, D.C., to Miami, the average distance between places where it could expect to find sleeping accommodations is 141 miles. . . . What does such a family do if a child gets sick midway between towns where they will be accepted? What if there is no vacancy? . . .

Ironically, the very people who complain most bitterly at the prospect of Federal action are the ones who have made it inevitable. . . . This proposed legislation is here only because too many Americans have refused to permit the American Negro to enjoy all the privileges, duties, responsibilities and guarantees of the Constitution of the United States.

5 | *Senator Thomas Kuchel (R-California),* March 30, 1964

In this speech, Senator Kuchel, as Republican floor leader for H.R. 7152, presented his economic analysis of the bill.

Every American is aware that discrimination in public accommodations has motivated most of the 2,100 demonstrations which occurred in the last half of 1963. Public accommodations legislation is certainly nothing new. . . . Thirty of the fifty States and the District of Columbia have laws of this kind. . . . There can be no question but that segregation in public accommodations obstructs and restricts interstate travel and the sale of related goods and services. The market for national entertainment such as community concerts, athletic competitions and motion pictures is surely restricted by such a situation. National industries seeking new sources of manpower and availability to growing urban markets are inhibited from locating their offices and plants in areas where racial strife is likely to occur.

. . . Logically and unquestionably, any businessman should have the right to refuse to serve the drunk, the disorderly, the disreputable. He still will be free to refuse to serve the drunk, the disorderly and the disreputable. He will still be free to set standards for dress and conduct for persons in his establishment. But, under the mandate of the Constitution, he would have to apply these same standards to all customers and thus could not deny service to anyone solely because of his race, religion, or national origin. What is wrong with that?

Source: Senator Thomas Kuchel, March 30, 1964, H.R. 7152, 88th Cong., 2nd sess., *Congressional Record* 110, pt. 5 (1964), 6556–58.

6   *Senator Sam Ervin (D-North Carolina),* April 11, 1964

In this speech, Senator Ervin argued against Title II of H.R. 7152, the prohibition on racial segregation in public accommodations. Ervin would gain new fame and popularity in 1973 when he chaired the special Senate committee investigating the Watergate burglary. Senate Leader Mike Mansfield appointed him to the chair because Ervin was so strict about the Constitution.

If the bill is passed in its present form, it will signal the destruction of constitutional government in the United States as we have known it. . . . There would be a complete end of the Federal system which divides the powers of government between the Federal government on the national level and the States on the local level. . . . This bill, and especially the public accommodations provision of the bill . . . does not attempt to regulate interstate commerce at all. It undertakes to regulate the use of privately owned property and the rendition of personal services within the borders of the States. It has been acknowledged from the very beginning of the establishment of the Republic to this date by every court that has dealt with the subject that the power to regulate the use of privately owned property and the rendition of personal services within the borders of the States is a power which belongs to the States, not to Congress. . . .

I wish to call the attention of the Senate to the Federal Food, Drug and Cosmetic Act of 1937. This act is based upon the power of Congress, under the interstate commerce clause [of the Constitution], to prohibit commerce in adulterated or deleterious or misbranded drugs, food, and the like. . . . In that respect, that act of Congress is entirely different from the proposals of the pending bill, for the pending bill does not constitute an effort to regulate or exclude the transmission across State lines of anything. Instead, the pending bill constitutes a brazen effort to regulate the use of privately owned property and the rendition of personal services within the borders of a State.

Source: Senator Sam Ervin, April 11, 1964, H.R. 7152, 88th Cong., 2nd sess., *Congressional Record* 110, pt. 6 (1964), 7700, 7703.

7   *Senator Strom Thurmond (D-South Carolina),* April 14, 1964

In this speech, Senator Thurmond argued against Title VII of H.R. 7152, the prohibition against racial or sexual discrimination in employment. Thurmond had led a prosegregation defection from the Democratic Party in 1948 when Senator Humphrey had introduced a civil rights plank into the party

Source: Senator Strom Thurmond, April 14, 1964, H.R. 7152, 88th Cong., 2nd sess., *Congressional Record* 110, pt. 6 (1964), 7903.

platform. That year, Thurmond ran for president on the "Dixiecrat" ticket and won 2 percent of the popular vote.

I agree that a man should be permitted to operate his own private business in the way he wishes. He should also be permitted to hire all white people, if he wishes to do that; or all Chinese, or all Filipinos, or people of any other race; or to hire some of each. He should be permitted to hire people in whatever proportion he wants to hire them. Our Government was founded on the theory of freedom. . . . When we deny a man the right to choose his own employees for his own business, we are denying him a very vital right of freedom. He knows better than anyone else what kind of people he wants to have work with him in his line of work. . . .

I believe most Negroes are happier among their own people. . . . I believe people generally are happier among their own kind. Arabs are probably happier among other groups of Arabs. I think the Jews are happier among their own people. I believe that white people are happier among their own people. It does not mean they dislike anybody. It does not mean that they have prejudice against anybody. Nature made us like that. The white men inhabit Europe; the yellow men, Asia; the red men inhabited America; the black men, Africa. I do not know what God had in mind; but He must have had something in mind. . . .

The southern people have warm affection for the Negro. They understand the Negroes and have tried to help them. . . . The Negroes are much better off as a result of their coming to this country. The progress they have made has not been the result of activities on the part of people who are seeking votes by defending the so-called civil rights legislation. The people who are primarily responsible for the progress of the Negroes are the southern people, because the South is where most of the Negroes have lived until recent years. The South has had this problem. It is familiar with it and has had to bear it. The people of the South have borne up bravely. They have done much for the Negroes.

8   *Senator James O. Eastland (D-Mississippi),* April 18, 1964

It was Senator Eastland's Judiciary Committee that Senator Mansfield navigated past to get the civil rights bill heard on the floor of the Senate. Here Eastland argued against the view that government-mandated segregation was a form of force and intimidation.

Mr. President, H.R. 7152 . . . is, in my judgement, the most monstrous and heinous piece of legislation that has ever been proposed in the entire history of the

Source: Senator James O. Eastland, April 18, 1964, H.R. 7152, 88th Cong., 2nd sess., *Congressional Record* 110, pt. 6 (1964), 8355–56.

U.S. Congress. It is inconceivable that the great mass of American people would not repudiate this bill out of hand if they were advised and understood its exact character and nature. . . . It is my duty to resist enactment. . . . Government by force and intimidation either borders on or crosses the border into anarchy, and today in many areas of the United States we are witnessing . . . a concerted and deliberate effort by certain minority groups to frighten and intimidate elected and appointed representatives of the people into giving them advantages, privileges, jobs and preferment. . . . We are witnessing a character of conduct that is lawless in its nature and designed to teach the children of this country to be disrespectful of authority; to violate the law; to invade the private and personal property of others, and to take by force that which they do not own and have no right to acquire. We can say what we please, but the proposed Civil Rights Act is a direct result of this widespread unlawful agitation, and those who would give it their whole-hearted support are, in a very real sense, unwittingly supporting anarchy itself. Appeasement was the road that led to World War II.

9   *Senator Everett Dirksen (R-Illinois),* June 10, 1964

Although Senator Kuchel was technically in charge of persuading Republicans to support H.R. 7152, Senator Dirksen proved to be the pivotal Republican figure in the debate. For weeks, he negotiated revisions in the bill's federal powers that made it more acceptable to rural Republican voters. In this speech, Dirksen argued, after fifty-seven days of Senate filibuster, to end the debate on H.R. 7152 by voting for cloture. When he spoke these words in his deep, melodious voice, every member of the Senate was present to hear him.

Mr. President, . . . To argue that cloture is unwarranted or unjustified is to assert that in 1917, the Senate adopted a rule which it did not intend to use. . . . It was adopted as an instrument for action when all other efforts failed. . . . There are many good reasons why cloture should be invoked and a good civil rights measure enacted. . . .

First. It is said that on the night he died, Victor Hugo wrote in his diary, substantially this sentiment: "Stronger than all the armies is an idea whose time has come." The time has come for equality of opportunity in sharing in government, in education, and in employment. It will not be stayed or denied. It is here. . . .

Second. Years ago, a professor who thought he had developed an incontrovertible scientific premise submitted it to his faculty associates. Quickly they

Source: Senator Everett Dirksen, June 10, 1964, H.R. 7152, 88th Cong., 2nd sess., *Congressional Record* 110, pt. 10 (1964), 13319–20.

picked it apart. In agony he cried out, "Is nothing eternal?" To this one of his associates replied, "Nothing is eternal except change." . . . America grows. America changes. And on the civil rights issue we must rise with the occasion. . . .

Third. . . . For many years, each political party has given major consideration to a civil rights plank in its platform. . . . Were these promises on civil rights but idle words for vote-getting purposes or were they a covenant meant to be kept? If all this was mere pretense, let us confess the sin of hypocrisy now and vow not to delude the people again. . . .

Fourth. . . . There is another reason why we dare not temporize with the issue which is before us. It is essentially moral in character. It must be resolved. It will not go away. Its time has come. Nor is it the first time in our history that an issue with moral connotations and implications has swept away the resistance, the fulminations, the legalistic speeches, the ardent but dubious arguments, the lamentations and the thought patterns of an earlier generation and pushed forward to fruition. . . .

Today is the one-hundredth anniversary of the nomination of Abraham Lincoln for a second term for the presidency on the Republican ticket. . . . At Gettysburg 101 years ago he spoke of "a new nation, conceived in liberty and dedicated to the proposition that all men are created equal." . . .

That has been the living faith of our party. Do we forsake this article of faith, now that the time for our decision has come?

There is no substitute for a basic ideal. We have a firm duty to use the instrument at hand; namely, the cloture rule, to bring about the enactment of a good civil rights bill.

I appeal to all Senators. We are confronted with a moral issue. Today let us not be found wanting in whatever it takes by way of moral and spiritual substance to face up to the issue and to vote cloture.

10 *Senator Barry Goldwater (R-Arizona),* June 18, 1964

In this speech, Senator Goldwater explained his decision to vote against H.R. 7152 the day before the final vote was taken and the bill passed, 73 to 27. Goldwater led a conservative resurgence within the Republican Party in 1964 and, just a few weeks after delivering this speech, was nominated to run as the Republican candidate for president against the Democrats' President Johnson. He won only 39 percent of the popular vote, doing best in the Southern states.

Mr. President, there have been few, if any, occasions when the searching of my conscience and the reexamination of my views of our constitutional system

Source: Senator Barry Goldwater, June 18, 1964, H.R. 7152, 88th Cong., 2nd sess., *Congressional Record* 110, pt. 11 (1964), 14318–19.

have played a greater part in the determination of my vote than they have on this occasion.

I am unalterably opposed to discrimination or segregation on the basis of race, color, or creed, or on any other basis; not only my words, but more importantly my actions through the years have repeatedly demonstrated the sincerity of my feeling in this regard. . . . .

I realize fully that the Federal Government has a responsibility in the field of civil rights. . . . The two portions of this bill to which I have constantly and consistently voiced objections, and which are of such overriding significance that they are determinative of my vote on the entire measure, are those which would embark the Federal Government on a regulatory course of action with regard to private enterprise in the area of so-called public accommodations and in the area of employment—to be more specific, titles II and VII of the bill. I find no constitutional basis for the exercise of Federal regulatory authority in either of these areas; and I believe the attempted usurpation of such power to be a grave threat to the very essence of our basic system of government; namely, that of a constitutional republic in which 50 sovereign States have reserved to themselves and to the people those powers not specifically granted to the Central or Federal Government. . . .

I repeat again: I am unalterably opposed to discrimination of any sort and I believe . . . some law can help—but not law that embodies features like these, provisions which fly in the face of the Constitution and which require for their effective execution the creation of a police state. . . . If my vote is misconstrued, let it be, and let me suffer its consequences. Just let me be judged by the real concern I have voiced here. . . . My concern is for the entire Nation, for the freedom of all who live in it and for all who will be born into it.

Analyzing Senate Speeches

1. What were the supporters' arguments in favor of H.R. 7152? Did they focus on the evils of race discrimination or on the particular features of this bill?

2. What were the opponents' arguments against H.R. 7152? Did they focus on the virtues of race discrimination or on the problems they saw in this bill?

3. How do you think the rules of the filibuster game shaped the differences in emphasis between supporters and opponents of the bill?

4. What evidence can you locate in the speeches to show that members of the Senate were paying attention to the grass-roots civil rights movement?

5. Do you have any reason to think that opponents or supporters of H.R. 7152 were emphasizing different points in their Senate speeches than they would emphasize in political speeches back home? What other types of sources would you use to test your hypothesis?

6. Numerous opponents of the Civil Rights Act of 1964 stayed in the Senate for many years and enjoyed considerable esteem among their colleagues and the voters. Using online resources, write a one-page profile of one of the following senators: Sam Ervin (D-North Carolina), Herman Talmadge (D-Georgia), Strom Thurmond (D-South Carolina), or Robert Byrd (D-West Virginia). What was notable about your subject's political career after 1964? Alternatively, you may wish to investigate Hubert Humphrey's political career after 1964.

The Rest of the Story

The most immediate and dramatic effect of the Civil Rights Act of 1964 was in the desegregation of public accommodations throughout the South. Many had predicted violent resistance to the integration of restaurants, swimming pools, hotels, and movie theaters, but a survey of fifty-three Southern cities in the summer of 1964 found "widespread compliance" and only scattered cases in which whites assaulted blacks for integrating a public place. Resistance was quelled in December 1964, when the Supreme Court ruled unanimously in *Heart of Atlanta Motel v. United States* that the commerce clause of the Constitution empowered Congress to enact Title II of the 1964 Civil Rights Act, which proscribed racial segregation in public accommodations throughout the nation. Since 1964, no one has mounted a credible legal challenge to Title II; those who desire racial segregation of public places have no credibility in the political debate in the United States.

Race did not simply disappear as a political issue in the United States, however. Just weeks after passage of the 1964 Civil Rights Act, the Republican Party nominated as its presidential candidate Barry Goldwater, one of the very few Republicans in the Senate who had voted against the bill. Goldwater was defeated by President Johnson in one of the biggest landslides in U.S. electoral history, but five of the six states Goldwater won were traditionally segregated Southern states. That election launched a realignment of the Democratic and Republican parties; the once "solid" Democratic South became a region where Republicans like Richard Nixon, Ronald Reagan, and George W. Bush dominated the national political scene in subsequent decades. Although none of these post–Civil Rights Act presidents supported the practice of racial discrimination (and, indeed, Nixon's administration brought more suits against segregated school districts in the South than Johnson's had), they all expressed ideological sympathy for the view that strong federal legislation on matters like race represented an unfortunate intrusion into personal liberty and states' rights.

The Democratic Party maintained a strong presence in the South because the Voting Rights Act, passed just a year after the Civil Rights Act, ended the region's legal disenfranchisement of blacks. Black voter registration in Southern states increased from 2.1 million in 1964 to 3.8 million in 1975, and those black voters tended to vote for Democratic candidates and for a strong federal role in monitoring and regulating racial equity. Indeed, many black candidates were elected to local, state, and national offices after passage of the Voting Rights Act. Before 1964, only twenty-seven blacks had ever served in the House of Representatives, and twenty of them had served during the Reconstruction Era. Since 1964, sixty-seven black men and twenty-seven black women have been elected to the House. By striking contrast, in the years since passage of the Voting Rights Act, only four African Americans have served in the U.S. Senate; three of those four were from the state of Illinois, including Barack Obama.

In addition to the changes in racial practices, the Civil Rights Act wrought another major change in American society. Title VII, dealing with businesses with fifteen or more workers, prohibited discrimination in employment on the basis of race, color, religion, sex, or national origin. The category "sex" was included in the House by a prosegregation congressman who thought his colleagues would defeat the whole bill rather than give women equal employment rights. He miscalculated, however, and women gained the right, alongside men, to file a complaint with the Equal Employment Opportunity Commission if they believed that an employer had based a hiring or promotion decision on applicants' sex, color, religion, or national origin.

Women's inclusion in the Civil Rights Act, although appearing to be a fluke, was actually the result of women's lobbying for employment equity for decades. A year before the Civil Rights Act, Congress passed the first federal legislation ever to deal with sex discrimination, the Equal Pay Act, which prohibited different pay for men and women doing the same job. These legislative gains in regard to women's employment were part of a societal shift in attitudes toward women's capacities and their public role, including their role in politics. Since the 1960s, white women and women of color have made great gains in winning electoral office. Before 1964, only sixty-two women had served in the House of Representatives; all were white and many of them were completing the terms of husbands who had died in office. Since 1964, one hundred and forty-four white women and twenty-four black women have served in the House. Again, though, the Senate has proved more resistant to change. Before 1964, just ten women had served in the Senate. Since 1964, twenty-seven white women and one black woman have served in the Senate, including Muriel Humphrey, who served out the term of her husband, Hubert Humphrey, after he died in 1978. (For more on the topic of women, employment, and the law since 1950, see the Capstone chapter).

The Senate has changed in other ways since 1964. The rule for cloture was changed in 1975; today the rule is that the votes of sixty, not sixty-seven, of the Senate's one hundred members are required for cloture. In 1964, when one political party was dominant in the nation and in Washington, D.C., sixty votes was not as difficult to get as it is in today's closely divided political climate, where presidential races are decided by slim margins and control of the Senate can change with one state's election. Sixty votes are also difficult to achieve in the current climate because of a notable shift in the relationships among U.S. senators. In 1960, Everett Dirksen won the post as Republican minority leader in the Senate precisely because he advocated for cooperation with the Democrats.

Back in 1964, at the height of the civil rights debate, Hubert Humphrey, Everett Dirksen, and Richard Russell could all go to a baseball game together. That sort of collegiality across ideological lines is not common today. Former Indiana senator Evan Bayh grew up in Washington, D.C., in the 1950s and 1960s as the son of Indiana senator Birch Bayh and as a childhood member of the Senate's social community. When Evan Bayh decided not to run for his Senate seat again in 2010, he gave as one of his reasons the dispiriting decline in mutual respect, trust, and friendship in the Senate and argued that a decline in senatorial socializing, as friends and families, had a negative effect on senators' ability to negotiate, cooperate, and compromise.

It would be a mistake to exaggerate the level of harmony in the Senate in 1964. There was as much division then over racial policies and the role of the federal government and as much rhetorical exaggeration of the socialistic, communistic, or racist implications of legislation as there is today. As colleagues, however, senators maintained a level of civility and collegiality that many observers would like to see brought back to Washington, D.C.

To Find Out More

Legislative Sources on the Civil Rights Act of 1964

Civil Rights Act of 1964. http://202.41.85.234:8000/InfoUSA/laws/majorlaw/civilr19.htm. Includes the entire text of the law.

Congressional Record. 88th Cong., 2nd sess., 1964. Vol. 110, pts. 3–11. Includes the 3,000 pages of Senate debate on H.R. 7152, from February 17 to June 19, with an index of important names and terms. For a list of locations that house printed copies of the 1964 *Congressional Record* (online versions are available only for 1994 and later sessions), see the Federal Depository Library Directory, http://catalog.gpo.gov/fdlpdir/. For online versions of the *Congressional Record* from 1994 and later, see the Government Printing Office, Federal Digital System, http://www.gpo.gov/fdsys/browse/collection.action?collectionCode=CREC.

"Legislative History of H.R. 7152." *CongressLink.* Dirksen Congressional Center. http://congresslink.org/civil/cr10.html.

Secondary Sources on the Civil Rights Act of 1964

Hulsey, Byron C. *Everett Dirksen and His Presidents: How a Senate Giant Shaped American Politics.* Lawrence: University Press of Kansas, 2000.

Loevy, Robert D., ed. *The Civil Rights Act of 1964: The Passage of the Law That Ended Racial Segregation.* Albany: State University of New York Press, 1997.

Loevy, Robert D. *To End All Segregation: The Politics of the Passage of the Civil Rights Act of 1964.* Albany: State University of New York Press, 1990.

Mann, Robert. *The Walls of Jericho: Lyndon Johnson, Hubert Humphrey, Richard Russell, and the Struggle for Civil Rights.* New York: Harcourt Brace, 1996.

Schapsmeier, Edward L., and Frederick H. Schapsmeier. *Dirksen of Illinois: Senatorial Statesman.* Urbana: University of Illinois Press, 1985.

Solberg, Carl. *Hubert Humphrey: A Biography*. New York: Norton, 1984.

Thurber, Timothy N. *The Politics of Equality: Hubert Humphrey and the African American Freedom Struggle*. New York: Columbia University Press, 1999.

Whalen, Charles, and Barbara Whalen. *The Longest Debate: A Legislative History of the 1964 Civil Rights Act*. Washington, DC: Seven Locks Press, 1985.

Selected Sources on the Civil Rights Movement

Branch, Taylor. *Pillar of Fire: America in the King Years, 1963–65*. New York: Simon and Schuster, 1998.

Civil Rights Documentation Project. University of Southern Mississippi. http://www.usm.edu/crdp. Includes dozens of oral histories by Mississippi residents who were active in the civil rights movement.

Garrow, David. *Bearing the Cross: Martin Luther King, Jr., and the Southern Christian Leadership Conference*. New York: William Morrow, 1986.

CHAPTER 12

Introducing the Seventies

Historians Explore Economic Decline

CBS was so nervous about offending viewers with its new series, *All in the Family*, that it launched the January 12, 1971, premiere with a warning label, which ran before the opening credits: the show's purpose, it said, was "to throw a humorous spotlight on our frailties, prejudices and concerns. By making them a source of laughter, we hope to show—in a mature fashion—just how absurd they are." Earlier that day, a *New York Times* article declared the effort a failure. It was simply not funny, wrote the sophisticated reviewer, to watch Archie Bunker, the show's working-class white antihero, spew racist epithets and sexist platitudes at his long-suffering wife Edith, his short-skirted, hip-but-not-hippie daughter Gloria, and her left-leaning student husband Mike. That opening night, CBS hired extra phone operators to take the angry calls it anticipated, but few came in. Instead, Americans across the nation's conflicted political and cultural spectrum embraced the Bunkers' weekly debate about politics, the economy, religion, sex, race, and the "American way of life," making it one of the most beloved television series in U.S. history.

At just the moment when the sixties' upheavals in race, class, and gender were spreading from college campuses and city streets into the living rooms and bedrooms of ordinary American families, *All in the Family* gave its audience a humorous and surprisingly sympathetic lens for watching the personal effects of social change. Viewers could laugh at Archie's illogical bigotry but could also glimpse his sadness and confusion over losing his place of white, male privilege. Many of the show's most loyal viewers were men like Archie who felt more represented by his character than by anyone on the political scene. At the same time, middle-aged wives who, like Edith, had been told to "stifle yourself" just once too often, could root for her, and the liberal children of such parents

Figure 12.1 All in the Family In this photo, taken during the filming of a segment of All in the Family, *Archie Bunker is delivering one of his characteristic rants about all that is wrong in 1970s America to his daughter Gloria and her husband Michael. Edith Bunker is quietly watching; if she spoke up to express her opinion, Archie would order her to "stifle yourself." Despite the cultural conflicts at the heart of this show, it was popular because the characters expressed views that were common in the United States at the time but were much funnier than most of us are in our living rooms.* Source: © Bettmann/CORBIS.

could nod in agreement with Gloria and Mike while, perhaps, grasping why their fathers disdained egalitarianism and their mothers fretted over liberated morals.

When *All in the Family* first aired in 1971, the nation's Archie Bunkers were still enjoying the prosperity of the 1950s and 1960s. Their anger was directed at anti–Vietnam War protestors, Black Power advocates, and sexual liberationists, a trio of critics who sneered at the picket-fenced safety that World War II veterans like Archie had patriotically built and defended. President Richard Nixon was their champion with a 60 percent approval rating, despite the continuation of the unpopular Vietnam War, and men like Archie Bunker applauded the New York City construction workers who violently attacked antiwar protestors the previous spring. They did not protest President Nixon's creation of the Environmental Protection Agency in 1970 or the first Earth Day since Republican voters were not (yet) squarely antigovernment and workers like Archie did not (yet) feel economically threatened. But members of the older, white, working class in 1971 did chafe at court orders to desegregate public schools via mandatory busing of students; did worry when younger workers adopted the dress styles, long hair, drug use, and sexual mores emblematic of anti-Establishment youth; and did resist the message of the women's liberation movement, which reached its tipping point in 1971, becoming a mass movement that would change the Ediths and Glorias of the nation as much as it changed more privileged women.

By 1976, when *All in the Family* was ending an unprecedented five-year run as the top-rated television show in the United States, its viewers had endured the two-year trauma of the Watergate scandal and Nixon's ignominious resignation as president along with the nation's humiliating withdrawal from its ten-year war in Vietnam. Further, Americans had faced a stunning series of blows to the economy, including the 1973 oil embargo that occurred when the Organization of Oil Exporting Countries (OPEC) reacted to U.S. support for Israel in the Yom Kippur War with Egypt and Syria by withholding oil shipments on which the U.S. economy had become dependent. The resulting increase in the price of oil from $3 per barrel in 1970 to $31 per barrel in 1980 was one of the main causes of "stagflation"—a peculiar combination of rising unemployment and rising prices—which proved impervious to both Republicans' and Democrats' frantic efforts to use the regulatory tools of government that had maintained stable prosperity in the three decades following World War II. So in 1976, when Americans were supposed to be celebrating the nation's bicentennial, two-thirds of those eligible did not even vote. Fed up, millions of Americans, from liberal to conservative, applauded a moment in the film *Network* when the hero roused his television audience to open their windows and scream, "I'm mad as hell and I'm not going to take it anymore."

For the first time since the Great Depression, American productivity declined, the United States imported more goods than it exported, businesses moved their manufacturing overseas even as the real income of American workers dropped by 2 percent every year from 1973 through 1981, and personal debt tripled. Every week at the checkout counter, women like Edith Bunker faced the effect of 11 percent inflation on the price of their entire shopping list. Just at the moment when nonwhite men and all women were demanding an equal place in the workforce, the opportunities in that workforce were shrinking. Meanwhile, environmentalists were blaming industrial growth—the one-time ticket to prosperity—for causing pollution, and rebellious women were itemizing male leaders' manifest failures in war, government, and the economy. White men had not simply lost their cultural privilege; they had lost their security, pride, and confidence. Who was to blame? The blacks? The Arabs? The corporations? The feminists? Themselves? It was a hard time to be Archie Bunker.

All in the Family went off the air in the spring of 1979, still in the top ten of television ratings. That summer, President Jimmy Carter gave a televised address on a subject, he said, "even more serious than energy or inflation." In what he admitted was "not a message of happiness or reassurance," Carter delivered what he saw as "the truth and . . . a warning." Americans, he reported, at the end of the seventies, were suffering "a crisis of confidence . . . that strikes at the very heart and soul and spirit of our national will . . . threatening to destroy the social and political fabric of America."

Is it really possible then that commentators in the 1980s and 1990s described the 1970s as the decade in which nothing happened? Historian Peter Carroll tried to counter that claim as early as 1982 with his book *It Seemed Like Nothing Happened,* but the seventies' reputation as the dull decade persisted, largely because its chronological neighbors—the 1960s and the 1980s—captured the limelight as the decades of dramatic social protest, sweeping social reforms, and economic prosperity. We can look at the historiography—the body of historical writings—on the seventies, however, and see a change starting in 2000, when historians began to publish books with titles like *How We Got Here: The 70's: The Decade That Brought You Modern Life (For Better or Worse); The Seventies: The Great Shift in American Culture, Society, and Politics; Something Happened; Decade of Nightmares;* and *Pivotal Decade.* Just the titles alone tell us that, thirty years after the start of the seventies, historians gained sufficient perspective to recognize the profile of a distinctive and decisive era.

That is not to say that historians of the 1970s claim that all Americans woke up on January 1, 1970, thinking and acting differently than they had on December 31, 1969. Rather, historians of the seventies, like historians of other decades, aim to identify clusters of change over time that constitute actual trends and genuine patterns. They then draw on our common sense of chronological markers, such as decades, to name the era they have defined as different from what came before and what came after. This makes for plenty of historiographical debate over precisely when the era of the seventies began, but the current consensus is that the seventies began in 1973, when the United States formally ended its role in the Vietnam War, when the Watergate scandal moved to the center of national attention, and when the oil crisis signaled the start of a prolonged recession; in short, the era began when the wealth-driven optimism of the sixties gave way to political disillusionment and economic contraction. Historians trace that trend with news stories and economic indicators as well as polls showing that 80 percent of those surveyed in 1966 trusted the government to do the right thing, but by 1981, only 25 percent of respondents had such trust.

All in the Family reflected key ways in which the seventies were notably different from the sixties. It was the era in which the cultural revolution we associate with the sixties actually spread into the mainstream culture; what began as underground experiments with sex, drugs, hair, clothing, music, and film in the sixties became part of everyday commerce and family experience in the seventies. It was also in the 1970s that sixties' demands for individual rights and equal treatment across race, ethnicity, and gender were enacted in social policies like school busing, affirmative action, and equal access to school athletics. Ironically, however, the sixties' demands for egalitarian opportunity presumed that U.S. wealth would continue to expand as it had since World War II, that the economic pie would continue to grow, and that women and nonwhite men could be given a more fair slice without depriving white men. As it turned out, the economic pie started to shrink in the seventies, and many white men blamed that outcome on the encroachment of women and non-white men. Archie Bunker began the seventies already angry about challenges to white male dominance and American honor. When that honor was tarnished by events, when industrial jobs started to disappear and white men's real incomes declined, the target of Archie's anger was already scripted—and it would not have been nearly as entertaining to watch him rant about deindustrialization or globalization as it was to hear his rage at anyone who did not look or think like him. So Americans fought the cultural wars in the seventies, at home and on television, while under their boots the shared economic ground crumbled.

Using the Source: Introductions to Books on History

In all other chapters of this book, you are examining different sorts of primary sources. As you now know, these are the original documents that writers of history draw on to reconstruct the past and to develop their own arguments about the meaning of the primary sources. Historians typically publish their interpretations of primary sources in books or in articles for historical journals. Because these published works are one step removed from the primary material, we call them secondary sources.

In this chapter, we will examine one very particular aspect of secondary sources: the introduction to book-length works of history. We do this because an author's introduction to her book is, quite literally, the place where she introduces herself, her description of her topic, her interest in the topic, her reasons for limiting the scope of her study in this way or that, the types of primary sources she used, and, most important, her argument. Unfortunately, readers of secondary works often make the big mistake of skipping the introduction to a book, thinking it is just a few pages of polite fluff. But right here, in this introductory paragraph, we make the argument that you should never skip the introduction to a book. Now that you have been introduced to that argument, you are positioned to decide whether the following paragraphs persuade you that ours is a sound argument. If you had not read this introduction, how would you know where we are taking you or why?

Just as there are techniques for reading primary sources—such as noting their origin, purpose, and standpoint—so, too, there are techniques for reading secondary sources. These techniques aid us in grasping the three things that historians offer: topic, information, and interpretation. (We might also refer to these as "subject" or "focus"; "evidence" or "data"; and "argument" or "thesis.") Mastery of techniques for reading secondary sources helps us to understand how the author's subject has logically shaped the choice of information presented and to assess how well the evidence does—or does not—support the author's argument. When we realize that reading involves more than taking in one word after another, that reading a scholarly book involves seeing it as a whole before diving into the particular chapters, then we become readers who can track an author's moves on the page and see the significance of those moves for the author's focus and thesis.

What Can Introductions Tell Us?

Reading a book's introduction is an essential technique for seeing a book as a whole. If the book is a map, the introduction pinpoints the destination. This is useful when we are simply looking for an interesting book to read; it is especially helpful when we are doing research on a historical topic and want to find out what other historians have discovered and argued about this topic.

Let's say you are writing a paper on popular music in the 1970s. One of the introductions you will read in this chapter is from Jefferson Cowie's book *Stayin' Alive*. You might grab this book off the shelf, knowing that "Stayin' Alive" was a hugely popular Bee Gees song from the 1977 film *Saturday Night Fever*. The subtitle of the book — *The 1970s and the Last Days of the Working Class* — might raise doubts about the book's direct relevance to your topic, but you could efficiently and confidently confirm those doubts by reading the introduction and finding out that Cowie's book is about the working class, not about popular music, in the seventies. But what if his introduction is so interesting to you that you decide to narrow your research focus to the impact of workers' economic problems on seventies music? You turn to Judith Stein's *Pivotal Decade: How the United States Traded Factories for Finance in the Seventies*, whose introduction is also included in this chapter. On the first page you encounter Stein's view of secondary histories that focus on the popular culture of the seventies:

Stein concedes the value of popular culture but, again, reveals her skepticism about the validity of claiming a meaningful pattern in such individualized, variegated data

By the bottom of the first page of Stein's introduction, she has told you that her book will not be offering you information or arguments about popular music in the 1970s

Some written accounts of the decade descend to [kitsch], whereas others contain interesting insights on sex, music, films, and drugs. But what do they add up to? Philip Jenkins portrayed a liberal culture that assimilated the social movements of the 1960s, while Bruce Schulman concluded that American culture became more southern, a synonym for conservative. Still, Schulman's depiction of ethnic, sexual, race, and New Age ideas and movements made American culture seem more sprawling than constricting. . . . Country music was more ambiguous than Schulman made it out to be. Was Loretta Lynn's "Coal Miner's Daughter" a conservative anthem, a reassertion of "southern chauvinism," as he claims? Whatever we conclude, it is risky to deduce politics from popular culture.

This derogatory term, referring to trivial, sloppy, superficial efforts, alerts us immediately to Stein's skepticism about "history through popular culture"

Stein is arguing that artistic expressions are, by definition, open to different interpretations and so are not a stable data set for historical analysis

Source: Judith Stein, *Pivotal Decade: How the United States Traded Factories for Finance in the Seventies* (New Haven, CT: Yale University Press, 2010), ix.

You might decide to put Stein's book back on the shelf since she will not be discussing popular culture in the seventies or even using popular culture sources. On the other hand, you might decide to read the rest of her introduction to find out whether her focus on economic issues is relevant to your understanding workers' struggles in the seventies. Either way, Stein has introduced you to a criticism of historical generalizations based on popular culture, and that gives you something more to consider as you pursue your research topic.

As the excerpt from Stein demonstrates, book introductions are a great place to go when you want to learn the names of other historians who work on a particular topic and want to get a sense of the debates among historians on that topic. Introductions to books on history (and the citations that accompany them) can quickly orient you to the historiography of a topic; they literally introduce you to different approaches that have been taken to a topic and different interpretations that have been put forth. In *They Say, I Say: The Moves That Matter in Academic Writing*, Gerald Graff and Cathy Birkenstein Graff explain that an author makes a particular "move" on the page when positioning himself within a field of study: he pivots from talking about what "they say" to defining what "I say." That informative pivot often occurs in a book's introduction.

The philosopher Kenneth Burke compares reading an academic study on an unfamiliar topic to being a stranger at a party where the other guests are engaged in intense conversations and you are trying to figure out who is friends with who, who disagrees with who, where your host (or book author) fits into this intellectual network, and what issues animate all these conversations. A historical work's introduction is often the site of that party. It is there that the author/ host talks about what others have said on his topic and then announces where his book differs from others and agrees with others. Just as you cannot trust everything you hear at a party, you cannot trust every historian's characterization of other historians' arguments; academic lines can be drawn in highly partisan ways. But even a biased introduction, dripping with praise for some and venom for others, can tell you a great deal about the author and alert you to hot-button issues in the field.

And then there are those books whose introductions do not make the explicit "they say/I say" move on the page but instead discuss historiography in the citations. Cowie's introduction to *Stayin' Alive* is an example of such a book. At over eighteen pages, Cowie's introduction is thirteen pages longer than Stein's. While Stein offers a brisk defense of her focus on powerful decision makers and the policies they set in the seventies, dismissing others' focus on "cultural conflicts" as "beside the point," Cowie slowly unwinds a narrative about the political (and cultural) evolution of one auto worker, Dewey Burton. This is Cowie's way of showing his reader that his book will consider cultural conflicts alongside economics and politics in arguing (like Stein) that the American working class was abandoned by the Democratic Party, the Republican Party, and labor unions themselves in the 1970s. Rather than discuss other historians' work on the pages of his introduction, Cowie chooses to draw his reader into Dewey Burton's story and let the reader decide about reading the historiography in the thirty-three endnotes that accompany his introduction.

Introductions not only differ in style and length, they even differ in what they are called. Stein's introduction, for example, is called the "preface"; her book has no "introduction." Cowie has no preface, and he calls his narrative on Dewey Burton his "introduction." Bruce Schulman includes both a preface and an introduction in his book, *The Seventies: The Great Shift in American Culture, Society, and Politics*. Schulman's preface offers his argument and positions his book in relation to other works on the seventies; his introduction gives the reader a twenty-page review of what he calls "The Sixties and the Postwar Legacy." The dictionary tells us that *preface, foreword,* and *introduction* are synonyms for that part of a book that explains its purpose, but a book's foreword is usually written by someone other than the author while prefaces and introductions are always written by the author. Distinctions about terminology are informative, but they do not change the basic point: before you start reading the content chapters of any history book, read the introductory material. Get to know the author, learn what her interests are, figure out where she positions herself in relation to others, get a sense of the book's style and contents, locate the book's thesis. In short, see the book as a whole to prepare yourself for active, inquisitive engagement with the book's topic, information, and interpretation. Reading the introduction will make you a confident player at the scholarly party rather than an awkward observer.

To assist in reading Judith Stein's introduction to *Pivotal Decade* and an excerpt from Jefferson Cowie's *Stayin' Alive*, see the Source Analysis Table on page 276. For guidelines on assessing book introductions in general, look over the following Checklist of questions.

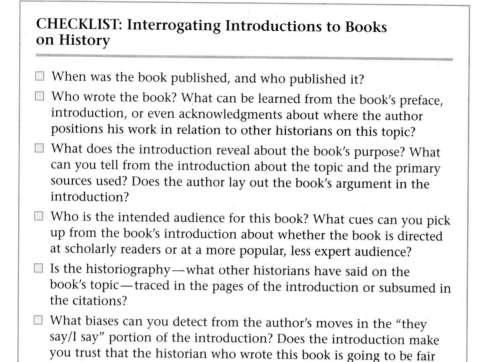

CHECKLIST: Interrogating Introductions to Books on History

☐ When was the book published, and who published it?

☐ Who wrote the book? What can be learned from the book's preface, introduction, or even acknowledgments about where the author positions his work in relation to other historians on this topic?

☐ What does the introduction reveal about the book's purpose? What can you tell from the introduction about the topic and the primary sources used? Does the author lay out the book's argument in the introduction?

☐ Who is the intended audience for this book? What cues can you pick up from the book's introduction about whether the book is directed at scholarly readers or at a more popular, less expert audience?

☐ Is the historiography—what other historians have said on the book's topic—traced in the pages of the introduction or subsumed in the citations?

☐ What biases can you detect from the author's moves in the "they say/I say" portion of the introduction? Does the introduction make you trust that the historian who wrote this book is going to be fair and open-minded in presenting her own and others' research?

Source Analysis Table

In the "Source" section of this chapter, you will find most of the preface to Judith Stein's 2010 book, *Pivotal Decade: How the United States Traded Factories for Finance in the Seventies*, followed by an excerpted version of Jefferson Cowie's introduction to his 2010 book, *Stayin' Alive: The 1970s and the Last Days of the Working Class*. The excerpt of Cowie's introduction omits some discussion of Dewey Burton's life and political events in the seventies; it does not omit any aspect of Cowie's overall argument. Space limitations prevent inclusion of all fifteen citations in Stein's preface or all thirty-three of the citations in Cowie's introduction. In each case, sample citations are included to show how authors use the citations section to supply basic information on sources, to introduce readers to related publications, and to align with and differ from other scholars in the field.

You can use the following Source Analysis Table to compare these two books' contents and arguments and to compare what the authors reveal in their introductions about their approach to their topics.

	Judith Stein *Pivotal Decade*	Jefferson Cowie *Stayin' Alive*
Book's topic		
Book's sources		
Book's overall argument		
Author's areas of agreement with other authors		
Author's areas of disagreement with other authors		
Signs of the author's political ideology		
Signs the author's political ideology does or does not dictate findings		

The Source: Introductions to Books on the Seventies

1 | *Preface to* Pivotal Decade: How the United States Traded Factories for Finance in the Seventies
by Judith Stein

Ask people old enough to recollect the 1970s and they will amuse you with tales of the flamboyant culture of garish clothes, big hair, and disco. Some will recall the therapeutic culture of TM and Esalen. A few may recount the experience of being "born again." Many will remember the political cynicism spawned by the Watergate scandal. And a number will evoke the social strife over race and gender. Writers have followed popular recollections. Some written accounts of the decade descend to kitsch, whereas others contain interesting insights on sex, music, films, and drugs.[1] But what do they add up to? Philip Jenkins portrayed a liberal culture that assimilated the social movements of the 1960s, while Bruce Schulman concluded that American culture became more southern, a synonym for conservative. Still, Schulman's depiction of ethnic, sexual, race, and New Age ideas and movements made American culture seem more sprawling than constricting. The film and music of the 1970's revealed profound critiques of authority—notably Martin Scorcese's *Taxi Driver* (1976) and the Talking Heads. Country music was more ambiguous than Schulman made it out to be. Was Loretta Lynn's "Coal Miner's Daughter" a conservative anthem, a reassertion of "southern chauvinism," as he claims?[2] Whatever we conclude, it is risky to deduce politics from popular culture.

Historians often psychologize the decade's conflicts. One book is called *Nervous Breakdown,* another, *Decade of Nightmares.* A collection of essays, *America in the 1970s,* declared, "It was during the 1970s in the backlash of political and economic crisis that Americans dealt with a productive uncertainty about the meanings of happiness, success, patriotism, and national identity."[3] . . .

Other scholars trace rightward trends, culminating in the election of conservative Ronald Reagan as president in 1980. Since 1992, when Michael Kazin enjoined historians to write more about conservatism, the profession has answered

---

[1] Mark Lytle, "Review, Berkowitz, *Something Happened," The Historian* 69 (2007), 522.

[2] Bruce J. Schulman, *The Seventies: The Great Shift in American Culture, Society, and Politics* (New York: Free Press, 2001).

[3] Beth Bailey and David Farber, eds., *America in the 1970s* (Lawrence: University Press of Kansas, 2004), 2.

the call.[4] Because most historians today are closer to the left than to the right, many treat their subjects the way anthropologists do theirs. A few argue that post–World War II political culture was never as liberal as assumed. They write about conservative communities or conservatives in general, a new Right, leading up to the 1964 presidential campaign of Barry Goldwater.[5] But the key fact about Goldwater was not that he presaged a future but that he lost massively in 1964. If Goldwaterites were the only people who voted for Ronald Reagan in 1980, he would have lost. There is a thread that links conservative ideas. But the significant question is why the ideology convinced majorities in some eras and not in others.

Writers who locate the growth of conservatism in the 1970s attribute it to backlash politics and conservatives' "concerted institutional and grassroots struggle to reshape the rhetoric and policies of America."[6] In the first, "working-class whites and corporate CEO's, once adversaries at the bargaining table, found common ideological ground in their shared hostility to expanding government intervention."[7] White workers abandoned liberalism because they identified it with African Americans. In the second, conservatives massively organized with political action committees, radio talk shows, think tanks, and clever communications networks to dislodge postwar liberalism.[8] Each makes Keynesian liberalism and the Democratic Party victims of right wing ideological and institutional assault. They assume that [Keynesian] ideology and the [Democratic Party] were up to the task of confronting the nation's challenges and that the rise of conservatism had nothing to do with their failures. These . . . stories of rising conservatism do not intersect with any political or economic event.

I start with different assumptions. I began this book after I learned that the 1970s was the only decade other than the 1930s wherein Americans ended up poorer than they began.[9] As the *Economist* recently observed, "Other than sarto-

---

[4] Michael Kazin, "The Grass-Roots Right: New Histories of U.S. Conservatism in the Twentieth Century," *American Historical Review* 97 (Feb. 1992), 136–55.

[5] Lisa McGurr, *Suburban Warriors: The Origins of the New American Right* (Princeton, NJ: Princeton University Press, 2001); Rick Perlstein, *Before the Storm: Barry Goldwater and the Unmaking of the American Consensus* (New York: Hill and Wang, 2001).

[6] Bruce J. Schulman and Julian E. Zelizer, eds., *Rightward Bound: Making America Conservative in the 1970s* (Cambridge, Mass.: Harvard University Press, 2008), 3–4

[7] Thomas B. Edsall and Mary E. Edsall, *Chain Reaction: The Impact of Race, Rights, and Taxes on American Politics* (New York: Norton, 1992), 154. In contrast, Thomas Edsall's earlier *New Politics of Inequality* (New York: Norton, 1984) attributed the New Politics to business mobilization and labor weakness, which had nothing to do with race. For a critique of Edsall and Edsall, see Larry M. Bartels, *Unequal Democracy: The Political Economy of the New Gilded Age* (Princeton, NJ: Princeton University Press, 2008), 64–97.

[8] Kim Phillips-Fein, *Invisible Hands: The Making of the Conservative Movement from the New Deal to Reagan* (New York: Norton, 2009).

[9] Earnings for nonagricultural workers declined over the 1970s by nearly 13 percent; median family income was level largely because more wives entered the labor force.

rially, the 70s weren't funny."[10] The decade featured the deepest recession since World War II, growing and permanent trade deficits, anemic productivity, rising oil prices, and high unemployment and inflation. The economy is the foreground. But every economy is shaped by politics. So the government response to these challenges was as important as the changes themselves. Could the practices and ideas of postwar liberalism meet the new circumstances?

Postwar U.S. liberalism, created by the New Deal, was rooted in the notion that high wages and regulated capital created and sustained U.S. prosperity. During the Age of Compression, 1947–73, income and wealth were mildly redistributed, even as economic growth soared. At the same time, the nation's leaders cemented Cold War alliances with foreign access to the U.S. market. In 1945, U.S. economic superiority was so vast that one-sided trade policies did not matter. Over time, they ultimately did. And when high oil prices and economic competition from Japan and Germany battered the economy in the 1970s, new policies—international and domestic—were needed. The fire bell in the night came in 1971 when the U.S. suffered the first trade deficit since 1893. The Age of Compression officially ended in 1973 when wages began to stagnate, largely because of a sharp drop in productivity.[11] Restoring growth was a project on the left and right throughout the 1970s. No one imagined that the productivity decline would continue until 1995 and the wage growth would continue to fall short of the achievements of the postwar period. Few predicted that U.S. trade deficits would remain and grow, producing the global imbalances between consuming nations (United States) and producing nations (China) that are at the root of the contemporary global economic crisis.

Yet telltale signs of this future were visible during the 1970s. First, the Democratic Party, which enjoyed a two-to-one advantage over the GOP at the beginning of the decade, was less responsive to the economy and to workers. New Democrats, often from suburban, affluent districts, made it a badge of honor that they were not New Dealers. Coming of age during the affluent 1960s, they believed that posteconomic issues—foreign policy, race, gender, political process, and environment—were the important ones. They ignored or misread the new industrial competition with Europe and Japan and high energy prices that challenged the affluence that held the party together. They produced incoherent policies that neither protected labor nor promoted growth. The critical moments occurred in 1979 and 1980 when a Democratic president chose in vain to battle inflation, not unemployment, and promote a balanced budget, not growth. The defeat of President Jimmy Carter gave another man, Republican Ronald Reagan, an opportunity to restore growth and prosperity.

The new GOP was a conservative party, affirming that capital freed from taxation, regulation, and trade barriers would produce national and labor

---

[10] Bagehot, "Through a Pint Glass, Darkly," *Economist* (April 11, 2009), 58.

[11] Between 1947 and 1973, productivity rose 103.5 percent; between 1973 and 2003 it rose 71.3 percent. Robert Kuttner, *The Squandering of America* (New York: Knopf, 2007), 21.

prosperity. The effects of such policies in a global economy shifted resources away from manufacturing—the "tradables"—into finance and housing. The recipe, aided by high-tech innovations, worked for a while, even as it produced what I call an Age of Inequality.[12] Financing from abroad allowed Americans to maintain consumption despite stagnating wages and huge trade deficits. Recently, this model has failed to sustain its foremost selling point, prosperity. Signature industries, housing and financial services, placed the "world on the edge" in fall 2008.[13] The worst never happened, but, as this is written, the nation is experiencing the nastiest and most intractable economic recession since the Great Depression.

This book explains how the Age of Compression became the Age of Inequality. Why did the nation replace the assumptions that capital and labor should prosper together with an ethic claiming that the promotion of capital will eventually benefit labor—trading factories for finance—a very different way of running a nation that produced very different results? The Age of Compression was a product of the Democratic Party, but Republican Richard Nixon governed according to its ethic. The Age of Inequality was created by the GOP, but Democrat Bill Clinton lived by its rules. Party and ideology are close but do not always coincide. Thus, unlike other historians who draw a sharp line in 1980, my key period is 1976-1980, when the Democrats controlled both houses of Congress and the presidency. The challenges of the globalizing world were played out within the governing Democratic Party. When Democrats failed to restore prosperity, the electorate voted for Republicans, who then claimed that their victory was a rejection of the ideas and practices of the Age of Compression. Simply saying it didn't make it true. But with the power of his office, President Reagan did create a new national blueprint. The new principles took hold. And, in many ways, they are still with us. . . .

My analysis draws from the primary sources of the period. The presidential records of Richard Nixon, Gerald Ford, and Jimmy Carter, including the papers of key aides, were crucial. Examining presidential decision-making convinced me that the cultural conflicts that dominate some of the books on the decade were beside the point. The records do not demonstrate rising conservatism, but a contentious polity. Understanding business thinking was crucial. The records of the National Association of Manufacturers and the Chamber of Commerce . . . congressional testimony on tax and labor legislation . . . offered an important source for international political and economic opinion during this period.

---

[12] In the 1980s, every group lost out to the top fifth. This pattern continued up to the present, except for the years from 1995–2000, when the lowest fifth outpaced the top fifth. Still, even in the second half of the Clinton presidency, the top 5 percent did better than everyone else. Lawrence Mishel, Jared Bernstein, and Sylvia Allegretto, *The State of Working America, 2006–2007* (Ithaca, N.Y.: Cornell University Press, 2006), 58; Ian Dew-Becker and Robert Gordon, "Where Did the Productivity Growth Go?" paper presented at the Eighty-first Meeting of the Brookings Panel on Economic Activity, Washington, DC, Sept. 8–9, 2005, 72.

[13] *Economist* (Oct. 4–11, 2008), 11.

The records of the American Federation of Labor and Congress of Industrial Organization (AFL-CIO) . . . are indispensable for documenting the changing politics of organized labor. Until 1981, the AFL-CIO was a major player in every important economic decision. I used, too, the National Urban League, National Association for the Advancement of Colored People (NAACP), Leadership Conference on Civil Rights, and Bayard Rustin papers . . . for the views of African Americans. . . . At the end of the 1970s and during the 1980s, monetary policy became important. Federal Reserve chief Paul Volcker has become the national hero as the slayer of inflation. Nevertheless, few scholars who applaud the bank's actions have read its deliberations. The Federal Open Market Committee minutes are online and reveal a much more uncertain and stumbling Volcker. Key senatorial papers were useful for understanding individual pieces of legislation. . . .These sources were supplemented with newspapers, especially the *Wall Street Journal,* magazines, and the secondary literature on various topics.

2 *Excerpted Introduction to* Stayin' Alive: The 1970s and the Last Days of the Working Class
by Jefferson Cowie

At only twenty-six years of age, sporting long sideburns, slicked back hair, and mod striped pants, autoworker Dewey Burton could barely contain his rage over the state of politics or his frustration with his job in the spring of 1972.

Dewey loved nothing more than customizing and racing automobiles, transforming old parts into dazzling metallic-flake creations, but he could barely tolerate his job at the Wixom Ford plant just outside of Detroit where he felt sentenced to a trivial role in assembling them. Satisfied with his pay, he was part of a widespread movement across the heartland fighting the mind-numbing tedium of industrial production. Reflecting the broad discontent on the floors of the nation's factories, some of which grew into open revolt, he remarked, "I hate my job, I hate the people I work for. . . . It's kind of stupid to work so hard and achieve so little."

Politically, Burton identified himself as a committed New Deal Democrat, but he was livid over plans to bus his son across Detroit in order to conform to the Supreme Court's ideal of racial integration—policies driving his politics quickly to the right. Like the nation as a whole, Burton was simply being torn in too many directions at once. . . . [The 1968 presidential race] was the last time Burton would call himself an unwavering Democrat as busing all but shattered his faith in the mainstream of the party. Extending the separate-is-not-equal logic of *Brown v. Board of Education* (1954), the Supreme Court decided in *Swann v. Charlotte-Mecklenburg Board of Education* (1971) that integrating school children through mandatory busing was an appropriate remedy for racial segregation in the public schools. And in Burton's Detroit, plans were to integrate not just the schools within the city, but the suburbs with the city.[1] "What burns me to the bottom of my bones is that I paid an excessive amount of money so that my son could walk three blocks to school," he explained about his family's small bungalow on the edge of Detroit. . . .

Burton decided that the answer to the busing threat was to pull the lever for the pivotal political figure of the era, George Wallace, for the Democratic nomination for president in 1972. The governor of Alabama, who famously stood in the schoolhouse doorway to defend segregation and who swore never to be "out niggered" in politics, was busy rattling the stale presumptions of both major parties. As an independent candidate in 1968, Wallace drew together the segregationist South with anti-liberal northerners concerned about blacks moving into their neighborhoods, fearful of the riots, and feeling simply forgotten. His candidacy enabled the political transformation of a substantial slice of white working people to become dislodged from the Roosevelt coalition and move toward what Kevin Phillips famously called *The Emerging Republican Majority* (1969). By the time George Wallace returned as an insurgent candidate in the fragmented Democratic primaries in 1972, his performance was roughly equal to any major candidate. . . .

Separating George Wallace's race baiting from his "stand up for the common man" theme is as difficult as untangling race from class in U.S. history, but his blue-collar rhetoric spoke to themes that no one else on the national stage addressed. Among northern wage earners like Burton, Wallace's populist anti-elitism, anti-crime, and anti-busing messages worked best, but his overt embrace of segregation, his snarling rhetoric, and petty resentments failed. . . . At the heart of the Wallace phenomenon was ambiguity about his cause. As one trucker explained, "I'm for either him or the Communists, I don't care, just somebody who wouldn't be afraid of the big companies. . . ."[2]

Many . . . dismissed votes like Dewey's as clear racism, but his political choices cannot be dismissed so simply. Raised poor (the first indoor running water he had was when he moved from southern Illinois to Detroit as a teenager), Dewey nonetheless profited from generations of segregated housing patterns, silent white privilege, and occupational segregation. Still, he felt open to black people as both leaders and neighbors. He touted his black union local leader as "the best president we've ever had" and claimed that he would welcome anyone into his neighborhood. "If a black mom and daddy buy or rent a

---

[1] In 1974, the Supreme Court ruled in *Miliken v. Bradley* that the Detroit suburbs were exempt from busing for desegregation in the Detroit city schools.—Eds.

[2] Kim Phillips-Fein, *Invisible Hands: The Making of the Conservative Movement from the New Deal to Reagan* (New York: Norton, 2008), 155.

house here and send their kids to [my son] David's school and pay their taxes, that's fine. Busing black kids to white neighborhoods and white kids to black neighborhoods is never going to achieve integration. It's upsetting. It's baloney." Like Wallace, Burton detested "welfare freeloaders," pointing to an unruly white family that lived down the block. His protest against liberalism had as much to do with control of his life, the fate of his family, and his modest and tenuous place in the social ladder as it did with anything else.[3]

For working people, the social upheavals associated with the sixties actually took root in most communities in the seventies, which was not simply a different decade but a distinctly less generous economic climate. From a policy perspective, the Democratic Party faced a dilemma that it could not solve: finding ways to maintain support within the white blue-collar base . . . while at the same time servicing the pressing demands for racial and gender equity arising from the sixties. Both had to be achieved in the midst of two massive oil shocks, record inflation and unemployment, and a business community retooling to assert greater control over the political process. Placing affirmative action onto a world of declining occupational opportunity risked a zero-sum game . . . issues like busing forced black and white residents to square off in what columnist Jimmy Breslin called "a Battle Royal" between "two groups of people who are poor and doomed and who have been thrown in the ring with each other."[4] . . .

The early seventies' political confusion had its analogue in the discontent boiling up on the shop floors. Employees at the Wixom Ford plant where Burton worked were a minor part of a national epidemic of industrial unrest in the first half of the 1970s. They fought with supervisors on the line, clogged up the system with grievances, demanded changes in the quality of work life, walked out in wildcat strikes, and organized to overthrow stale bureaucratic union leadership. . . .

Commentators often referred to the unruliness on the assembly line as the "Lordstown syndrome," after the infamous three-week-long strike in 1972 by a group of young, hip, and inter-racial autoworkers at a General Motors (GM) plant in Lordstown, Ohio, who battled the fastest—and most psychically

---

[3] *New York Times,* May 14, 1972; *New York Times*, November 7, 1972; Burton Oral History [conducted by author in Fort White, Florida, September 30, 2006].

[4] Breslin, quoted in Ronald P. Formisano, *Boston Against Busing: Race, Class, and Ethnicity in the 1960s and 1970s* (Chapel Hill: University of North Carolina Press, 2004 [1991]), 177; on white ethnic revival, see Matthew Frye Jacobsen, *Roots Too: White Ethnic Revival in Post–Civil Rights America* (Cambridge, MA: Harvard University Press, 2006), Michael Novak, *The Rise of the Unmeltable Ethnics* (New York: Macmillan, 1971); on the transformation in gender and race in the workplace, see Nancy MacLean, *Freedom Is Not Enough: The Opening of the American Workplace* (Cambridge, MA: Harvard University Press, 2006), 2; Katherine Van Wezel Stone, "The Legacy of Industrial Pluralism: The Tension between Individual Employment Rights and the New Deal Collective Bargaining System," *University of Chicago Law Review* 59 (Spring 1992): 576; Judith Stein, *Running Steel, Running America: Race, Economic Policy and the Decline of Liberalism* (Chapel Hill: University of North Carolina Press, 1998), 195.

deadening—assembly line in the world. "With all the shoulder-length hair, beards, Afros and mod clothing along the line," explained *Newsweek* of the notorious GM plant, "it looks for all the world like an industrial Woodstock.". . . The union bureaucracy saw the upheavals as threatening to its power. . . . Yet the insurgencies of the early seventies, resisted so mightily by the union hierarchy, were the main source of whatever hope there may have been for updating the old order. . . .

The 1970s might appropriately be thought of as half post-1960s and half pre-1980s, but they were also more than that—they served as a bridge between epochs. A broad spectrum of observers . . . have formed a consensus that within the gloomy seventies we can find the roots of our own time. The period has been named "pivotal" not because of its monumental events, its great leaders, or its movements, but because society, from its economic foundations to its cultural manifestations, really did move in a new direction. It stands as a bookend to the New Deal era: that which was built in the thirties and forties—politically, economically, and culturally—was beginning to crumble barely two generations later. More than a time of mere fads for which it is mercilessly teased, it was a time of fundamental realignments. . . .

Above all, the mid-1970s marked the end of the postwar boom. The years prior to the 1973–74 crisis had been the most economically egalitarian time in U.S. history, the point on the graph where the bounty was shared most equitably, and unemployment was at historic lows. The year 1972 was also the apex of earnings for male workers. Starting in the 1973–74 years, real earnings began to stagnate and then slide as workers began their slow and painful dismissal from their troubled partnership with postwar liberalism. By mid-decade the record-breaking strikes, rank-and-file movements, and vibrant organizing drives that had once promised a new day for workers were reduced to a trickle in the new economic climate. They were then replaced by layoffs, plant closures, and union decertification drives. White male workers' incomes had risen an astonishing 42 percent since 1960, but those incomes stagnated or fell for the next quarter century following the early seventies. Real earnings first stagnated and then were driven down by oil shocks and inflation; deindustrialization, plant closings, and anti-unionism; and a global restructuring of work itself that would continue over the ensuing decades. . . .[5]

[5] Robert Collins, *More: The Politics of Economic Growth* (New York: Oxford University Press, 2000), 132–65; Daniel H. Weinberg, "A Brief Look at Postwar U.S. Income Inequality," *Current Population Reports,* June 1996, Bureau of the Census (P60-191); Daniel H. Weinberg, Charles T. Nelson, and Edward J. Welniak Jr., "Economic Well-Being in the United States: How Much Improvement—Fifty Years of U.S. Income Data from the Current Population Survey: Alternatives, Trends, and Quality," *American Economic Review* (May 1999): 18–22; for a brief overview of postwar Gini coefficients, see Thomas Frank, *One Market Under God* (New York: Doubleday, 2000), 6; David Frum, *How We Got Here: The 70's: The Decade That Brought You Modern Life (For Better or Worse)* (New York: Basic Books, 2000), 331–32; U.S. Census Bureau, *Income, Poverty, and Health Insurance Coverage in the United States: 2005* (Washington, DC: GPO, 2005), 38; Francine D. Blau and Lawrence M. Kahn, "Gender Differences in Pay," *Journal of Economic Perspectives* 14 (Fall 2000): 84–85.

Burton too saw little hope or opportunity in the emerging reality at mid-decade. Peering out from underneath what he called his "despondency," he framed the problem as effectively as any of the sociologists of the time. "Something's happening to people like me—working stiffs, as they say—and it isn't just that we have to pay more for this or that or that we're having to do without this or make do with less of that. It's deep, and hard to explain, but it's more like more and more of us are sort of leaving all our hopes outside in the rain and coming into the house and just locking the door. . . ."[6]

By 1980 Burton completed the most significant transformation in postwar political history: from New Deal faithful to icon of discontent to Reagan Democrat. . . . Burton's choice for the presidency in 1980 helped usher in a new and complex era of working-class political history. . . . At a time when the traditional working-class ally, the Democratic Party, offered precious little material comfort to working people, Ronald Reagan's New Right offered a restoration of the glory days by bolstering morale on the basis of patriotism, God, race, patriarchy, and nostalgia for community. The Reagan administration did squeeze inflation out of the economy but only by allowing historic levels of unemployment, industrial decline, and the decimation of the collective bargaining system—all of which combined to fight inflation by lowering wages and raising unemployment. After the president's attack on organized labor, most dramatically in the firing of over ten thousand striking members of the Professional Air Traffic Controllers Organization, and the restructuring of the tax schedule in favor of the wealthy, he looked a lot less like the working man's champion. . . . As Dewey later confessed, "Reagan blindsided us. . . ."[7]

What many pegged as the promise of a working-class revival in the early 1970s turned out to be more of a swan song by decade's end. The fragmented nature of the labor protests—by organization, industry, race, geography, and gender—failed to coalesce into a lasting national presence. The mainstream labor movement failed in its major political initiatives. Market orthodoxy eclipsed all alternatives, and promising organizing drives ended in failure. Deindustrialization decimated the power of the old industrial heartland. . . .

One of the great constructs of the modern age, the unified notion of a "working class" crumbled [in the 1970s], and the new world order was built on the rubble. . . . It ultimately died of the many external assaults upon it, yes, but mostly of its own internal weaknesses.

[6] *New York Times,* October 17, 1974.
[7] Burton Oral History; see also Gil Troy, *Morning in America: How Ronald Reagan Invented the 1980s* (Princeton, NJ: Princeton University Press, 2005), 50–83.

Analyzing Popular History

1. Both Judith Stein and Jefferson Cowie are examining U.S. economic decline in their books on the 1970s. But what do the introductions reveal about differences in the actual topics of the two books?

2. Looking over the information on your Source Analysis Table, which of these two introductions tells you more about the author's sources and position in the relevant historiography? Does this difference cause you to want to read one of these books more than the other? Why or why not?

3. What is Stein's argument for the cause of the shift from what she calls the Age of Compression to the Age of Inequality in the "pivotal decade" of the seventies? According to her introduction, where did she decide to focus her research for answering her question about the cause of the shift?

4. What is Cowie's argument for the cause of the shift from working-class support of Democrats to working-class support of Republicans? Is he saying that this political shift caused or resulted from the economic decline of the seventies?

5. Based on their introductions, which of these books would you choose to read for a paper on the impact of workers' economic problems on seventies' music and why? Do you think the introductions give you enough information to make that decision?

6. Both Stein and Cowie appear to be liberal in their political ideology. Both probably vote for Democratic candidates and both likely support unionization of workers. In what specific ways do their introductions tell you that these ideological leanings do or do not bias their arguments about economic decline in the seventies? Do your findings on this question increase or decrease your trust in these authors' interpretation of information?

The Rest of the Story

In August 1974, Carroll O'Connor—the actor who played Archie Bunker on *All in the Family*—refused to participate in the filming of new episodes for almost a month because the electrical equipment operators at CBS were on strike over wages, and the network had hired nonunion replacement workers, or "scabs." O'Connor, a member of the Screen Actors Guild and other labor unions, said he could not cross a picket line or undermine unionists' bargaining position by working with strikebreakers; "I could no more go into a building and work with scabs than I could play handball in church."

So even though O'Connor's views were different from Archie Bunker's on virtually everything, from race and gender to electoral politics, they shared an increasingly old-fashioned belief that the decline of labor unions was bad for them and their kind. Ironically, the four episodes whose filming was delayed due to the real strike were about a fictional strike over wages at Archie Bunker's workplace.

Two years later, in a 1976 episode, Archie expressed his unhappiness that Jimmy Carter had won the presidential election against Gerald Ford. In what was supposed to be a joke revealing Archie's political naiveté, he declared that liberals were not going to be so happy when Ronald Reagan defeated Carter in 1980. In that case, Archie Bunker got the last laugh. By 1980, only 52.6 percent of eligible voters in the United States actually went to the polls (compared to 62.8 percent in 1960, when John F. Kennedy defeated Richard M. Nixon), but among those who voted, Ronald Reagan garnered just over 50 percent of the votes. In a historic shift of allegiance, many of those Reagan voters were white, male, working-class refugees from the Democratic Party, like Dewey Burton. They believed that Reagan was their champion because of his skepticism about government solutions to social problems, such as his opposition to affirmative action and the Equal Rights Amendment, his disdain for the spread of cultural trends from the sixties, and his pro-labor past as president of the Screen Actors Guild. When President Reagan's words and deeds did not support labor unions, and when his tax policies shifted national wealth from 80 percent of the population to the top 20 percent, most Reagan Democrats did not blame him because they still felt a strong cultural affinity for the man and still shared his doubts about government activism.

Looking at the electoral shift that occurred with Reagan's election to the presidency in 1980, historians ask whether this means the 1970s ended with chronological precision in 1980. Some say yes, arguing that Reagan's defeat of the Democratic incumbent, Jimmy Carter, marked a decisive conservative triumph in the debate that had raged throughout the seventies. They see 1980 as the start of a new era—the Reagan Revolution—when liberals moved from the offensive to the defensive position. Other historians dispute this, but only slightly, by arguing that the seventies ended not in 1980 but in 1984, when President Reagan was reelected by 58.8 percent of the 53 percent of eligible voters. It was at that point, they argue, that even Democrats had to embrace Republican faith in free-market solutions, placing supporters of government activism in the clear minority. But there are still other analysts of recent history who emphasize the persistence of the U.S. debate over the role of government policy and the role of the free market in distributing wealth to all who share in creating it. In their eyes, we are still living in the seventies—but without the bad hairstyles.

To Find Out More

Bailey, Beth, and David Farber, eds. *America in the Seventies.* Lawrence: University Press of Kansas, 2004.

Berkowitz, Edward D. *Something Happened: A Political and Cultural Overview of the Seventies.* New York: Columbia University Press, 2006.

Borstelmann, Thomas. *The 1970s: A New Global History from Civil Rights to Economic Inequality.* Princeton, NJ: Princeton University Press, 2013.

Carroll, Peter N. *It Seemed Like Nothing Happened: America in the 1970s.* New York: Holt, Rinehart and Winston, 1982.

Frum, David. *How We Got Here: The 70's: The Decade That Brought You Modern Life (For Better or Worse).* New York: Basic Books, 2000.

Jenkins, Philip. *Decade of Nightmares: The End of the Sixties and the Making of Eighties America.* New York: Oxford University Press, 2006.

Kaufman, Will. *American Culture in the 1970s.* Edinburgh, Scotland: Edinburgh University Press, 2009.

Killen, Andreas. *1973 Nervous Breakdown: Watergate, Warhol, and the Birth of Post-Sixties America.* New York: Bloomsbury USA, 2006.

Schulman, Bruce J. *The Seventies: The Great Shift in American Culture, Society, and Politics.* New York: Free Press, 2001.

CHAPTER 13

Drawn to Summits

Political Cartoons on President Reagan and the Arms Race

"My fellow Americans, I am pleased to tell you I just signed legislation which outlaws Russia forever. The bombing will begin in five minutes." President Ronald Reagan was joking, of course. It was a Saturday morning in the late summer of 1984; he was vacationing at his ranch in Santa Barbara, California, and having a bit of fun while he tested the sound levels on the microphone set up to record his weekly radio message. The president was, in effect, drawing an oral cartoon of himself: his joke grossly exaggerated his critics' view of him as a "commie hater" and warmonger, making the criticism so ridiculous that even the radio technicians in the room laughed. The only problem was that the microphone was on, and it was broadcasting. The whole world, including officials in the Soviet Union, heard the "joke," and they took it as evidence of the president's genuine feelings; his humor, they said, revealed his authentic hatred for the Russian people and his desire to destroy them. Some of Reagan's critics in the United States agreed with that analysis; other critics viewed the gaffe as proof that the president was too clumsy and simpleminded to handle delicate diplomacy.

The irony in the story is that 1984, the year Reagan ran for reelection, marks a turning point in his relationship with the Soviet Union and the start of Reagan's open dialogue with the Soviet leadership on the subject of nuclear arms limitation. In his first term, the president had reversed a twenty-year trend toward "détente"—the relaxing of tensions between the world's two military superpowers—and had emphasized instead his ideological view of communism as a corrupt political and economic system bent on global domination. In that first term, Reagan had used aggressive rhetoric to describe the Soviet Union, calling it an "evil empire" and promising that the West would not simply contain communism, which had been its policy since the 1940s, but would "transcend communism" and relegate the Soviet system to the "ash heap of history." Beyond the warlike language, Reagan's first term in office was marked by the first complete breakdown of arms limitations talks in twenty years and was the first time since Harry Truman's presidency that there was no "summit," or top-level meeting between the two superpower leaders. Those who worried about this pattern in Reagan's first term had trouble dismissing as a "joke" his accidental on-air remark about bombing the Russians.

Ronald Reagan brought to the presidency two long-standing convictions: that Soviet military power was a grave threat to the United States and to world peace and that the Soviet economic system was on the verge of collapse. Arguing that a buildup of U.S. military power either would scare the Soviets into arms control negotiations or would bankrupt their economy by forcing them to match U.S. spending, Reagan insisted on massive increases in the defense budget. In his first year in office, he won congressional approval for a 25 percent increase, producing the largest military authorization bill in U.S. history. By the end of Reagan's two terms, his administration's highly publicized weapons expenditures had expanded the defense budget by 40 percent. "We must keep the heat on these people," he told one political ally in 1982. "What I want is to bring them to their knees so that they will disarm and let us disarm; but we have got to do it by keeping the heat on."

The American people had mixed feelings about Reagan's "heat on" strategy. The dramatic expansion in military spending, when coupled with Reagan's tax cuts for upper-income earners, produced soaring federal budget deficits as well as a barrage of criticism for "Reaganomics." Massive cuts in social spending for the poor, elderly, and children did not offset increases in military expenditures, and tax cuts intended to spur the economy failed to generate enough revenue to pay for all the new weapons. In 1981, Reagan's first year in office, only 20 percent of Americans responding to one poll said that the United States spent "too much" on defense; by 1985, that figure had risen to 66 percent. By then, the federal deficit had grown 134 percent, from $907 billion to more than $2 trillion, and many feared that Reaganomics would bring the United States to its own economic knees.

Impervious to public opinion on foreign and military policy, Reagan continued to pursue his own agenda of peace through military strength. In early 1983, he announced that his Defense Department would pursue an expensive line of research and development on a strategic defense initiative (SDI) — quickly dubbed "Star Wars" — which the president envisioned as a space-based shield against nuclear attack. For Reagan, SDI was the ultimate expression of his desire to avoid nuclear war, but opponents of nuclear weapons did not perceive this hard-line, anticommunist, promilitary president as their ally and scoffed when he promised to share SDI with the Soviets. Many in the scientific community, meanwhile, regarded SDI as science fiction, a product of the president's experience as a Hollywood actor.

Few were aware in 1983 that President Reagan was increasingly convinced of the need for arms control talks with the "evil empire." The United States military buildup had, as intended, frightened the Soviets, not into submission but into greater certitude that the United States was about to attack. Events in late 1983 impressed upon Reagan the high stakes of his military gamble. In September, the Soviets accidentally shot down a civilian Korean airliner, causing temporary panic among U.S. leaders. Concerned that the president did not fully appreciate the risks involved in nuclear war, Pentagon officials forced Reagan to listen to briefings on possible nuclear war scenarios; the Soviets' near-fatal overreaction to a large-scale U.S.-led military war game in November made those scenarios seem more plausible. Fear of nuclear annihilation also made its way into popular culture and into the screening room at the White House. In November 1983, Reagan viewed a television drama, *The Day After*, which imagined life in Lawrence, Kansas, following a nuclear war. In his diary, he said that the film was "very effective and left me greatly depressed." He later claimed in his autobiography that the drama moved him to alter U.S. policy on a nuclear war.

In a major address favoring nuclear arms control in January 1984, Reagan signaled that his priorities were shifting away from defeating the Soviet Union and toward reducing nuclear weapons. Some questioned the sincerity of his call for talks to "begin now," noting that it coincided with his run for reelection, but historians with access to internal memos and Reagan's own diary find that Reagan was indeed reordering his priorities.

No U.S. president can single-handedly bend world events to his will. Reagan's new priorities would not have mattered had there not been, simultaneously, a remarkable series of developments in the Soviet Union. Leonid Brezhnev, leader of the Soviet Union since 1964, died in 1982 at age seventy-five. He was followed in quick succession by two equally elderly, equally conservative representatives of the communist regime: Yuri Andropov and Konstantin Chernenko. Then, in March 1985, the Soviet Politburo elected reform-minded Mikhail Gorbachev to the government's top post. Twenty years younger than Reagan, Gorbachev emphasized *glasnost* (openness) and *perestroika* (economic restructuring), insisting that reduced military spending was vital to make the communist economic system more globally competitive with U.S. capitalism and calling for a negotiated end to the arms race. The American public responded positively to Gorbachev's vision as well as to his winning personal style. The Soviet leader, whose broad smile and prominent forehead birthmark made him instantly recognizable, was affectionately nicknamed "Gorby," and he became a real personality match for the famously charming U.S. president.

In November 1985 in Geneva, Switzerland, Reagan and Gorbachev held their first summit meeting. The great achievement of that summit was that the two world leaders actually talked alone, with only two translators in the room, for more than two hours, engaging in the most honest exchange of ideas in U.S.-Soviet history. They spoke seriously of a 50 percent reduction in long-range missiles and of drastic reductions in "intermediate" weapons. Although the two leaders got along and believed that they could work together productively, Reagan's commitment to pursuing the still-untested SDI was unacceptable to Gorbachev. Reagan viewed SDI as a guarantor of peace: both sides would have a shield rendering nuclear weapons useless. Gorbachev viewed it as a costly

Figure 13.1 Ronald Reagan and Mikhail Gorbachev Meet in Geneva, 1985 This *photograph captures the mood at the first Reagan-Gorbachev summit, held in Geneva, Switzerland, on November 19, 1985. The two men met with only interpreters for an hour in the morning and then participated in more public discussions. In the late afternoon, they walked alone to a pool house on the shore of Lake Geneva and, with only interpreters present, held a genuine conversation about their mutual need for trust and a reduction in weapons. At the end of the day, Reagan told a diplomatic aide, "You're right, I did like him."* Source: Universal History Archive/Getty Images.

extension of the arms race, arguing that eliminating nuclear weapons would make SDI unnecessary. Still, they ended their first meeting with the remarkable joint statement that nuclear war "cannot be won and must never be fought" and with the promise that neither nation would "seek to achieve military superiority."

The Reagan-Gorbachev summit meeting in Reykjavik, Iceland, just one year later, brought the two nations to the brink of peace; the two leaders seriously negotiated a plan to eliminate all nuclear weapons. Private conversations between the two leaders and group meetings between arms negotiators were bold, innovative, and rather impetuous. It appeared that the euphoric momentum of the meeting was headed toward a 50 percent cut in strategic long-range weapons, an elimination of Soviet and U.S. intermediate weapons in Europe, and a commitment to more reductions in the future. Although the two-day meeting was scheduled to end at noon on the second day, Reagan and Gorbachev, and their negotiating teams, kept working until 7:30 p.m., believing a deal was imminent. In the end, however, the two leaders left Reykjavik with nothing to show for their labors. The whole package unraveled over SDI. Reagan insisted that the United States be allowed to continue research and development of this still-hypothetical system, both in laboratories and in space. Gorbachev, worried that the Soviet budget could not fund SDI research in space, insisted that research be limited to laboratories. Neither leader would budge on this point.

The collapse of the Reykjavik summit did not mean the end of U.S.-Soviet discussions over arms control or the end of Reagan-Gorbachev summits. The two leaders met again in Washington, D.C., in December 1987, at a time when both were in political trouble at home and in need of a foreign policy success. Reagan's stature had been diminished by a political scandal involving illegal weapons deals with Iran and Nicaraguan "contra" fighters. Meanwhile, Gorbachev was becoming increasingly unpopular with antireformist Soviet politicians, and he faced a costly quagmire in Afghanistan, where the Soviet attempt to control that country was losing to U.S.-funded Islamic fundamentalists. The Washington summit produced an agreement to eliminate certain intermediate nuclear weapons, accounting for just 4 percent of each nation's arsenals. It was a small step toward strategic arms reduction talks, or START, a step aided by the fact that Gorbachev now regarded SDI as a technical impossibility. He was quite willing to let the United States waste billions of dollars on a defense shield that could be breached for far less money.

Ronald Reagan and his wife, Nancy, traveled to Moscow, Russia, in May 1988 for his fourth summit with Gorbachev. The U.S. president had eight months left in office. Dreams of eliminating all nuclear weapons had been replaced by modest arms control talks, and Congress and the Joint Chiefs of Staff had agreed to shelve SDI and write off the $12 billion spent on exploring that failed idea. The Moscow summit was more a celebration of four years' worth of good intentions than a true negotiating session. At a well-staged walkabout for photographers in Red Square, Reagan told reporters that he no longer thought of the Soviet Union as the "evil empire" that he had described just five years earlier. He had used such language, he said, when "talking about another time in another era." Now, in 1988, Reagan joined Gorbachev in a Moscow toast to "the hope of holding out for a better way of settling things."

Using the Source: Political Cartoons

Jeff MacNelly was a prize-winning political cartoonist facing professional trouble when his candidate, Ronald Reagan, emerged victorious from the 1980 election. MacNelly later admitted, "That was hard for me because I can't go around saying, 'Gee, isn't the president doing a great job?' That's not what a political cartoonist does."

What a political cartoonist "does" in a democratic society is provide citizens with pointed, pictorial satire. Ever since Ben Franklin published the first American political cartoon in 1754 (admonishing the colonies to unite in fighting the

French and Indian War), journalists have been using irony, sarcasm, ridicule, and exaggeration to stimulate readers' engagement with current events. Certainly since the late nineteenth century, when Thomas Nast's drawings mocked political corruption, cartoonists have been using visual humor to provoke citizen outrage and action. Provocation is their job; that is what newspapers and magazines pay them to do, and that is why the public pays attention to them. No matter what their political position, all political cartoonists agree with one of the profession's great figures, Bill Mauldin, who said his role was to "jar, shake, needle people out of their fat-headedness."

In a democracy, any public figure and any public policy can be "drawn and quartered" by a political cartoon, and cartoonists' duty is to put politicians and citizens on notice that their hypocrisies, conceits, and missteps are subject to visual ridicule and graphic mockery. When Florida governor Jeb Bush warned Gary Trudeau to "walk softly" in his *Doonesbury* cartoons, Trudeau commented that "telling a cartoonist to walk softly is like asking a professional wrestler to show a little class. It's just not a productive suggestion."

What Can Political Cartoons Tell Us?

To be effective, a political cartoon must capture the essence of a complex situation in a clever drawing that the viewer can understand in about twenty seconds. Cartoonists make their arguments by drawing the most ridiculous, most absurd, most extreme version of a political situation; they illuminate their sober editorial points with the aid of outrageous drawings and comedic devices. So great is the cartoonist's potential to make a powerful statement that acerbic editor H. L. Mencken once announced, "Give me a good cartoonist and I can throw out half the editorial staff."

The key to effective political cartooning is "caricature"; cartoonists must draw an image of a person or place or thing so realistically that viewers instantly recognize it, but cartoonists must, at the same time, distort their subject, exaggerate its features, and transform it in a way that is not only funny but also meaningful. In deciding which features to distort, which visual qualities to exaggerate, the cartoonist must be guided by the editorial point of the cartoon. "Caricature does not deal merely with faces and forms," explained nineteenth-century cartoonist Joseph Keppler. "It has to deal with character as well. If a man is notoriously stingy, that stinginess must be pictured in his caricature, and pictured extravagantly so that it will stand out as the most prominent feature of the portrait."

Included in the cartoonist's tool kit are sight gags, puns, dialogue, labels, stereotypes, cultural references, and clichés. Each of these tools is potentially useful to the cartoonist, but each also runs the risk of offending or alienating its readers. For example, less than six months after the terrorist attacks of September 11, 2001, cartoonist Mike Marland outraged many subscribers to the *Concord (N.H.) Monitor* because of a drawing he used to criticize President George W. Bush's Social Security proposals. Marland depicted the president flying a plane labeled

"Bush Budget" into twin towers labeled "Social" and "Security." To quell the public outcry, the *Monitor* apologized to its readers. But strong public reactions are part of the history and daily life of political cartooning.

Above all, every cartoonist must assume that viewers are sufficiently informed about current events to have some idea of what a particular cartoon is about, even if they do not grasp every reference or gag. When Adrian Raeside, cartoonist for *The Colonist* in Victoria, British Columbia, drew the cartoon you see here, he was obviously assuming that his Canadian viewers knew that President Reagan's joke about bombing Russia had been mistakenly broadcast over the radio airwaves that August morning in 1984. Raeside greatly exaggerated the event in order to mock Reagan's attempt at humor but also to make a serious point about the potential effect of such gaffes by a U.S. president.

How does the image of missiles firing outside the Oval Office make this drawing a true cartoon?

Would a viewer need to notice this sight gag to get the point of the cartoon?

What is the purpose of the word *heck* in this cartoon's speech bubble?

How are the technicians being stereotyped here?

How does the drawing of Reagan's face advance the cartoonist's point?

Source: ©raesidecartoon.com.

Because political cartoons must be accessible to a broad spectrum of the public, cartoons from past decades can give us a window on what ideas and images were widely available and shared in the popular culture. If a cartoonist in 1981 used the image of jellybeans in a cartoon about Reagan, we can conclude that it was well known that the president loved jellybeans and kept a jar of them on his desk. Similarly, if cartoonists in the 1980s typically drew Mikhail Gorbachev with a birthmark on his forehead, we can conclude that Americans were quite familiar with the Soviet leader's visage. So, the most obvious advantage to political cartoons as a source of information about the past is that they offer a quick, entertaining index to popular culture.

Political cartoons also offer an accessible guide to political developments and debates that were so well known that they could be abbreviated into a single drawing using few, if any, words. If a cartoonist in the 1980s could use the abbreviation "SDI" in a drawing or simply refer to "Star Wars" without further explanation, then we can conclude that the debate about Reagan's strategic defense initiative was a frequent topic in political debate and that these shorthand references were widely used and understood. We cannot, however, assume that a collection of political cartoons from a particular era reflects the whole span of views in U.S. political debate. Despite the First Amendment, there are often limits on how far a publisher will go in ridiculing a public figure or mocking a political proposal. Since cartoonists' job is to be outrageous, they endeavor not to censor themselves, but since their job depends on getting published, cartoonists must consider whether an editor will accept a particularly biting image.

You can keep track of your ideas about political cartoons by using the table on pages 297–98. The following Checklist questions will help you examine cartoons as primary sources that can provide some insight about a society's values, assumptions, popular culture, and political controversies in a given historical moment.

CHECKLIST: Interrogating Political Cartoons

☐ When was the cartoon published?

☐ Who drew the cartoon? Is the cartoonist known to have a particular political viewpoint?

☐ In what publication did the cartoon appear? Is the publication known to have a political agenda?

☐ For what purpose was the cartoon created? To entertain? Persuade? Praise? Criticize?

☐ Who was the intended audience for the cartoon?

☐ What topic does the cartoon cover? What is its message? What hidden assumptions or biases does the cartoon contain?

Source Analysis Table

Use the table that follows to track changes in the story of Reagan's foreign policy and to record different tools that cartoonists use to make their points.

Source	Reagan Promilitary	Reagan Pro–Arms Control	Physical Exaggeration	Pop Culture References	Spoken Words	Labels
1. "Can't you see . . ." (1981)						
2. "He's got to eat . . ." (1982)						
3. "Surely they'll not be so stupid . . ." (1982)						
4. "I'm surprised . . ." (1983)						
5. "Go on, Yuri . . ." (1984)						
6. "Say, here comes the new blood . . ." (1984)						

(continued)

Source	Reagan Promilitary	Reagan Pro–Arms Control	Physical Exaggeration	Pop Culture References	Spoken Words	Labels
7. "The U.S. bargaining chip . . . " (1985)						
8. "The Soviets are a bunch of . . . " (1985)						
9. "Hey, maybe we should do this . . . " (1985)						
10. Reykjavik summit . . . (1986)						
11. "Little Ronnie . . . " (1987)						
12. Reagan and Gorbachev emerging . . . (1987)						
13. Evolution (1988)						

The Source: Political Cartoons from the Reagan Era, 1981–1988

1 **"Can't you see I'm trying to fill a hole?"**
by Bill Sanders, *Milwaukee Journal*, 1981

In his first year as president, Ronald Reagan pleased some Americans and angered others by advocating sharp increases in defense spending and large cuts in spending on social services. In October 1981, Reagan advocated an expensive speedup in the deployment of the "MX" missile, a land-based inter-continental ballistic missile approved under President Jimmy Carter. This proposal, which involved redesigning the basing plan for the MX, was hotly debated in Congress and in the press throughout 1981. Ultimately, Congress rejected the new basing plan.

Source: William Sanders.

2

"He's got to eat to have the strength to start reducing"

by Jim Mazzotta, *Fort Myers News Press,* 1982

In February 1982, President Reagan submitted a federal budget that included $200 billion in defense spending alongside reductions of $63 billion in programs such as food stamps, Medicare, and Medicaid. The 1982 budget projected a federal deficit of $91.5 billion. Reagan argued that cuts in social spending would reduce waste and fraud in social programs, whereas increases in defense spending would bring victory in the Cold War and an end to the need for large defense budgets.

Source: Jim Mazzotta.

3

"Surely they'll not be so stupid as to keep on coming!"
by Bob Artley, *Worthington Daily Globe*, 1982

The Reagan administration argued that a large defense buildup was a spending strategy to defeat the Soviet Union, either economically or militarily. Critics argued that the strategy fueled a risky arms competition in which neither country could back down.

Source: Used by permission of the Bob Artley estate.

The nuclear arms race

4

"I'm surprised at how the president dealt with the Russians . . . "
by Walt Handelsman, *Catonsville Times*, 1983

On September 1, 1983, a Soviet fighter shot down Korean Air Lines Flight 007 when the civilian plane mistakenly flew 500 kilometers off course into Soviet airspace. All 269 passengers and crew were killed, including Congressman Lawrence McDonald (D-Georgia). Four days later, President Reagan denounced the shooting as "an act of barbarism" and revoked the license of Aeroflot Soviet Airlines to operate in and out of the United States but ordered no further retaliation. Cartoonists had lampooned Reagan's tough stance toward the Soviet Union during his first three years in office, but this incident offered a chance to mock anti-Soviet conservatives who were disappointed in the president.

Source: Walt Handelsman.

5

"Go on, Yuri, make my day . . . "
by Mike Peters, *Dayton Daily News*, 1984

Sudden Impact, the fourth of Clint Eastwood's Dirty Harry movies, was a big hit in early 1984. In the film, Detective Harry Callahan aims his gun at the head of a thief who is holding a gun at a hostage's head and growls, "Go ahead, make my day." By referencing that quote, cartoonist Mike Peters was playing on some Americans' perception of President Reagan as a tough leader and on others' perception of Reagan as someone who would relish a military confrontation with Soviet leader Yuri Andropov. At the same time, Peters was invoking the president's own Hollywood career as an actor who had made fifty-three movies between 1937 and 1964.

Source: Mike Peters Editorial Cartoon used with the permission of Grimmy, Inc. and the Cartoonist Group.

6   *"Say, here comes the new blood now. . . . "*
by Jack Higgins, *Chicago Sun-Times*, 1984

Konstantin Chernenko, age seventy-two, was immediately appointed to replace
Yuri Andropov as the Soviet president after the sixty-nine-year-old Andropov
died in February 1984. Chernenko was the same age as President Reagan, but
he did not enjoy Reagan's robust health. Many, including cartoonists, viewed
the physical contrast between the two leaders as a metaphor for U.S. strength
and Soviet weakness. Indeed, Chernenko died in office in March 1985.

Source: Jack Higgins.

7 ***"The U.S. bargaining chip! The Soviet bargaining chip, chip, chip, chip!"***
by Chuck Asay, *Colorado Springs Sun*, 1985

This cartoon, which appeared just a few days after Gorbachev came to power in the Soviet Union, indicates that the press was immediately expecting some attempt at arms negotiations between President Reagan and this new, young Soviet leader. Chuck Asay, who drew this cartoon, was a supporter of Reagan's SDI. He believed that because Gorbachev lacked any new weapons system he could trade away to eliminate SDI, he would simply try to prevent the United States from developing a defense system.

Source: Chuck Asay.

8   *"The Soviets are a bunch of rabid, murdering . . . "*
by Mike Graston, *Windsor Star*, 1985

In July 1985, just four months after Mikhail Gorbachev became the leader of the Soviet Union, he and President Reagan announced that they would hold a summit in Geneva, Switzerland, in November of that year. This summit would be Reagan's first meeting with a Soviet leader since taking office, and his four years as president had been marked by angry rhetoric from both sides of the Cold War. As a result, there was considerable skepticism about whether the summit was a serious meeting or merely a diplomatic performance by both politicians in response to public pressure to meet.

Source: Mike Graston.

9

"Hey, maybe we should do this more often"
by Hy Rosen, *Albany Times-Union*, 1985

Ronald Reagan's 1984 reelection campaign theme, "It's morning in America," suggested a new start for an incumbent president. Hy Rosen may have been invoking that theme in this cartoon, which appeared immediately after the Geneva summit, amid optimistic reports of genuine discussions between Reagan and Gorbachev.

Source: Hy Rosen, *Albany Times-Union*, 1985.

10   *Reykjavik summit destroyed by Star Wars*
by Jerry Fearing, *St. Paul Dispatch-Pioneer Press*, 1986

Ronald Reagan and Mikhail Gorbachev held their second summit in October 1986. The news coming out of the first day of meetings on October 11 raised high hopes for dramatic reductions in the number of intermediate-range missiles in Europe and the intercontinental ballistic missiles in the United States and Soviet Union, but these hopes were dashed on October 12 when the two leaders could not agree on a plan for research and deployment of Reagan's strategic defense initiative, which skeptics of the hypothetical system had dubbed "Star Wars."

Source: Pioneer Press Copyright © 2015. All rights reserved.

11   *"Little Ronnie Reagan and his imaginary friend"*
by Mike Keefe, *Denver Post*, 1987

In the aftermath of the Reykjavik summit, commentators continued to fear that Reagan's commitment to SDI and Gorbachev's resistance to it would ruin the potential for arms limitation that the two leaders' relationship seemed to promise. Only in retrospect, with the aid of documents and recollections, is it clear that in 1987 Gorbachev came to the conclusion that SDI would never be a viable defense shield and that he did not need to link arms limitation to controls on SDI development.

Source: Mike Keefe, InToon.com.

12 | *Reagan and Gorbachev emerging from a missile as doves*
by Dick Wallmeyer, *Long Beach Press-Telegram*, 1987

The third Reagan-Gorbachev summit, in Washington, D.C., in early December 1987, was less ambitious in its goals for arms reduction than the Reykjavik summit, but it did successfully achieve some reductions in actual nuclear weapons. More important for the mood of the time, the summit made clear that the two leaders of the world's nuclear superpowers were still committed to arms reductions and that the failure at Reykjavik had not spoiled the Reagan-Gorbachev partnership for peace. At the start of the summit, President Reagan said, "Americans believe people should be able to disagree and still respect one another, still live in peace with one another. That is the spirit, the democratic spirit, that I will bring to our meetings."

Source: Richard Wallmeyer.

13 | *Evolution*
by Joe Majeski, *Wilkes-Barre Times-Leader*, 1988

By the time of the fourth Reagan-Gorbachev summit, this time in Moscow in May 1988, even Reagan's critics were admitting that he had made great strides in mending the relationship with the Soviet Union. The president who had called the Soviet Union the "evil empire" and had revived production of the neutron bomb now referred to the Soviets as "allies" and sought to eliminate all nuclear weapons.

Source: Wilkes-Barre Times Leader, 1988.

Analyzing Political Cartoons

1. Exaggeration and distortion are basic tools that cartoonists use to make their editorial points. How are Ronald Reagan's physical features exaggerated in these political cartoons? What messages did the cartoonists convey with their distorted drawings?

2. Cartoonists argue about artistic techniques among themselves. Some take the view that a cartoonist who draws labels on people or objects in a cartoon is somehow cheating or insulting the reader's intelligence. Look over the cartoons in this set that include labels. Do you think that they detract from or enhance the effect of these cartoons?

3. If this set of cartoons were your *only* source of information on U.S. military policy and Soviet policy during the Reagan administration, what story would you be able to construct from the cartoons?

4. Cartoonists' work must be readily accessible to viewers, but cartoonists must also assume that their audience is somewhat informed about political events. Which cartoons in this set could have been grasped by a person who did not pay much attention to the news? Which cartoons required a more advanced knowledge of current events?

5. The cartoons in this chapter were all selected from a series of books published annually entitled *Best Editorial Cartoons of the Year*. Which cartoon do *you* think is the "best" in this set? Write an explanation of your choice. Be sure to discuss the mix of content and style that influences your evaluation. Is your selection based on the editorial opinion expressed in the cartoon, or is it based on the cartoonist's use of exaggerated visual imagery to make a point? Does your favorite cartoon include a lot of detail, or is it very spare? Do you pay more attention to the words in the cartoon or to the drawing itself?

6. When Reagan was elected, cartoonist Jeff MacNelly lamented that it would be hard to satirize a president whose policies he agreed with. Which cartoons directly attack Reagan's policies? Which ones favor Reagan? Which appear neutral? How did you reach these conclusions?

The Rest of the Story

Three years after Ronald Reagan left office, the Union of Soviet Socialist Republics ceased to exist, its presidency was eliminated, and Mikhail Gorbachev no longer held any official power. The fifteen republics that made up the Soviet Union all became independent states in December 1991. Two years earlier, the Warsaw Pact nations of East Germany, Poland, Bulgaria, Czechoslovakia, Hungary, and Romania (which had operated under Soviet control since 1955) had all declared independence from Moscow. At the same time, the Berlin Wall came down, and the reunification of East Germany and West Germany began. As one historian put it, "A political avalanche had changed the face of Europe" in the space of just over two years, and only in the case of Romania was any blood spilled.

The U.S. president who witnessed these dramatic events and devised U.S. foreign policy in response to them was George Herbert Walker Bush, formerly Ronald Reagan's vice president and a public official whose experience in foreign affairs included appointments as U.S. ambassador to the United Nations, chief U.S. diplomatic representative in China, and director of the Central Intelligence Agency. As a product of the U.S. foreign affairs establishment, Vice President Bush had been uncomfortable with President Reagan's harsh denunciations of the Soviet Union and equally uncomfortable with Reagan's wide swing toward eliminating nuclear weapons. When George H. W. Bush moved into the Oval Office, he intended to deal slowly and cautiously with the Soviet Union, Gorbachev, and the apparent thaw in the Cold War.

In 1988, the Bush administration articulated a U.S. policy that looked beyond Cold War "containment" of the Soviet Union and its Warsaw Pact countries and proposed "integration" of the Soviet Union and its satellites "into the community of nations." Even as that new U.S. policy was being devised, the Warsaw Pact was unraveling. Commentators at the time criticized Bush for being too reserved in his reaction to the demise of Soviet power in Eastern Europe, but the president believed that prudence dictated a fairly closed-mouth approach. Because independence movements within the Warsaw Pact put Gorbachev in political danger inside the Soviet Union, Bush believed that he should avoid any celebratory comments that conservatives in Moscow could interpret as a U.S. declaration of victory in the Cold War. Rather than gloat over the Soviet loss of regional power, Bush sought to protect Gorbachev from his internal enemies and to assist Gorbachev's democratizing efforts by staying out of the way. Bush announced major cuts in conventional weapons and military forces stationed in Europe but did not otherwise interfere in the Eastern Europeans' tumultuous political process.

Even though the international ground was shifting below their feet, George Bush and Gorbachev did hold four summit meetings, the last four of a total of sixteen summits ever held between a U.S. president and a Soviet leader. The agendas at each of those summits reveal a shift from the Cold War to what Bush optimistically described as the "new world order."

The first summit was held on a ship off the island of Malta in December 1989, just as Soviet control over Eastern Europe was collapsing. Although the agenda focused on old, familiar issues—strategic arms limitation plans and military installations in Europe—the whole thrust was new. Gorbachev told Bush that the Soviet Union's stability relied on continued U.S. military presence in Europe; faced with the prospect of a reunited, independent Germany, Gorbachev told Bush, "We don't consider you an enemy any more. Things have changed."

Indeed, things had changed so much that by the time of the second summit in the United States in 1990, the focus of discussion was not on weapons but rather on trade and Gorbachev's need for economic assistance from the United States to survive the political and economic dislocations resulting from Soviet policies of *glasnost* and *perestroika*. It was the third summit, a one-day meeting in Helsinki, Finland, in early September 1990, that marked for many observers the end of the Cold War and a new chapter in international history. Bush and Gorbachev met in Helsinki for one purpose: to solidify their shared opposition to

Iraqi leader Saddam Hussein's recent invasion of Kuwait. Gorbachev agreed to vote with the United States at the United Nations to denounce the Soviets' former ally, Iraq, but did not agree to join a military attack on Iraq should diplomacy fail. Gorbachev warned Bush that invasion of Iraq could lead to the sort of quagmire the Soviets had faced in Afghanistan and the United States had faced in Vietnam. Still, they spoke as partners in Helsinki, not as rivals.

Viewed from the perspective of the Cold War, the cooperation around the Iraq problem looked to George H. W. Bush like the start of a new world order in which the two world powers, working together through the United Nations, would be able to guarantee world peace. So great was Bush's desire to stabilize this new world order that his final summit with Gorbachev in Moscow in the summer of 1991 was most notable for the U.S. president's efforts to hold the Soviet Union together by discouraging the independence movement in Ukraine.

President Bush's new world order did not evolve out of the Cold War as he had envisioned it. A cautious approach to the Soviet Union did not prevent the demise of that world power or the end of Gorbachev's influence, and a decision not to invade Iraq did not prevent later U.S. adventures in that country. The four Bush-Gorbachev summits did mark the end of the Cold War, but the new world order was beyond these two leaders' reach.

To Find Out More

Political Cartoon Collections

Brooks, Charles, ed. *Best Editorial Cartoons of the Year*. Gretna, LA: Pelican, published annually. The 1980 through 1989 editions were the source for cartoons in this chapter.

Cagle, Daryl. *Political Cartoonists Index*. MSNBC. http://www.cagle.com.

Secondary Sources on Political Cartooning

Bok, Chip. *The Recent History of the United States in Political Cartoons*. Akron, OH: University of Akron Press, 2005.

Hess, Stephen, and Sandy Northrup. *Drawn and Quartered: The History of American Political Cartoons*. Montgomery, AL: Elliott and Clark, 1996.

Lamb, Chris. *Drawn to Extremes: The Use and Abuse of Editorial Cartoons*. New York: Columbia University Press, 2004.

Primary Source on the Reagan-Gorbachev Summit

"The Reykjavik File: Previously Secret Documents from U.S. and Soviet Archives on the 1986 Reagan-Gorbachev Summit." National Security Archive, George Washington University. www.gwu.edu/~nsarchiv/NSAEBB/NSAEBB203/index .htm.

Secondary Sources on the Reagan-Gorbachev Era and the End of the Cold War

Fischer, Beth A. *The Reagan Reversal: Foreign Policy and the End of the Cold War.* Columbia: University of Missouri Press, 1997.

Garthoff, Raymond. *Great Transition: American-Soviet Relations and the End of the Cold War.* Washington, DC: Brookings Institution, 1994.

Hutchings, Robert L. *American Diplomacy and the End of the Cold War: An Insider's Account of U.S. Diplomacy in Europe, 1989–1992.* Baltimore: Johns Hopkins University Press, 1998.

Lettow, Paul. *Ronald Reagan and His Quest to Abolish Nuclear Weapons.* New York: Random House, 2005.

Matlock, Jack, Jr. *Reagan and Gorbachev: How the Cold War Ended.* New York: Random House, 2004.

Oberdorfer, Don. *From the Cold War to a New Era: The United States and the Soviet Union, 1983–1991.* Baltimore: Johns Hopkins University Press, 1998.

Schweizer, Peter. *Victory: The Reagan Administration's Secret Strategy That Hastened the Collapse of the Soviet Union.* New York: Atlantic Monthly Press, 1996.

Shultz, George P. *Turmoil and Triumph: My Years as Secretary of State.* New York: Charles Scribner's Sons, 1993.

Organizing Their Lives

Women, Work, and Family, 1950–2000

On January 25, 1971, Ida Phillips heard the good news: the justices of the United States Supreme Court had ruled unanimously that the Martin Marietta Corporation broke the law when it refused to hire her into a factory position in Orlando, Florida. When applying for the job, Phillips told the company that she had seven children and that the youngest child was in a day nursery. In response, Martin Marietta told Phillips that its policy was not to hire women with preschool-age children, even when the job involved building the monorail for a child's paradise: Disney World.

Ida Phillips, at age thirty-five, was not a feminist firebrand, but she told a reporter for the *Ladies' Home Journal*, "It's not just for myself that I'm doing this; it's for all mothers." Along with her husband, a truck mechanic, Phillips was working to support her family, and the simple fact was that assembly-line jobs at Martin Marietta paid twice what she earned in her waitressing job. When Phillips found out that the company hired men with preschool-age children for those assembly-line jobs, she filed a complaint with the Equal Employment Opportunities Commission (EEOC). The commission's purpose is to investigate charges that employers have violated Title VII of the 1964 Civil Rights Act, the portion of the law that prohibits employment discrimination on the basis of race, color, religion, national origin, or sex. Phillips's 1970 complaint launched the first sex discrimination case under Title VII to reach the Supreme Court.

Phillips's victory in the case, which came with the support of President Richard Nixon's Justice Department, marks just one moment in American women's ongoing struggle to integrate their income-earning and child-rearing responsibilities. By tracing that struggle over the last five decades of the twentieth century, we can begin to appreciate its practical challenges and cultural complexities.

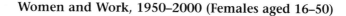

Women and Work, 1950–2000 (Females aged 16–50)

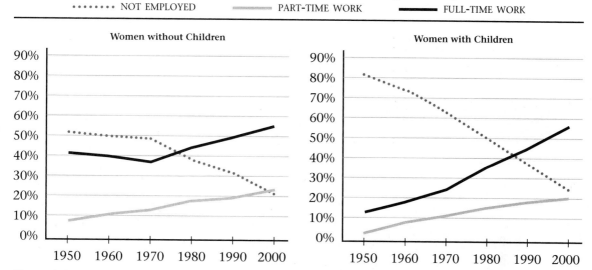

Figure 1 Women and Work, 1950–2000 *The percentages in these charts were compiled from IPUMS-USA, which offers carefully designed samples of anonymous information on individual American households drawn from the U.S. Bureau of the Census. The sample size for the 1950–1970 data is 1 percent of the U.S. population, yielding a 0.2–0.3 percent margin of error; the sample size for the 1980–2000 data is 5 percent of the population, yielding a 0.1 percent margin of error. Source:* Steven Ruggles, J. Trent Alexander, Katie Genadek, Ronald Goeken, Matthew B. Schroeder, and Matthew Sobek, *Integrated Public Use Microdata Series: Version 5.0* (Minneapolis: University of Minnesota, 2010), http://usa.ipums.org/usa.

Born in 1935, Ida Phillips was in elementary school at the end of World War II, that watershed in U.S. labor history when married women first outnumbered single women in the workforce. She grew up in a postwar world in which American wives and mothers, across class and across race, persistently participated in paid labor. Between 1940 and 1960, the number of working mothers increased by 400 percent, and by 1960, one third of all female workers had children below the age of eighteen (see Figure 1). This economic trend is remarkable because it unfolded in a cultural climate that claimed to disapprove of mothers working for pay outside the home. In 1950, for example, when almost one-fourth of all U.S. wives were employed, a *Fortune* magazine poll reported that two-thirds of its middle-class respondents opposed wives working. Such attitudes were often reflected in television shows and advertising campaigns of the era, and yet the trend of workforce participation by wives and mothers continued upward, especially among middle-class women.

Contrary to our image of the 1950s as a time of stress-free gender conformity, the reality is that the decades between 1945 and 1965—between the end of World War II and the start of the modern feminist movement—were a time of genuine conflict over the American mother's role. At the ideological extreme, Freudian theory claimed that any woman who sought paid employment suffered

Figure 2 Working Mothers and Their Children, 1952 *The end of the day at a child care center looks very much the same today as it did in 1952. Although mothers of preschool children were far less likely to work in the 1950s than they are today, those who did work relied on private child care providers, neighbors, or family members, especially grandmothers, to take care of their children during the work day.*
Source: Nina Leen/The LIFE Picture Collection/ Getty Images.

from "penis envy" and a "masculinity complex," while Cold War rhetoric insisted that the American man's success at supporting his wife and children with an individual "family wage" was proof of capitalism's superiority. In the eyes of these conservative critics, mothers who took paid jobs were either neurotic or subversive. More mainstream opponents of maternal employment simply ignored the economic need to work. They emphasized the social importance of women's child rearing and insisted that modern labor-saving devices did not render home-making obsolete.

Defenders of mothers' employment in the 1945–1965 era agreed on the importance and the difficulty of child rearing and housekeeping. But working moms and their supporters challenged the idea that a single "family wage" was adequate to provide an American standard of living and upheld a woman's right to pursue work outside the home. In labor union meetings and in the pages of popular magazines, in women's organizations and in political party conferences, advocates for working mothers called for profamily reforms like maternity leave (without loss of seniority), flexible hours, and childcare centers that would allow women to better perform all their responsibilities to their families.

In the competitive Cold War climate of the 1950s and 1960s, U.S. policy-makers began to voice their own concerns about full-time female domesticity. They worried that household duties were depriving society of women's economic contribution. According to a 1957 report by the National Manpower Council, women performed vital service as teachers, nurses, and clericals in the sex-segregated labor market, but a postwar pattern of early marriage and early childbearing was taking too many women off the track to these female jobs. Since many women were in their early thirties when their youngest child started school, the Manpower Council recommended that society provide ways for these youthful mothers to move into these vital, traditionally female occupations. It also observed that women with five or more years of postsecondary school were twice as likely to be in the workforce as women with no high school degree, but these women were often underused by being denied promotions and excluded from traditionally male jobs. How could the United States compete with the Soviet Union, asked the Manpower Council, if our best and brightest women were systematically confined to the kitchen and the typing pool?

Amidst this debate over women's roles, President John F. Kennedy bowed to pressure from women in labor unions and, in 1961, appointed a Presidential Commission on the Status of Women to study the barriers and opportunities for women in American society. The commission's 1963 report, showing a national pattern of sex discrimination against women in all walks of life, launched a wave of female organizing that triggered the feminist movement of the 1960s and 1970s. This modern movement is often referred to as the "second wave" out of respect for the "first wave" woman suffrage movement, a seventy-two year struggle that culminated in the ratification of the Nineteenth Amendment in 1920. In contrast to the first-wave women's movement, the second wave gained grass-roots popularity with dizzying speed. Its rise in popularity was so rapid in part because the second wave included a wide array of viewpoints, from the members of the National Organization of Women, who sought gender equality within the existing political and economic systems, to more radical feminists who sought salaries and Social Security for all homemaker-mothers or who envisioned communal rearing of test-tube babies.

For millions of women and men, however, riding the second wave of feminism in the 1970s meant agreement on three basic principles. First, that "gender," not "sex," defines our social roles—that is, culture, not biology, dictates who rears children, who tends the house, who makes the money—and gender roles are quite malleable. Second, that the personal is highly political; our individual freedom in organizing our households, our families, our work lives, our sex lives, and our reproductive lives is profoundly shaped by the nation's public policies. And third, men as well as women should be engaged in the socially important work of child rearing and housekeeping. Although some vocal members of the more radical "women's liberation movement" defined domesticity and motherhood as oppressive to women, the vast majority of second-wave Americans agreed with the position most consistently articulated by African American feminists that both work and motherhood are empowering for women and that disregard for either is simply unrealistic. Across gender, race, and class, feminists in the United States found common ground on the same issue that had fueled debate in the 1950s: how to design public policies that will allow for the integration of paid employment and family life.

The economic troubles of the 1970s and 1980s created a climate that was both hospitable and hostile to feminism. On the one hand, the tripling of federal, business, and personal debt, the rise in oil prices, and an unfavorable balance of payments in foreign trade meant "stagflation": prices went up, unemployment went up, and real earnings went down. Husbands and wives did not have to become card-carrying members of the National Organization for Women to recognize that a family's economic security demanded that both parents work and earn as much as possible. Ida Phillips was not alone in calculating that sex discrimination in employment materially injured her family and that antidiscrimination laws were needed to remove that injury. It was a mix of feminist conviction and economic need that fueled the expansion of mothers' workforce participation: in 1970, only 10 percent of mothers of preschool children worked full time; by 1990, almost 30 percent did so. Similarly, in 1970, 25 percent of mothers of school-age children worked full time; by 1990, 40 percent did so. Over the course of these twenty years, feminist activism brought improvements in the jobs these mothers could get and the pay they received.

At the same time, however, a new movement of Christian conservatives and limited-state libertarians was coalescing, partly in response to feminism but also in reaction to the 1960s counterculture and the government spending of President Lyndon Johnson's Great Society programs. As early as the election of Richard Nixon to the presidency in 1968, advocates for the "New Right" aimed to improve the economy by reducing government programs. So, just at the moment when feminists sought to expand public support for child care, the economic downturn and the New Right were exerting joint resistance to such expensive entitlement programs. Conservatives predicted that a reduction in government spending and taxes would produce such prosperity that Americans would be able to afford their own, private solutions to their child care needs or, better yet, mothers would be able to stay home with their children. Those predictions did not prove accurate, however. A survey of readers by *Better Homes and Gardens* in February 1982 found genuine anger that the New Right's Reagan Revolution had not made it possible for middle-class families to either afford high-quality private day care or survive on one parent's income.

Throughout the conservative Reagan years and into the more liberal years of the Clinton presidency, Americans continued to struggle with competing sets of values and goals. On the one hand, they accepted the feminist view that women have the need, the right, and the ability to operate as breadwinners for their families. On the other hand, they accepted the libertarian view that individuals, not tax-supported programs, should manage the costs associated with child care, which can consume more than 35 percent of a single parent's income. For example, the welfare reform act of 1996 ended the federal government's six-decade commitment to aid single mothers. Called the Personal Responsibility and Work Opportunity Reconciliation Act, this legislation embraced the feminist idea that women are capable workers but not the feminist call for universal state-subsidized child care as an extension of public school.

Throughout all the swings in the political pendulum in the second half of the twentieth century, mothers in the United States kept on raising their kids and going to work. Sometimes the government, the culture, and the economy assisted mothers in performing these dual roles; sometimes mothers persevered in the face of resistance. Despite dramatic changes in women's access to occupations they were once denied, despite real increases in women's income, and despite general acceptance of the reality of maternal employment, Americans still struggled to find individual, affordable, responsible solutions to the conflict between earning an income and child rearing.

Using Multiple Sources on Women, Work, and Family, 1950–2000

Social attitudes and social realities are, by definition, interactive and dynamic. To analyze social attitudes in the past, multiple sources from multiple social positions must be considered. Using only situation comedies from the 1950s, for example, to analyze social attitudes toward working mothers leads to the conclusion that all American mothers worked at home and were delighted to do so. That conclusion is not only wrong, it is boring and unrealistic. Multiple readings from multiple sources over time give us the complicated, conflicted, contradictory picture that we all know, from our own experience, to be the real story of social attitudes.

Up to this point in the second volume of *Going to the Source*, we have concentrated on the advantages and disadvantages of just one type of historical source per chapter. We have explored visual and printed sources, public and private sources, and primary and secondary sources. In addition, we have focused on particular places and moments in post–Civil War U.S. history, such as the Blackfeet Indian reservation at the beginning of the twentieth century, the 1894 Pullman rail strike, Japanese internment during World War II, and economic decline in the 1970s. In this chapter, we apply lessons learned along the way to analyze a range of different source types over a longer span of time.

What Can Multiple Source Types Tell Us?

All historical analyses draw on multiple types of sources to tell the story. A book on the New Deal's post office murals might put the visual evidence at the center of the analysis, but it would also have to draw on Treasury Department press releases and policy papers, letters between artists and local communities, and newspaper reports on new murals to place the murals in historical context. Similarly, a complete analysis of the Senate speeches during the filibuster of the Civil Rights Act would have to use government records of previous civil rights bills, biographies of Senate members, presidential memos, letters, and tape recordings, national and local polling data, and both print and film news reports on the civil rights movement to explain the content of the speeches and the outcome of the filibuster. Close analysis of one source type is necessary in historical analysis, but never sufficient. Multiple sources are needed to provide a fully furnished view of any moment in time.

Examining a range of sources rather than a single source type can produce a more complete picture and a broader perspective on a historical episode, but tracking down a wide variety of sources can be a challenge. Staying focused on a specific research question and limiting the scope to a meaningful time period are critical in preventing the research task from becoming overwhelming. For this chapter, our goal is to present different positions as expressed in different types of sources, allowing you to draw on the analytical skills acquired from previous chapters to construct your own argument about women, work, and motherhood in the United States in the second half of the twentieth century.

You will find, for example, that a presidential veto message can be analyzed like Senate speeches: it may not tell you what the person in power actually thought, but it will tell you what arguments that person regarded as most persuasive with his or her constituency, and that in itself serves as a window on public opinion. Public opinion polls, of course, give us the most direct access to information on attitudes and can provide surprising evidence of the gap between what people say they believe in and what they actually do. For example, a majority of poll respondents may say that they do not approve of mothers working for pay even though objective data on employment shows that a majority of mothers do, in fact, hold paying jobs.

Cultural products, like songs or cartoons, can also be used as a gauge of popular opinion. The creators of these products, like the federal sponsors of the post office murals, hope to appeal to a broad audience, but they also want to express a particular view of the world. When creative works, including children's songs or comic strips, become very popular, historians can conclude that their creators were in sync with the culture's dominant values. They do not, of course, represent everyone's views, but they can be used as evidence of what was marketable, popular, and mainstream at a particular moment in time. Articles from mass-marketed magazines seek to strike a balance, offering enough individual viewpoints to be interesting for readers but presenting those views in a way that will not offend a broad readership. They can give us a sense of what is acceptable to discuss, but we cannot conclude that every reader agreed with each article's position.

When we turn to sources like labor union debates, political newsletters or position papers, government reports, and even letters to the editor, we know that the views expressed are those of the individuals or organization members who hold particular ideological positions. Their aim is to persuade others, but their views are not necessarily those of the majority of Americans. From such sources, historians can round out their understanding of the society's discussion of a topic like work and motherhood, bringing in the voices of those who might not sell a lot of products or recordings but who are actively engaged in influencing social attitudes and who may signify a passing stage or the next stage in those attitudes.

All historical sources, of course, must be read with sensitivity to the cultural and political climate in which they were created. However familiar the issues of motherhood, housewifery, and employment may sound, debate on these issues in the 1950s took place in a world where both the technology of domestic life and scientific assumptions about sex differences were different from today's. Housewifery did, objectively, take more time in an era that offered fewer time-saving food and cleaning products than are available today, and unsophisticated research on sex differences did promote now-disproven beliefs about intellectual and "temperamental" differences between men and women. Although the issues under debate have persisted, the social and material context has changed considerably. A housewife arguing for the value of her domestic labor was not as old-fashioned in 1956 as she would be today.

Source Analysis Table

The various sources included here represent a range of views expressed in public discussions of women, work, and motherhood in the years between 1955 and 1998. This chapter is your opportunity to review the principles of source analysis that we have been developing throughout *Going to the Source* and then build on your source analysis to develop your own interpretation of the sources. For that reason, the table on pages 324–25 operates as your Checklist questions to ask of each source. Completion of this table will help you sort out the array of sources; identify differences and similarities in the purposes, audiences, points of view, and biases in these sources; and work toward building your own argument about the pattern, meaning, and significance that you find in this material.

Source	Source Type	Source Audience	Source Purpose	Source Viewpoint	Source Bias
1. UAW-CIO Workers' Debate, 1955					
2. "Modern American Housewife," 1956					
3. Florida Scott-Maxwell, "Women Know They Are Not Men," 1958					
4. *American Women: Report of the President's Commission on the Status of Women*, 1963					
5. Dr. Benjamin Spock, "Should Mothers Work?" 1963					
6. National Organization for Women, "Why Feminists Want Child Care," 1969					
7. President Richard M. Nixon, Veto of the Comprehensive Child Development Act, 1971					
8. *The Phyllis Schlafly Report*, "What's Wrong with 'Equal Rights' for Women?" 1972					

Source	Source Type	Source Audience	Source Purpose	Source Viewpoint	Source Bias
9. Carol Hall, "Parents Are People," 1972					
10. Miriam Wosk, *Ms.* magazine cover, 1972					
11. Betty Friedan, *The Second Stage*, 1981					
12. Claudia Tate, "Should We Expect Black Women to Be Supermothers?" 1984					
13. Lynn Johnston, *For Better or For Worse*, 1984					
14. National Opinion Research Center Poll: Women, Work, and Family, 1972–1998					
15. Richard Morin and Megan Rosenfeld, "The Politics of Fatigue," 1998					

The Sources: Documents on Women, Work, and Family, 1950–2000

1 Meeting of Union of Auto, Aerospace, and Agricultural Implement Workers of America (UAW-CIO)
Public debate. March 27–April 1, 1955

The members of this UAW affiliate were debating a resolution that upcoming contract negotiations include the requirement that employers end customary discrimination in hiring and wages based on sex and marital status.

DELEGATE BARRY, LOCAL 835: I urge the adoption of this resolution for the reason that . . . many women . . . are the breadwinners of the family. In the case of Negro women, if they don't work in the plant they are forced to go out and do day work [domestic service] for $6 a day and carfare. In some instances that I personally know about some of them are taking care of crippled husbands and a lot of children that nobody else will help to support. . . .

DELEGATE CARRIGAN, LOCAL 887: In my Local there are approximately 2,000 women members. . . . Many of us have ten or more years seniority in our jobs and are still in the lowest classifications. . . . The resolution states that an average income is forty-four percent less for women than for men. This forty-four percent represents purchasing power which should be in the workers' pockets instead of in management's till. . . .

DELEGATE HILL, LOCAL 961: I rise to oppose the particular resolution on the floor at this time for the simple reason that I think our International Union is trying to create a condition whereby it will require two paychecks in every home in order that we might live like decent human beings. . . .

I am not opposed to single women and widows working in the shop, but I am opposed to married women working. . . .

DELEGATE MURPHY, LOCAL 3: Two paychecks in a family are fine. I happen to be married. My husband happens to be one of those unfortunate people with twenty-two years seniority in Hudson Local Union No. 154. Today he has no job. What would happen if I wasn't able to work? My family would be going hungry. . . .

DELEGATE RUTT, LOCAL 195: . . . . as long as there are single women looking for jobs the married woman's place is in the home. . . . As long as the husband is working it is his place to provide for his wife and family.

Source: Excerpt from transcript of Meeting of Union of Auto, Aerospace and Agricultural Implementation Workers of America (UAW-CIO). Reprinted by permission of United Auto Workers.

DELEGATE SZURE, LOCAL 174: . . . Who is to say a woman should work or not? Where is our democracy in this country if a woman cannot be a free individual and make up her own mind? I think that when you start telling women you can or cannot work, you are infringing on their civil rights, which I as a woman resent.

2   *Modern American Housewife*
Letter to the editor.
Ladies' Home Journal, March 1956

Dear Editors: I am furious! I have just read an article in which a psychologist says that the American male has spoiled his wife and made her *useless* by the purchase of automatic equipment in the home. He then adds, "Women don't feel needed. They know the house will almost run itself."

I am one of those women lumped together as a group of nonworkers. I am an average American housewife. I have laborsaving equipment in my home. The wife of a county official, I have three children. And I have found none of these four to be a laborsaving device. I find that it is I who must change bed linens, wash clothes, hang clothes, take clothes down, iron clothes, mend clothes and put them away. No one has invented a laborsaving device for these chores, or an automatic diaper-changing device! I have yet to find on the market an automatic push-button control for picking up articles not in the proper place.

I prepare three meals a day, by the best methods revealed in the women's magazines. I make most of our pastry and our freezer has a considerable supply of fresh fruit pies ready to bake, corn on the cob, and a side of beef. All were prepared by me, usually at night. . . .

The activities one gets into to provide a happy, wholesome life for her children are all time-consuming. As mother of a boy, I was a Cub Scout assistant den mother. As mother of two daughters, I have co-led a Brownie troop. As a member of the community, I have been twice elected to our elementary-school board of trustees. . . . As a member of a church, I have taught in the Sunday school. For none of these activities am I paid. . . .

We American women need every laborsaving device there is. There are more demands on our time than it is humanly possible to fill, and we are anything but *useless*. . . .

SINCERELY YOURS, A Reader from Castro Valley, California

3 | *Women Know They Are Not Men: When Will Business Learn This Valuable Secret and Arrange Women's Working Conditions Accordingly?*

Survey report. Florida Scott-Maxwell,
Ladies' Home Journal, **November 1958**

In this article, Scott-Maxwell reported on the results of a survey the *Ladies' Home Journal* conducted with "hundreds of young mothers." Ninety percent of the respondents had experience working for pay; half were working outside the home when the survey was taken. Although the survey itself did not ask women for solutions to their problems, the title and conclusion of the article imply that the author thought that there were tangible solutions.

Whether they work at outside jobs or not, today's young mothers find their greatest satisfaction in home, husband and children. They realize they are not men, and they don't want to be. . . . And yet they are faced with a dilemma peculiar to women and to our times. . . . Will their families, and they themselves, be better off and happier if they work, or if they remain at home? . . .

Can a mother of young children satisfactorily fulfill her family responsibilities and hold a full-time job besides? A majority of those who are doing it say yes, though they admit the dual role produces considerable strain. On the other hand, can a young woman who has enjoyed the stimulation and contacts of outside employment find satisfaction when and if she quits to devote herself full time to home and children? Again, the answer is yes, though not without some qualifications.

All agreed that the first responsibility is to home and family. . . . Those who do not work feel that they could not earn enough to justify the added strain and expense of being away from the children while they are young. . . . Meanwhile, they sometimes feel restless, frustrated, that they are wasting special talents and training. . . .

Young mothers who now hold jobs show conflicting feelings. Nine out of ten give finances as a major reason for working, yet . . . fifty-eight percent of these women say that they prefer working at a paid job to staying at home! . . .

On the debit side of the ledger, most young working mothers suffer to some degree from the fear that they are not adequately fulfilling their duties to husband, home and children. And yet eighty-one percent say they are satisfied with the arrangements they have made for the children's care, and sixty-one percent think the children would be no better off if their mothers had more time with them. . . . The young working mother's second problem is . . . she returns from work to take over the housework herself. . . . Her race with the clock goes on from Monday to Monday, evenings and weekends included. . . .

The present situation presents no problem to the young mother who never did like working and who doesn't need to. She simply doesn't work. The opposite decision is almost as simple (not quite) for the woman who is highly trained and talented in a specialized field. But for the majority of women in between the question is difficult, and the answer not likely to be entirely satisfactory. One thing is certain: if women had organized business and industry, the system would be different. And it might be better.

 ## 4   *American Women: Report of the President's Commission on the Status of Women*
Government report. October 1963

> From 1961 to 1963, twenty-six prominent men and women with experience in labor, economics, politics, race relations, education, and social services served on the President's Commission on the Status of Women. Their deliberations were informed by research submitted by numerous subcommittees. President Kennedy appointed former First Lady Eleanor Roosevelt to chair the commission, a position she held until her death in November 1962. The final, seventy-five page report was issued in October 1963, just weeks before Kennedy was assassinated.

American women work in both their homes, unpaid, and outside of their homes, on a wage or salary basis. Among the great majority of women, as among the great majority of men, the motive for paid employment is to earn money. For some, work has additional—or even primary—value as self-fulfillment. . . . Women's participation in paid employment importantly increases the Nation's labor force: 1 worker in 3 is a woman. . . .

Because personnel officers believe that women are less likely than men to want to make a career in industry, equally well-prepared young women are passed over in favor of men for posts that lead into management training programs and subsequent exercise of major executive responsibility. . . . Reluctance to consider women applicants on their merits results in underutilization of capacities that the economy needs and stunts the development of higher skills. . . .

The Commission recognizes the fundamental responsibility of mothers and homemakers and society's stake in strong family life. Demands upon women in the economic world, the community, and the home mean that women often simultaneously carry on several different kinds of activity. If the family is to continue to be the core institution of society . . . new and expanded community

Source: American Women: Report of the President's Commission on the Status of Women, 1963 (Washington, DC: U.S. Government Printing Office, 1963), 18, 19, 27, 29–30.

services are necessary. Women can do a far more effective job as mothers and homemakers when communities provide appropriate resources. . . .

Child care services are needed in all communities, for children of all kinds of families who may require day care, afterschool care, or intermittent care. In putting major emphasis on this need, the Commission affirms that child care facilities are essential for women in many different circumstances, whether they work outside the home or not. It is regrettable when women with children are forced by economic necessity or by the regulations of welfare agencies to seek employment while their children are young. On the other hand, those who decide to work should have child care services available. . . .

The gross inadequacy of present child care facilities is apparent. Across the country, licensed day care is available to some 185,000 children only. In nearly half a million families with children under 6 years, the mother is frequently the sole supporter. . . . Failure to assure such services reflects primarily a lack of community awareness of the realities of modern life.

5   *Should Mothers Work?*
Advice column. Dr. Benjamin Spock, *Ladies' Home Journal*, January–February 1963

> Dr. Spock was an American pediatrician whose child-rearing manual, *The Common Sense Book of Baby and Child Care*, first published in 1946, is the seventh best-selling book of all time. He regularly delivered advice to mothers in the pages of popular magazines in the 1950s and 1960s. The subhead for this column stated, "A drastic change has taken place—half of our mothers have given birth to their last child by the age of twenty-six."

For years I've shied away from writing on the subject of working mothers. It has so many prickly aspects that there is no simple way to tackle it. But the proportion of mothers working has risen steadily, especially since the beginning of World War II, so there's no use my trying to dodge the topic. . . .

If it's essential from a financial point of view for a mother of a young child to work, she is spared some of the doubts and guilt that are apt to trouble the woman who wants a job primarily for her own adjustment. For guilt about leaving a child will cut down on the satisfaction she receives from working, and it will complicate the mother-child relationship. . . .

Quite a few mothers say that they work to help meet the payments on the house and its equipment, or to give their children special advantages, even though their husbands are earning ordinary salaries. . . . [These mothers][1] seem to be saying that the things they can earn are more important for their

---

[1] Bracketed text has been added by the editors to fill in a gap.

Source: "Should Mothers Work?" Advice column by Dr. Benjamin Spock, *Ladies Home Journal*, January–February, 1963. Originally published in the January–February, 1963 issue of *Ladies Home Journal*,® magazine. All rights reserved.

children than taking care of them themselves. This line of thought doesn't make too much sense to me unless the mother is referring to a very temporary financial emergency, or unless her real reason is that she would be miserable taking care of her children all day long. . . .

Most of us who are fairly well adjusted—men as well as women—have an enjoyment of accomplishment. The real question is why one job gives it and another does not. In most parts of the world women feel thoroughly fulfilled in having motherhood as their main career. . . .

I'm one of those who believe that women are basically different from men in temperament as well as in anatomy and physiology. In some cultures and in some periods in history these differences have been exaggerated. I think that in America they have been unnaturally minimized. How is this process carried out in the rearing of each generation? Lots of girls from infancy are dressed like boys, encouraged to play like boys. Their mothers don't think of giving them a sense of pride and distinction in being female. . . . There are very few teachers who emphasize or even hint that motherhood (or fatherhood) is potentially, in itself, an exciting and distinguished career. The academic focus is all on the work of the world that exists outside the home. . . . Then when these young women's feminine instincts lead them into marriage and child rearing, they feel shut out of the world they envisioned. Never having thought of motherhood as demanding high skills or bringing rich rewards, knowing that any uneducated female above the age of fourteen can enter into it with no credentials at all, they may come to regard it more as a chore than as a challenge. . . .

I am not trying to dissuade any woman from having a career in addition to child rearing. I am only expressing the opinion that since most women will spend at least fifteen years of their lives mainly rearing their children, they themselves should be brought up and educated in such a way that they will derive the maximal satisfaction and enjoyment from it, even if they have other strong aspirations in addition.

6 *Why Feminists Want Child Care*
Position paper. National Organization for Women (N.O.W.), 1969

The National Organization for Women was founded in 1966 in Washington, D.C., during a national conference of members of state commissions on the status of women whose task was to extend the work of the presidential commission. When conference participants learned from Representative Martha Griffiths (D-Michigan) that the Equal Employment Opportunities Commission (EEOC) was not investigating the thousands of sex discrimination complaints it was receiving, they decided to form a nongovernmental lobbying

Source: Position Paper, "Why Feminists Want Child Care." Position paper. National Organization for Women (N.O.W.) 1969. (New York City Chapter, Paper, Box 10, Taminent Library). Reprinted by permission of NOW-NYC.

organization, made up of both men and women, to press for compliance with existing laws and passage of new laws aimed at equal rights.

A basic cause of the second-class status of women in America and the world . . . has been the notion that woman's anatomy is her destiny . . . that because women bear children, it is primarily their responsibility to care for them and even that this ought to be the chief function of a mother's existence. Women will never have full opportunities to participate in our economic, political, cultural life as long as they bear this responsibility almost entirely alone and isolated from the larger world. A child socialized by one whose human role is limited, essentially, to motherhood may be proportionately deprived of varied learning experiences. In a circular fashion, the development of children has been intimately influenced by the development of women.

N.O.W. believes that the care and welfare of children is incumbent on society *and* parents. We reject the idea that mothers have a special child care role that is not shared equally by fathers. Men need the humanizing experiences of nurturance. . . .

Developmental child care services are a right of children, parents, and the community at large, requiring immediate reallocation of national resources. In general, existing day care programs are a national disgrace in quality and availability. Therefore, the National Organization for Women, Inc. (N.O.W.) proposes the following. . . .

- Comprehensive child care and developmental services available to all children whose families seek it. . . .
- Government support of a coordinated network of developmental child care services as an immediate national priority. . . .
- Major responsibility for planning and operating the services must be a function of local control. . . .
- Developmental child care service is to be interpreted as including family child care, group home child care, child care centers, home visiting programs, and other innovative approaches to be developed in the future.

N.O.W. is committed to work for universally available, publicly supported, developmental child care and raising the national consciousness to public investment in this national priority. As interim steps, we support flexible fees, if any, to reflect the urgent needs and various resources of families now.

7 *Veto of the Comprehensive Child Development Act*

Presidential message. President Richard M. Nixon, December 9, 1971

The Comprehensive Child Development Act sought to make prekindergarten programs available to all children, as a matter of right, regardless of economic status. Programs were to be free to families earning less than half the median U.S. income; other families would pay according to a sliding scale based on income. Its across-class design conflicted with President Nixon's Family Assistance Plan, which proposed a guaranteed annual income and child care for the nation's poorest families. In late 1971, heading into a reelection campaign, Nixon needed to appeal to right-wing members of his Republican Party. They were concerned about the Family Assistance Plan and about Nixon's friendly overtures to communist China. For that reason, Nixon's veto message argued beyond the practicalities of fiscal restraint and appealed to anticommunists' cultural devotion to the self-supporting, male-headed nuclear family.

I return herewith without my approval S.2007, the Economic Opportunity Amendments of 1971. . . .

The most deeply flawed provision of this legislation is Title V, "Child Development Programs." Adopted as an amendment to the OEO[1] legislation, this program points far beyond what this administration envisioned when it made a "national commitment to providing all American children an opportunity for a healthful and stimulating development during the first five years of life."

Though Title V's stated purpose, "to provide every child with a full and fair opportunity to reach his full potential," is certainly laudable, the intent of Title V is overshadowed by the fiscal irresponsibility, administrative unworkability, and family-weakening implications of the system it envisions. We owe our children something more than good intentions.

We cannot and will not ignore the challenge to do more for America's children in their all-important early years. But our response to this challenge must be a measured, evolutionary, painstakingly considered one, consciously designed to cement the family in its rightful position as the keystone of our civilization. . . . Specifically, these are my present objections to the proposed child development program:

---

[1] The Office of Economic Opportunity (OEO) was a federal agency created in 1964 as part of the Great Society programs of President Lyndon B. Johnson's administration. Its original focus was on improving economic opportunities for Native Americans (such as the Blackfeet profiled in Chapter Two of this volume). Soon, however, the OEO was charged with administering other Great Society Programs, including the Job Corps, the Community Action Program, and Head Start. In 1974, three years after delivering this message, Nixon dismantled the OEO, transferring oversight of its programs to other federal agencies.

Source: John T. Woolley and Gerhard Peters, *The American Presidency Project,* http://www.presidency.ucsb.edu/ws/?pid=3251.

- neither the immediate need nor the desirability of a national child development program of this character has been demonstrated.

- day care centers to provide for the children of the poor so that their parents can leave the welfare rolls . . . are already paid for in H.R. 1, my workfare legislation.[2] . . .

- given the limited resources of the Federal budget, and the growing demands upon the Federal taxpayer, the expenditure of two billions of dollars in a program whose effectiveness has yet to be demonstrated cannot be justified. . . .

- for more than two years, this administration has been working for the enactment of welfare reform . . . to bring the family together. This child development program appears to move in precisely the opposite direction. . . .

- good public policy requires that we enhance rather than diminish both parental authority and parents involvement with children— particularly in those decisive early years when social attitudes and a conscience are formed, and religious and moral principles are first inculcated. . . .

- for the Federal Government to plunge headlong financially into supporting child development would commit the vast moral authority of the National Government to the side of communal approaches to child rearing over, against the family-centered approach.

[2] Nixon was referring to his Family Assistance Plan (FAP), which would have guaranteed a government subsidy to any family earning less than $2,960, rewarding those who worked at low-paid jobs with the incentive of government assistance and free child care, while promising mothers of preschool children that they did not have to work to get the subsidy. For a variety of political reasons, including the Watergate scandal, Nixon and the Democratic Congress never passed the FAP.

8   *What's Wrong with "Equal Rights" for Women?* Political newsletter. *The Phyllis Schlafly Report,* February 1972

Phyllis Schlafly has been a prominent conservative since the mid-1960s. A lawyer, author, public speaker, and mother of six, Schlafly has advocated for the preservation of women's private domestic role throughout her long public career. In 1972, she founded the Eagle Forum, a lobbying and fund-raising organization, and started publishing her newsletter, *The Phyllis Schlafly Report,* which is now published online. In her successful STOP ERA campaign, Schlafly articulated her beliefs that women in the United States had a

Source: "What's Wrong with 'Equal Rights' for Women?" by Phyllis Schlafly, February, 1972. Reprinted by permission of the author.

guaranteed right to economic support from their husbands and that the Equal Rights Amendment would abolish that right.

Of all the classes of people who ever lived, the American woman is the most privileged. We have the most rights and rewards, and the fewest duties. . . . We have the immense good fortune to live in a civilization which respects the family as the basic unit of society. This respect is part and parcel of our laws and customs. It is based on the fact of life—which no legislation or agitation can erase—that women have babies and men don't.

If you don't like this fundamental difference, you will have to take up your complaint with God because He created us this way. The fact that women, not men, have babies is not the fault of selfish and domineering men, or of the establishment, or of any clique of conspirators who want to oppress women. It's simply the way God made us.

Our Judeo-Christian civilization has developed the law and custom that, since women must bear the physical consequences of the sex act, men must be required to bear the *other* consequences and pay in other ways. These laws and customs decree that a man must carry his share by physical protection and financial support of his children and of the woman who bears his children. . . . The family gives a woman the physical, financial, and emotional security of the home—for all her life. . . . American women are . . . the beneficiaries of a tradition of special respect for women . . . the traditions of the Christian Age of Chivalry. In America, a man's first significant purchase is a diamond for his bride, and the largest financial investment of his life is a home for her to live in. . . .

Under present American laws, the man is *always* required to support his wife and each child he caused to be brought into the world. . . . By law and custom in America, in the case of divorce, the mother always is given custody of her children unless there is overwhelming evidence of mistreatment, neglect, or bad character. This is our special privilege because of the high rank that is placed on motherhood in our society. Do women really want to give up this special privilege and lower themselves to "equal rights." . . . ? I think not. . . .

Women's libbers are trying to make wives and mothers unhappy with their career, make them feel that they are "second-class citizens" and "abject slaves." . . . If women's libbers want to reject marriage and motherhood, it's a free country and that is their choice. But let's not permit these women's libbers to get away with pretending to speak for the rest of us. Let's not permit this tiny minority to degrade the role that most women prefer. Let's not let these women's libbers deprive wives and mothers of the rights we now possess.

9 *Parents Are People*

Children's song. Carol Hall for
***Free to Be You and Me*, 1972**

Free to Be You and Me **is an album of eighteen original children's songs produced and performed by profeminist artists. Actress Marlo Thomas organized the project to raise funds for the Ms. Foundation, an offshoot of** *Ms.* **magazine, that funds educational programs for women and girls. As of 2006, the album had sold more than half a million copies. In 2010, the Target company used the title track in children's clothing advertisements. To hear "Parents Are People" (performed by Marlo Thomas and Harry Belafonte) and other selections from the album, visit http://www.freetobefoundation.org.**

Mommies are people, people with children
When mommies were little, they used to be girls
Like some of you, but then they grew
And now mommies are women, women with children
Busy with children, and things that they do
There are a lot of things a lot of mommies can do

Some mommies are ranchers, or poetry makers
Or doctors or teachers, or cleaners or bakers
Some mommies drive taxis, or sing on TV
Yeah, mommies can be almost anything they want to be

Well, they can't be grandfathers, or daddies

Daddies are people, people with children
When daddies were little, they used to be boys
Like some of you, but then they grew
And now daddies are men, men with children
Busy with children, and things that they do
There are a lot of things a lot of daddies can do

Some daddies are writers, or grocery sellers
Or painters or welders, or funny-joke tellers
Some daddies play cello, or sail on the sea
Yeah, daddies can be almost anything they want to be

They can't be grandmas or mommies

Parents are people—Parents are people
People with children—People with children
When parents were little, they used to be kids
Like all of you, but then they grew
And now parents are grown-ups—Parents are grown-ups

Grown-ups with children—Grown-ups with children
Busy with children, and things that they do
There are a lot of things a lot of mommies
And a lot of daddies, and a lot of parents can do

10   *Ms.* Magazine Cover (next page)
Illustration. Miriam Wosk, Spring 1972

Ms. magazine was the mass media face of the feminist movement in the 1970s and 1980s. For this cover of the preview issue in the spring of 1972, artist Miriam Wosk adapted the image of the multiarmed Hindu goddess Kali to the modern image of the multitasking American mother. The hugely successful preview issue included articles that have become icons of feminist literature, including "The Housewife's Moment of Truth," "Down with Sexist Upbringing," and "De-sexing the English Language." Indeed, the magazine's title referred to a long-standing movement to confer a title on women that, like the title "Mr.," indicates gender but not marital status. *Ms.* magazine is still published today and continues to advocate for feminist reform around the world.

Source: Ms., Spring 1972.

Source: Reprinted by permission of *Ms.* Magazine, © 1972.

11 | *The Second Stage,* Book. Betty Friedan, 1981

Betty Friedan was the author of *The Feminine Mystique*, a best-selling 1963 book that was instrumental in launching the second-wave women's movement. Friedan was a founding member and first president of the National Organization for Women and continued to be an outspoken feminist until her death in 2006. In *The Second Stage*, Friedan focused on the needs of the family and reported, in one section, on the 1980 White House Conference on Families, held at the end of President Jimmy Carter's administration, which brought together activists from both feminist and antifeminist organizations.

Though the women's movement has changed all our lives and surpassed our dreams in its magnitude, and our daughters take their own personhood and equality for granted, they—and we—are finding that it's not easy to *live*, with or without men and children, solely on the basis of that first feminist agenda. I think, in fact that the women's movement has come just about as far as it can in terms of women alone. . . . And yet the larger revolution, evolution, liberation that the women's movement set off, has barely begun. How do we move on? What are the terms of the second stage? . . .

I believe that feminism must, in fact, confront the family, albeit in new terms, if the movement is to fulfill its own revolutionary function in modern society. . . . To the degree that feminists collude in assuming an inevitable, unbridgeable antagonism between women's equality and the family, they make it a self-fulfilling prophecy. In fact, the media, which take that antagonism for granted now, reported about the White House Conference in those terms, and missed the significance of what really happened. For when we feminists broke out of our own rhetoric and dealt with women's most basic concerns within the larger family context, we were able to bridge that polarization and win overwhelming majority support for second-stage solutions. . . .

The most strongly supported demands of the entire conference, along with action to counter drug and alcohol abuse, were "the development of alternative forms of quality child care, both center and home based" (547 to 44), and "creative development" (by business, labor, and government) of "policies that enable persons to hold jobs while maintaining a strong family life," including "such work arrangements as flex-time, flexible leave policies for both sexes, job-sharing programs, dependent-care options, and part-time jobs with pro-rated pay and benefits," which passed 569 to 21.

12 | *Should We Expect Black Women to Be Supermothers?* Magazine article. Claudia Tate, *Ebony*, September 1984

Ebony **has been a successful monthly magazine since its founding in 1945. It is directed at the African American audience, both male and female. When this article was published, Claudia Tate was a professor of English at Howard University.**

The label "supermother" refers to . . . an extremely competent working mother, who both works and mothers with a singularly high degree of proficiency. She always seems in control of the situation, whether she's fixing breakfast and applying mascara after four hours of sleep, or preparing dinner after working eight hard but successful hours, or engaging in stimulating conversation with her husband after checking homework and tucking the children in their beds. . . . But no one is "super" successful on one front, let alone so many, without making difficult choices and paying high prices. That simply is the way of the world. Although the role of the working mother, let alone "supermother," is a difficult one filled with stress and exhaustion, the degree to which she is even moderately successful may dictate whether many households survive, let alone prosper. . . . [But] is the supermother image a nurturing one for Black mothers and the Black community?

First, the mythic supermother is very destructive, for it promotes the erroneous belief that Black women (who are ready victims for both racial and gender discrimination) have somehow "got it made." Consequently, many people mistakenly believe there is no need to eliminate racial and gender discrimination for Black women because they are already free as women and free as Blacks. This myth . . . makes Black women, as a group, appear to have social and economic advantages they do not, in fact, possess.

Second, the mythic supermother image is self-destructive because it is a delusion. It sets Black women up for defeat by encouraging them to believe that they can provide for their families alone, when most of them can do nothing more than contribute to the growing number of poor households. Before a Black woman (or any woman) decides to maintain a household alone, she'd better check her resources as well as her emotional needs. To leap before checking is foolhardy. . . .

But the demythologized supermother, known as the hardworking, working mother, is an exemplary figure in the Black community. She is not only real, she is someone we must support if the Black community is to prosper. We must celebrate her success, applaud her ambition, acknowledge her hard work, comfort her pain, and provide her willing assistance.

Source: From "Should We Expect Black Women to be Supermothers?" by Claudia Tate, *Ebony*, September 1984. Used by permission of the author's estate.

13 | *For Better or For Worse,* Cartoon strip. Lynn Johnston, 1984

Johnston began publishing her widely read comic strip about the Patterson family in 1979 and followed the family's development in real time until 2008. In the early 1980s, Elly Patterson, married mother of three, took a job outside the home. Johnston chronicled that change in the family's life in her newspaper comic strip and published portions of that chronicle in her 1984 collection, *Just One More Hug*, from which these examples are taken.

Source: FOR BETTER OR FOR WORSE © 1984 Lynn Johnston Productions. Dist. By UNIVERSAL UCLICK. Reprinted with permission. All rights reserved.

14   *National Opinion Research Center Poll: Women, Work, and Family*
Survey data. 1972–1998

From 1970 to 1998, researchers conducted a survey about women, work, and politics; Figure 1 shows the results. The solid line, "Women should take care of homes," reflects the percentage of people who agreed with the statement "Women should take care of running their homes and leave running the country up to men." The dashed line, "Disapprove of married women working," reflects the percentage of people who said they disapproved "of a married woman earning money in business or industry if she has a husband capable of supporting her." The dotted line, "Would not vote for woman for president," reflects the percentage of people who answered "no" to the following question: "If your political party nominated a woman for president, would you vote for her if she were qualified for the job?"

Source: Tom W. Smith, Peter Marsden, Michael Hout, and Jibum Kim, *General Social Surveys, 1972–2010* (Chicago: National Opinion Research Center, 2011).

Figure 1
Responses to Questions about Women's Employment

AGREE THAT WOMEN SHOULD RUN HOMES AND LET MEN RUN GOVERNMENT

DISAPPROVE OF MARRIED WOMAN WORKING IF SHE HAS CAPABLE HUSBAND

WOULD NOT VOTE FOR WOMAN FOR PRESIDENT

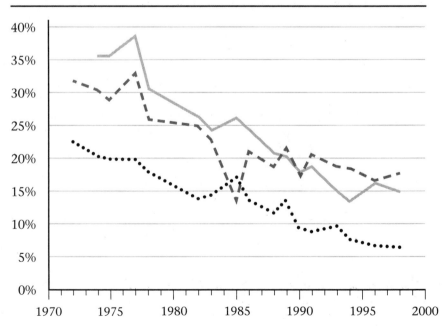

Figure 2 shows the results of a survey conducted from 1975 to 1998, in which researchers asked respondents about women, work, and home life. The dotted line, "Not more important for wife to help husband's career," reflects the percentage of people who disagreed with the statement, "It is more important for a wife to help her husband's career than to have one herself." The dashed line, "Working mothers can establish warm relationships with their children," reflects the percentage of people who agreed with the statement, "A working mother can establish just as warm and secure a relationship with her children as a mother who does not work." The solid bold line, "Preschooler is not likely to suffer if mother works," reflects the percentage of people who disagreed with the statement, "A preschool child is likely to suffer if his or her mother works." The solid light line, "Not necessarily better for everyone if man achieves outside the home," represents the percentage of people who disagreed with the statement, "It is much better for everyone involved if the man is the achiever outside the home and the woman takes care of the home and family."

Figure 2
Responses to Questions about Women Combining Work and Family

• • • • •   DO NOT AGREE THAT HUSBAND'S CAREER IS MORE IMPORTANT THAN WIFE'S

▬ ▬ ▬   AGREE THAT WORKING MOTHERS CAN ESTABLISH WARM RELATIONSHIP WITH CHILDREN

━━━━━   DO NOT AGREE THAT PRESCHOOL CHILD WILL SUFFER IF MOTHER WORKS

▬▬▬▬   DO NOT AGREE THAT FAMILY IS MUCH BETTER OFF IF MAN WORKS AND WOMAN STAYS HOME

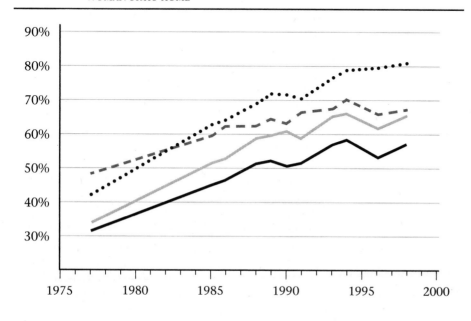

15   *The Politics of Fatigue,* Newspaper article.
Richard Morin and Megan Rosenfeld, *Washington Post,* April 20, 1998

Men and women have declared a cease-fire in the war that raged between the sexes through much of the last half of this century. In its place, they face common new enemies—the stress, lack of time and financial pressure of modern life.

A new national survey has found that after nearly a generation of sharing the workplace and renegotiating domestic duties, most men and women agree that increased gender equity has enriched both sexes. But both also believe that the strains of this relatively new world have made building successful marriages, raising children and leading satisfying lives ever more difficult. . . .

Surprisingly, although men and women agreed they should have equal work opportunities, and men said they approve of women working outside the home, large majorities of both said it would be better if women could instead stay home and just take care of the house and children. . . .

Most men in the polls said they were happy to share child care and domestic chores with wives who work outside the home. Yet household duties remain sharply divided along gender lines. Working mothers still do twice as much housework as their husbands, and more than half of all women questioned expressed at least some dissatisfaction with the amount of help their husbands provide around the house. . . .

But rather than emphasizing their differences and blaming life's problems on each other, men and women share a sense of conflict and confusion about how to make it all work under today's pressures. To a large extent, the politics of resentment have become the politics of fatigue. . . .

In important ways, the survey suggests that we have yet to find new patterns of living that recognize the real workloads of two-career couples with children, and some resentment, nostalgia and fatigue are reflected in the survey results. . . .

Age, more than sex, shapes attitudes toward the changing roles of men and women, the survey suggests. Younger men and women are far more likely than their elders to say the change in gender roles has made their lives better. . . .

"There's too much pressure on everyone, period, whether they're men or women," says Karen Mapp, a 42-year-old Ph.D. candidate and researcher in Boston.

In response to those pressures, four in ten of those surveyed said it would be better to return to the gender roles of the 1950's, a dimly remembered world of television's *Ozzie and Harriet* and their blithe suburban existence.

"I definitely think it would be good to go back," says Rose Pierre-Louis, 40, a social worker in Brooklyn, N.Y., who was among those interviewed in the poll. . . . But just as many Americans say they aren't eager to go back—particularly young people, who do not bear the burden of their parents' nostalgia. . . . "I think a lot of the problems we hear of now are because we have raised our standards," says Christopher M. Moeller, 22, a radio reporter in Des Moines. "We're more involved in each other's lives. . . . We value equality, we value everybody wanting to have self-esteem, to get everything they want, and I don't see where imposing a limit on more than half of our population accomplishes that."

Analyzing Sources on Women, Work, and Family

1. In Source 15, "The Politics of Fatigue," people surveyed in 1998 expressed nostalgia for the less-exhausting 1950s. How would the authors of the documents from the 1950s included in this chapter respond to this nostalgia?

2. A union debate, a presidential commission report, a children's song, and a comic strip are very different types of sources. What do we gain by including them all in one analysis?

3. In creating an argument that captures key themes in the debate about women, work, and motherhood, what are the potential problems with incorporating evidence from very different types of sources?

4. "An American housewife" extolled the importance of the family in the 1950s, and Claudia Tate did the same in the 1980s. The two women are also similar in their use of a very personal voice in their writing. How are their assumptions about women's family role different, across the divide of thirty years?

5. Gender politics often produces strange alliances and disagreements. Dr. Benjamin Spock was a liberal Democrat, Phyllis Schlafly is a conservative Republican, and President Richard Nixon was a moderate Republican. How were these very different individuals similar in their beliefs about the role of mothers? Why do you think their views did not prevail in recent U.S. history?

6. Write a three- to five-page historical analysis, using the documents presented in this chapter, to argue *either* that the second-wave women's movement significantly altered the American discussion about mothers and employment or that it had no significant effect on that discussion. If you do not find either of those positions consistent with the evidence from the 1955–1998 documents, develop an alternative argument.

7. Write a two- to three-page policy paper in which you draw on these documents to argue for or against the use of tax dollars to support a national, publicly funded child care system. To persuade your modern American audience of your position, you must reconcile these historically competing desires:

   - to achieve full adult employment

   - to encourage female economic self-sufficiency

   - to pay less in taxes

   - to nourish healthy child development regardless of economic status

   - to allow for individual rights to choose a life path

The Rest of the Story

Books directed at mothers, talking about paid work and child rearing, have been a staple of the publishing world since the 1940s. But since the 1980s, such books and their authors have achieved blockbuster status because Americans are so eager for advice on "the balancing act" (a title used more than once for such books) or so hungry for bitter diatribes about the deficiencies of working moms or the failures of fathers and the government to help working moms. Top sellers in the mommy market since 2000 have included such titles as *The Motherhood Manifesto*, *The Mommy Myth*, and *The Price of Motherhood*.

The blogosphere is now a gathering space for mothers seeking personal advice and opportunities to influence public policy. **MomsRising.com** is one of many Web sites devoted to telegraphing the voices of women who agree with the concluding lines of the 1958 *Ladies' Home Journal* article: "If women had organized business and industry, the system would be different. And it might be better." According to the headline of a 2009 *New York Times* article on these maternal blogs, "Mom's Mad. And She's Organized." Time will tell if these Web-linked moms can enact their belief that American society should better serve families in the twenty-first century through some mix of affordable child care, accommodating the schedules of working parents, and making it easier for one parent to temporarily step out of the workforce for child rearing.

Today, most families in the United States rely on the tax-supported public school system for the bulk of their child care needs. Well over half of the mothers of preschool children are employed, however, and they turn to private providers and receive a child care tax credit from the federal government at the end of the year. Although the average annual cost of child care in the United States is more than $8,000 per year, the tax credit is capped at 30 percent of no more than $2,400 per child, and low-income workers who pay for child care but owe no taxes do not receive this credit. As middle-income taxpayers felt the burden of their own child care bills in the 1980s and 1990s, many were increasingly resentful of public welfare that paid enough for poor women to stay at home but not enough for them to work and pay for child care. The welfare reform enacted during President Bill Clinton's administration, known as the Personal Responsibility and Work Opportunity Reconciliation Act of 1996, did not go as far as the Family Assistance Plan envisioned by President Nixon insofar as it did not guarantee every family a base income, nor did it go as far as the Comprehensive Child Development Act of 1971 and make publicly subsidized child care available to all Americans. Instead, welfare codified the expectation that mothers work to support their families, including the 15 percent of families with children in poverty. Key to this expectation is access to child care, which can consume more than 35 percent of a single parent's income. Consistent with President Nixon's vision, the federal government now provides a subsidy to families who are employed but whose low wages put them below the poverty line so that they can purchase child care on the open market.

As for accommodating the schedules of working parents or making it easier for one parent to step out of the workforce for a period of time, Americans' efforts are too scattered, too individualized, and too dependent on employers' largesse or families' incomes to allow for generalization. The second stage of women's liberation that Betty Friedan called for in 1981 is yet to be enacted. The Family and Medical Leave Act of 1993 guarantees that a full-time employee can take up to twelve weeks of unpaid leave for personal health reasons or to care for a new child in the family or a family member who is seriously ill, but beyond that, workers must negotiate their own arrangements with employers, either as individuals or through their labor unions.

In the last decade, the upper-middle-class media has devoted considerable attention to whether mothers with high-paid spouses are "opting out" of the workforce because full-time, at-home motherhood is less stressful and more satisfying than work as, say, a corporate lawyer. The current employment data demonstrates, however, that most mothers do not have the luxury of opting out full time. Two-parent working-class families cannot afford the immediate loss of one income, and two-parent professional families cannot risk the effect of extended time out on a woman's lifetime career earnings. Every year, tens of thousands of mothers, and a few thousand fathers, trade job security, promotions, health benefits, and seniority to work part-time while their children are young, often jeopardizing the family's long-term economic mobility for children's real and immediate needs. Moreover, evidence is now emerging that employers still evaluate job applicants and employees differently if they know that they are mothers than if they do not know, largely because they assume that mothers are less committed to the workplace and face more demands on their energies outside of work.

Americans find themselves in a serious dilemma in the second decade of the twenty-first century. Culture, politics, and economics have normalized attitudinal support for the working mother while, at the same time, normalizing a citizen resistance to tax-supported national programs like child care, after-school care, and parental leaves that child advocates define as the solution to the family-work tension. The economic recession has, at the same time, created such a competitive workforce climate that employees are afraid to ask for any accommodation to their parental duties for fear that they will be relegated to the dreaded "mommy track" or, worse, the unemployment line. Indeed, on the day this chapter of *Going to the Source* was completed, the *New York Times* published an article on the job market with the headline, "A Market Punishing to Mothers."

To Find Out More

Books Written for Working Mothers, 1963–2010

Albrecht, Margaret. *A Complete Guide for the Working Mother.* Garden City, NY: Doubleday, 1967.

Benjamin, Lois. *So You Want to Be a Working Mother.* New York: McGraw-Hill, 1966.

Callahan, Sidney Cornelia. *The Working Mother*. New York: Macmillan, 1971.

Correll, Shelley J., Stephen Benard, and In Paik. "Getting a Job: Is There a Motherhood Penalty?" *American Journal of Sociology* 112 (March 2007): 1297–1338.

Cotton, Dorothy Whyte. *The Case for the Working Mother*. New York: Stein and Day, 1965.

Critttenden, Ann. *The Price of Motherhood: Why the Most Important Job in the World Is Still the Least Valued*. New York: Henry Holt, 2001.

Douglas, Susan J., and Meredith W. Michaels. *The Mommy Myth: The Idealization of Motherhood and How It Has Undermined All Women*. New York: Free Press, 2004.

Gerson, Kathleen. *Hard Choices: How Women Decide about Work, Career, and Motherhood*. Berkeley: University of California Press, 1985.

Hewlett, Sylvia, and Cornel West. *The War Against Parents*. Boston: Houghton Mifflin, 1998.

Hochschild, Arlie. *Second Shift*. New York: Viking Penguin, 1989.

Nye, Ivan F., and Lois Wladis Hoffman. *The Employed Mother in America*. Chicago: Rand McNally, 1963.

Nye, Ivan F., and Lois Wladis Hoffman. *Working Mothers*. San Francisco: Jossey-Bass, 1974.

Risman, Barbara, ed. *Families as They Really Are*. New York: Norton, 2010.

Spain, Daphne, and Suzanne M. Bianchi. *Balancing Act: Motherhood, Marriage, and Employment among American Women*. New York: Russell Sage Foundation, 1996.

Williams, Joanne. *Unbending Gender: Why Family and Work Conflict and What to Do about It*. New York: Oxford University Press, 2000.

Selected Secondary Sources on the History of Working Mothers

Barnes, Riché Jeneen Daniel. "Black Women Have Always Worked: Is There a Work-Family Conflict among the Black Middle Class?" Chap. 9 in *The Changing Landscape of Work and Family in the American Middle Class*, edited by Elizabeth Rudd and Lara Descartes. Lanham, MD: Lexington Books, 2008.

Blackwelder, Julia Kirk. *Now Hiring: The Feminization of Work in the United States, 1900–1995*. College Station: Texas A&M University Press, 1997.

Cobble, Dorothy Sue. *The Other Women's Movement: Workplace Justice and Social Rights in Modern America*. Princeton, NJ: Princeton University Press, 2005.

Coontz, Stephanie. *The Way We Never Were: American Families and the Nostalgia Trap*. New York: Basic Books, 1992.

Critchlow, Donald T. *Phyllis Schlafly and Grassroots Conservatism: A Woman's Crusade*. Princeton, NJ: Princeton University Press, 2007.

Goodwin, Joanne L. " 'Employable Mothers' and 'Suitable Work': A Re-Evaluation of Welfare and Wage-Earning for Women in the Twentieth-Century United States." *Journal of Social History* 29 (Winter 1995): 253–74.

Harrison, Cynthia. " 'A Revolution but Half Accomplished': The Twentieth Century's Engagement with Child-Raising, Women's Work, and Feminism." Chap. 9 in *The Achievement of American Liberalism: The New Deal and Its Legacies*, edited by William H. Chafe. New York: Columbia University Press, 2003.

Keller, Kathryn. *Mothers and Work in Popular American Magazines*. Westport, CT: Greenwood, 1994.

Kinser, Amber E. *Motherhood and Feminism: Seal Studies*. Berkeley, CA: Seal Press, 2010.

MacLean, Nancy. "Postwar Women's History: The 'Second Wave' or the End of the Family Wage?" Chap. 13 in *A Companion to Post-1945 America*, edited by Jean-Christophe Agnew and Roy Rosenzweig. Malden, MA: Blackwell, 2006.

Meyerowitz, Joanne. "Beyond the Feminine Mystique: A Reassessment of Postwar Mass Culture: 1946–1958." *Journal of American History* 79 (March 1993): 1455–82.

Orleck, Annelise. *Storming Caesar's Palace: How Black Mothers Fought Their Own War on Poverty*. Boston: Beacon Press, 2005.

Polatnick, M. Rivka. "Diversity in Women's Liberation Ideology: How a Black and a White Group of the 1960's Viewed Motherhood." *Signs: Journal of Women in Culture and Society* 21 (1996): 679–706.

Rose, Nancy E. *Workfare or Fair Work: Women, Welfare, and Government Work Programs*. New Brunswick, NJ: Rutgers University Press, 1995.

Thistle, Susan. *From Marriage to the Market: The Transformation of Women's Lives and Work*. Berkeley: University of California Press, 2006.

Weiner, Lynn Y. *From Working Girl to Working Mother: The Female Labor Force in the United States, 1820–1980*. Chapel Hill: University of North Carolina Press, 1985.

Avoiding Plagiarism

Acknowledging the Source

If you have taken classes that involve writing, particularly writing and research, chances are good that you have heard the term *plagiarism* before. You may have received syllabi that mention plagiarism and describe the penalties for it, such as a failing grade in the course or even suspension from school. You also may have read your school's plagiarism policy, which most likely offers a brief definition of plagiarism and issues dire warnings about what will happen if you plagiarize. And if you read or watch the news, you may have noticed that plagiarism is an important issue not only within academic settings but in the larger world as well. Clearly, plagiarism is serious business, but what is it, exactly? And how do you avoid doing it?

Defined simply, plagiarism is the unattributed use of someone else's words or ideas. This apparently simple definition can be quite complicated, however. It tends to change across contexts and may be understood differently by different readers. Despite the slipperiness of the definition, every writer has the responsibility to learn how to navigate it and to attribute sources accurately and fully. Ethical researchers must acknowledge their sources because writers and readers depend on one another's honesty. To use someone else's words or ideas without sufficient acknowledgment breaks that trust. Writers in academia are interdependent, with each of us depending on everyone else to help uphold the integrity of the group. Every person engaged in academic writing, from the first-time research writer to the seasoned professor, shares this responsibility. For this reason, the penalties for an academic writer who fails to practice academic integrity are severe.

Source: Adapted from *The St. Martin's Tutorial on Avoiding Plagiarism* by Margaret Price, University of Massachusetts–Amherst.

Why Acknowledgment of Sources Is Important

Within the Western academic tradition, new ideas are built on older ones. Writers give acknowledgment in writing to their sources for a number of reasons:

- **To indicate that you are a responsible and careful researcher.** Acknowledging your sources increases your credibility as a researcher.
- **To give your writing added relevance.** When you refer to others' ideas and show how your own ideas fit into that framework, readers can see more easily what is significant about your work.
- **To help define your research project.** Sources help indicate what topic you are addressing, what approach you are taking, with whose ideas you are aligning yourself and from whose ideas you are distancing yourself, and (in some cases) what discipline you are writing in. In sum, citation helps situate *you* as a unique researcher.

Keeping Track of Source Materials: The Research Portfolio

As an ethical researcher, you should establish good research habits and stick to them. A research project, even a relatively small one involving only a few sources, quickly accumulates materials. There is no firm rule for how to keep these materials organized, but keeping some form of research portfolio is important. This portfolio should include

- photocopies or electronic copies of your source information
- your notes
- your annotated bibliography
- drafts of the paper or project you are working on
- any feedback you have received

Organize your portfolio so that it is both comprehensive (containing all your materials) and manageable (designed for easy retrieval of information). With experience, you will develop a type of research portfolio that works for you. As you collect data, however, keep in mind some basic principles that will help you organize your research materials and avoid inadvertent plagiarism. Recording your research findings precisely and accurately reduces the chances that you will unintentionally express and claim someone else's idea as your own.

1. **Create a structure for your portfolio.** One example is the folder system. Hanging file folders represent large categories that can be subdivided

using folders to represent smaller categories. As you discover more information through your research, you will add more folders or perhaps revise the categories altogether. Keep your working bibliography (see the next section) in a separate folder. Also, keep your notes and annotations for each source. Another possible structure for a research portfolio is the notebook system, in which materials are kept in a three-ring binder, with dividers separating the categories. The system you use will be governed by how much material you accumulate as well as your own organizational preferences.

2. **Keep backup materials.** Your portfolio should include backup copies of everything to guard against loss or computer failure. If a lot of your information resides on a computer, keep hard copies of everything and at least one electronic backup.

3. **Make a hard copy of each source for your own use.** You should print out any articles that you download from an online periodical database, photocopy articles or chapters of books, and print out all Web sites. (Most printouts of Web sites will automatically note the URL and date of access. If that does not occur, note this information.) These printouts will be very useful for checking quotations, paraphrases, and bibliographic information.

4. **Take notes on every source you collect.** This step is crucial. If you simply read a source over and later consult the source directly while writing your paper, your chances of plagiarizing are much greater than if you consult your notes on the source. Moreover, you cannot truly digest a source's information unless you take notes in your own words on what you read.

Maintaining a Working Bibliography

A working bibliography is a list of all the sources you consult as you work on a research project. You may not need to include every source in your project, but you should keep a list of every work you have consulted so that your records are complete. If you develop this habit, you will avoid the problem of wondering where you found certain facts and ideas. A working bibliography also may come in handy for future research projects. After you complete your research, keep your working bibliography so that you can consult it again if necessary.

Your working bibliography should include complete information for each source so that you can write your citations easily (see Appendix II, Documenting the Source). This information includes the author's name, the title of the work, the title of the book or periodical the work comes from (if applicable), the volume or issue number, the place of publication, the publishing company, the date of publication, and inclusive page numbers. Note any other information that pertains to the work's publication, such as whether it is a volume in a series, an edition other than the first, or a translation. Write down the information for each source as you begin using it. You can also keep your working bibliography on a computer file; this technique allows you to easily transfer the bibliography into your final draft later on.

Taking Notes: Knowing Where Each Idea and Word Comes From

It is easy to assume that the research process and the writing process are separate—"First I research, and then I write"—but in fact, researching and writing should be intimately intertwined. As you read and research, new ideas occur to you. Your research question begins to change shape and sometimes to change direction. The development of your own thoughts in turn leads to a different reading of your sources. Taking notes and writing drafts while you research are essential. If you wait to begin note-taking and drafting until you have "finished" your research, the rich mixture of ideas and thoughts you created while researching will never be captured on paper.

You may be surprised to learn that research involves so much writing before you begin writing your "real" paper, but note-taking is not an optional or extra step. All responsible researchers write notes before (and while) drafting their projects. They are crucial building blocks of an effective research project. A detailed note-taking system makes writing a paper much easier.

To master each source's information and argument—and avoid plagiarizing—it is best to take concise notes in your own words, including page numbers for the location in each source. When you come to a comment in the source that you think you will want to quote in your paper, be sure to write it out accurately, with quotation marks around it and the page number from the source.

Taking careful notes while you are researching also makes it easier to determine which ideas are your own. Any plagiarism policy that you read will say that plagiarism is the act of representing someone else's words or ideas as your own. Summarizing or paraphrasing requires that you take another person's idea and put it into your own words.

Clearly, then, it is better to write as you go rather than to save the writing for the end of a research project, but how do you go about doing it? Here are some concrete note-taking strategies.

- **Write an instant draft.** Before you begin researching, or as early in the research process as possible, write a draft that describes what argument you want to make or what question you want to explore. Writing professors Charles Moran and Anne Herrington call this an "instant draft." An instant draft will be a tentative, somewhat disorganized piece of writing since you have not yet done your research. Its purpose is to capture what you know about a subject before you begin consulting other people's ideas. In your instant draft, address the following questions: *What do I* *already know about this topic? Where have I gotten my information from so far? Do I have a strong feeling or stance on this topic? What questions do I have about the topic? What is (are) the main thing(s) I want to find out through my research? Where will I begin looking for this information? What do I need help with? Whom can I ask for that help?* An instant draft is a research memo to yourself and is enormously helpful in providing a recorded baseline for your knowledge. As you learn more and more through your research, you will always know where you started out and hence which ideas you have acquired through researching.

- **Annotate each source.** Before you begin taking more detailed notes, annotate each source you have just read. That is, write a brief summary of the source's main point and key ideas. It is helpful to include annotations in your working bibliography (which turns it into an *annotated bibliography*). Some instructors will ask you to turn in an annotated bibliography with your final draft.

Summarizing, Paraphrasing, and Quoting

You can record someone else's words or ideas in your notes by using three techniques: summarizing, paraphrasing, and quoting. Summarizing and paraphrasing involve putting a source's words into your own; quoting involves recording a source's exact words. After you practice these techniques independently, it is a good idea to show your notes to your instructor and to ask for his or her comments on the effectiveness of your note-taking. Is it complete? Is it accurate? When summarizing and paraphrasing, do you put other authors' ideas into your own words effectively?

1. **Summarizing.** To summarize is to rephrase a relatively large amount of information into a short statement in your own words. Although some information will inevitably be lost, your job is to record what you see as the main idea of the passage. Summarizing is useful when you want to give a reader the gist of a relatively lengthy passage without going into every detail.

2. **Paraphrasing.** To paraphrase is to restate something with your own words and sentence structure. Unlike a summary, a paraphrase is generally about as long as the original passage. Because you are changing the language, you will also inevitably change the meaning of the passage *slightly*, but your job is to keep the meaning as intact as possible. Paraphrasing is useful when you want to convey another author's exact idea but not his or her exact words, perhaps because the language is highly technical or perhaps because a quote would be distracting.

3. **Quoting.** To quote is to state a source's exact words, signaled by the use of quotation marks. If you change a quotation in any way, you must indicate

this change by including three-dot ellipsis points (when you omit part of a quotation) or square brackets (when you make a slight change or addition for clarification). In a final draft, quotations are often less useful than summaries or paraphrases because quotations break up the flow of your writing and often require fairly extensive explanation. Quotations are useful, however, when you want to capture a source's exact wording.

Knowing Which Sources to Acknowledge

Beginning researchers often ask, "Do I have to cite *everything*?" It is a good question because not every piece of information in a research paper must be cited. Figuring out what to cite can be difficult, even for experienced researchers. Generally, if you are unsure, include a citation. It is always better to have an unnecessary citation in your paper than to omit one that is necessary.

Materials That Do Not Require Acknowledgment

Here are some types of materials that usually do not require acknowledgment in research projects:

- **Common knowledge.** It is often easy to spot pieces of common knowledge. For example, the sky is blue, the United States has fifty states, and the 1996 presidential candidates were Bill Clinton and Bob Dole are all pieces of information that appear in various sources, but because they are known to just about everyone, you do not need to cite a source. Sometimes, however, recognizing common knowledge becomes tricky because common knowledge for one person may not be common knowledge for another. Identifying your audience is the key to recognizing common knowledge. If you know what audience you are writing to, you will have a clearer idea of what your readers would consider common knowledge. As always, if you are unsure, be more conservative rather than less so.

- **Fact.** Uncontested pieces of information that can be found in many different sources—particularly reference sources such as encyclopedias—do not require acknowledgment. In *The St. Martin's Handbook*, writing professor Andrea Lunsford gives an example of one such fact: that most of the Pearl Harbor military base, except oil tanks and submarines, was destroyed on December 7, 1941, by Japanese bombers. She adds an example of information on the same topic that *does* require citation: "a source that argued that the failure to destroy the submarines meant that Japan was destined to lose the subsequent war with the United States" (394). The distinction Lunsford makes here is between fact (something commonly accepted as true) and opinion (something that is arguable).

- **Your own ideas.** Recognizing that an idea is your own can sometimes be difficult, especially during the research process, when you are reading and absorbing so many others' ideas. A good way to capture your own ideas is to write a draft *before* you begin researching.

- **Your own field research.** Knowledge that you create by conducting a field study such as a survey, an interview, or an observation is considered your own work. You do not need to cite this sort of information, but another kind of ethics guides the field researcher. You should be clear about how you collected the information. In addition, you should be scrupulous about protecting your participants' autonomy (be sure to quote them accurately, and ask for their feedback when possible).

Materials That Do Require Acknowledgment

Anything that you draw from another source, unless it falls into one of the categories described above (common knowledge, fact, your own ideas, and your own field research), must be cited. Your citations should appear in two places: in the body of your paper and in a list at the end of the paper. The style of citation your instructor has asked you to use will affect the formatting of these citations. Complete bibliographic information for each source will appear in a section titled "Bibliography" (see Appendix II, Documenting the Source).

The following list is suggestive, but not exhaustive. New kinds of information are always emerging. Generally speaking, however, here are the types of materials that require acknowledgment in academic writing:

- **Another person's words.** Direct quotations must always be cited.

- **Another person's ideas.** Even if you rephrase someone else's idea by paraphrasing or summarizing it, you must cite it. Citations for paraphrases and summaries look just like citations for quotations, except that no quotation marks are used.

- **Judgments, opinions, and arguments.** Arguable information, such as the idea about the effect of the Pearl Harbor bombing discussed previously, must be cited. Whenever you offer an idea from another source that could be argued, acknowledge that it is this individual's point of view. You should do so even if you thought of the idea and *then* encountered it through your research. You can indicate in your writing that you came to the idea independently of the other author, but you cannot omit mention of the other author.

- **Visual information.** If you use a chart, graph, or picture from another source—or if you use the information from that chart, graph, or picture—acknowledge the source.

- **Information that can be attributed to a company or organization rather than a single person.** Web sites and corporate publications often do not list individual authors. In this case, the organization that sponsored the Web site or publication should be listed as the author. If the author is unknown, your citation should indicate that.

- **Information gathered from class lectures or from another aural source.** If you heard information rather than saw it, you must still cite it. You can cite information you have heard in various ways, including as a lecture, as a personal communication, or as an interview.

- **General help offered by readers.** Sometimes the feedback you receive from readers (such as your teacher, classmates, and friends) will affect the shape of your work, but not its content. For instance, a classmate might offer a suggestion for making your introduction more interesting. In this case, the best way to acknowledge your classmate's contribution is in a note of thanks appended to the paper. Such "Acknowledgments" notes generally appear at the end of academic papers or in a footnote added to the title or first paragraph. If you look at a refereed history journal, you will see examples of less formal acknowledgments of this kind.

Learning these rules and following them appropriately is one of your responsibilities as a member of an academic or writing community. Even if you plagiarize unintentionally, the penalties for plagiarism—which can be very severe—still apply to you. For more information on plagiarism, consult your school's or your department's guidelines. For more detailed and constructive information, speak with your instructor, who probably has a good idea of what sort of citation is expected. You should also find out if your school has a writing center with tutoring available. Tutors can discuss ways of citing information and often can refer you to other sources of information if you need additional help. A third resource to consider is a writing handbook that includes the rules of academic citation as well as guidelines on conducting research, managing information, and citing sources responsibly.

APPENDIX II

Documenting the Source

Whenever you use another researcher's work as a source in your own writing, whether you quote the researcher's words directly or rely on the researcher's evidence and theories to support your arguments, you must include documentation for that source. This requirement is equally true when using a map, photograph, table, or graph created by someone else. The reasons for this are twofold. First, to avoid any possibility of plagiarism, you must always include proper documentation for *all* source materials (see Appendix I, Avoiding Plagiarism). Second, a proper citation gives important information to your reader about where to find a particular source, be it on a Web site, in a book at the library, or in an archive in your local community.

When documenting sources, historians use a standard form based on the recommendations published in *The Chicago Manual of Style*. All the documentation models presented here are consistent with the guidelines published in the sixteenth edition of *The Chicago Manual of Style* (Chicago: University of Chicago Press, 2010). For each source type, you will see a citation style that can be used for either a footnote, which appears at the bottom of the page of text, or an endnote, which appears at the end of a chapter or at the end of the whole text. These model notes are indicated by an "**N**" in the margin. Each note is followed by an example of how this source type would be cited in a bibliography. Model bibliography entries are marked by a "**B**" in the margin. Two examples are provided because footnote/endnote citation style is slightly different from bibliography citation style.

The examples provided here illustrate how to cite the various types of sources that appear in *Going to the Source*, and they will help you address many of the documentation issues associated with sources that you come across in your research. This guide is not a comprehensive list, however, and as you dig further into the past, you may uncover source types that are not covered in this brief guide. For additional information about documenting sources in the *Chicago* style, please see **bedfordstmartins.com/resdoc**.

Documentation Basics

When you are wondering what to include in a citation, the question to keep in mind is, "What does my reader need to know to *find* this source?" When citing sources internally, you should use the footnote or endnote style. Footnotes and endnotes are used to document specific instances of borrowed text, ideas, or information. The first time you cite a source, you need to include the full publication information for that source—the author's full name, source title (and subtitle, if there is one), and facts of publication (city, publisher, and date)—along with the specific page number you are referencing.

1. David Paul Nord, *Communities of Journalism: A History of American Newspapers and Their Readers* (Urbana: University of Illinois Press, 2001), 78.

If you refer to that source later in your paper, you need to include only the author's last name, an abbreviated version of the title, and the page or pages cited.

4. Nord, *Communities of Journalism,* 110–12.

A bibliography is used in addition to footnotes or endnotes to list all the works you consulted in completing your paper, even those not directly cited in your footnotes. The sources included in your bibliography should be listed alphabetically, so the citation style for a bibliographic entry begins with the author's last name first.

Nord, David Paul. *Communities of Journalism*: *A History of American Newspapers and Their Readers*. Urbana: University of Illinois Press, 2001.

BOOKS

■ *1. Standard format for a book*

The standard form for citing a book is the same whether there is an editor or an author, the only difference being the inclusion of "ed." to indicate that an editor compiled the work.

Directory of Documentation Models

1. Tim Johnson, ed., *Spirit Capture: Photographs from the National Museum of the American Indian* (Washington, DC: Smithsonian Institution Press, 1998), 102. N

Johnson, Tim, ed. *Spirit Capture: Photographs from the National Museum of the American Indian.* Washington, DC: Smithsonian Institution Press, 1998. B

2. Book with two or more authors or editors

When citing a source from a book with two or three authors or editors, you need to include the names of all the authors (or editors) in the order that they appear on the title page. If a work has more than three authors, you need to include all the names in your bibliography. In your footnotes or endnotes, you need only include the name of the lead author followed by "and others" or "et al.," with no intervening comma.

2. Graham Russell Hodges and Alan Edward Brown, eds., *"Pretends to Be Free": Runaway Slave Advertisements from Colonial and Revolutionary New York and New Jersey* (New York: Garland, 1994), 58. N

B   Hodges, Graham Russell, and Alan Edward Brown, eds. *"Pretends to Be Free": Runaway Slave Advertisements from Colonial and Revolutionary New York and New Jersey.* New York: Garland, 1994.

◼ *3. Edited book*

Sometimes a book will have an author and an editor. In that case, you need to include both the author's and the editor's names.

N   3. Hilda Satt Polacheck, *I Came a Stranger: The Story of a Hull-House Girl*, ed. Dena J. Polacheck Epstein (Urbana: University of Illinois Press, 1991), 36.

B   Polacheck, Hilda Satt. *I Came a Stranger: The Story of a Hull-House Girl.* Edited by Dena J. Polacheck Epstein. Urbana: University of Illinois Press, 1991.

If the edited book does not have an author, list it according to the editor's name.

3. Robin Wright, ed., *The Iran Primer* (Washington, DC: United States Institute of Peace Press, 2010), 59–60.

Wright, Robin, ed. *The Iran Primer.* Washington, DC: United States Institute of Peace Press, 2010.

◼ *4. Multivolume book*

If you are referring to a specific volume in a multivolume work, you need to specify which volume you used. This information should come before the page reference toward the end of the citation.

N   4. Bernard Bailyn, ed., *The Debate on the Constitution: Federalist and Anti-Federalist Speeches, Articles, and Letters during the Struggle over Ratification* (New York: Library of America, 1993), 2:759–61.

B   Bailyn, Bernard, ed. *The Debate on the Constitution: Federalist and Anti-Federalist Speeches, Articles, and Letters during the Struggle over Ratification.* 2 vols. New York: Library of America, 1993.

Sometimes individual volumes in a multivolume work have separate volume titles. When citing a particular volume, you should include the volume title first followed by the name of the complete work.

◼ *5. Book with an anonymous author*

Many books printed in the nineteenth century were published anonymously. If the author's name was omitted from the title page but you know from your research who the author is, insert the name in square brackets; if you do not know who the actual author is, begin the citation with the work's title. Avoid using "Anonymous" or "Anon." in citations. As originally published, the author of *The Mother's Book* was listed as "Mrs. Child," so this citation includes that information along with the full name in brackets.

5. Mrs. [Lydia Maria] Child, *The Mother's Book* (Boston: Carter, Hendee, and   N
Babcock, 1831), 23.

Child, [Lydia Maria]. *The Mother's Book*. Boston: Carter, Hendee, and Babcock, 1831.   B

SECTIONS OR DOCUMENTS WITHIN BOOKS

■ *6. Book-length work within a book*

Sometimes, the source you are using may be a book-length work that has been reprinted within a longer work. In that case, you need to include both titles along with the editor of the longer work.

6. Álvar Núñez Cabeza de Vaca, *The Narrative of Cabeza de Vaca*, in *Spanish*   N
Explorers in the Southern United States, 1528–1543, ed. Frederick W. Hodge (New York:
Charles Scribner's Sons, 1907), 52–54, 76–78, 81–82.

Cabeza de Vaca, Álvar Núñez. *The Narrative of Cabeza de Vaca*. In *Spanish Explorers in the*   B
   Southern United States, 1528–1543, edited by Frederick W. Hodge. New York:
   Charles Scribner's Sons, 1907.

■ *7. Chapter or article from a book*

If you want to cite a particular chapter from a book, you should include the title of the chapter in quotation marks before the title of the book.

7. Vicki L. Ruiz, "The Flapper and the Chaperone," in *From Out of the Shadows: Mexican*   N
Women in Twentieth-Century America (New York: Oxford University Press, 1998), 12–26.

Ruiz, Vicki L. "The Flapper and the Chaperone." In *From Out of the Shadows: Mexican*   B
   Women in Twentieth-Century America. New York: Oxford University Press, 1998.

■ *8. Published letter or other correspondence*

When citing published letters, memoranda, telegrams, and the like, you need to include the name of the sender and the recipient along with the date of the correspondence. Memoranda, telegrams, and other forms of communication should be identified as such in your citation after the recipient's name and before the date, but letters do not need to be specifically noted as such.

N   8. James Buchanan to Juan N. Almonte, March 10, 1845, in *Diplomatic Correspondence of the United States: Inter-American Affairs, 1831–1860*, ed. William R. Manning (Washington, DC: Carnegie Endowment for International Peace, 1937), 8:163.

B   Buchanan, James. James Buchanan to Juan N. Almonte, March 10, 1845. In *Diplomatic Correspondence of the United States: Inter-American Affairs, 1831–1860*, edited by William R. Manning. Washington, DC: Carnegie Endowment for International Peace, 1937.

■ *9. Table, graph, or chart*

Whenever you incorporate statistical data into your work, it is important to document your evidence. If you borrow a table, graph, or chart from another source, you must cite it just as you would quoted material in your text. Include a citation in appropriate footnote format to the source of the borrowed information directly below it. If you change the table, graph, or chart in any way (for example, eliminating unnecessary information or adding another element such as a percent calculation to it), use the phrase "adapted from" in your citation, which signals to the reader that you have altered the original. If a number is used to identify the data in the original source, that information should also be included at the end of the citation.

N   9. Adapted from Hinton R. Helper, *The Impending Crisis of the South: How to Meet It* (New York: Burdick Brothers, 1857), 71, table XVIII.

Because you would not cite any one particular table in your bibliography, you would follow the style for citing the book, periodical, or Web site where the data you consulted first appeared.

■ *10. Illustration*

When citing drawings, paintings, and other images that appear in a book, include the illustration title and author followed by the publication information for the book. In the note, include the page number for the item as well as any figure or plate number assigned to it.

N   10. Theodore de Bry, "Birds and Fish of New England," Michael Alexander, ed., *Discovering the New World: Based on the Works of Theodore de Bry* (New York: Harper and Row, 1976), 202.

B   de Bry, Theodore. "Birds and Fish of New England." In *Discovering the New World: Based on the Works of Theodore de Bry*, edited by Michael Alexander. New York: Harper and Row, 1976.

PERIODICALS

Journals are scholarly publications that are usually published a few times a year. Popular magazines are written for the general public and are most often published on a monthly or weekly basis. Most newspapers are published daily, although some small local papers are published weekly. The following examples demonstrate the style for citing each type of periodical. If you consult an online periodical, the style for citing this source would be the same, with the addition of the URL at the end of your citation.

■ *11. Journal article*

When citing an article from a journal, you need to include the volume number, issue number (when given), and date of publication.

> 11. Elizabeth A. Fenn, "Biological Warfare in Eighteenth-Century North America: N
> Beyond Jeffery Amherst," *Journal of American History* 86, no. 4 (2000): 1552–80.

> Fenn, Elizabeth A. "Biological Warfare in Eighteenth-Century North America: Beyond   B
>   Jeffery Amherst." *Journal of American History* 86, no. 4 (2000): 1552–80.

■ *12. Popular magazine*

When citing material from a popular magazine, you need to include only the magazine title followed by the date of publication and the page number(s) for the material. If you are citing from a regular feature of the magazine, you should include the title of the feature in the citation. If there is an author of the magazine article or the magazine's regular feature, the author's name would appear first in your citation, followed by the name of the feature.

> 12. Benjamin Spock, "Should Mothers Work?" *Ladies' Home Journal*, January–   N
> February, 1963, 16, 18, 21.

> Spock, Benjamin. "Should Mothers Work?" *Ladies' Home Journal*, January–February, 1963.   B

■ *13. Newspaper article*

When citing newspaper articles, you must include the day, month, and year of publication, and the author if the article had a byline. *Chicago* style allows for page numbers to be omitted because newspapers often publish several editions each day and these editions are generally paginated differently.

> 13. John Dickinson, "The Liberty Song," *Boston Gazette*, July 18, 1768.   N

> Dickinson, John. "The Liberty Song." *Boston Gazette*, July 18, 1768.   B

■ *14. Letter to the editor*

For letters to the editor published in newspapers and magazines, include the letter title (if any) as well as the words "letter to the editor."

N   14. Evalyn F. Thomas, "Modern American Housewife," letter to the editor, *Ladies' Home Journal*, March 1956, 6, 8.

B   Thomas, Evalyn F. "Modern American Housewife." Letter to the editor. *Ladies' Home Journal*, March 1956.

INTERNET SOURCES

■ *15. A document from a Web site*

To cite a document found on a Web site, you need to provide as much of the following information as possible: the author, the name of the document with original date of publication, the name of the site, the sponsor or owner of the site, and the URL. Also include the date that the site was last revised or modified; if that is unavailable, include the date that you accessed the site. Sometimes a Web archive will include a document number; when available, you should include this cataloging number as well.

N   15. William Plumer, "An address, delivered at Portsmouth, N.H., on the Fourth of July, 1828," *Fourth of July Orations Collection*, University of Missouri Special Collections and Rare Books, last revised October 20, 2009, E286.P65, http://mulibraries.missouri .edu/specialcollections/fourth.htm.

B   Plumer, William. "An address, delivered at Portsmouth, N.H., on the Fourth of July, 1828." *Fourth of July Orations Collection*, University of Missouri Special Collections and Rare Books. Last revised October 20, 2009. E286.P65. http://mulibraries.missouri .edu/specialcollections/fourth.htm.

■ *16. An entire Web site*

To cite an entire Web site, you need include only the author of the site (if known), the name of the site, the sponsor or owner of the site, the date of the last revision or modification (or, if unavailable, the access date), and the URL.

N   16. University of Minnesota College of Liberal Arts, *Immigration History Research Center*, University of Minnesota, last modified December 8, 2010, http://ihrc.umn.edu/.

B   University of Minnesota College of Liberal Arts. *Immigration History Research Center*. University of Minnesota. Last modified December 8, 2010. http://ihrc.umn.edu/.

PUBLIC DOCUMENTS

◼ *17. Executive department document*

For government documents issued by the executive branch, include the name of the department or commission that created the document, the name of the document, and the publication information.

> 17. President's Commission on the Status of Women, *American Women: Report of the President's Commission on the Status of Women, 1963* (Washington, DC: U.S. Government Printing Office, 1963), 27, 29–30, 18, 19.   N

> President's Commission on the Status of Women. *American Women: Report of the President's Commission on the Status of Women, 1963*. Washington, DC: U.S. Government Printing Office, 1963.   B

◼ *18. Congressional testimony*

Testimony given before a congressional committee is usually published in a book. The exact name of the committee is given in the title of the work in which the testimony appears.

> 18. United States Congress, *Report of the Joint Select Committee to Inquire into the Condition of Affairs in the Late Insurrectionary States*, vol. 2, *South Carolina, Part I* (Washington, DC: Government Printing Office, 1872), 25–28, 33–34.   N

> United States Congress. *Report of the Joint Select Committee to Inquire into the Condition of Affairs in the Late Insurrectionary States*. Vol. 2, *South Carolina, Part I*. Washington, DC: Government Printing Office, 1872.   B

◼ *19. Court records*

When citing legal cases in historical writing, the name of the plaintiff appears first, followed by the name of the defendant, and both names are italicized. The first time you cite the case, you should also include the court and year in which the case was decided. Supreme Court decisions are published by the government in a series called *United States Reports*. When citing Supreme Court decisions, you need to include the name of the case in italics followed by the number of the volume that contains the particular case, the abbreviation "U.S." for *United States Reports*, page numbers, and the year of the decision.

> 19. *Korematsu v. United States*, 323 U.S. 242, 242–48 (1944).   N

> *Korematsu v. United States*. 323 U.S. 242, 242–48. 1944.   B

■ *20. Online government document*

For government documents accessed online, include everything you would for a print publication, as well as the date of last modification (or your access date) and the URL.

N   20. Civil Rights Act of 1964, Document PL 88-352, *International Information Programs*, U.S. State Department, page revised August 13, 1996, http://202.41.85 .234:8000/InfoUSA/laws/majorlaw/civilr19.htm.

B   Civil Rights Act of 1964. Document PL 88-352. *International Information Programs*, U.S. State Department. Page revised August 13, 1996. http://202.41.85.234:8000 /InfoUSA/laws/majorlaw/civilr19.htm.

OTHER SOURCES

■ *21. Advertisement*

To cite an advertisement, provide the name of the company or institution, the name of the ad, and the publication information for the periodical in which the ad appeared. Advertisements should be included in notes, but not bibliographies.

N   21. Mutual of New York, "Life insurance? For a wife? That's money down the drain!" advertisement, appeared in *Newsweek*, May 6, 1968, 57.

■ *22. Audio recording*

For citing an audio recording, include information as you would for a print source. If you retrieved the recording online, include the latest modification date (or your access date) and the URL.

N   22. "Executive Committee Meeting of the NSC on the Cuban Missile Crisis," October 24, 1962, transcript and Adobe Flash audio, 37.4, *Presidential Recordings Program*, Miller Center of Public Affairs, University of Virginia, accessed February 22, 2011, http:// millercenter.org/scripps/archive/presidentialrecordings/kennedy/1962/10_1962.

B   "Executive Committee Meeting of the NSC on the Cuban Missile Crisis." October 24, 1962. Transcript and Adobe Flash audio, 37.4. *Presidential Recordings Program*. Miller Center of Public Affairs, University of Virginia. Accessed February 22, 2011. http:// millercenter.org/scripps/archive/presidentialrecordings/kennedy/1962/10_1962.

■ *23. Painting*

When citing paintings that appear in a catalog, archive, or database, you need to include the artwork's catalog or accession number if available. This documentation will help other researchers locate the original source. Generally, specific works of art are not included in your bibliography, but if a particular painting is important to your research, you may list it in your bibliography by the painter's name first.

23. George Catlin, *Shón-Ka-Ki-He-Ga, Horse Chief, Grand Pawnee Head Chief*   N
(1832, Smithsonian American Art Museum: 1985.66.99).

Catlin, George. *Shón-Ka-Ki-He-Ga, Horse Chief, Grand Pawnee Head Chief*. 1832.   B
    Smithsonian American Art Museum: 1985.66.99.

■ *24. Photograph or other archival material*

Any material found in an archive or depository—be it a photograph, diary, letter, or map—needs to be cited just as published material would be. The name of the author (or photographer, in the case of photographs) should appear first, followed by the title of the image or document being cited in quotation marks, the date, and the name of the archive or depository. If a source from a collection is important enough to your work, you can mention that source specifically in your bibliography. If you make use of more than one photograph or other type of source from a particular collection, however, you need only cite them generally in your bibliography.

24. George P. Barnard, "Ruins of Charleston, S.C.," 1866, Beinecke Rare Book and   N
Manuscript Library, Yale University.

Photographs. Beinecke Rare Book and Manuscript Library, Yale University.   B

■ *25. Unpublished letter or other correspondence*

Unpublished letters and those that have not been archived should include some indication of this fact, such as "in the author's possession" or "private collection." If the letter was found in an archive, the location of the depository would be included as well. (For information on how to cite material found in an archive, see the section "Photograph or other archival material," above.)

25. Jeff Rogers to William and Adele Rogers, November 10, 1968, in the author's   N
possession.

Rogers, Jeff. Jeff Rogers to William and Adele Rogers, November 10, 1968. In the author's   B
    possession.

Acknowledgments (continued)

CHAPTER 4

Pages 87–90 (Source 1): From *I Came a Stranger: The Story of a Hull-House Girl.* Copyright 1989 by the Board of Trustees of the University of Illinois. Used with permission of the University of Illinois Press.

Pages 93–96 (Source 3): From *Rosa: The Life of an Italian Immigrant,* by Marie Hall Ets, University of Wisconsin Press, 1999. Used by permission of the University of Wisconsin Press.

CHAPTER 6

Pages 140–143 (Source 3): Sergeant Elmer Straub, *A Sergeant's Diary in the World War,* volume 3, Indiana World War Records (Indianapolis): Indiana Historical Commission, 1923), 11– 343.

CHAPTER 7

Pages 158–159 (Source 1): "Despedida de un Norteño/An Emigrant's Farewell" from Paul S. Taylor, "Songs of the Mexican Migration." *Puro Mexicano,* J. Frank Dobie, ed. Publications of the Texas Folklore Society, no. 22. Austin: Texas Folk-Lore Society, 1935. 222–24.

Pages 159–160 (Source 2): "Advice to the Northerners" (Consejos a los norteños). María Herrera-Sobek.

Pages 161–162 (Source 3): "The Northerners" (Los norteños). María Herrera-Sobek.

Pages 162–164 (Source 4): "Defense of the Emigrants" (Defensa de los norteños). María Herrera-Sobek.

Pages 164–165 (Source 5): "Ballad of Pennsylvania" (Corrido de Pensilvania). Benjamin J. Galina.

Pages 165–166 (Source 6): "Verses of the Beet-Field Workers" (Versos de los betabeleros). Benjamin J. Galina.

Page 166 (Source 7): "Mexicans Who Speak English" (Los Mexicanos que hablan ingles). Benjamin J. Galina.

Pages 167–168 (Source 8): "Radios and Chicanos" (Radios y chicanos). Benjamin J. Galina.

Pages 168–169 (Source 9): "The Ranch" (El rancho). Benjamin J. Galina.

Pages 169–170 (Source 10): "Red Bandannas (Los paños colorados)." "Los paños colorados/Red Bandannas (Los paños colorados)" from Mario Gamio, *Mexican Immigration to the United States: A Study in Human Migration and Adjustment* (New York): Dover, 1971).

CHAPTER 12

Pages 277–281 (Source 1): *Pivotal Decade: How the United States Traded Factories for Finance in the Seventies,* by Judith Stein. Yale University Press, 2010.Copyright © 2010 by Judith Stein. Used by permission of the publisher.

Pages 281–285 (Source 2): Excerpt from *Stayin'Alive: The 1970s and the Last Days of the Working Class.* Copyright © 2010 by Jefferson Cowie. Reprinted by permission of The New Press. www.thenewpress.com.

CAPSTONE CHAPTER

Pages 326–327 (Source 1): Excerpt from transcript of Meeting of Union of Auto, Aerospace and Agricultural Implementation Workers of America (UAW-CIO). Reprinted by permission of United Auto Workers.

Page 327 (Source 2): "Modern American Housewife," letter to the editor, written by a reader from Castro, Valley, CA. Originally published in the March 1956 issue of *Ladies Home Journal,*® magazine. All rights reserved.

Pages 328–329 (Source 3): "Women Know They Are Not Men: When Will Business Learn This Valuable Secret and Arrange Women's Working Conditions Accordingly?" by Florida Scott-Maxwell. Originally published in the November 1958 issue of *Ladies Home Journal,*® magazine. All rights reserved.

Pages 330–331 (Source 5): "Should Mothers Work?" Advice column by Dr. Benjamin Spock, *Ladies Home Journal,* January-February, 1963. Originally published in the January-February, 1963 issue of *Ladies Home Journal,*® magazine. All rights reserved.

Pages 331–332 (Source 6): Position Paper, "Why Feminists Want Child Care." Position paper. National Organization for Women (N.O.W.) 1969. (New York City Chapter, Paper, Box 10, Taminent Library). Reprinted by permission of NOW-NYC.

Pages 334–335 (Source 8): "What's Wrong with 'Equal Rights' for Women?" by Phyllis Schlafly, February, 1972. Reprinted by permission of the author.

Pages 336–337 (Source 9): "Parents Are People," by Carol Hall from *Free To Be . . . You and Me.* © 1972 Free To Be Foundation, Inc. Used by permission.

Page 339 (Source 11): *The Second Stage,* by Betty Friedan. Copyright © 1981. Reprinted by permission of Curtis Brown, Ltd.

Page 340 (Source 12): From "Should We Expect Black Women to be Supermothers?" by Claudia Tate, *Ebony*, September 1984. Used by permission of the author's estate.

Pages 344–345 (Source 15): From *The Washington Post,* April 20, 1998 © 1998 Washington Post Company. All rights reserved. Used by permission and protected by the Copyright Laws of the United States. The printing, copying, redistribution, or retransmission of this Content without express written permission is prohibited.

Index

Letters in parentheses following page numbers refer to:
(f) figures
(i) illustrations
(m) maps
(t) tables

Working with Sources on Your Own

Avoiding Plagiarism

See Appendix I, "Avoiding Plagiarism: Acknowledging the Source," for important information on how to work with sources effectively without unintentionally borrowing the work of another author.

Documenting Sources

See Appendix II, "Documenting the Source," for guidelines on how to cite sources you use in your papers. The following is a list of model citations included in Appendix II.

Directory of Documentation Models